MICROSOFT® CERTIFIED SYSTEMS ENGINEER

MCSE Windows® Server 2003 Active Directory Infrastructure Study Guide

(Exam 70-294)

MCSE Windows® Server 2003 Active Directory Infrastructure Study Guide

(Exam 70-294)

Dennis Suhanovs

McGraw-Hill/Osborne

New York   Chicago   San Francisco   Lisbon   London   Madrid
Mexico City   Milan   New Delhi   San Juan   Seoul   Singapore   Sydney   Toronto

The McGraw·Hill Companies

McGraw-Hill/Osborne
2100 Powell Street, 10th Floor
Emeryville, California 94608
U.S.A.

To arrange bulk purchase discounts for sales promotions, premiums, or fund-raisers, please contact **McGraw-Hill**/Osborne at the above address. For information on translations or book distributors outside the U.S.A., please see the International Contact Information page immediately following the index of this book.

**MCSE Windows® Server 2003 Active Directory Infrastructure Study Guide
(Exam 70-294)**

1234567890 DOC DOC 019876543

Book p/n 0-07-222320-0 and CD p/n 0-07-222321-9
parts of
ISBN 0-07-222319-7

Publisher Brandon A. Nordin	**Acquisitions Coordinator** Jessica Wilson	**Composition** Apollo Publishing Services, George Charbak, Elizabeth Jang
Vice President & **Associate Publisher** Scott Rogers	**Technical Editors** Todd Logan, Dave Field	**Illustrators** Kathleen Edwards, Melinda Lytle, Lyssa Wald
Acquisitions Editor Timothy Green	**Copy Editor** Judith Brown	**Series Design** Roberta Steele
Project Editor Elizabeth Seymour	**Proofreader** Mike McGee	**Cover Series Design** Peter Grame
	Indexer Jack Lewis	

This book was published with Corel VENTURA™ Publisher.

I would like to dedicate this book to my friends and family, all of whom were supportive of the project. Mom and Dad, I've been a wayward son lately. Thank you for putting up with me all this while; I did not make it easy for you.

Dennis Suhanovs has been in the IT industry since 1996, specializing in Microsoft operating systems and server products such as Microsoft Exchange and Microsoft SQL Server. He received his first technology certification in 1997 and went on to achieve another seven over the course of several years, passing well over 20 Microsoft, Cisco, and Novell exams. After serving for five years as a Microsoft systems engineer, Dennis resigned to establish a consulting and outsourced development practice. His first Exchange 2000 co-authoring project was published in 2001; since then Dennis has been the co-author of several books and author study guides for companies like Brainbench and Self Test Software. When he is not busy helping his public company clients achieve their technology goals, Dennis is learning new riffs on his Fender Strat. Feel free to visit his web site at www.flexecom.com.

About LearnKey

LearnKey provides self-paced learning content and multimedia delivery solutions to enhance personal skills and business productivity. LearnKey claims the largest library of rich streaming-media training content that engages learners in dynamic media-rich instruction complete with video clips, audio, full motion graphics, and animated illustrations. LearnKey can be found on the Web at www.LearnKey.com.

CONTENTS AT A GLANCE

CONTENTS

6 Planning and Implementing Group Policy **375**

Analyze Your Environment 376

    Group Policy Scope in Active Directory 377

    Resource Location on the Network 378

    Security Requirements 379

    Corporate Policies 379

    Network and Storage Capacities 379

    Ease of Administration 380

Plan Group Policy Strategy 381

    Analyze Requirements 381

    The Group Policy Management Tools 389

    Resultant Set of Policy (RSoP) Tool 400

    User Environment Considerations 406

    Computer Environment Considerations 411

    Exercise 6-1: Creating, Editing, and Applying Group

    Policies 414

Configure the User Environment by Using Group Policy 414

    User Software Distribution 415

    User Certificate Enrollment and Digital Signatures 423

    Exercise 6-2: Certificate Enrollment Using Group Policies . 429

    Folder Redirection 431

    User Security Mechanisms 435

Deploy a Computer Environment by Using Group Policy 442

    Computer Software Distribution 442

    Exercise 6-3: Software Distribution Using Group Policies . . 442

    Computer Certificate Enrollment 443

    Computer Security Mechanisms 444

    ✓ Two-Minute Drill 452

Q&A   Self Test 453

    Lab Question 457

    Self Test Answers 459

    Lab Answer 461

7 Managing and Maintaining Group Policy **463**

Troubleshoot Issues Related to Group Policy Application and

  Deployment 464

    Viewing Effective Group Policy Settings 464

ACKNOWLEDGMENTS

I t is an interesting contrast to recall what you planned on saying in the Acknowledgments section of your book the day you sign the contract, and what actually gets written when the book is about to be published. Many people contributed their time and effort to this project, and so my heartfelt gratitude goes out to: Jawahara Saidullah of Waterside and Tim Green of McGraw-Hill/Osborne for making this project possible; Jessica Wilson, Elizabeth Seymour, Gareth Hancock, Judith Brown, and all the folks at McGraw-Hill/Osborne for their contributions to the process; technical editors Todd Logan and Dave Field for making sure the content is technically accurate—thank you kindly. On my side of things, my partners Alex Zotov and Alex Golovine deserve a lot of praise for their contributions, which proved to be instrumental to the project—you guys rock. This has been an interesting endeavor. To all the folks who contributed to our collective effort: I salute you.

In This Book

This book is organized in such a way as to serve as an in-depth review for the MCSE Windows Server 2003 Active Directory Infrastructure exam (Exam 70-294) for both experienced Windows Server 2003 Active Directory professionals and newcomers to Microsoft networking technologies. Each chapter covers a major aspect of the exam, with an emphasis on the "why" as well as the "how to" of working with and supporting Windows Server 2003 Active Directory as a network administrator or engineer.

On the CD

For more information on the CD-ROM, please see Appendix C.

Exam Readiness Checklist

At the end of the Introduction you will find an Exam Readiness Checklist. This table has been constructed to allow you to cross-reference the official exam objectives with the objectives as they are presented and covered in this book. The checklist also allows you to gauge your level of expertise on each objective at the outset of your studies. This should allow you to check your progress and make sure you spend the time you need on more difficult or unfamiliar sections. References have been provided for the objective exactly as the vendor presents it, the section of the study guide that covers that objective, and a chapter and page reference.

In Every Chapter

We've created a set of chapter components that call your attention to important items, reinforce important points, and provide helpful exam-taking hints. Take a look at what you'll find in every chapter:

- ■ Every chapter begins with the **Certification Objectives**—what you need to know in order to pass the section on the exam dealing with the chapter topic.

The Objective headings identify the objectives within the chapter, so you'll always know an objective when you see it!

- **Exam Watch** notes call attention to information about, and potential pitfalls in, the exam. These helpful hints are written by authors who have taken the exams and received their certification—who better to tell you what to worry about? They know what you're about to go through!

- **Practice Exercises** are interspersed throughout the chapters. These are step-by-step exercises that allow you to get the hands-on experience you need in order to pass the exams. They help you master skills that are likely to be an area of focus on the exam. Don't just read through the exercises; they are hands-on practice that you should be comfortable completing. Learning by doing is an effective way to increase your competency with a product. The practical exercises will be very helpful for any simulation exercises you may encounter on the MCSE Windows server 2003 Active Directory Infrastructure exam.

- **On The Job** notes describe the issues that come up most often in real-world settings. They provide a valuable perspective on certification- and product-related topics. They point out common mistakes and address questions that have arisen from on the job discussions and experience.

- **Inside the Exam** sidebars highlight some of the most common and confusing problems that students encounter when taking a live exam. Designed to anticipate the what the exam will emphasize, getting inside the exam will help ensure you know what you need to know to pass the exam. You can get a leg up on how to respond to those difficult to understand questions by focusing extra attention on these sidebars.

- **Scenario and Solutions** sections lay out potential problems and solutions in a quick-to-read format.

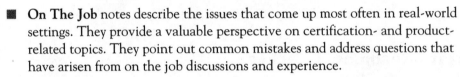

SCENARIO & SOLUTION

James must be available to troubleshoot the computers in any office in the four buildings of the company that he works for…	Implement a roaming profile for James so that he can access his desktop no matter what computer he is using. This is especially handy. since his roaming profile can include the mapping to a network drive that holds his diagnostic tools.

- The **Certification Summary** is a succinct review of the chapter and a restatement of salient points regarding the exam.

- The **Two-Minute Drill** at the end of every chapter is a checklist of the main points of the chapter. It can be used for last-minute review.

Q&A

- The **Self Test** offers questions similar to those found on the certification exams. The answers to these questions, as well as explanations of the answers, can be found at the end of each chapter. By taking the Self Test after completing each chapter, you'll reinforce what you've learned from that chapter while becoming familiar with the structure of the exam questions.

- The **Lab Question** at the end of the Self Test section offers a unique and challenging question format that requires the reader to understand multiple chapter concepts to answer correctly. These questions are more complex and more comprehensive than the other questions, as they test your ability to take all the knowledge you have gained from reading the chapter and apply it to complicated, real-world situations. These questions are aimed to be more difficult than what you will find on the exam. If you can answer these questions, you have proven that you know the subject!

Some Pointers

Once you've finished reading this book, set aside some time to do a thorough review. You might want to return to the book several times and make use of all the methods it offers for reviewing the material:

1. *Re-read all the Two-Minute Drills*, or have someone quiz you. You also can use the drills as a way to do a quick cram before the exam. You might want to make some flash cards out of 3 x 5 index cards that have the Two-Minute Drill material on them.

2. *Re-read all the Exam Watch notes*. Remember that these notes are written by authors who have taken the exam and passed. They know what you should expect—and what you should be on the lookout for.

3. *Review all the S&S sections* for quick problem solving.

4. *Re-take the Self Tests*. Taking the tests right after you've read the chapter is a good idea, because the questions help reinforce what you've just learned. However, it's an even better idea to go back later and do all the questions in the book in one sitting. Pretend that you're taking the live exam. (When you

go through the questions the first time, you should mark your answers on a separate piece of paper. That way, you can run through the questions as many times as you need to until you feel comfortable with the material.)

5. *Complete the Exercises.* Did you do the exercises when you read through each chapter? If not, do them! These exercises are designed to cover exam topics, and there's no better way to get to know this material than by practicing. Be sure you understand why you are performing each step in each exercise. If there is something you are not clear on, re-read that section in the chapter.

INTRODUCTION

This book is written with Exam 70-294 in mind. This being said, the book is not solely an exam guide; if you master the topics we present herein, chances are you are going to do well not just on the exam but also in the corporate world.

Microsoft is positioning Exam 70-294 towards field engineers and system architects. This exam will test your planning and concept skills and it will jog your memory of how and where to use Active Directory tools, how to configure certain settings or policies, and so forth. This is a bit different from Windows 2000 series exams, where two sets of exams were administered: planning (to test your conceptual knowledge) and administration (to test your hands-on experience). Exam 70-294 is a mixture of both.

To address this shift in exam strategy, we put together this book so that it first explains the concepts involved in architecting an Active Directory environment, and then provides you with a few exercises and step-by-step walkthroughs of how to perform certain procedures in this latest revision of the OS. Although there have not been a lot of fundamental changes as far as Active Directory is concerned, rest assured, being aware of the small changes will make a big difference when you take the exam.

In addition to the concepts and step-by-step elements of each chapter, we included "On the Job" and "Exam Watch" tips to draw your attention to points of information we feel are important to remember. To paint an even clearer picture for you, the book features dozens of screenshots and figures. In the middle and at the end of each chapter, a short question and answer section will help you refresh important points and make sure we are still on the same page.

At the end of each chapter you will find a quiz and a lab question. The quizzes are designed to test your conceptual knowledge while the lab questions present on-the-job scenarios in an attempt to test your hands-on knowledge. Don't be alarmed: The exam does not contain any of those 10-page scenarios Microsoft was running in Windows 2000 design exams, but there will be plenty of lab-like questions. Try to answer our questions before you look up the answers—and feel free to disagree with our reasoning, but make sure to go back and review if you feel confused.

Included with the book is a CD-ROM disc that contains a sample exam and the exercise videos in AVI format. The exam mimics the actual Windows Server 2003 Active Directory exam in that it contains approximately the same number of questions that follow a similar format. This will give you a rough idea of what to expect on the actual exam and help you evaluate how well you are prepared for it. Make sure you thoroughly understand concepts such as group policy and Active Directory sites before attempting to take this test, and do not register for your live exam until you are comfortable answering the questions on the CD-ROM.

Exam Readiness Checklist

Official Objective	Certification Objective	Ch #	Pg #	Beginner	Intermediate	Expert
Planning and Implementing the Active Directory Infrastructure						
Plan a strategy for placing global catalog servers.	3.01	3	124			
Evaluate network traffic considerations when placing global catalog servers.	3.01	3	131			
Evaluate the need to enable universal group caching.	3.01	3	133			
Plan flexible operations master role placement.	3.02	3	135			
Plan for business continuity of operations master roles.	3.02	3	136			
Identify operations master role dependencies.	3.02	3	145			
Implement an Active Directory directory service forest and domain structure.	3.03	3	147			
Create a child domain.	3.03	3	150			
Create the forest root domain.	3.03	3	152			
Create and configure Application Data Partitions.	3.03	3	154			
Install and configure an Active Directory domain controller.	3.03	3	157			
Set an Active Directory forest and domain functional level based on requirements.	3.03	3	162			

Exam Readiness Checklist

Official Objective	Certification Objective	Ch #	Pg #	Beginner	Intermediate	Expert
Establish trust relationships (external trusts, shortcut trusts, and cross-forest trusts.)	3.03	3	165			
Implement an Active Directory site topology.	3.04	3	171			
Configure site links.	3.04	3	175			
Configure preferred bridgehead servers.	3.04	3	176			
Plan an administrative delegation strategy.	3.05	3	178			
Plan an organizational unit (OU) structure based on delegation requirements.	3.05	3	180			
Plan a security group hierarchy based on delegation requirements.	3.05	3	182			
Managing and Maintaining an Active Directory Infrastructure						
Manage an Active Directory forest and domain structure.	4.01	4	202			
Manage schema modifications.	4.01	4	203			
Manage trust relationships.	4.01	4	212			
Add or remove a UPN suffix.	4.01	4	220			
Manage an Active Directory site.	4.02	4	224			
Configure site boundaries.	4.02	4	225			
Configure replication schedules.	4.02	4	228			
Configure site link costs.	4.02	4	235			
Monitor Active Directory replication failures. Tools might include Replication Monitor, Event Viewer, and support tools.	4.03	4	239			
Monitor Active Directory replication.	4.03	4	240			
Monitor File Replication service (FRS) replication.	4.03	4	243			
Restore Active Directory directory services.	4.04	4	251			

Exam Readiness Checklist

Official Objective	Certification Objective	Ch #	Pg #	Beginner	Intermediate	Expert
Perform a nonauthoritative restore operation.	4.04	4	254			
Perform an authoritative restore operation.	4.04	4	255			
Troubleshoot Active Directory.	4.05	4	259			
Diagnose and resolve issues related to operations master role failure.	4.05	4	259			
Diagnose and resolve issues related to Active Directory replication.	4.05	4	263			
Diagnose and resolve issues related to the Active Directory database.	4.05	4	264			
Planning and Implementing User, Computer, and Group Strategies						
Plan a security group strategy.	5.01	5	286			
Plan a user authentication strategy.	5.02	5	324			
Plan a smart card authentication strategy.	5.02	5	331			
Create a password policy for domain users.	5.02	5	334			
Plan an OU structure.	5.03	5	337			
Analyze the administrative requirements for an OU.	5.03	5	338			
Analyze the Group Policy requirements for an OU structure.	5.03	5	340			
Implement an OU structure.	5.04	5	341			
Create an OU.	5.04	5	342			
Delegate permissions for an OU to a user or to a security group.	5.04	5	344			
Move objects within an OU hierarchy.	5.04	5	347			
Planning and Implementing Group Policy						
Plan Group Policy strategy.	6.01	6	381			

Exam Readiness Checklist

Official Objective	Certification Objective	Ch #	Pg #	Beginner	Intermediate	Expert
Plan a Group Policy strategy by using Resultant Set of Policy (RSoP) Planning mode.	6.01	6	400			
Plan a strategy for configuring the user environment by using Group Policy.	6.01	6	406			
Plan a strategy for configuring the computer environment by using Group Policy.	6.01	6	411			
Configure the user environment by using Group Policy.	6.02	6	414			
Distribute software by using Group Policy.	6.02	6	415			
Automatically enroll user certificates by using Group Policy.	6.02	6	423			
Redirect folders by using Group Policy.	6.02	6	431			
Configure user security settings by using Group Policy.	6.02	6	435			
Deploy a computer environment by using Group Policy.	6.03	6	442			
Distribute software by using Group Policy.	6.03	6	442			
Automatically enroll computer certificates by using Group Policy.	6.03	6	443			
Configure computer security settings by using Group Policy.	6.03	6	444			
Managing and Maintaining Group Policy						
Troubleshoot issues related to Group Policy application and deployment. Tools might include RSoP and the gpresult command.	7.01	7	464			
Troubleshoot the application of Group Policy security settings. Tools might include RSoP and the gpresult command.	7.01	7	466			
Configure automatic updates for network clients by using Group Policy.	7.02	7	483			

1
Introduction

CERTIFICATION OBJECTIVES

This chapter serves as an introduction to directory technologies in general and Active Directory in Windows Server 2003 in particular. For the purposes of exam 70-294, it is safe to skip the chapter if you are a seasoned professional. Try the quiz at the end of the chapter.

CERTIFICATION OBJECTIVE 1.01

A Little Bit of History

Throughout history, humans have always sought ways of systematizing information, and in the contemporary world, we now have the technology not only to store a huge set of data accumulated over time and supplemented on a daily basis, but also to search and access that information instantaneously. Several implementations of such technology appeared right after people first realized all the benefits of that concept. Early versions specialized in storing objects of predefined types only. The purpose of directories in the early days was to introduce flexibility and simplify administration, using those predefined object types.

The first attempts to create such systems were MVS PROFS and the Michigan Terminal System (MTS). Later, the operating system UNIX, with its own approach to storing user accounts, came along. UNIX is a multiuser operating system with access-restriction mechanisms, which allows multiple concurrent interactive user sessions at any given moment. Information about users is stored in the file /etc/passwd, with each line adhering to a certain predetermined format. Each line in the file describes a particular user of the system, and it constitutes the *user account*. One acceptable format that the user account definitions can follow is shown here:

```
login_name: encryptd_password: user_ID: group_ID: user_information:
login_directory: login_shell
```

Each user account must have a unique name (login_name). To access the resources managed by the operating system, users must log on (or authenticate) to the system by providing their username and password. Information they supply is passed on to the operating system module that is responsible for validating user logon requests.

In simple terms, this module then proceeds and searches the /etc/passwd file for that specific user account. If a matching entry is located, it reads all of the parameters defined in the file for that user (encryptd_password: user_ID, and so on). It then compares the password entered by the user with the password read from the user account entry, and if they match, the module issues the necessary system calls to allow the user into the system.

This simple yet powerful approach, in its fundamental form, is present in the systems we use today. Of course, if you think of this solution in terms of today's level of computer use, it certainly has its problems—such as performance (try searching a flat file with a few million user entries) and security. But way back when, it served as a great start.

CERTIFICATION OBJECTIVE 1.02

Definition of a Directory and Directory Services

Directories appeared as a result of the logical continuation of attempts to normalize data storage and create some sort of standard that could be used by any system regardless of implementation. The definition of *directory* as we know it today has expanded a great deal beyond its original purpose. In the beginning, a directory was equivalent (and is often compared to) a catalog of information, such as a telephone directory, where records are normalized (last name, initials, phone number, address) and listed in a certain order (alphabetically, descending.) Thus, using a telephone directory, with a bit of effort you can locate a telephone number based on a known parameter—last name in this example. Directories of today include the same fundamental characteristics and serve the same fundamental purpose—we still have some data in some format sorted in some way—but the functionality far exceeds that of a simple search.

A simple definition of a directory could be given as a file or a database that organizes resources or information in a hierarchical manner. As a software implementation, it has some defining characteristics, some of which are listed here. Most people would agree that a directory must, at a minimum, allow the following:

- Ability to store user data
- Extensive ability to search data
- Ability to identify users of data (authentication)
- Ability to set permissions and control access to data (authorization)

Directory characteristics are implemented within directory software, which also defines and implements the structure of the directory, commands that can be executed against this directory, and communication protocols and rules supported by this directory. *Directory service*, therefore, is more of a functionality provided by directory software: it involves interaction with other software programs, called *clients*, which users of the system employ to interact with the directory. For example, these clients may allow reading and writing from, and to, the directory, searching, comparing, and deleting data. So in essence, directory service can also be defined as an interface between users and data that is organized and stored in the directory. Clients can be implemented as graphical user interface applications and also as command-line applications.

Storing User Data

Usually, information stored in the directory represents some real-world data. Modern implementations of directory software organize and store information in units called *objects*. For now, we won't worry about exactly how those objects are implemented within the directory—technically, this can be a text file, relational database record, or an actual object created using a high-level programming language. To store these units of data—objects—the directory must be configured accordingly.

For instance, it is neither easy nor practical to store information about people in a directory that was initially created for automobiles. This brings up another very important requirement for a directory: its structure and object definitions must be easily modifiable to add support for new objects. If we have an automobile directory, it could make sense to keep track of potential and existing owners, and we should be able to add this support with a minimal amount of effort.

Further on in this chapter, we will revisit the concepts of directories, how their structures can be modified, and other reasons why this is so important. Objects (instances and classes) and attributes are also covered in more detail in later sections.

Searching User Data

We know that searching data is as integral to directories as storing it. The search facility is implemented by the client-side software, which formulates search requests, sets up search parameters, and forwards specifically formatted search requests to the directory. Users can search for objects based on property values, or *attributes*—the date the object was created or modified, the object's unique identifier, for example—and their location within the directory.

The client itself does not conduct the search; it would be too inefficient in terms of wasted network bandwidth and unused directory server resources. Instead, clients submit the definition of objects they are looking for, and get the resulting set of references to matching objects in response. Directory servers are tasked with conducting the actual search using all the processing power they usually have. Directory structures and servers are constructed with this in mind; search times must be minimized to provide an adequate level of service.

Note that creating new instances of existing object classes and populating their attributes (in other words, writing new information to the directory) is usually significantly faster than searching for existing data. Ultimately, it depends on how well a particular directory is implemented, how much data is stored and searched, what performance optimization mechanisms were utilized by the developers, and exactly how much processing power is available to the directory server.

Authentication and Authorization

It is unlikely that owners of directories would want just anyone to be able to access their information (unless, of course, that is exactly what they need done). Security and access control have rapidly become the key features of any server product on the market these days. Access restriction and control is usually implemented on two levels, the first being authentication. Before you can grant or deny access in response to an incoming request, you need to unambiguously identify users or computers submitting those requests. A valid form of identification could be a unique combination of a username and a password, digital signature, or even a smart card.

Therefore, *authentication* can be defined as an access control mechanism, responsible for establishing and verifying user (or computer) identity.

Once the identity of the access-requesting entity has been established, authorization— the second mechanism of access control—kicks in. *Authorization* is the process by which the directory establishes access rights or rules that apply to the access-requesting entity and determines whether or not access to particular objects is allowed or denied.

Access rights consist of a set of security parameters used in authorization processes, and most commonly they include rights such as "read," "write," "modify," and "delete." All of the objects stored in the directory have certain access rights defined and "attached" to them. The access-requesting entity, upon requesting a certain object, is checked against that particular object's access list. Access rights and permissions are two terms that can be used interchangeably, and the same goes for access control lists (ACLs) and access lists. If an ACL on any given resource states that User A has read-only access rights and User B has read access plus the ability to modify object attributes, when User A attempts to modify an attribute of that particular object, he or she should fail. This is authorization in action.

Contrary to a one-time deal, as is the case with authentication, authorization is persistent; users are constantly subjected to authorization as they request access to more and more objects within the security model of a directory.

As you can infer from the discussion so far, weak authentication code jeopardizes authorization, for we can no longer be sure that User A is really User A. Likewise, there is no point in strong authentication if authorization mechanisms are weak, because it doesn't matter who User A is, if User A can retrieve objects that she should otherwise not have access to. You may hear people compare this to a chain being only as strong as its weakest link.

Example: Windows Server 2003

The characteristics of a directory can be summarized using one example that is directly related to exam 70-294: Windows Server 2003 Active Directory (AD). Suppose you are using a directory client, in this case, either a Windows XP Professional or Windows 2000 Professional that belongs to the AD 2003 domain. When you boot up your workstation, it prompts you for a username and a password. If you enter a valid username and a correct password, your information is matched with a user account object in the Active Directory, and the logon completes successfully.

Without going into technical details of the process, let's say that authentication completes successfully. From this point on, every resource you request (files, directory objects, printers, network services, and so on) is subjected to verification of your identification information against individual ACLs of the resource in question. Should the ACL permissions seem insufficient, the operating system will flash an error message stating that you cannot access the requested resource. Authorization enforces permissions.

Reasons to Implement Directories

Modern companies have vast amounts of resources, such as computers, peripherals, and office equipment, that they must keep track of. To do this, they often have to implement different software packages, not necessarily developed by a single vendor. To store information about employees, they need yet another application. Eventually, it may become necessary to track the use of renewable supplies or rather costly services, such as color laser toner or peak hours of overseas faxing. In other words, the need to keep track of things mounts, as does the volume and type of information, and existing applications designed to track specific things may not necessarily be flexible enough to adapt quickly and cost effectively.

It follows that since companies resort to using several software packages to track similar things, some information is bound to be duplicated. That, in turn, may result in omissions and leakages—in other words, complete inconsistency. Administrators become overburdened by having to maintain multiple user accounts, each of which may have access controls implemented. Not only could this result in serious security oversights, but a simple change like a new phone number can require changing it several times in several applications—not very efficient to say the least.

Now, consider users. They have access to several different applications, and they have several different pairs of user accounts and passwords to remember. Experienced administrators know what this results in—not only forgotten passwords but users having to write their usernames and passwords on sticky notes and attaching these to their monitors. Very secure.

As time goes by, problems are compounded, administrators spend more time fixing things that were "working yesterday," instead of proactively managing a unified environment. The net result is an overblown TCO (total cost of ownership) of technology, with the company spending more and working less efficiently—the exact opposite of what technology aims to deliver.

Directories come to the rescue by aiming to solve all of the problems just identified. They deliver a unified storage facility for all these objects, which now only have to be stored in a single instance. Since directories are flexible in terms of what kinds of information they store, both automobile and owner data (to use the earlier example) can be stored. Finally, security is no longer a concern for applications. By fully delegating this to the directory, each object can be restricted in terms of who can access it, and administration is centralized. The only thing remaining on our checklist is directory and application compatibility.

Example: Application of Directory Services

Suppose a company has implemented directory services and employs their directory to store hundreds and thousands of objects—its employees, office equipment, applications, network configuration, and so on. User Sandra logs on to her computer, which is associated with the security perimeter created and maintained by this directory, and attempts to print a document. The printer queue is a directory object. It is maintained on a print server, and it has an ACL associated with it. When Sandra submits a print job to the queue from her workstation, the authorization process compares her identity against a set of printer queue permissions; and if access is allowed, the print job goes through.

The directory makes sure that the authentication process established Sandra's identity; and because the printer queue and Sandra's user account are associated with the same security perimeter, the authorization process accepts Sandra's security ID and trusts it to be valid.

CERTIFICATION OBJECTIVE 1.03

Directory Standards

There is an alphabet soup of standardization bodies, each of which is responsible for its own area of technology. Some of the most prominent are listed here:

- **ISO**   International Organization for Standardization
- **ECMA**   European Computer Manufacturers Association (information and communication systems standards association)
- **CCITT**   International Consultative Committee on Telephony and Telegraphy (Comité Consultatif International Telegraphique et Telephonique)

Efforts to create a unified directory standard were initiated by a partnership of ISO and ECMA, who were developing a name resolution system for applications based on the OSI (Open Systems Interconnection) model. Around the same time, CCITT was working on implementing white pages based on the new standard. White pages serve as a catalog of network service subscribers on the Internet; they contain information such as assigned network addresses, telephone numbers, and mailing addresses.

Objectives of the two teams were, obviously, very different, but their technical implementation had many common areas. As a result, they united their efforts and formed a single ISO/CCITT task force in 1986, which proceeded to develop directory standards. The first version of the standard, called X.500, was finalized in October 1988.

X.500 has become the de facto standard in directory technologies, in spite of the fact that not a single software development company implemented the original standard in its entirety. The standard was so comprehensive that it was difficult to implement in full. So, in the early days of X.500, while many portions of it did find its way into the software, it was really just a set of recommendations.

After several improvements and modifications, X.500 has not yielded to competition; quite the opposite, it has become the dominating specification for how directories and directory services should function. The X.500 standard is of particular interest to us because it was used in laying the engineering groundwork for Active Directory.

CERTIFICATION OBJECTIVE 1.04

Overview of X.500

In basic terms, the purpose of X.500 was to standardize the following components of a directory:

- Fundamental structure model
- Security model
- Distributed model
- Data replication
- Access protocols

The Fundamental Structure Model

The less traditional fundamental structure of a directory is perhaps the single characteristic that makes it so different from its relational and object database peers.

You have already been introduced to the units of information stored in groupings, referred to as objects. Object definitions in the directory can be anything they need to be—correlating to existing objects in the real world, or not. Objects can describe cars and any other physical objects, or abstractions such as mathematical expressions and formulas.

Attributes and *values* of an object are used to describe properties of that object. An attribute without a value has no significance, and vice versa.

Each *entry*—a unit of data in the directory—is a set of attribute/value pairs, describing one particular instance of the object type. One user account is represented by one object, which has attributes and values, which in turn describe the user.

The Directory Information Base (DIB) is the structure of the database, used to store entries. It follows a hierarchical model, similar to that of a tree, and hence is sometimes referred to as the Directory Information Tree (DIT). Each DIB node represents a directory entry. Like other hierarchical databases, the DIT is usually presented as an upside-down tree. The top of the tree, where all other entries stem from is called the *root*.

A *distinguished name* (DN) is a unique identifier and hence a unique reference to an entry. DNs can be *relative* or *absolute*, referring to their uniqueness within their own branch or the entire tree, respectively. Absolute DN uniquely defines an object in the context of the entire directory, and when you see references to a distinguished name, you can usually assume absolute DN unless stated otherwise. The DN of each entry is constructed as a listing of all nodes beginning from the root to the entry in question (absolute DN).

Some examples of objects, attributes, and values are presented in Table 1-1.

Given that the basic idea of the structure, followed in the design of an X.500-compliant directory, is that of a tree, it follows that all of the objects within that tree must be grouped into a category or entity that initially serves as the root. The root entity may be subdivided into several units, called *organizational units* (OUs), which may be further subdivided into third-level OUs, fourth-level OUs, and so on. (The greater the number of levels, the more negative impact on performance.) Each of the second-level OUs is sometimes referred to as a *subtree*. OUs often contain objects of the same or different types; hence, OUs are also called *containers*. Containers are structural units of the directory that help organize objects; they are not actual objects.

Each object in the tree must have its container, and in order to describe the relationship between nodes, that container is called the *parent* in respect to the object, and the object is referred to as a *child* in respect to the container (its parent).

Distinguished Names

Let's revisit distinguished names for a moment. DNs are defined as a list of all nodes from the root to the node in question. Well, all those nodes in between have to be containers, for one object cannot contain another object (although it may reference another object in one of its attributes). So, for example, CN=Administrator, OU=Technology, O=Flexecom,

Object	**Attribute**	**Value**
User Administrator	Account Name	Administrator
	SecurityID	S-1-5-21-1275210071
	First Name	Richie
	Last Name	Sambora
	Date Created	May 21, 2003
Computer MobileDude	Computer Name	MobileDude
	DNS name	mobiledude.flexecom.com
	Operating System	Windows XP Professional
	Service Pack	Service Pack 1

TABLE 1-1 Sample User and Computer Objects (Directory Entries)

C=US is a reference to object Administrator, which is located in the Technology subtree of our organization. OU=Technology in this example is the top of the Technology subtree. If we had further subdivisions of the Technology unit, our record would look similar to CN=Administrator, OU=Santa Barbara, OU=Technology, O=Flexecom, C=US. Figure 1-1 shows a typical distinguished name.

We also need to differentiate between absolute DN and relative distinguished names (RDNs). The difference between the two lies in how uniquely they define the object in the context of the root. Absolute distinguished names, as we have already established, are unique directory-wide references. RDNs are unique only to the container of the object; an example of an RDN is a common name (CN) portion of a sample DN (as shown in the preceding illustration).

For purposes of performing read/write/delete and search operations, you do not really need to use absolute DNs. Relative DNs are accepted as well, although in that case you are limiting the context of these operations. This can be useful in the case of read/write/delete operations, but it may or may not be a good thing when you are searching for something. User Administrator from OU=San Francisco, OU=Technology will not match your query for all accounts named "Administrator" if the context of

FIGURE 1-1

Distinguished name

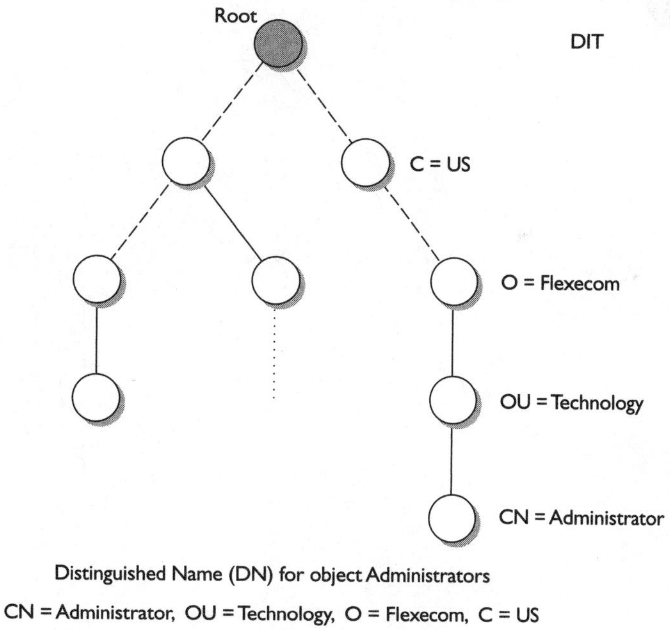

Distinguished Name (DN) for object Administrators

CN = Administrator, OU = Technology, O = Flexecom, C = US

Distinguished Name (DN) example

your search is limited to OU=Santa Barbara. At the same time, if you only need to find matching objects from a specific area of the directory, limiting the context of the search will save you time. In this case, you would need to submit the DN of a container you wish to use as a context root with your search. This is shown in Figure 1-2.

Whether or not it is possible to have two accounts with the same name depends on the design and implementation of your directory. Traditionally, you are allowed to have more than one object with the same name, providing that these objects do not reside in the same container. (Otherwise, it would be impossible to construct an absolute DN, which violates the definition of DNs.) Objects *can* have identical common name (CN) portions in their absolute DNs. Objects with the same name in different containers have absolute DNs.

Do not confuse object names (used in DN "paths") and unique object identifiers (OIDs, the serial number of an object). In the context of Active Directory, you are allowed to have only one unique login name (which is used in DNs) per domain. For example, you cannot have an administrator@flexecom.com user account in Santa Barbara OU *and* in San Francisco OU at the same time. These OUs would have to be

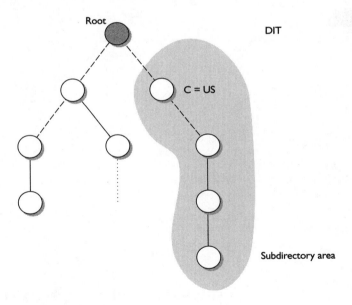

FIGURE 1-2

DN of a container used as a context root

Subdirectory example

in different domains and carry different UPN suffixes. (This topic is covered in greater detail in Chapter 3.)

Given all the definitions just covered, we can now conclude that a directory is based on a hierarchical, object-oriented database. The smallest unit of data is a pair consisting of an attribute and its corresponding value, clusters of which define an object.

Example: Distinguished Name   Consider a randomly chosen individual who has a corresponding user account object defined in the directory. His location in the structure of the organization can be described using an absolute distinguished name. Beginning with the common name, which must be unique within its container, we add the names of object and container nodes until we reach the top of the organization tree. However, that is not the root of the X.500 directory; we continue by adding a country abbreviation. The level that follows the two-letter country abbreviation to the right of the DN is the root of the directory.

Directory operations are specific to the context. If your directory search client defaults to the root of the organization and you run a search for all user accounts that contain the string value "Natasha" in the "First Name" attribute, the search will return references to all matching user accounts in the entire organization. It may also take some time to run, depending on the number of objects and OU levels in the structure. On the other hand, you can narrow the scope of the search by specifying a certain subtree you might be interested in (this includes all subcontainers beginning with the container you set as the context root) or even a certain container (this does not include any of the subcontainers regardless of where in the structure the search is conducted). Specific search options are subject to client implementation and need not be similar in different directory systems.

Directory Schema

Now that we have the long view of the directory structure, let's take a closer look at individual components of the structure.

An *object class* is a template for objects of the same type that contain no end-user data. It is a skeleton that defines what properties each object type has, how many properties an instance of the object should have, which properties are mandatory, and which ones are optional. Think of an orange. Your mind almost instantly pictures a spherical edible object and associates it with a specific color, smell, class (citrus, fruit, food), and perhaps some memories or past experiences, trips, novels, and so on. Likewise, when we define a new object type in the system, we must describe it to the system. Now picture a bowl of oranges—those are *instances* of an object class, in other words, actual objects created from "orange" template. User class and user account objects are no different from oranges in this example.

Then we have *attribute types*. Our oranges have many attributes and corresponding values associated with orange class; they fully describe the object. However, in certain cases, values aren't predictable or even constant. For instance, oranges are probably not very orange in the early stages and also when they are rotten, so the "color" attribute in this case may not be constant, but it has no more than three or four probable values that we want to allow. Note that our oranges cannot be transparent and must have some color, so the "color" attribute is not optional. (However, memories associated with oranges are not something that is naturally attached to oranges, so that is an optional attribute.) By the same token, blue or gray oranges do not make a lot of sense, so those values are not an option. Also note that we may have two colors present at the same time, so we want to construct this attribute to respect that fact.

Attribute types also describe which actions we should be able to perform on the values. Getting back to our example, in simple terms, we have no control of the natural color of oranges. We could probably paint them burgundy, but it would not change their natural color, so that attribute is likely to be read-only.

A *directory schema* (*schema*) is the entire collection of all object classes in the directory. The schema effectively defines what objects can be stored in the directory. Modern directories must provide some flexibility here; Active Directory 2003 allows extending schema. Genetically modified oranges—you know, those white, cubic ones—will probably need a new object class in our directory.

It follows that if two objects have the same properties, they belong to the same class. Each object must have at least one class associated with it. Associations between structure elements are depicted in Figure 1-3.

FIGURE 1-3

Associations between structure elements

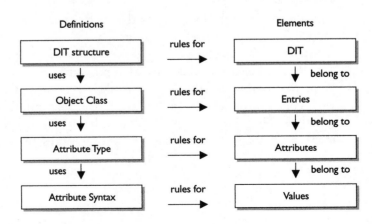

The Security Model

At first glance, the security model in X.500 seems fairly simple. It is based on the two main access control mechanisms discussed earlier in the chapter—authentication and authorization. X.500 refers to these two mechanisms as the Access Control Scheme (ACS). In practical implementations though, this simple scheme is not so simple. It includes, but is not limited to, the following areas:

- Access Control Specific Administrative Area
- Access Control Inner Administrative Area
- Directory Access Control Domains
- Autonomous Administrative Area

Modern implementations of the standard tend to support this general approach, but they all seem to have their own way of handling the details. For the purpose of our discussion, we will concentrate on the *Autonomous Administrative Area* (AAA), since it is common to all implementations.

In simple terms, AAA is a concept that allows delegating certain portions of directory trees—such as OUs—to different administrators. It would be difficult to overstate the value this brings to directories. For example, say that you work for a midsize-to-large corporation, and each geographical division has its own IT department and IT personnel. These departments are fairly autonomous, yet they manage one directory that is the backbone of the entire infrastructure.

It may simply be impossible for one person (or even department) to manage hundreds, if not hundreds of thousands, of directory objects, and field help desk calls from geographically dispersed production departments. Obviously, these departments must be able to take care of password resets and user account configuration in their jurisdiction, while people from the corporate HQ IT department oversee the backbone itself from a central location. Planning new containers and managing common schema are tasks that come to mind for those folks. Delegation is perhaps the only feasible and cost-effective solution in this case.

From the technical perspective, delegation is defined at the administrative unit level, such as containers and subtrees. Delegated authority begins where it is defined and spans all the child containers and leaf objects of the tree, unless there is another AAA, demarcated by one of the lower-level containers.

AAA is a real asset when it comes to merging previously disparate IT infrastructures of merging or acquired companies. Two existing AAAs are simply migrated into one tree, while existing IT departments retain control of their territory. Again, if that is

in the best interests of the company, two AAAs may be merged into one. It is a matter
of company policy at this point, not technical feasibility.

The Distributed Model

The distributed model portion of the X.500 standard describes the rules and algorithms
necessary to make directory clients independent of the distributed nature of the directory
itself. In all likelihood, companies will need a lot more than one directory server.
(Remember from the beginning of the chapter, one of the reasons for creating a directory
was information overload; massive amounts of data are waiting to be stored somewhere.)

Clients need not pay attention to "which server they are tuned to"; they should
have seamless access to the entire data store. Furthermore, users do not even need to
be aware of the technical implementation of their environment; all they want is to get
their email on time and print documents without delay.

The distributed model essentially makes all of the resources available to users with
as little as one directory server being accessible at a time.

Directory System Agent (DSA)

Each server in the group of directory servers runs specialized software that maintains the
directory on the local server. Besides providing its own database to network users, each
server also has a *Directory System Agent* (*DSA*) running in addition to the directory itself.
Although X.500 does not describe the specifics of how DSAs should be implemented,
they have plenty of responsibilities; the core responsibilities that are relevant to our
discussion are covered here.

Each of the servers running directory software serves its own DITs to network users
and applications, and end users access those local DITs on a regular basis. Now suppose
these previously disparate DITs are united into a single logical resource network. Users
of the system will not reap the benefits of a single resource network until each directory
server learns about other directory servers in the neighborhood and, more importantly,
until they learn to understand the information in previously isolated DITs.

That is precisely the purpose of DSAs. Once DSAs are configured, end users will
be able to access any resource from any DIT in a transparent fashion while using the
same server they were configured to use, providing that it is part of the united resource
network. They do not need to know which directory server they are connected to and
which DIT has the resource they are about to use; it will be made available as if it were
stored in a local DIT.

The physical location of the resource may actually matter. Imagine the frustration of submitting your lengthy print job to a printer queue located in a company office in a neighboring country. Of course, even in the case of an error like this, users still do not care about which directory server provided printer queue information. So long as all of them are able to access the same set of resources, all they have to do is be careful about physical locations of those resources. (When I say "able to access" in the context of DSA, I'm referring to security controls that may exist.)

DSA implements this functionality using chaining and referrals. When a user requests a resource, the directory server that services the request checks it against its own local DIT first (local in respect to the user). If it is determined that the server has no information about the resource in question, the request is passed on to a neighboring directory server. The neighboring server checks the requested resource in its own DIT, which is remote with respect to the user, and the process repeats. It goes on until one of the servers locates the requested information. At that point, it is passed back to the requesting entity in exactly the opposite direction, using the same path, until it reaches the client. This method is called *chaining*.

Referrals serve a similar purpose in a different way: in the process of establishing which remote server has the information requested by the user, some servers may already know of another server that has that information. So instead of continuing to follow a chain of requests, the process may skip a server or two and cut directly to the remote server that has the information. This saves quite a bit of time, especially in large directory implementations supporting a vast amount of data on many servers. The Directory System Protocol (DSP) is a high-level communication protocol used between the DSAs in X.500.

Directory User Agent (DUA)

X.500 also has provisions for the user portion of the directory service—in other words for a directory client. The purpose of the *Directory User Agent (DUA)* specification is to provide a simple and convenient user interface that allows interaction between the user and one of the DSAs. As described earlier, this can be a GUI-based or command-line application, but it can also be a set of the programming libraries that other developers could use to incorporate DUA functionality in their applications. DUAs and DSAs communicate with each other using the Directory Access Protocol (DAP). See "Access Protocols" later in the chapter for a more detailed discussion of protocols.

Data Replication

Replication is a process of synchronization of the additions and changes made to data in two or more data repositories. X.500 recommends implementing a *single master replication* model, in which one directory server is designated as the *master*, its DIT becomes a *master copy* of the directory database, and the rest of the servers in the infrastructure synchronize their changes with the master copy. The X.500 standard does not specify the sequence of replications that have to take place before the DIT information is considered synchronized. It likewise provides no recommendations for what a pause between synchronization cycles should be. Consequently, directory solution vendors make their own judgments in regard to what these should be. The standard describes such a replication model as a "weak consistency of the data" scheme.

Synchronized copies of the master repository, which are located on other directory servers participating in the scheme, are called *replicas*. Replicas are read-only copies of the directory. Thus, a user request can be serviced by the closest replica. If the user decides to make changes to an object served from the replica, the changes will be written to the only read/write copy of the repository—the master copy. Through the natural course of replication, this updated information will eventually find its way to every replica maintained by directory servers.

X.500 requires that users be given the ability to look up information directly on the master server. This may be handy at times when you suspect that the information served by the replica is out of date. Directory vendors should, in theory, respect this requirement.

Access Protocols

As noted in the discussion of the Directory User Agent, DAP (Directory Access Protocol) is a communication protocol used between DUAs and DSAs. DAP is based on a *connection-oriented* protocol, which means that parties have to agree on certain parameters before initiating data communications. If both parties accept requirements set forth by either of the participants, a communication session will go through. Parties can negotiate network addressing and communication protocol parameters, security information, transfer speeds, and other pertinent information. After the session is over, the connection is torn down.

Once the connection has been established, the client side submits formulated requests, such as the Read Operation, Search Operation, Compare Operation, AddEntry Operation, RemoveEntry Operation, ModifyDN Operation, and some others.

The DAP specification in the context of X.500 describes all possible communication error states. Connection error messages are delivered to the initiating party. This is good news for both users and developers. The user camp benefits from knowing

when they specify a nonexistent resource. The developer camp benefits by having access to error information, which can further be used to eliminate or contain conditions that cause errors.

DAP respects the OSI networking model. The Lightweight Directory Access Protocol (LDAP), which is a revision of the DAP, is covered in the following sections.

Lightweight Directory Access Protocol (LDAP)

The LDAP directory service is a simplified version of the X.500 counterpart, DAP. X.500 defines the directory structure, as well as the DAP protocol, which is used to access the directory. DAP turned out to be a complicated protocol, which was not feasible to implement in TCP/IP networks. People at the University of Michigan first developed, and IETF later standardized, the answer to the problem—LDAP—which enabled Internet users to work with the data stored in X.500 directories.

The LDAPv1 standard emerged and was described in RFC1487. LDAPv1, the first revision of LDAP, introduced the LDAP client entity and LDAP gateway entity, which were used as communication middlemen between TCP/IP LDAP clients and DAP X.500 directories. Soon after, LDAPv2 came along (RFC1777 and others). LDAPv1 assumes interoperability between X.500 directories and TCP/IP-based clients, but LDAPv2 introduces the capability of adding autonomous LDAPv2 directories (autonomous in respect to X.500 directories) as well as the LDAP server.

These days, we no longer rely on the first two revisions of the LDAP standard. LDAPv3, described in RFC2251 and some others, is the standard of choice for modern directory systems based on TCP/IP. It eliminates many shortcomings of its predecessors, transforming an otherwise great theory into a practical instrument for building distributed information systems. LDAPv3 allows extending the directory schema, which, as discussed earlier in the chapter, is sometimes necessary. It makes it possible to modify existing object classes and introduce new object classes to the system.

Since the LDAP standard is really a subentity of a wider X.500 standard, I will not spend much time describing it, but only cover a few key areas and improvements.

LDAP Functionality   Functional operations supported by LDAP directory services are based on client-server architecture, and provide mechanisms for establishing client-server connections, authenticating clients, performing searches and modifications of directory objects, and ending connections.

A set of LDAP utilities can be used with any LDAP directory regardless of the server operating system, and each vendor of LDAP directories provides some of those tools, such as ldapsearch, ldapmodif. These tools can be used manually or in automated scripts to search for specific information in the distributed environment. In addition to utilities, there are some LDAP browsers on the market, which provide visual representation and navigation of the LDAP structure and data, as well as other more traditional functions such as search and modification.

The ability to access LDAP servers and data through a regular web browser using URL references is yet another improvement, or rather innovation, introduced with LDAPv3. This is described in RFC1959. A new prefix was introduced to URL formatted references, ldap://. The latest versions of Microsoft Internet Explorer fully support LDAP URLs and extend the classical functionality of a web browser by making it possible to search distributed directories.

LDAP Schema   The directory schema consists of object class definitions. New classes are described using a class name and a set of attributes and acceptable values that are inherited by objects of this class. For each object class you can also define one or more parent classes, definitions of which will be *inherited*. All attributes defined as mandatory for the parent class are likewise inherited by the child class, as mandatory. The same holds true for optional attribute inheritance.

Another improvement of the LDAP schema is dealing with the way object classes are defined. In X.500, you need to describe all of the properties of objects in the class, and also define value constraints for those attributes in the class. In LDAP, the process is somewhat different. Instead of defining attributes in the class, you define attributes separately as part of the schema, unrelated to object classes. When you later build object classes, you establish class attributes based on this set of attributes that is kicking around in the schema. This ensures that you do not create new class attributes with the same names, which may end up having different value types and constraints. This makes the whole development and support process a bit easier and more consistent.

Extending schemas is a fairly straightforward operation. One example that comes to mind is Microsoft Active Directory 2000 and Microsoft Exchange 2000. When you install the first instance of Exchange service in your directory, you must first extend its schema to support new types of objects introduced with Exchange, as well as extend existing user object classes to support Exchange-specific attributes, such as multiple email addresses and mail delivery rules and restrictions.

A problem arises when you have distributed, heterogeneous environments—how do you synchronize or manage objects of the same class that have different sets of attributes? LDAPv2 did not address this problem due to the assumption that it was not an independent system, but rather a middleman between clients and X.500. LDAPv3 provides a universal solution to this issue: it employs subschemas. This allows publication and exchange of schema information between LDAP servers, and before any synchronization can take place between any two LDAP servers that are part of the same directory, they must exchange schemas first.

Security Improvements   One of the most important improvements introduced with LDAP is support for more secure authentication mechanisms, most of which are also industry standards. The LDAP standard specification allows using the popular Secure Sockets Layer (SSL) as well as Simple Authentication and Security Layer (SASL) mechanisms. SSL can be used to secure plain-text passwords inherent to LDAP. It is also a viable alternative to third-party centralized authentication systems, such as Kerberos (although it is more of a standard these days), if there is a need to replace such systems.

CERTIFICATION OBJECTIVE 1.05

Windows Implementations of Directory Services and Windows Server 2003 Active Directory

Microsoft implemented directory services based on X.500 and LDAP standards in Windows 2000 Active Directory (AD 2000). Major competitors were already introducing second or even third generations of their directory services at the time. Nevertheless, it is safe to say that Microsoft found itself among the leaders in the directory space in a short time, and also introduced a series of products ranging from "directory aware" to "cannot install without it." Active Directory is here to stay.

Recall that application and directory integration is one of the reasons directories were developed some 15 years ago. Industry experts argue that Microsoft is one of the very few companies that, in fact, achieved this objective successfully.

Early Competitors

Many companies attempted their own directory implementations for commercial use after X.500 was finalized. Predictably, these first versions did not win much popularity. This was partly due to lack of user acceptance—developers saw an opportunity that companies were slow to acknowledge and even slower to spend resources on implementing. Developers argued that it was similar to a telephone directory, containing a large amount of very specific information, and that they were facilitating access to that information. "All you have to do is write a simple application," they added.

Novell introduced its own version of directory services in 1993. NetWare Directory Services (NDS) was first used to store NetWare-specific information. Later on, Novell extended NDS functionality to apply to many other enterprise resources, and so they renamed NDS to Novell Directory Services (likewise NDS) in 1996. NDS developers successfully implemented a centralized authentication system dubbed *single sign-on* (SSO). SSO enabled users to access any network resource while having to supply their authentication information only once, as the name implies.

It was not long after that Microsoft realized the full potential of directory services. Microsoft and Novell were fierce competitors in the network operating systems (NOS) arena right around the same time, fielding Windows NT and NetWare, respectively. Microsoft first moved to provide an add-on directory for Windows NT, released in a resource kit. Quite naturally, Novell was gaining ground as a result of Microsoft's patchwork approach, and was claiming as recently as 1998 that they managed the Windows NT environment better than Microsoft themselves (referring to Windows NT client and server integration into networks managed by NDS). Corporations were rolling out NetWare en masse.

Microsoft, still playing catch-up, had to come up with something more credible, like a version of directory service that is inherent to a network operating system. In 2000, Microsoft shipped its first code of Windows 2000, the next-generation enterprise operating system built on Windows NT. Its headline feature? Active Directory.

Windows 2000 and Active Directory

This book, of course, is about Active Directory planning and administration with Windows Server 2003. However, a lot of what is true about Windows 2000 Active Directory is still true about Windows Server 2003 Active Directory. Let's pay a brief visit to AD 2000.

Active Directory is a vehicle for storage and retrieval of information in a distributed environment that has its own security mechanisms. There is no distinction between users and applications in terms of who can access AD resources and how they are allowed to access them (subject to security settings).

AD is used in Windows 2000 in many different ways. Operating systems store user accounts and refer to the directory during authentication. Exchange servers store address book objects and digital certificates in the directory. DCOM applications use the directory to locate remote objects and applications. In other words, AD is the main reason why we have a distributed environment in the Windows world.

As you know, one of the main benefits of standardized directories is that they simplify integration of heterogeneous environments. Information stored in the AD can be used by applications that have their own directories, such as Lotus Notes. Likewise, AD can import NDS objects, and vice versa, allowing easy migration and coexistence of the two directories.

Windows 2000 AD supported X.500 and LDAP naming standards, as well as LDAP URL requests and the more familiar universal naming convention (UNC) references. Perhaps the strongest feature of Active Directory is its much improved manageability and security. These are the main benefits of using AD:

- **Single logon (SSO)** Users have to authenticate only once. Successful authentication grants access to all system resources, regardless of their location in a distributed environment.

- **Global catalog (GC)** *Global catalogs* store a limited set of attributes for all objects in the entire directory. They respond to search requests by returning LDAP references to real locations of objects. Administrators can control which attributes to make available to the GC, and therefore control which attributes can be used in searches. The GC optimizes query times by reducing the number of chained requests.

- **Lowered TCO through centralized administration** AD is perhaps the first viable solution to centralizing administrative control in the Windows world.

- **Delegated administrative authority** It follows from the previous point that if it is possible to centralize administrative control, it should be a lot easier to control and manage delegation of administrative authority.

- **IntelliMirror** This technology makes it possible for data to follow users, wherever they go. It spans features such as remote installation services (RIS), roaming user profiles, automated software rollout and management, and offline folders and synchronization. To end users, this means their data is available regardless of which workstation they use, and sometimes even regardless of whether they are currently connected to the network.

- **Automated software rollout and management** Administrators can assign applications either to computers or users, and let Windows do the rest.

- **Multimaster replication** Active Directory implements a multimaster replication model, allowing simultaneous modifications of objects on more than one directory server.

- **Group policies** Group policies are security and configuration templates that can be linked to local computer objects, sites, domains, or OU containers. They allow tighter control of what users are allowed to do and how their computers should behave in a distributed environment.

- **Security** Active Directory implements ACLs not only on the resource (object) level but also on the object attribute level. This allows more flexible control of which information should be made available to users. AD uses industry-standard authentication mechanisms such as Kerberos, SSL, smart cards, and PKI/X.509 digital certificates.

- **DNS integration** Active Directory uses DNS for its namespace, service location, and resource reference needs. Integration of the two systems makes the best use of resources, since users are already somewhat familiar with DNS name formats and administrators have fewer namespaces to plan, deploy, and support. The fact that DNS is the industry-standard naming system only adds more weight to the argument.

- **Scalability** Active Directory provides adequate response times serving millions of objects. Forests, trees, domains, and OUs allow segmentation of network resources and also directory schema, which translates into a theoretical possibility of building distributed systems of virtually unlimited size.

- **Schema extensibility** Administrators can easily extend existing object classes and add new classes to Active Directory. This works great for new, directory-integrated applications that are written to take full advantage of the fact.

- **Active Directory Service Interfaces (ADSI)** Active Directory provides an easy way to access its resources through APIs. Custom administrative scripts are easily written to take full advantage of the time- and cost-saving features of AD from the IT management perspective. Custom applications can be easily written to look up or modify data in AD.

Windows Server 2003 Active Directory

While many improvements and features are certainly worth the wait, in many respects the difference between Active Directory 2000 and 2003 may be best described as evolution, not revolution. Windows Server 2003 improves Active Directory in four different categories of the product: interoperability, manageability, security, and performance. What follows is a brief first look at AD 2003.

Interoperability

The main interoperability gains are achieved by overall improvements in the area of API and GUI interfaces. AD 2003 supports new industry-standard object classes out of the box; it adds service integration with Passport; it implements broader support for newer industry standards such as XML; and delivers an enhanced Active Directory Migration Tool (ADMT v2).

Manageability

Manageability gains come from improvements in Windows Management Instrumentation (WMI) and more mature scripting support. AD 2003 has a revised replication topology generation, and now allows directory replicas to be inserted from media, as opposed to waiting for replication cycles. AD 2003 improves management by introducing application partitions. For the first time, administrators can control replication and availability of certain portions of AD data on directory servers of choice. New MMC-based consoles have also been written and are available out of the box.

Security

AD 2003 introduces new types of previously unavailable interforest trusts. Among other new features, authentication request routing, cross-forest authentication, and credential management features stand out. Less fundamental but still apparent improvements are present in security management tools and controls, and new wizards are shipped as well.

Performance

Perhaps the single biggest advantage of Windows Server 2003 technology is its support for 64-bit computing. Although the 64-bit platform is still price-prohibitive for some organizations, it will eventually become more common. Several improvements in the amount of control administrators have over the AD replication process also have performance implications. For example, administrators will be able to suppress intersite replication compression, reducing the CPU use on domain controllers at the expense of bandwidth use. Windows Server 2003 and AD have better support for clustered nodes, and a new cluster computer object class is introduced.

CERTIFICATION SUMMARY

This introductory chapter provided an overview of what we mean when we say "directory." Professionals new to Active Directory will find it most helpful; however, experienced professionals may also find it worthwhile to review the underlying concepts of what makes software a directory.

Defining precisely what makes software a directory is no trivial task, except we know that some common features and characteristics must exist in all directories. Directories allow locating and accessing resources in a way that is transparent to the end user. Users do not have to know or care which server has the resource they are looking for, nor do they need to know how the search and access processes work. All they have to do in order to be granted some form of access is to authenticate to the directory. Once authentication succeeds, the directory will ensure that ACLs on individual resources are honored, and users who are not explicitly authorized to use the resources will not be able to access them. Companies implement directory services to provide better resource and security management, both of which become a significant problem the bigger and more geographically decentralized the company becomes.

X.500 is the single most important standard that serves as a blueprint for many implementations of directories, including Active Directory. The standard further suggests that there is no simple definition of directory. Several companies have commercial directory products that implement most of the suggestions made by the standard; however, some deviations exist.

Not surprisingly, Microsoft incorporated many of the existing directory standards in its implementation of directory services, some of which date back as far as the 1980s. Industry standards benefit both consumers and developers, and the longer the standard has been out there, generally, the more mature it is.

Eventually, LDAP transformed the previously unfeasible elements of X.500 into something more easily attainable. The first version of LDAP was purely a modification of access to existing X.500 legacy systems. By the time LDAPv3 was introduced, it had become apparent that to make it a serious commercial project, developers needed a way to create directories for the TCP/IP network protocol environment. LDAP introduced that possibility, along with numerous improvements to, and modifications of, X.500. Over time, LDAP was transformed from being a gateway service to X.500 into something completely independent of the legacy system.

The last part of this chapter described what Microsoft did in the first implementation of directory services in its flagship Windows product and how it eventually became a leader in the directory marketplace. A review of Windows 2000 AD covered the main features of the directory, which are still in Windows Server 2003 Active Directory. The point was made that Windows Server 2003 includes an evolutionary, not revolutionary, version of Active Directory. The new version introduces security, performance, management, and interoperability enhancements that were not available in Active Directory 2000. Things are getting faster, more reliable, and easier to use.

TWO-MINUTE DRILL

Definition of a Directory and Directory Services

❑ There is no single unambiguous definition of directory.

❑ Most of us think of a directory as something that can store and search data, and authenticate and authorize users.

❑ Authentication is the process that establishes user identity.

❑ Authorization is the process that controls access to resources.

❑ ACL is a listing of permissions defined on each individual resource.

❑ Reasons to implement directories include ease of locating resources, ease of management, and access control.

❑ A directory is a building block of every large or global enterprise or any environment that is distributed in nature.

Directory Standards

❑ Industry needs standards to foster growth and user acceptance.

❑ X.500 was formulated in the early days of directories and became a blueprint for many years to come.

Overview of X.500

❑ X.500 deals with the fundamental structure model, security model, distributed model, data replication, and access protocol aspects of directories.

❑ Object instances are collections of properties that represent a unit of data.

❑ Attributes and attribute values define properties of objects.

❑ An entry is a record in a directory database (same as object).

❑ DIB is a structure used to store entries. It is hierarchical and object-oriented in nature.

❑ DIB is presented in the form of an upside-down tree and is sometimes termed DIT. It contains three types of nodes: root, containers, and leaf objects.

❑ Root is the beginning of a DIT-like structure.

❑ Container is a unit of the structure that can host other containers and objects.

❑ Leaf objects are units of the structure that cannot host other containers (same as objects).

❑ DN is a path that unambiguously refers to the object.

❑ DNs can be absolute or relative. Relative DN is a CN, and it uniquely refers to the object in the context of its container.

❑ Parent-child relationship describes how objects and containers are linked to other containers.

❑ Inheritance is the flow of properties from upper levels to lower levels of DIT.

❑ OU is a type of container that organizations define in order to subdivide their resources in manageable groups. All OUs are containers; the opposite need not be true.

❑ Subtree is the name for a collection of downstream containers and objects that use another container as a root point of reference, instead of the DIT root itself.

❑ Directory schema is a set of object classes and attributes that describe what objects can be stored in the directory.

❑ Object class is a definition of a particular type of object.

❑ Attribute type describes whether a value must be set for a particular attribute, and also what type of value is permitted.

❑ Schemas can be extended and modified as a company's needs change.

❑ AAA is a term used in X.500 to describe autonomous units of a directory, the administration of which can be delegated.

❑ A DSA's (directory server agent's) function is to be aware of other directory servers.

❑ DSAs use chaining and referrals for directory-wide searches.

❑ DUA is a user agent, a particular implementation of a directory client.

❑ DAP is a protocol originally defined in X.500 that governs communications between DUAs and DSAs.

❑ Replication is the process of copying directory information to other servers participating in the infrastructure.

❑ Master copy is a database where all modifications are committed.

❑ Single master replication establishes one instance of the master copy.

❑ Replicas are read-only copies of master databases.

❑ LDAP is a simplified and enhanced version of X.500 that evolved to replace X.500 and adapt it to TCP/IP networks.

❑ Active Directory is Microsoft's version of directory services based on LDAP, and hence, X.500.

Windows Implementations of Directory Services and Windows Server 2003 Active Directory

❑ Windows Server 2003 Active Directory is the second version of directory from Microsoft.

❑ Significant improvements have been made, but they are evolutionary, not revolutionary.

❑ Major areas of improvement span security, performance, manageability, and interoperability.

SELF TEST

The following questions will help you measure your understanding of the material presented in this chapter. Read all the choices carefully because there might be more than one correct answer. Choose all correct answers for each question.

Definition of a Directory and Directory Services

1. Which of the following properties are common to all directory services implementations? (Choose all that apply.)
    A. Store and search user data
    B. Store and search administrator data
    C. Authenticate users
    D. Authorize requests to access resources

2. A user successfully logs on to the system and proceeds to work on her projects. After a few hours of work she attempts to save her work to a different location on the network, but fails. In the directory framework, this is an example of which one of the following issues?
    A. Authentication issue
    B. Authorization issue
    C. Resource access issue
    D. Permissions issue

3. A user logs on to his machine locally. He proceeds to work on his projects. After a few hours of work he attempts to save the work to a network location, but whenever he tries to access it, he gets a prompt to enter a username and a password. He tried a few combinations and they did not work, preventing him from saving the work on a network share. In the directory framework, this is an example of which one of the following issues?
    A. Authentication issue
    B. Authorization issue
    C. Resource access issue
    D. Permissions issue

4. What is the primary purpose of an ACL?
    A. It controls access to resources.
    B. It explicitly allows or denies access to a particular resource.
    C. It explicitly defines users and their respective access rights to a particular resource.
    D. All of the above.

5. Which of the following reasons may be valid "pro" arguments in deciding whether or not to go with directory services? (Choose all that apply.)

   A. Keep a better track of resources

   B. Set up a common security context or boundary

   C. Lower the TCO of information systems

   D. Enable highly distributed computing

Directory Standards

6. X.500 is a standard that first described directory services using which of the following communication protocols? (Choose all that apply.)

   A. NetBEUI

   B. TCP/IP

   C. IPX/SPX

   D. DAP

Overview of X.500

7. DIT is an abbreviation used to refer to which of the following? (Choose all that apply.)

   A. DIT, Directory Information Tree

   B. DIT, Directory Instance Tree

   C. DIB, Directory Information Base

   D. DIB, Directory Information Bit

8. XYZ Corp. has been growing steadily in the last few years and reached a point where centralized administration of directory resources is no longer practical. An administrator wishes to delegate some authority to manage user account objects to another administrator in a different location. Assuming that they have a flat department-level DIT structure, and speaking in general terms of directory services, what should they do? (Choose all that apply.)

   A. Create a separate root and populate it with the objects that need to be delegated.

   B. Create a separate subtree and populate it with the objects that need to be delegated.

   C. Instruct fellow administrators to use a workstation in their geographical location to administer the objects in their jurisdiction.

   D. Delegate necessary administration rights to the person who needs to manage the objects in question.

9. In terms of directory structure units, what would most closely describe a sound your guitar makes on a certain string at a certain fret?

    A. An attribute of a property

    B. A value of an attribute

    C. A value of a property

    D. An attribute type

10. The object reference CN=Kimi Raikkonen,OU=Race Drivers,O=McLaren,C=UK would be an example of which of the following? (Choose all that apply.)

    A. Relative distinguished name

    B. Relative distinct name

    C. Absolute distinguished name

    D. Absolute distinct name

11. Protocols and technologies such as SSL and Kerberos would correlate best with jurisdiction of which of the following X.500 models?

    A. Distributed model

    B. Authorization model

    C. Authentication model

    D. Security model

12. XYZ Corp. has been using LDAP-compliant directory services for quite a while with a certain amount of success. They now wish to implement a directory-integrated emailing system, meaning that email address information needs to be stored with existing user objects. Currently, these objects feature no such options. What should XYZ plan on doing prior to installing email software? (Choose all that apply.)

    A. Extend the directory schema

    B. Expand the directory schema

    C. Extend the directory DIT structure

    D. They cannot do this with the existing directory

13. In the context of directory services, AAA stands for which one of the following?

    A. Authentication, Authorization, and Accounting

    B. Autonomous Administrative Areas

    C. Autonomous Authentication and Authorization

    D. Administrative Area Accounting

14. A user account in a directory can be described as which of the following? (Choose all that apply.)

    A. Object instance

    B. Object class instance

    C. Collection of attribute and value pairs

    D. Entry in a directory database

15. A user logs on to the system and pulls up a program that, among other things, is a GUI implementation of DUA. She belongs to the Accounting OU in her organization and wants to find a fancy color printer in marketing's offices. Marketing has its own OU container, and the printer resource in question is assigned to that OU. The default search context is set to the user's home container. She searches but finds no color printers. What should be the first step in trying to troubleshoot this issue?

    A. Check if all DSAs are configured properly.

    B. Check if replication is working.

    C. Try a less specific search context.

    D. Try moving the user object to the directory server that has a printer resource.

Windows Implementations of Directory Services and Windows Server 2003 Active Directory

16. Windows Server 2003 does not introduce revolutionary, but rather evolutionary, technologies in several areas of Active Directory. Which areas are these? (Choose all that apply.)

    A. Administration

    B. Migration

    C. Integration

    D. Performance

17. The IntelliMirror set of technologies used in Active Directory allows which of the following functionalities? (Choose all that apply.)

    A. Remote installation services

    B. Automated software rollout and management

    C. Offline folder synchronization

    D. Roaming profiles

18. Which of the following advantages does the multimaster replication model provide? (Choose all that apply.)

    A. It reduces the number of directory servers.

    B. It makes LDAP queries faster.

    C. It allows more efficient modification of objects.

    D. It consumes less network bandwidth.

19. Global catalog servers are integral to the Active Directory environment. In the context of directory terminology and standards, which of the following best describes GC? (Choose all that apply.)

    A. It reduces query times, cutting the traditional DSA chaining mechanism.

    B. It stores a limited set of object attributes.

    C. It minimizes replication traffic.

    D. It minimizes query traffic.

20. The ADSI interface in Windows 2000/2003 serves which of the following purposes? (Choose all that apply.)

    A. It enables custom directory-aware applications.

    B. It enables custom directory administration mechanisms.

    C. It promotes integration and interoperability.

    D. It honors X.500 directives.

SELF TEST ANSWERS

Definition of a Directory and Directory Services

1. ☑ **A, B, C,** and **D.** All of the answers describe the use of a typical directory. Note that user data and administrator data carry the same meaning in the context of directory.
   ☒ None

2. ☑ **B.** This is a typical authorization issue, which deals with resource access after user identity is established.
   ☒ **A, C,** and **D.** A is incorrect because authentication deals with logon and verification of user identity. While **C** and **D** may be correct in principle, they are incorrect in the context of directory terminology.

3. ☑ **A.** Authentication issue is a correct description of the problem. The question is the opposite of question 2.
   ☒ **B, C,** and **D.** B is incorrect because authorization has not kicked in yet due to lack of identity verification. While **C** and **D** may be correct in principle, they are incorrect in the context of directory terminology.

4. ☑ **C.** ACL is responsible for the definition of who can do what with a particular resource.
   ☒ **A, B,** and **D.** A is incorrect because directory security mechanisms verify user actions and effectively control access, not ACL. **B** is incorrect because it uses different language to state the same thing as in **A**. **D** is incorrect because **C** is correct.

5. ☑ **A, B, C,** and **D.** All of the reasons listed are good arguments in support of implementing directory services.
   ☒ None

Directory Standards

6. ☑ **D.** DAP was initially described as the communication protocol between X.500 directory servers and clients.
   ☒ **A, B,** and **C.** A is incorrect because NetBEUI is a nonroutable protocol that cannot be used in distributed environments. **B** is incorrect because LDAP introduced TCP/IP to the directory world. **C** is incorrect because IPX was Novell's proprietary protocol.

Overview of X.500

7. ☑ **A** and **C.** A and C refer to the same directory structure. DIT is a more specific description because it reflects on the fact that DIB is represented as a tree.
   ☒ **B** and **D.** Both **B** and **D** are nonexistent terms.

8. ☑ **B and D.** B would be necessary to establish an AAA. D, in turn, would take advantage of the fact and establish delegation.

☒ **A and C.** A is incorrect because a directory always has only one root. C is incorrect because in a directory environment, physical locations of resources do not matter.

9. ☑ **B.** Working with the given answers, **B** is best because that is the only combination of attributes and values which together describe properties. In an ideal world, however, we might think of introducing a new object class that would describe sound, and then link the two.

☒ **A, C, and D.** A is incorrect because "properties" is not a directory term, and because properties do not have attributes—properties *are* attributes paired with values. C is incorrect for a similar reason. D is incorrect because an attribute type defines an attribute itself in the object class, not a particular attribute of an object instance.

10. ☑ **C.** The example is an absolute distinguished name.

☒ **A, B, and D.** A is incorrect because a relative distinguished name only provides a unique reference within the object's own container; in this case it would be CN=Kimi Raikkonen. B and D are incorrect because they are not directory terms.

11. ☑ **D.** The given security protocol examples are covered in the security model.

☒ **A, B, and C.** A is incorrect because the distributed model deals with technologies such as DSA and replication, not security. B and C are incorrect because these models do not exist.

12. ☑ **A.** Extending the directory schema is the most appropriate answer—the company needs to modify the user object class to include email address properties.

☒ **B, C, and D.** B is incorrect because expansion of schema is not a term. C is incorrect because extending the DIT structure of directory will not modify the object class in question. D is incorrect because **A** is correct.

13. ☑ **B.** Autonomous Administrative Areas correctly describes AAA.

☒ **A, C, and D.** While these terms may exist in other areas of computing, they do not belong in a directory services discussion.

14. ☑ **B, C, and D.** All correctly describe a user account object.

☒ **A.** A is incorrect because you cannot have an instance of an instance. One of the definitions of objects is that they are instances of their respective object classes.

15. ☑ **C.** A less specific search will do the trick, unless there is a technical problem with the directory, in which case real-world administrators would have a much bigger problem to deal with.

☒ **A, B, and D.** A and B are incorrect because while these are plausible actions in theory, they are not the first steps to try. D is incorrect because the physical location of users and resources is irrelevant from a directory's perspective.

Windows Implementations of Directory Services and Windows Server 2003 Active Directory

16. ☑ **A, B, C,** and **D.** All of the areas feature improvements. Note that migration and integration mean interoperability.
    ☒ None

17. ☑ **A, B, C,** and **D.** All of the choices presented relate to IntelliMirror.
    ☒ None

18. ☑ **C. C** is correct because the ability to write changes to any of the servers improves response times for administrators and balances the load, resulting in improved performance for users.
    ☒ **A, B,** and **D. A** and **B** are incorrect because multimaster replication has no effect either on the number of servers required to maintain the infrastructure or on the speed of LDAP queries, at least not in a good way. **D** is incorrect because any given change still has to find its way through from the server it was committed to, to any given number of directory servers.

19. ☑ **A, B,** and **D. A, B,** and **D** correctly describe the role of the global catalog in the Active Directory environment.
    ☒ **C. C** is incorrect because global catalog replication can be viewed as duplication of effort in some ways, which at the very minimum will not add to existing Active Directory replication, never mind reducing it. The real need for GC is in its ability to minimize query times and traffic.

20. ☑ **A, B, C,** and **D.** All of the statements correctly describe the purpose of ADSI.
    ☒ None

2

Planning and Implementing the DNS Infrastructure

Although this chapter does not cover any certification objectives per se, it lays the groundwork necessary to plan and implement a robust Windows 2003 Active Directory infrastructure. Microsoft Exam 70-294 makes certain assumptions about namespace proficiency among candidates. In addition, some Active Directory topics are simply synonymous with DNS due to a close integration and dependency between the two. Exam candidates should assume the possibility that questions covering DNS could be presented on the actual exam.

Let's say you log on to your workstation, launch an Internet browser application, and type in the address of your favorite news provider website. Before the homepage starts loading, dozens of domain name system servers around the globe will have done all the name resolution work required for translating a common address of the website to its IP address, which is what your browser needs in order to initiate the download and display the homepage of the site. Your computer submits a request to a domain name database server by providing the name of the resource, and expects to receive its IP address.

Gone are the days when entire contents of such a database could be stored on a single computer in a single flat "hosts" file, and likewise gone are the days when short and simple domain names were readily available. Domain naming has been transformed from a single, centralized, flat repository into a highly distributed, hierarchical system, where no single server or area of the system is responsible for the system's operation.

CERTIFICATION OBJECTIVE 2.01

Overview of DNS

From Chapter 1, we know that large, distributed environments are impossible or at least extremely expensive to manage without directory services. In the early days, DNS was used in a few dozen universities in the United States, but things have changed. These days, it is safe to assume that every corporate network with over ten computers uses some form of DNS resolution. DNS in Windows 2003 is effectively a backbone for building Active Directory, acting as a middleman between directory servers; therefore, some form of interoperability between different domain name systems will have to be implemented, even more so when the enterprise has some sort of connectivity to the Internet.

This chapter deals with topics and questions directly related to resource name resolution—what these resource names consist of and why; how to set up a resolution service and enable Internet users to request resources provided by your network; and how to properly configure the system and prepare it for Active Directory implementation. You will see that DNS and X.500/LDAP directory have a lot in common as far as design and structure are concerned. They feature the same "." root; then several levels of domain names, such as .com or .net; and finally, familiar leaf objects—hostnames—which together with domain names and the root are termed *fully qualified domain names* (*FQDNs*). These elements of the DNS structure map directly to the elements of a typical X.500 directory.

The domain name system is an open standard, supported by virtually all vendors of Internet-capable software, Microsoft included. In addition to getting ready for Active Directory implementation, which relies heavily upon name resolution provided by the domain name system, you will learn (or review) the concepts of zones—types of zones in Windows 2003, the main differences between them, and transfer and replication implications—which, in turn, will make you more adept at planning and implementing larger-scale DNS systems, possibly involving other vendors and systems such as UNIX.

The name resolution system is maintained on DNS servers responsible for their own areas of the network. These servers maintain a local database of host-to-IP address mappings and respond to queries performed by DNS clients. Administrators must ensure that DNS servers respond to queries in a timely fashion, and that these servers are reliable and secure. As we review each of these areas in greater detail in the chapter, the focus will be on Windows 2003, and we will review the main differences between Windows 2003 DNS and its predecessor, Windows 2000 DNS. DNS is implemented on a common base of standards, so this knowledge is not really OS specific, although some elements may suggest that.

Whereas Active Directory emerges as a successor to the Windows NT 4.0 domain model and its SAM user and computer account database, DNS in Windows emerges as a successor to the NetBIOS name resolution system, implemented in Windows Internet Name Service (WINS). WINS was very convenient in smaller networks, where it provided dynamic mapping of IP addresses to NetBIOS names; however, in larger environments this service proved to be unreliable and inefficient. DNS implemented in Windows 2000 and 2003 borrowed some of the features found in WINS to accommodate ease of use in smaller networks—for example, Dynamic DNS (DDNS), which allows dynamic registration of DNS hostnames, and the ability to map IP addresses to network services in addition to hostnames. AD clients learn about domain controllers (and directory services they provide) based on special DNS registrations, which we will review later in the chapter. IP addresses-to-network services mappings are implemented using SRV (service locator) records.

Crucial technical aspects notwithstanding, perhaps the main learning objective of this discussion is to understand how a distributed directory-like system, located on thousands of servers around the world and administered by as many independent operators, works as a unified system, allowing any user on the Internet to unambiguously resolve any resource made available for the general public.

Purpose of DNS

The vast majority of corporate and interconnected networks (such as the Internet) use the TCP/IP protocol to transfer information between network nodes involved in data communications. Each of the participating nodes must have a valid IP address assigned to it in order to communicate; a valid IP address must be unique within the TCP/IP subnet where it is used. (There are other conditions that make IP addresses invalid even if they are unique, as well as some exceptions when two or more nodes can share the same IP address—this goes well beyond the scope of our chapter.)

Version 4 of TCP/IP addresses are 32 bits long, and most of the time they are presented in a dotted-decimal format, such as 192.168.0.250, where four sets of numbers are separated by dots, with each of the sets representing 8 bits and therefore being called an *octet*. It follows that acceptable value ranges for octets are between 0 and 255, inclusive. IP addresses are "easily understood" by TCP/IP software implemented on network nodes such as computers and routers, but it's a different story when it comes to people trying to remember them.

To facilitate access to network resources, besides a unique IP address, certain easy-to-remember names, or *hostnames*, et al are assigned. However, we now have another problem—devices that connect our computers do not know what we mean by hostnames; in most cases, they are optimized to route traffic based purely on IP addresses. Chapter 1 mentioned a telephone directory as an example of a directory service, and this situation is analogous to telephone numbers. Telephone numbers usually are not easily remembered and do not follow an obvious hierarchical or other sort of visual pattern as to how they are assigned (not obvious to most of us at least). Imagine calling a local telco and asking to be connected with Mr. Jones from the customer service department of XYZ Inc. Most likely, all you will get in response is a continuous carrier tone. You (or your phone) need to know the number to dial.

The solution to this problem is the printed telephone directory and a directory assistance number. In the case of computer communications, directory service is provided by the DNS system. To access the services of the DNS, each participating node on the network is configured with one or more DNS server addresses. Therefore, the DNS server is a point of access to the DNS network service (implemented on a Windows 2003 Server in the context of our discussion).

The domain name system allows users to access resources based on easily memorized names that follow a logical pattern and in most cases are intuitive. In Microsoft-based systems, DNS support has been included beginning with Windows NT 4.0 Server, but as an optional network service. It became a fundamental network service beginning with Windows 2000, and now it has been further improved in Windows 2003/ Windows XP.

DNS is also necessary for Active Directory to function. Network resources such as user or computer accounts, printers, and shared folders are stored in Active Directory. Addressing and identification of these objects are based on LDAP naming conventions and use so-called distinguished names, which were discussed in Chapter 1. Another naming format based on the same standard and also used in AD is *canonical name*—a reference to an object such as flexecom.com/administrators/superuser. Addressing of a domain controller's internal objects may appear even more complicated: flexecom.com/ System/MicrosoftDNS/flexecom.com/_ldap._tcp.Toronto-site._sites.gc._msdcs.

As you can see, these examples of canonical name references are based on DNS hostnames or domain names ("flexecom.com" in this particular example), and thus the logical conclusion is that LDAP directory implementation in Windows 2000/2003 must rely on DNS name resolution. Intradomain addressing, as well as interdomain addressing and interoperability, employs the DNS system and inherits its hierarchical structure.

DNS is one of the fundamental network services provided with Windows 2003. Its purpose is to service client queries and resolve domain names into IP addresses and, in some cases, IP addresses into domain names. Technically speaking, the service accepts specifically formatted requests from network nodes, conducts a search of its database for matching records, and then either forwards the request to an upstream DNS server or constructs a reply to be sent back to the requesting node. Basic DNS configuration information is stored in the HKEY_LOCAL_MACHINE\SYSTEM\ CurentControlSet\Services\DNS registry key.

DNS is based on the TCP/IP suite of protocols, and so clients and servers use TCP and UDP protocols to exchange information. Client queries are submitted to DNS servers via UDP port 53, whereas zone transfers between the servers are conducted using a TCP protocol, port 53. The difference is that transmission of client-to-server and server-to-client information is not critical for DNS operation, and thus the UDP connectionless mechanism provides significantly less network traffic and processing overhead. There is no need to establish and tear down connections, and if one query gets lost due to a network error, the client will submit it again after a time-out period expires. On the other hand, zone transfers happen less frequently as compared to client queries, and successful transfers are critical to ensuring stable and consistent DNS operation across all participating servers within a common administrative zone. The TCP protocol guarantees delivery in this case.

To summarize, the main purpose of DNS service in Windows 2003 is to resolve domain names and FQDN addresses to IP addresses and vice versa, and to locate network services and resources on the network. However, each DNS server does not know about every single network resource out on the Internet; instead, it only contains a small number of so-called zones, or subdirectories. The treelike structure of the DNS system, along with delegation of rights to administer subdirectory zones, allows clients to use any single DNS server to resolve any resource made available through the DNS. Recalling our directory service analogies, a DNS zone stored on a particular DNS server is just a local segment of an enormous directory database, and is preferred by clients of that particular server. However, clients do not need to know which DNS server they need to access in order to retrieve addressing information for a certain resource—DNS servers make sure that the process is fully transparent.

Elements of DNS

Name resolution in DNS is a fairly complicated process. Each part of this process involves several subroutines and deserves a separate discussion. Before proceeding with technical descriptions of DNS functionality, we need to define the elements and establish some terminology, specifically the purposes of zones and domains. In addition, this section covers the following:

- What makes each resource unique and distinguished from millions of other similar resources
- Which agents participate in resolving each resource
- What is the purpose of each type of resource

The logical boundary of all fully qualified domain names in each particular network is called the *namespace*. In this namespace, each host may belong to one of the domains—for example, hosts SRV1.flexecom.com and www.flexecom.com belong to the "flexecom.com" domain.

The definition of zone is a bit more technical and somewhat broader. A *zone* is a partition of a distributed database that is stored on the local DNS server and contains the actual DNS records. Zones may contain domains, subdomains, and perhaps even hostname records, which are identical to the domain name itself. For example, SRV1.flexecom.com, SRV12.sales.flexecom.com, and flexecom.com could all be stored in the same DNS zone. The following illustration depicts the relationship between zones and domains.

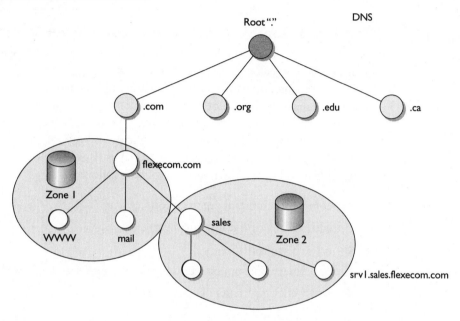

Domain Namespace

In the past, hosts on the Internet had certain distinguished, nongrouped hostnames that were used for unique identification of those hosts. Collectively, these hostnames belong to a *flat namespace,* where all names have equal weight and parity in the system; in other words, they do not depend on each other and are fully autonomous. A flat namespace in its entirety must be concentrated in a single location, perhaps on a single name server or cluster of name servers. Naturally, with the advance of the Internet, the size of this unified database would have exploded out of proportion and become unmanageable.

Another problem that quickly appeared was the finite number of meaningful, intuitive names that could be assigned to the hosts participating in the flat namespace. Hence, the technical community came up with a directory-like naming convention, effectively creating a *hierarchical namespace,* in which each hostname comprises several names separated by dots, such as exchange.farm1.flexecom.com.

The format of this type of hostname implies less specific location information on the right and more specific information on the left; thus reading from right to left, we start with the "dot," representing the root of the namespace, then .com, in our example, which is termed the *top level domain (TLD).* The full hostname beginning with the dot and ending with the "exchange" hostname is analogous to an absolute distinguished name in directory terms and is called the fully qualified domain name (FQDN) in DNS terms. Collectively, all FQDNs form the namespace.

Top Level Domain (TLD) and Second Level Domain (SLD)

Historically, TLDs were implemented in order to divide the namespace into autonomous areas for different sectors of the economy; for instance, government, education, commercial and nonprofit organizations, and the military all needed their own subdivision of namespace, independent of other participants in the namespace. Top level domains are governed by the Internet Corporation for Assigned Names and Numbers (ICANN), and the number of TLDs available for public use is limited. Queries between TLDs are serviced by the root domain servers, denoted as the dot before the TLD. The most commonly used North American TLDs are as follows:

- **com** Commercial organizations
- **edu** Educational institutions
- **org** Nonprofits
- **net** Network support centers and network service providers
- **gov** U.S. government
- **mil** U.S. military
- **two-letter ISO country code** Such as "us" for United States and "ca" for Canada. Each country has its own country-code TLD.

Thus, if you see a hostname or a domain name ending with .edu, it is most likely an educational institution in the United States. Likewise, a name ending with .ca more than likely represents an entity incorporated or registered in Canada—it could be either a university or a corporation.

Second level domain (SLD) is the next portion of an FQDN after the TLD, going from the root dot to the left. Continuing with our example, flexecom would be the SLD in www.flexecom.com. It wasn't long before short, descriptive, and intuitive SLD names were depleted, and remembering hostnames with three or four domain levels is tantamount to remembering IP addresses. So ICANN authorized a new set of TLDs in 2001, namely, .info, .biz, .name, .news, .pro, .museum, .aero, .inc, .mail, .games, .learn, and .coop. You can find a complete listing of new TLDs at http://www.icann.org/tlds.

To distinguish resources in local area networks from those located in the public portion of the namespace, companies are allowed to use the .local TLD name, which is invalid in the public sector, but it doesn't need to be registered with ICANN. For example, say we want to set up another namespace to be used locally in our imaginary organization. We could use flexecom.local, while flexecom.com is still maintained in parallel to support external requests that can be resolved using public namespace mechanisms. The .local TLD does not belong to the same root, so it cannot be resolved on the Internet. Note that individual companies in turn may still choose to resolve this name if they create static mappings in their DNS system. Technically, they can use any nonregistered TLD in this way.

DNS databases are also used for reverse resolution—that is, resolution of IP addresses into fully qualified domain names. To facilitate this, DNS uses a special service zone, in-addr.arpa. Although this may seem like a second level domain, the in-addr.arpa zone is as important from the reverse name resolution perspective as a top level domain is from the name resolution perspective. A reverse name resolution zone is named using octets denoting classified network ID numbers, ordered in reverse if you read from left to right. For example, IP address 192.168.10.1 is a class C IP address, where 192.168.10 represents the network ID and .1 represents the host ID.

So if we wanted to set up a zone for reverse mapping of IP addresses to hostnames, we would name the domain 10.168.192.in-addr.arpa. In essence, if you request the hostname of the 192.168.10.1 machine, you request addressing information for node "1" from domain 10.168.192.in-addr.arpa. Similarly, in the case of a class A address, such as 10.1.1.1, we would need the 10.in-addr.arpa domain, and in a class B address, such as 172.16.30.11, it would be 16.172.in-addr.arpa. In the latter example, the 16.172.in-addr.arpa domain would need to contain a 30. subdomain, where information about host "11" would be stored.

SLDs such as "flexecom.com" must be registered with any of the domain registrars to prevent name duplication and to set them up on the TLD servers, which in turn enable SLD name resolution by third-party agents on the Internet. Uniqueness of third level domains and lower is not crucial for name resolution on the Internet as a whole, and is usually the responsibility of the company or organization that owns the respective SLD.

Fully Qualified Domain Name (FQDN)

As is the case in searching a directory, requests in the DNS system can be absolute or relative: fully qualified domain name requests are absolute, and hostname requests are relative to the domain and subdomain (in other words, context) where the client host is located. The operating system will usually construct the queries to conform to the absolute format, which is what DNS servers expect to receive. Relative names must be identical within the boundaries of the subdomain or domain where they are registered (as in directories).

A fully qualified domain name, contrary to the hostname, includes all parent domains up to and including the root domain, which in turn guarantees their uniqueness in the DNS namespace. A prominent example is the "www" hostname you see everywhere you look. There are literally millions of hosts named www around the world, yet their FQDNs are unique because they include the company SLD domain, then TLD, and then the root.

Different operating systems handle FQDN requests in their own ways, but usually the name resolution request submitted with the dot at the end (to the right of the FQDN) means that the root domain is included in the request and there is nothing else left to be appended. If the dot at the end is missing, which means the request is relative and may include just the hostname, or hostname with a parent level domain appended, the client will usually attempt to append the missing portion of the FQDN. This missing portion is called the primary DNS suffix, and it is normally configured in the client settings.

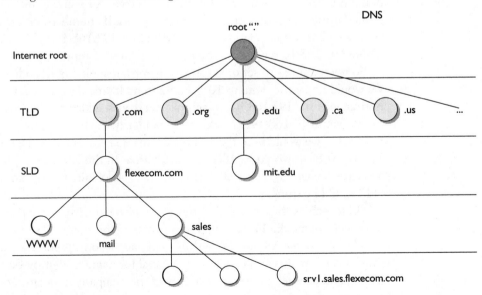

In the days of Windows NT 4.0, the NetBIOS name and DNS hostname were not related or dependent on one another. To ensure backward compatibility of applications in Windows 2000/2003/XP and also to reduce administrative overhead, hostname and NetBIOS names are being set identically. This means that the hostname portion of FQDNs must conform to NetBIOS name requirements. Assigning the same NetBIOS name and hostname is not mandatory, but it is recommended if your network still uses applications that rely on NetBIOS names. You must be sure in this case that you assign valid NetBIOS names that are compatible with host-naming RFCs. Microsoft recommends combining two namespaces (assigning identical names) or getting rid of NetBIOS entirely, whenever possible.

Valid hostnames in the case of coexistence of both namespaces are those consisting of letters and numbers. The first character must not be a number, and the total hostname length should not exceed 15 characters.

exam

watch

Hostnames in DNS can be up to 24 characters in length, but NetBIOS names can only be up to 15 characters in length. To avoid maintaining two conflicting namespaces, design your DNS namespace to honor the 15-character limit and assign the same NetBIOS hostname. This is not mandatory, but highly recommended.

Underscores are permitted in the NetBIOS namespace, but they are not a valid DNS hostname character. Underscores in DNS names are only permitted in service records, not host records (DNS RFCs: 1034, 1035, 1123, 1995, 1996, 2136, 2181, 2308, and some others). So if you have existing NetBIOS names with underscores, they will have to be changed to hyphens. Some recent revisions of the DNS standard also made it possible to use languages other than English when naming hosts; however, this technology is not very reliable outside the local area network.

Resource Records

Zone files contain numerous records that follow a certain format and describe specific types and addresses of the resources. These records are called *resource records* (*RRs*). Depending on the type, resource records may contain information about the zone itself, about other DNS servers maintaining the zone, about mail servers, network nodes, network services, and numerous other types of resources. To add, modify, or delete resource records in Windows 2000/2003, you can either use a DNS management tool (covered later in the chapter) or any text editor and then reload the content of the zone file directly into the file system. Figure 2-1 shows the content of a typical DNS zone.

You'll find a detailed description of the zone file format in RFCs 1035 and 2052. Among some of the mandatory resource record fields are Owner, TTL, Class, and Type. Table 2-1 gives brief descriptions of these fields.

The DNS management interface displays the structure of the DNS zones and domains in a familiar treelike structure and controls the input, preventing syntax errors when adding records; so if you have to edit the zone file directly, make sure you fully understand what is involved.

The following few sections review the most commonly used types of resource records. We'll begin with SOA and NS records, as they are regarded to be the most critical

FIGURE 2-1   A typical DNS zone

```
flexecom.com.dns - Notepad                                                              _ □ ×
File  Edit  Format  View  Help
;  Database file flexecom.com.dns for flexecom.com zone.
;      Zone version:  33
;
@                        IN   SOA  win2003srv.flexecom.com.  hostmaster.flexecom.com. (
                              33           ; serial number
                              900          ; refresh
                              600          ; retry
                              86400        ; expire
                              3600        ) ; default TTL


;  Zone NS records
;
@                        NS      win2003srv.flexecom.com.


;  Zone records
;
@                             600    A       192.168.0.254
b0869ebe-018a-44b5-b38f-647bcce67b7a._msdcs 600 CNAME   win2003srv.flexecom.com.
_kerberos._tcp.Default-First-Site-Name._sites.dc._msdcs 600     SRV     0 100 88        win2003srv.flexecom.com.
_ldap._tcp.Default-First-Site-Name._sites.dc._msdcs 600 SRV     0 100 389      win2003srv.flexecom.com.
_kerberos._tcp.dc._msdcs 600    SRV     0 100 88        win2003srv.flexecom.com.
_ldap._tcp.dc._msdcs    600     SRV     0 100 389       win2003srv.flexecom.com.
_ldap._tcp.2d42a6aa-34ac-4c97-b4e4-587d88f4f5cb.domains._msdcs 600      SRV     0 100 389       win2003srv.flexecom.com.
gc._msdcs               600     A       192.168.0.254
_ldap._tcp.Default-First-Site-Name._sites.gc._msdcs 600 SRV     0 100 3268    win2003srv.flexecom.com.
_ldap._tcp.gc._msdcs    600     SRV     0 100 3268      win2003srv.flexecom.com.|
_ldap._tcp.pdc._msdcs   600     SRV     0 100 389       win2003srv.flexecom.com.
_gc._tcp.Default-First-Site-Name._sites 600     SRV     0 100 3268      win2003srv.flexecom.com.
_kerberos._tcp.Default-First-Site-Name._sites 600       SRV     0 100 88        win2003srv.flexecom.com.
_ldap._tcp.Default-First-Site-Name._sites 600   SRV     0 100 389       win2003srv.flexecom.com.
_gc._tcp                600     SRV     0 100 3268      win2003srv.flexecom.com.
_kerberos._tcp          600     SRV     0 100 88        win2003srv.flexecom.com.
_kpasswd._tcp           600     SRV     0 100 464       win2003srv.flexecom.com.
_ldap._tcp              600     SRV     0 100 389       win2003srv.flexecom.com.
_kerberos._udp          600     SRV     0 100 88        win2003srv.flexecom.com.
_kpasswd._udp           600     SRV     0 100 464       win2003srv.flexecom.com.
DomainDnsZones          600     A       192.168.0.254
_ldap._tcp.Default-First-Site-Name._sites.DomainDnsZones 600    SRV     0 100 389       win2003srv.flexecom.com.
_ldap._tcp.DomainDnsZones 600   SRV     0 100 389       win2003srv.flexecom.com.
ForestDnsZones          600     A       192.168.0.254
_ldap._tcp.Default-First-Site-Name._sites.ForestDnsZones 600    SRV     0 100 389       win2003srv.flexecom.com.
_ldap._tcp.ForestDnsZones 600   SRV     0 100 389       win2003srv.flexecom.com.
win2003srv              A       192.168.0.254
```

TABLE 2-1	Resource Record Fields and Zone File Format
Owner	This field is used to define the association between the record and the domain it belongs to. The @ character can be used in the zone file as a pointer to the current domain.
Time to Live (TTL)	This field defines the resource's *time to live*, which is the period of time the record shall be made available through the secondary DNS servers in situations when it is not possible to update the zone information from the primary DNS server. The same TTL value is used by the caching DNS servers to identify the duration of validity of any record stored in the cache. This field is mandatory for the main zone record SOA (start of authority); and the records contained in the zone usually inherit the TTL of the SOA, unless a different value is configured explicitly.
Class	This is the class of the record. In Windows 2003, only one class is supported—IN, or Internet. This does not limit Windows 2003 DNS server abilities in any way, because other classes are practically unused.
Type	This field defines the type of record. Types of records correlate with client query types (QTYPE). Depending on the query type the server gets from a client, it searches for the record in question and returns the result in a way that the client expects. Some examples of record types are PTR, A, SRV.
Record-specific data	The information also included in records depends on the value of the Type field. Records may store specific information relevant only to that particular type of record.

ones for overall DNS operation. Fields of these records are displayed in the DNS management tool in the properties of each zone.

SOA and NS Resource Records

When you create a new DNS zone, it always automatically configures itself with an SOA record. SOA stands for "start of authority," and as the name implies, it denotes the starting point of authority for a particular zone in the namespace. As shown in Figure 2-2, this record contains information critical to zone operation. Most importantly, the SOA indicates which server is the primary name server for the zone in question. This information is then used in zone replication—the primary name server is the source of the most accurate and up-to-date zone information.

The serial number value of the zone is used in deciding whether it is time to synchronize the information between the primary and secondary name servers for the zone. When a change is committed to the zone file, the serial number value is incremented, signaling to replication partners that the primary server copy is more

FIGURE 2-2

SOA property
page

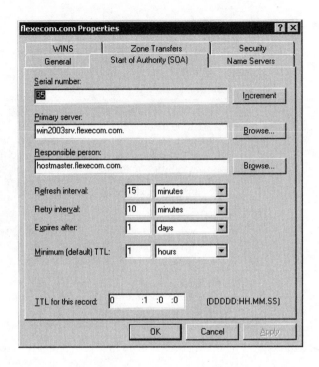

recent than what they received during the last replication cycle. (Replication is discussed in more detail later on.) This in turn means that if serial numbers on the primary server match serial numbers in the zone copies stored on the secondary servers, there is no need to replicate the zone, and hence no additional network bandwidth is used to achieve this unnecessary replication. (Note that it is possible to increment the serial number manually.)

The Expires After interval sets a time-out value for secondary zone servers, indicating how long they should store a copy of the zone and respond to client queries after connectivity to the primary zone server becomes unavailable. If the primary server cannot be contacted (and hence, zone information cannot be refreshed) for the duration of this interval, if secondary servers are no longer considered authoritative for the zone, and if local copies of the zone are no longer considered reliable, then secondary servers stop servicing requests for the zone. By default, the expire interval value allows 24 hours and is set in seconds (86,400 seconds).

The Refresh Interval sets a value for how often secondary servers should attempt to contact the primary server to verify their zone serial numbers. The less frequently you change information in the primary zone, the more sense it makes to increase this value. Less frequent attempts to refresh zone information will ultimately consume less network bandwidth, although given the bandwidth available to an average company today, this may turn out to be quite a trivial gain. This value is also set in seconds and is assigned 15 minutes by default.

The Retry Interval of the SOA record sets a value indicating how long secondary servers should wait before retrying a failed zone transfer attempt. This interval is generally shorter than the refresh interval, and is set in seconds to 10 minutes by default.

The Responsible Person field indicates the email address of the DNS administrator, who should be contacted if there is a problem with DNS setup that might be visible from external networks. If you wish to send an email to the DNS administrator, keep in mind that the usual @ sign is not featured in his or her email address due to the standardized format of the zone file. (The @ signs are used to indicate the beginning of a section in the zone file.) Instead of the @ sign, the responsible person's email address is listed with a "." character.

on the job

If you are tasked with setting up DNS zones in your company, keep in mind that it would not hurt to create mailboxes as indicated in the responsible person's SOA field, or to set contact information in the DNS to match an existing administrator's mailbox. That is, after all, the point of advertising this information through your DNS SOA record.

The last field of interest in SOA records is the Minimum (Default) TTL, sometimes referred to as M-TTL. The default TTL is used by the DNS server to automatically assign TTL values to individual records as you create them in the zone. If you specify a TTL that is less than the minimum TTL defined in the SOA, it will be ignored. Also keep in mind that SOA has its own TTL value, which equals the minimum TTL by default.

Here is an example showing a typical SOA record from a Windows Server 2003 zone file, configured with default values:

```
@                       IN  SOA win2003srv.flexecom.com.
hostmaster.flexecom.com. (
                            33          ; serial number
                            900         ; refresh
                            600         ; retry
                            86400       ; expire
                            3600    )  ; default TTL
```

NS resource records indicate which servers have been delegated authority for the domain in question. Delegation is a process of designating authoritative servers, which in plain terms means assigning servers to host a zone and service name resolution requests for that zone. Authoritative servers "own" records in the zone that has been delegated to them. Any server from the list of authoritative servers for a given domain is authorized to service queries for records in that domain. NS records may delegate authority not just to the primary server but to any name server.

In addition to domain delegation, NS records are used to delegate authority for subdomains. When you delegate authority for a subdomain, a list of NS servers is added to the zone file, and all of the servers on the list become authorized to service requests for that subdomain.

To summarize, SOA and NS records collectively form the backbone of DNS, serving as pointers and demarcations between numerous independent DNS subsystems, uniting them into a single distributed database. They allow navigating the DNS tree structure from the top down to lower levels of this structure, although that is about all they do—they do not represent any leaf objects in this structure, which is certainly not the point of having a directory. Leaf objects in DNS are various types of host records, which map hostnames to IP addresses within the structure (see Figure 2-3).

"A" Resource Records

The most basic type of mapping in the DNS, employed to map hostnames to IP addresses, is the "A" resource record. These simple mappings do not point to any network services, just plain network nodes. When you create a new "A" record, the DNS server

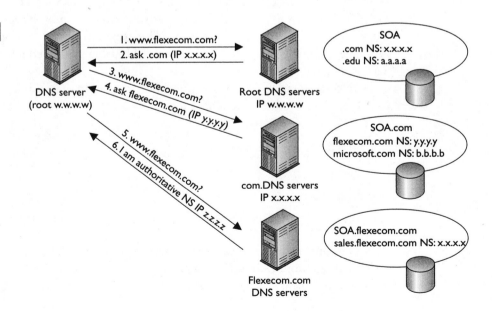

FIGURE 2-3

Leaf objects in DNS

automatically constructs an FQDN value for that host based on the context of the
zone by appending the parent portion of the DNS structure to the new hostname.
After you define the hostname, you need to provide an IP address before the record is
committed to the zone file. The Update Associated Pointer (PTR) Record option will
attempt to automatically add corresponding reverse mapping to the in-addr.arpa zone,
if that zone exists for the class of IP address you specify for the "A" record. Figure 2-4
depicts this.

In some cases, "A" records may be referred to as "glue records." The RFC standard
suggests not mapping service resource records directly to IP addresses, partly because
it will increase administrative overhead. As you will see later on, it is customary to
point service resource records to FQDNs; however, without creating an FQDN mapping
(which is an "A" record), the service record would be pointing nowhere. Then if you
map multiple network services to the same FQDN, and the IP address of that FQDN
changes later on, you would need to adjust just one "A" record, and this in turn will
have updated all the service records. In this way, "A" records glue service resource
records to actual hostname-IP mappings.

FIGURE 2-4

"A" resource
record

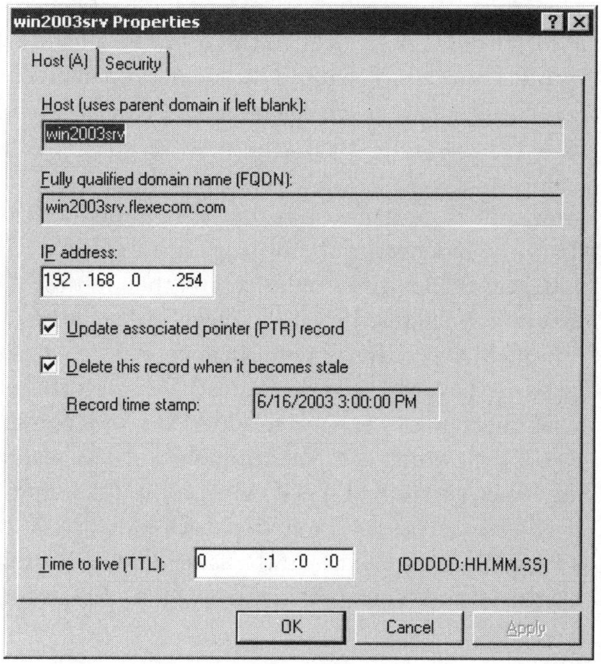

CNAME Resource Records

It may be necessary to assign more than one FQDN to the same physical host, or more specifically, to the same IP address. You could create multiple "A" records, but then you would have to update each of them every time the underlying IP address changes. To avoid this situation, you use CNAME resource records, also called aliases. Suppose you have a server with the hostname srv1.flexecom.com, and you want to make it available on the Internet for web and ftp services, at the same time providing intuitive addresses to users. You would create one "A" record, srv1.flexecom.com = [its IP address], and then add CNAME www.flexecom.com and ftp.flexecom.com and map it to srv1.flexecom.com's "A" record.

on the
job

While on the subject of making it easy to remember FQDNs, considering the example just given, you could also add an "A" record with an empty hostname field. This would map the domain name itself to an IP address and make it possible to refer to the server in question simply by using the flexecom.com domain name.

MX Resource Records

The MX resource record stands for Mail Exchanger, and it is one of the records used to locate network services, in this case, the email server responsible for mail delivery within a particular domain. The originating email server queries the destination domain for MX records, and gets one or more FQDNs in response. MX records point to one or more FQDNs of the email server(s), also indicating their priority, so that the originating email server picks the FQDN with the highest priority first (highest priority = lowest priority field value), resolves the FQDN into an IP address, and attempts delivery to that host. If delivery fails, the originating email server goes on to the next MX record with the second highest priority, and then retries, sending a piece of email through that host. Valid priority values fall within the range of two-digit decimal numbers. Equal priority MX records will result in approximately equal round-robin email distribution between these MX records. Figure 2-5 displays this process.

While it may be possible to add MX records pointing to IP addresses, this goes against RFC 1035, which describes the usage of MX records in detail. Some email server implementations will specifically prohibit delivery of email to MX records mapped to IP addresses. Therefore, you should always map MX records to FQDNs, and ensure that a valid "A" record exists in the same domain for that FQDN (so-called glue records). Figure 2-6 shows the property page for an MX record.

FIGURE 2-5

MX resource
records

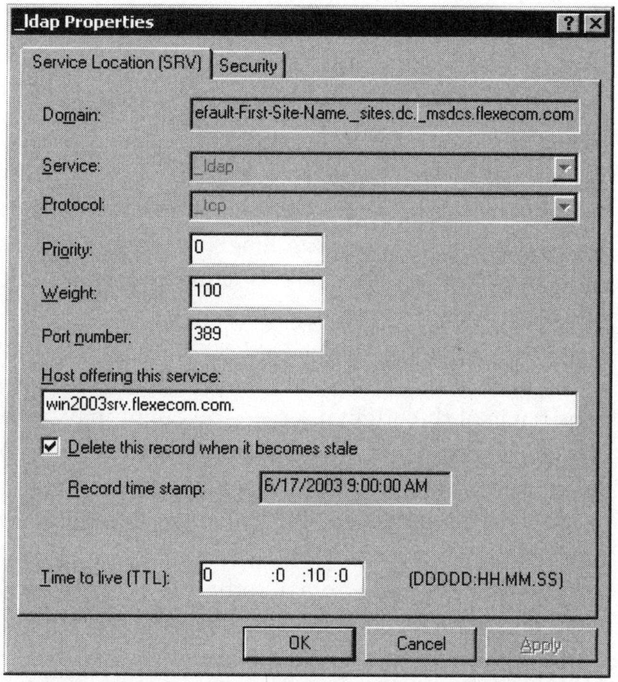

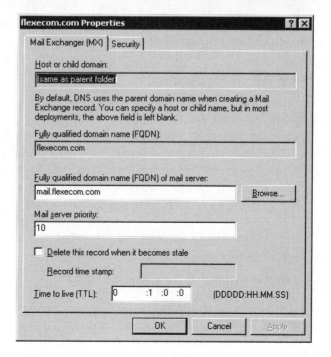

FIGURE 2-6

MX record
properties

PTR Resource Records

PTR records (PTR is short for "pointer"), provide the opposite functionality of "A" records. They provide reverse mapping of IP addresses to hostnames. This allows network nodes to obtain some information about the communicating party when only the IP address is known. For example, some Internet applications may use it to confirm the identity of the party, or collect domain names for the sake of statistics. It may be used as a rudimentary way of controlling some types of address spoofing and man-in-the-middle attacks, where server traffic gets redirected to a third-party node with an IP address different from the server.

In this case, the client may ask its own DNS server to resolve the third-party IP address into a hostname, and if the result does not match the advertised hostname of the original server, the client may opt to reject further communication. Internet servers, on their part, may also opt to block clients in certain domains from accessing their services, and they may rely on reverse DNS functionality to resolve IP addresses of clients into fully qualified domain names. (This is also one of the spam countermeasures.)

PTR records differ from all other types of records because they populate the in-addr.arpa zone used for reverse resolution. Zone types are covered in "DNS Zones," later in this chapter. As mentioned in the "A" record discussion, the easiest way to create PTR records is to ensure that a reverse resolution zone is created before you begin adding "A" records, and use the Update PTR Record option in the "A" record properties page. Figure 2-7 shows PTR record properties.

SRV Resource Records

Perhaps the most important addition to DNS service beginning with Windows 2000, the SRV record makes it possible for clients to locate Active Directory services. SRV is short for "service locator," and as the name implies, the records are used exclusively to locate services and not to resolve network hostnames. Windows 2000/2003/XP clients query their DNS servers for SRV records in order to identify which network hosts are running services of interest. Clients need to provide the following information when querying a DNS server for network services:

- Domain name that the client belongs to
- Globally unique identifier (GUID) of the domain (this is optional)
- Site name that the client belongs to

By submitting this information to their DNS server, clients get a list of matching SRV records that point to the closest domain controllers providing network services

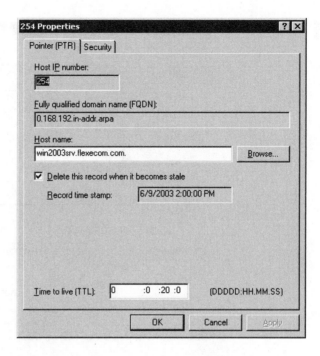

TR record
properties

that may be of interest—for example, LDAP, PDC emulator, Kerberos, and global catalog, to name a few. Here is a sample SRV record:

```
_ldap._tcp.ms-dcs     SRV  0 0    389 win2003srv1.flexecom.com
                      SRV 10 0    389 win2003srv2.flexecom.com
```

Each SRV record indicates which service it is advertising, what protocol and port number should be used, and what the priority of the record is. In networks where more than one domain controller is installed, priorities are similar to those found in MX records—that is, they help clients determine which server to pick from the list. The second number after priority is a weight value, which is used to distribute the load when priorities are equal.

SRV records are created dynamically when you install Active Directory, and also verified and added, if necessary, every time the NETLOGON service is restarted. This, however, only works if your DNS zone is configured to accept dynamic DNS registrations, which in some cases may be viewed as a security risk. (See the section "Dynamic DNS Updates" later in this chapter.) The NETLOGON service also creates a netlogon.dns file in the %systemroot%\system32\config directory; so if there is an issue adding these records dynamically, it can be done manually by copying records from the netlogon.dns file. Figure 2-8 demonstrates a typical SRV record.

FIGURE 2-8

SRV record
properties

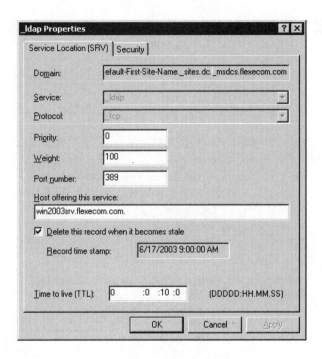

Microsoft recommends creating DNS zones and installing Active Directory on the same domain controller, as this allows you to take advantage of the dynamic registration and ensures that SRV records are created properly. If for any reason you must use a third-party DNS system such as those implemented in UNIX, you must make sure that they support SRV records. (Dynamic registration used to be a recommendation, and it has not become an absolute requirement.) DNS BIND versions 8.2.1 and later are considered compatible. Also note that Windows NT 4.0 servers prior to Service Pack 4 do not support SRV records.

WINS, WINS-R Resource Records

Legacy Windows systems, and hence the namespaces, are still around and are unlikely to go away anytime soon. Administrators have a bit of an issue here because older clients are "unaware" of the fact that they can, if not must, register themselves with the DNS system. Because of this, new clients using DNS may not be able to resolve the names of the older ones. The WINS record is used in cases like this to redirect failed hostname resolution queries to the WINS server, so in a way this reminds DNS delegation, where NS records point to other DNS servers which are authoritative for a certain subzone—except in this case delegation is to a different namespace.

Those hostname-IP address queries that did not find a match in the DNS zone are forwarded to the WINS server. If the WINS server finds a match in its database, this result is returned to the DNS server, the parent DNS domain name gets appended to the WINS-returned hostname, the result gets cached in the DNS server cache, and it is subsequently returned to the client who originated the query. This process is transparent to the new clients, and based on what they see, it really does not differ from a normal DNS query. Thanks to caching, it works faster for subsequent requests than if these new clients were querying the WINS server directly. Figure 2-9 shows the WINS record properties.

WINS-R records are similar to WINS in the sense that they are used as server-side interfaces between DNS and WINS namespaces, but they are opposite in the sense of what is being resolved. WINS-R records are used to resolve IP addresses into the NetBIOS names of WINS-registered NetBIOS clients. There is a problem though: WINS was not designed to support reverse name resolution, so instead of redirecting requests to the WINS server, DNS submits a *node adapter status request* to the host in question. Response to this request contains the NetBIOS name of the node, which is returned to the client. In the WINS-R record properties, you must indicate which domain should be appended to the returned name (see Figure 2-10).

FIGURE 2-9

WINS record properties

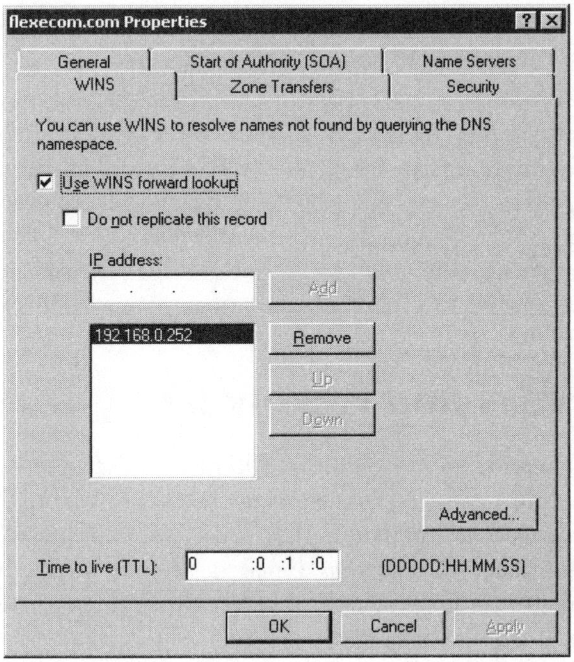

FIGURE 2-10

WINS-R record
properties

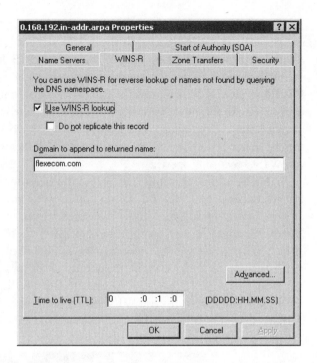

WINS and WINS-R records cannot be replicated to non-Windows DNS servers because they are proprietary to Microsoft and may not necessarily be supported elsewhere. It is possible to turn off replication for both WINS and WINS-R records by checking Do Not Replicate This Record in the properties of each of these records. This in turn will add a Local field to the record in the zone file. Lastly, as you probably noticed in Figures 2-9 and 2-10, WINS and WINS-R records are not added separately as if they were individual records; instead they are added through the master property pages of the forward or reverse lookup zones, respectively.

DNS Servers and Resolvers

The process of resolving a DNS name involves two parties—client and server. Before sending a request to the server, the client looks up the hostname in question in its local cache and then in the local copy of the "hosts" file, which is used for static DNS hostname–IP mappings. If matches are not found, the client proceeds by submitting a request to the primary DNS server listed in its network interface settings.

The hosts file is a flat text file, with each line representing a mapping between a DNS hostname and an IP address. In operating systems beginning with Windows NT 4.0 up to Windows Server 2003, it is located in %systemroot%\ system32\drivers\etc directory. If there is a matching hostname record in the hosts file, further attempts to resolve the name are unnecessary, so the resolution process stops.

The name resolution process on the server side may happen in a number of ways depending on the circumstances. Security, response times, and other technical factors influence this process as well. Overall, the process can be summarized as follows:

1. The DNS server receives the request to resolve a name into an IP address. It checks its local cache first, and then the zones supported on the server, in an attempt to issue an authoritative response.

2. If no matches are found, it proceeds to submit the requests to upstream DNS servers configured as forwarders.

3. If the latest effort produces no matching records, the DNS server invokes an iterative query process, sequentially submitting requests first to root servers, then TLD servers, then SLD servers, and so on, until a match is either found or not found in the zone of a server, which is authoritative for the domain in question.

The following sections review these concepts in more detail.

Authoritative Server

Authoritative servers are "owners" of the records in zones that they support, and as discussed earlier, this authority is bestowed by means of NS records. Answers from authoritative servers are considered authoritative for the zone and have the highest priority. In contrast to authoritative servers, nonauthoritative servers may store a copy of the zone but not be listed in the NS records for that zone. Nonauthoritative answers are also the ones being returned from the DNS cache, or from secondary servers for the zone, which are listed as NS servers, in cases where they are unable to refresh the zone information with the primary DNS server for longer than set in the Expires After field in the SOA record.

In practice, to designate a DNS server as authoritative for the zone, it must not only be added to the NS records in the zone itself, but also to NS records on DNS servers that are authoritative for the parent domain of the zone in question. For example, if you have a DNS server named ns1.flexecom.com in the flexecom.com domain and it is listed as an NS server for this domain, you also need to make sure that the registrar adds ns1.flexecom.com server as an NS record for your domain in the .com domain. This will make it possible for network clients on the Internet to locate the authoritative server for your domain and ultimately resolve hostnames from this domain.

Forwarder Server

As the name implies, forwarder servers are used to designate where to forward queries that cannot be resolved by a DNS server from its locally stored zones or subordinate DNS servers. Windows Server 2003 introduces *conditional forwarding,* whereby administrators may choose forwarder servers based on domains. For example, you can configure to forward all requests for sales.flexecom.com domain to be redirected (forwarded) to a certain DNS server (see Figure 2-11).

Slave Server

Slave servers are also called "caching-only" servers. When you install a DNS server on a fresh Windows Server 2003 installation, it configures itself as a caching-only server by default, until you configure forward lookup zones. Caching is integral to the DNS server, and in the absence of local zones, caching and resolving of domains through root servers is all they do; in essence, caching-only servers are DNS servers that are nonauthoritative for any of the zones. Caching servers are best used to decrease response times in local area networks with slow connections to the Internet.

For example, you can configure all your internal DNS servers with the same forwarder server and have that forwarder server query root servers and resolve resources outside your local area networks. When you start a caching-only server, its cache is naturally

FIGURE 2-11

Forwarder server

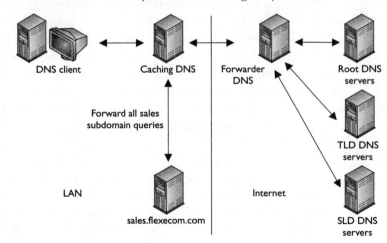

empty, but every request it fulfills gets cached. Consecutive requests for the same resources are fulfilled from the cache instead of directly through the root servers, so you save precious bandwidth and increase DNS performance by reducing query times for the clients.

This sounds like a great idea, but there is one inconvenience to caching: it detects changes to the records on authoritative DNS servers rather slowly, because cached records are valid until their TTL times expire. In your local network, this problem has a rather simple solution: you can clear the DNS cache by executing the **ipconfig/flushdns** command at the command prompt, or by selecting Clear Cache from the Action menu (see the following illustration). However, due to the extensively distributed nature of the DNS system, it may not help, because other servers participating in the name resolution on the Internet may also have these names cached.

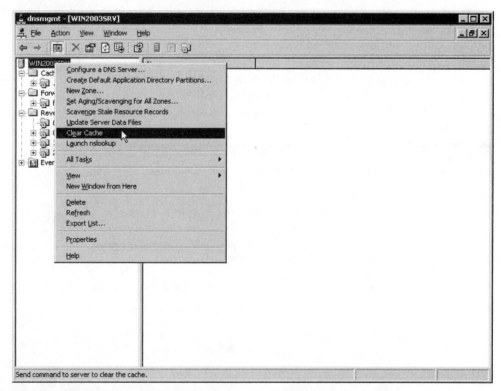

To make a caching-only server a slave to its forwarder server, you have to configure it not to resolve names on its own. The setting Do Not Use Recursion for This Domain on the Forwarders tab achieves this (see Figure 2-12). Note that the slave server in this configuration will not work correctly if its forwarder server(s) does not work correctly. A slave server simply forwards recursive queries to forwarder servers, which are capable of resolving a specified hostname into an IP address. If this process succeeds, the forwarder server returns the results to the slave server.

A slave and forwarder server combination is usually employed in DMZ ("demilitarized zone") network segments, as Figure 2-13 shows. Usually, forwarder servers are exposed to the outside world (at least DNS ports are), and a slave server is located within the secure area of the DMZ or inside the local area network, where it cannot be reached from outside, and it does not interact with the external DNS servers. A slave server can also be configured with Active Directory. Specific information and firewalls are configured to block all external DNS traffic destined to the slave server, which eliminates unwanted attempts to resolve resources on the local network.

Other possible uses for caching-only and slave servers exist within the Active Directory environment, where LAN segments are split apart and connected via slow WAN links, although they might still belong to the same DNS domain (if administrators have chosen not to maintain any separate zones for each of these segments). In this

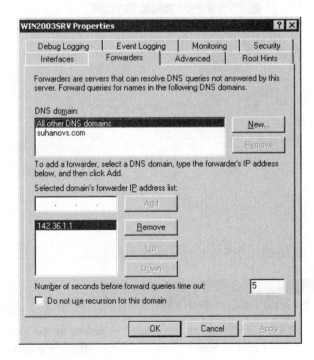

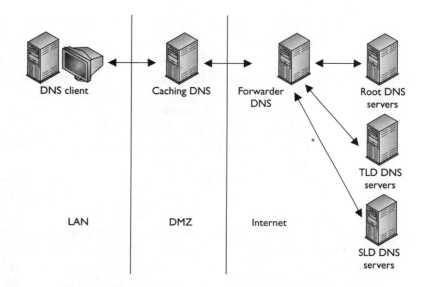

FIGURE 2-13

Slave and
forwarder
servers

case, the slave server is configured with a forwarder server that "knows" about all
Active Directory resources, which might be located in the HQ segment. Over time
it caches responses from that server locally, improving performance for local clients.
Depending on the circumstances, this may be better than transferring the entire zone
and maintaining a secondary DNS server in each segment.

Round-Robin Functionality

As mentioned earlier in the chapter, the DNS system has some load-balancing features,
namely, *round-robin* functionality. It may be helpful to distribute incoming connections
equally between a few network hosts, such as web servers. If one web server is getting
hit with lots of requests, it may be serving pages slowly or may even be rejecting or timing
out some of the requests. In this case, one solution may be to set up a twin web server
box and load-balance incoming traffic using DNS (a.k.a., *poor man's load-balancing*).
You have to figure out a way of referencing two different servers using the same FQDN;
if you create two separate "A" records pointing to different IP addresses, the DNS server
will simply return the first record it matches during its zone search.

Round robin comes to the rescue. It issues replies for the same FQDN containing
several IP addresses, which are ordered differently in each reply. This produces a
cycling effect. New to Windows Server 2003 is the ability to control round-robin
functionality based on record types—for instance, you may want to specifically turn off

round robin in certain cases. The DoNotRoundRobinTypes key in HKEY_LOCAL_ MACHINE\System\CurrentControlSet\Services\DNS\Parameters helps achieve this. So to prevent round robin for SRV and NS records, you simply modify the key value and enter these record types separated by a space. In addition, the Advanced tab of DNS Server Properties (shown in Figure 2-14) can be used to enable the netmask ordering feature. *Netmask ordering* forces the DNS server to issue the IP address closest to the requesting client from the pool of round-robined IP addresses, thereby reducing the length of the path that packets take from the client to the resource in question.

Note that round robin only works on authoritative servers. Nonauthoritative servers cache the order in which IP addresses were returned by the authoritative server and fulfill subsequent requests from the cache.

One of the obvious shortcomings of round robin is its unawareness of the status of load-balanced servers, so in essence it will go on issuing load-balanced IP addresses, even if one of the load-balanced nodes goes down or gets overwhelmed by incoming requests. Network load-balancing and clustering features in Windows Server 2003 deal with load-balancing in a more constructive way.

FIGURE 2-14

Enabling the netmask ordering feature

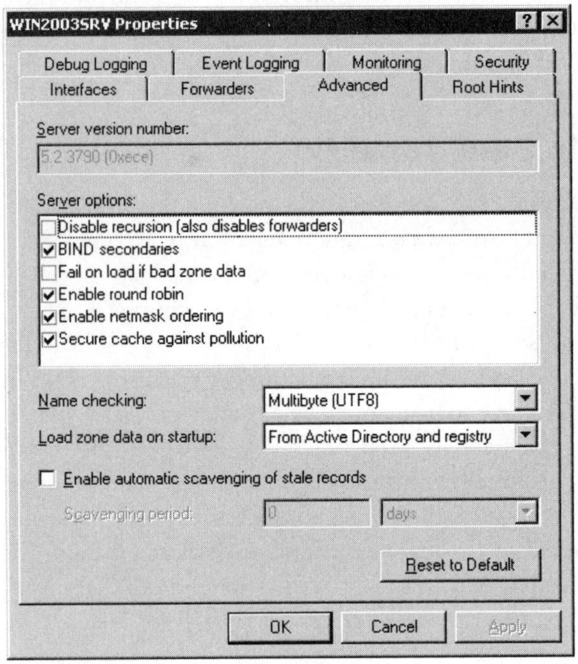

DNS Query Functionality

As we have established, the DNS query process is a dialogue between clients requesting IP addresses of resources and servers that are in possession of this information. Questions and answers are formatted in a special way, and the dialogue is constructed in a special manner depending on the situation. The client asks its designated server for the IP address of resource ABC. The server then uses its knowledge of the DNS hierarchy (and algorithms for acquiring missing parts of this knowledge) to help the client resolve the name. It first checks its cache, then its local zones, then if no forwarder servers were configured, it begins searching the DNS directory for the authoritative zone, beginning with the root (".") on the right (least specific location) and progressing to the left (most specific location). Root servers are preconfigured with the DNS and are loaded from the cache.dns zone file upon start-up. (There would be no DNS without this—DNS cannot learn of root servers on its own, because it needs root servers to do that.)

As an example, consider the process of resolving an external resource, msdn.microsoft.com, from your local network. If your local DNS server has no cached information or zone copies of the microsoft.com domain, it will query one of the root servers for the msdn.microsoft.com resource. The root server has no idea about this resource, but it knows where to look for the .com TLD and issues the IP address of .com's NS server. Then your DNS server submits another query to the IP address returned from the root server, asking for the same resource. The .com NS server does not know where this resource is, but it knows where the SLD microsoft.com is located, and issues Microsoft's NS IP address. Your DNS makes the third request on your behalf, this time directing it to Microsoft's NS servers, asking for the msdn.microsoft.com resource. This time you hit authoritative DNS servers, and they return the IP address you are looking for.

on the
job

When you install a DNS server where no Internet connectivity is available, the installation process may automatically configure the server as the root server and add the root domain ("."). If this happens, your DNS server will not be able to resolve external resources following the plan just described. It will also affect the ability to add forwarder DNS servers, and will not add root server addresses to the cache.dns. The root domain should be deleted from the server manually later on.

The process of resolving a resource on the Internet involves exchanging messages between clients and DNS servers. The following section deals with the types of these messages in greater detail.

Recursive Queries and Iterative Queries

When a client or server makes a recursive query, it expects a clear "yes/no" reply from the other party. Yes/no means that either a resolved IP address should be returned, or a message should be returned saying that this resource was not found.

Iterative queries (also called *nonrecursive*) behave more like a dialogue, where server A asks server B if it is aware of a certain resource. Server A does not necessarily need the IP address of the requested resource, although that would be accepted. In case server B does not know where the resource is, it will issue a reference to server C in the DNS hierarchy, which in server B's opinion might know better. Server A then issues a repeated request in search of the same IP address, but directs it to a different server based on the reply from the previous iterative query. Iterative queries eventually locate authoritative servers for the domains in question.

By default, the client always issues *recursive queries* to its DNS servers, beginning with the primary DNS server. The client expects either an address or an error message. DNS servers, on their part, prefer iterative queries, "talking" to each other to "figure out" the location of the requested resource. If the iterative process extends beyond a preconfigured period of time, either an error message is generated and returned to the client, or a recursive query is submitted to the forwarder server, if it is configured.

Why don't servers default to recursion? First of all, this would lead to an overload of the root servers, because they would have to know about every resource available on the Internet in order to service recursive queries—in essence, there would be no root servers. Second, an iterative process on the server side ultimately leads to more names being added to the cache, significantly speeding up execution of further searches for repeated domains and hostnames. If eventually DNS servers return neither an IP address nor the error message, clients may attempt an iterative process themselves. Figure 2-15 demonstrates how iterative and recursive queries work together to resolve a DNS name.

Reverse and Inverse Queries

Reverse queries are used to resolve IP addresses into hostnames. As discussed in "PTR Resource Records" earlier, regular zones are not designed for this purpose. Instead, special in-addr.arpa zones are used, and they contain PTR records, which correlate with "A" records in regular zones. The in-addr.arpa zones are called *reverse lookup zones*, and they are constructed to include the network address of the subnet; for example, 100.168.192.in-addr.arpa zone would be suitable for 192.168.100.0 class C network IP addresses. You have to add the octets in reverse order because the format of the FQDNs in the DNS mandates that the most-specific addressing information is on the left side of the name, becoming less specific going to the right.

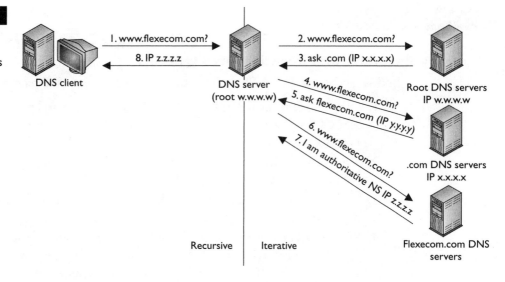

FIGURE 2-15

Iterative and recursive queries

DNS client

1. www.flexecom.com?

8. IP z.z.z.z

DNS server
(root w.w.w.w)

2. www.flexecom.com?

3. ask .com (IP x.x.x.x)

Root DNS servers
IP w.w.w.w

4. www.flexecom.com?

5. ask flexecom.com (IP y.y.y.y)

.com DNS servers
IP x.x.x.x

6. www.flexecom.com?

7. I am authoritative NS IP z.z.z.z

Flexecom.com DNS
servers

Recursive | Iterative

In addition to reverse queries, there are *inverse queries*, which are considered to be an outdated feature of the DNS standard. The purpose of this type of request is the same: to get the hostname based on the IP address. However, the server does not need the reverse lookup zone to service this query, and instead it searches for a matching IP address in the normal DNS zones—forward lookup zones. If a match is not found, an error is returned, and it is not clear whether the host does not exist in the zone, or does not exist on the network. Inverse query support is optional, and Microsoft DNS implementations beginning with Windows 2000 Server DNS accept inverse queries, but do not search the forward lookup zone in a standard for that type of request fashion—that is, the server does not search forward lookup zones. Instead, Microsoft DNS server returns a reverse reply formatted as an inverse reply.

Tracing DNS Queries with NSLOOKUP

NSLOOKUP is one of the most basic and widely used network troubleshooting tools. It allows checking server name resolution functionality and troubleshooting other DNS-related problems, such as erroneous functionality or name resolution on remote DNS servers. It is basically a DNS client that allows administrators to query DNS servers manually and get some debugging information in addition to query results. Among other things, you can use NSLOOKUP to view the content of the zone files and trace DNS queries.

on the **job**

The NSLOOKUP utility is used to troubleshoot DNS-related problems. You can launch it by issuing the nslookup *command at the command prompt, or by using the DNS management console's context menu (Launch nslookup).*

EXERCISE 2-1

CertCam & MasterSim ON THE CD

Observing Recursive and Iterative DNS Queries

In this exercise, you use NSLOOKUP to run traced iterative and recursive lookups.

1. Open the Start menu and click Run. Type **nslookup** and press ENTER. NSLOOKUP will start and connect to the DNS server as prescribed in the network settings, displaying the server name and IP address.

2. Type **server 142.77.1.1** and press ENTER. This command will switch to a public DNS server run by Worldcom Canada (UUNET).

3. Type **set debug** and press ENTER. This will set debugging information to display during the query execution.

4. Type **set recurse** and press ENTER. This will set recursion to be used in querying (the default behavior of a DNS client), which will cause a recursive query to be submitted to the current DNS server. We do not know how the server will process the query (because we do not know how it is configured).

5. Type **www.flexecom.com** and press ENTER. You should see a detailed output of the query request and returned results.

6. Type **set norecurse** at the command prompt and press ENTER. This command will switch NSLOOKUP into iterative mode.

7. Type **msdn.microsoft.com** and press ENTER. You should see a detailed output of the query request and the resolution process, beginning with the root servers and lower down the DNS tree.

8. Type **exit** and press ENTER.

DNS Message Types

The messages exchanged by clients and servers in the process of name resolution follow a predetermined standardized format, which includes five different sections, as shown in Table 2-2.

DNS messages always have a header with service information that identifies what kind of request or reply is contained in the message. The Questions section contains actual questions addressed to the DNS server, and they feature parameters such as QTYPE (query type), QCLASS (query class), and QNAME (query name). The Answer and Authority sections follow the same format: they provide addressing information in response to the query in the form of a list containing resource records of authoritative or nonauthoritative servers that happened to have requested information. Figure 2-16 shows a sample DNS packet as viewed in the network analyzer Network Monitor, provided with Windows Server 2003.

TABLE 2-2   DNS Message Format

Field	Description
Header	Supporting information, indicating how many requests or replies are provided, identification information, flags, and so on.
Question(s)	One or more name resolution request(s).
Answer(s)	One or more name resolution response(s).
Authority	Records pointing to the authoritative source of provided information.
Additional Information	This field is used for additional addressing information, if it is identified.

FIGURE 2-16   DNS packet structure captured in Network Monitor

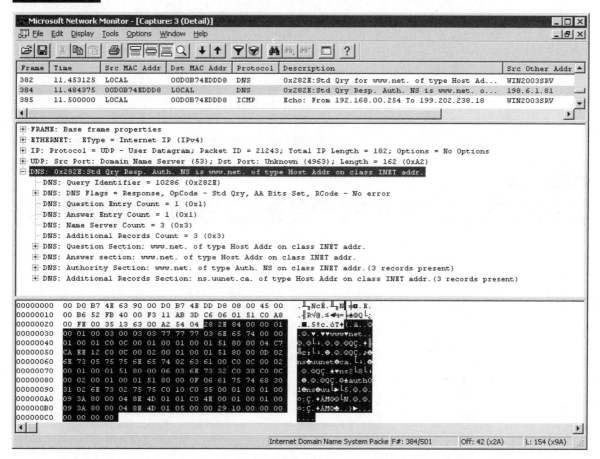

The figure shows a few packets captured from a network communication stream, using the **ping** command against www.net server. There are three sections: The first shows the DNS name resolution request (packet #3), DNS reply (packet #4), and subsequent ICMP ECHO request issued by the **ping** command (packet #5). The second section shows the structure of the reply received from the DNS server; you can actually see all five of the fields listed in Table 2-2. The third section displays the binary content of the packet selected in the first section. The OpCode flag value in the second section points out the function of this particular packet. Table 2-3 shows possible values and definitions of this flag.

DNS Zones

In the context of the DNS namespace, DNS zones are actual database files that contain FQDN records. Name servers are authoritative for FQDN records stored locally. Usually FQDNs are grouped by parent domain names, and hence the authority is "split" into several zones. Each of these zones contains resource records, which were described earlier in the chapter. The administrator must ensure that DNS service is highly available, fault tolerant, secure, and up-to-date, and Microsoft Windows Server 2003 has a few mechanisms that help to achieve this. This part of the chapter deals with different zone types and replication mechanisms available in DNS.

Classical implementations of DNS services used to have one primary zone and a few secondary zones, maintained as read-only copies of the primary zone. In Windows

TABLE 2-3 OpCode Flag Values

OpCode Value	DNS Operation	Definition
0	Query	Request, which is used in forward lookup and reverse lookup resolutions.
1	Iquery	Inverse request, which, as discussed earlier, is an outdated feature of DNS, still supported in Windows.
2	Status	Name server status.
3	Reserved	Reserved for future use.
4	Notify	This is designed for zone transfers and is a notification message that the content of a zone has changed. The primary DNS server issues this to notify its replicating partners.
5	Update	These messages are used for resource record updates between replicating partners.
6-15		Not used.

Server 2003 (and Windows 2000 Server as well), you can also use primary and secondary zones, as well as the third type of zone—Active Directory Integrated. Resource records in AD Integrated zones are stored as objects in Active Directory, not as records in the zone file.

Zone information can be stored in several ways, most commonly in .dns zone files, located in the %systemroot%\system32\dns directory. These zone files are close to being compatible with the BIND implementation of DNS servers. Information can also be stored in Active Directory in the form of entries in the LDAP database, in which case they can be viewed using the Active Directory Users and Computers management console. Select Advanced Features in the View menu (see Figure 2-17) to use this feature.

FIGURE 2-17   DNS information in Active Directory

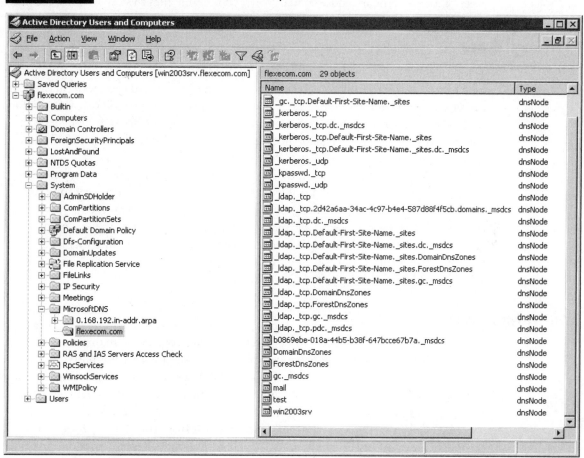

When you create a DNS zone, you are asked to select an appropriate type of zone and where it should be stored (AD Integrated is an exception). Active Directory Integrated zones are more complex to maintain, so first we will review the classic types of zones—primary and secondary—which use zone files to store resource records.

Primary Zone

The primary zone is a master read-write copy of a DNS hostname database, which is used to commit any sort of zone configuration or resource record changes. Changes can be made either by using notepad.exe (or any other text editor) to add text information to the zone file, or using the DNS management snap-in, in Microsoft management console (MMC). The third type of modification introduced with Windows 2000 Server was dynamic updates (DDNS).

The primary zone is the source of DNS information for all secondary zones. In a classical implementation of DNS, there can be only one primary zone for a domain in question. SOA domain records distinguish the primary server from other authoritative NS servers using a Primary Server field. The primary zone stored on your primary NS server should be used to maintain all domain names included in the zone, and if that is not the case, then delegation should be used to "outsource" subdomain maintenance to other NS servers.

Secondary Zone

It is very common to maintain information for the same zone on more than one server, and secondary zones—read-only copies of the zones—are used for this purpose. This achieves, among other things, reliability of the DNS service (eliminating single point of failure), as well as distribution of DNS query traffic between several network nodes in an attempt to improve response times.

Zone transfer is a process that replicates records from the primary zone to the secondary zones. As discussed in the "SOA and NS Resource Records" section earlier in this chapter, SOA record serial numbers are used as a comparison mechanism in zone transfer decision making. In addition to serial numbers, zone transfers may be triggered by any of the following conditions:

- The zone refresh interval elapses.
- The secondary server receives a Notify message from the primary server, informing it of a change.
- The DNS service starts on the secondary server.
- The administrator triggers an update manually using the DNS console on the secondary server.

exam

Ⓦatch *The same physical name server cannot function as primary server and secondary server for one zone.*

To receive a copy of the zone, you need to create a secondary zone on your secondary DNS server, and indicate the IP address of the primary server that will be used as the source. In theory, this server need not be the primary server; it could be any name server that has a local copy of the zone in question. Of course, if you transfer zones from secondary servers instead of the primary server, you increase zone propagation lag (the time it takes any single change to reach all servers maintaining the zone). Also, the probability that something will go wrong and get copied farther on is introduced with this scheme, which makes transferring from secondary servers generally not a worthwhile idea.

By default, all secondary name servers listed as NS servers for the zone are allowed to transfer the zone. However, if the situation so dictates, you can configure other non-NS-listed servers that should be allowed to transfer the zone on the Zone Transfers tab in the zone properties. Figure 2-18 shows that you can also allow any server to transfer the zone (not recommended for security reasons), not just a specific server based on its IP address.

Stub Zone

New to Windows Server 2003, *stub zones* are used to store information about authoritative DNS servers for other domains. No resource records can be stored in the stub zones other than references to authoritative servers, in the form of SOA and NS records (SOA for the domain in question, NS for the domain in question and its subdomains). A stub zone copies and then refreshes all NS records of authoritative servers for the zone from IP addresses specified in the zone configuration. The source servers, in stub zone terms, are called master servers. Both secondary and primary servers are allowed

FIGURE 2-18

Zone transfer
properties

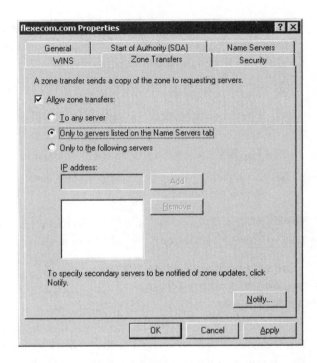

to play the role of master server when it comes to configuring a stub zone, but the same secondary zone propagation lag argument applies.

As you have probably guessed, stub zones increase performance of the DNS system by adding a name server list of often-referenced domains to a local zone. This makes it unnecessary for the DNS server to go out to the Internet and query first the root servers, then TLDs, SLDs, and so forth. A stub zone is a sort of shortcut in the DNS system. This works both ways: the primary DNS server may also be configured with a stub zone for nested child zones, which would maintain an updated list of NS servers used within an organization's DNS namespace. This also potentially saves query time. Figure 2-19 illustrates the use of stub zones. In essence, by using stub zones, you can set up delegation of zones that need not be in a parent-child relationship, and keep NS records up-to-date without having to manually configure their IP addresses.

e x a m
w a t c h
Be mindful of the fact that stub zones are not considered to be authoritative for anything, and hence they cannot be used for load-balancing in place of secondary zones. All they do is store pointers to authoritative servers for other domains locally, in an attempt to save time on iterative queries.

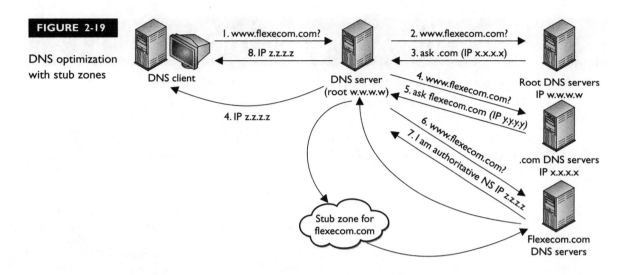

FIGURE 2-19

DNS optimization with stub zones

Last but not least, stub zones can be used for any other reason that would make it desirable to transfer name server information and store it locally in other segments of the network without actually transferring entire zones.

Active Directory Integrated Zone

In the classic implementation, one primary server stores the only copy of the primary zone. While secondary servers maintain redundant copies of the zone, they would not be able to support DNS zones and respond to queries for records in those zones for a lengthy period of time without being able to contact the primary server. In fact, SOA records contain Expires After fields that control this. Now this problem can be avoided using Active Directory Integrated zones.

As discussed previously, AD Integrated zones are stored in Active Directory, with every record represented as AD objects. Hence, the DNS server with an AD Integrated zone must also be a domain controller. AD Integrated zones are all master copies of the zone, meaning that changes can be made to any instance of the zone. To replicate the changes, or transfer zones in classic terms, Windows Server 2003 uses the AD replication engine, built for multimaster replication. This also means that failure of any one DNS server responsible for the zone does not incur any downtime for the DNS system as a whole, no matter how long it remains down, providing that more than one domain controller was configured as a DNS server.

DNS information can be stored either in a domain directory partition or in the new application directory partition (new to Windows Server 2003; covered in

SCENARIO & SOLUTION	
Which two types of queries are used in DNS?	Recursive and iterative queries.
What is the purpose of a Minimum TTL field in the SOA record?	The TTL value of this field is used by default by all resource records in the zone. Custom resource record TTL values less than the minimum TTL are ignored.
What is the main reason why WINS is no longer used for infrastructure name resolution in Windows 2000/2003?	DNS replaces WINS as the namespace registration system because of the push to phase out NetBIOS, which is inherently inefficient for midsize to large networks, and in routed or WAN environments. Domain controllers in Windows 2000 Server and Windows Server 2003 no longer register records that are used to resolve and locate critical network services, such as Active Directory, in WINS. Instead, this information is registered in the DNS using dynamic DNS. WINS registers which computers are domain controllers and master browsers, but it was not designed to register LDAP, Kerberos, and other AD-specific information.
Is it mandatory to configure forwarder servers?	No. By default, Windows 2000 and Windows Server 2003 use root servers to resolve hostnames on the Internet. Nonetheless, you may opt to force the DNS server to forward recursive requests to an upstream DNS server maintained, for instance, by your ISP. Most of the time when you configure forwarder servers, performance of resolution service provided by the DNS server is increased due to caching on the forwarder server. However, the likelihood of downtime also increases because you are introducing a single point of failure by relying on the forwarder server. This can be mitigated by allowing iterative root server queries in conjunction with recursive queries submitted to forwarder servers.

Chapter 3). The application partition allows better control of how application data stored in Active Directory is replicated to other domain controllers. Now you can control which domain and forest servers should receive this application information, separately from "regular" AD replication. Application partition data is not compiled into the global catalog service, designed primarily to speed up user searches for other users, folders, and printers. This reduces DNS replication overhead, while still using the same AD replication mechanism, thereby maintaining only one database replication

scheme in your infrastructure. The following illustration shows a domain property page with a prompt to select application partition replication scope (storage location).

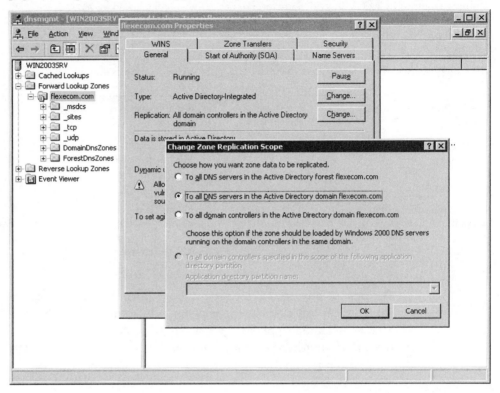

By default, two application partitions and one domain partition are used for this purpose. Table 2-4 shows the main aspects of storing DNS zones in Active Directory.

Reverse Lookup Zone

The topic of reverse lookup zones has come up throughout the chapter. They are not mandatory in the DNS system, and their absence will not affect the primary purpose of DNS—resolving hostnames into IP addresses. However, in some circumstances, these zones, and the PTR records they contain, may be required for applications that would want to make sure that a particular client is who she says she is.

From the looks of it, reverse lookup zones seem unnecessary, because we already have a valid mapping of an IP address to a hostname in the forward lookup zone. Indeed, it is possible to find a reverse match using the forward lookup zone. (Inverse queries do that.) In reality though, it is a fairly complicated and not very optimized process.

TABLE 2-4   DNS Zones in AD

Storage method of AD Integrated zone, configurable from the DNS management console	Partition used to store the zone	Zone objects addressing	Tools designed to view the records (objects) in AD Integrated zones
All DNS servers in AD forest	Application partition	forestdnszones.<domain name>	DNS console, dnscmd
All DNS servers in AD domain	Application partition	domaindnszones.<domain name>	DNS console, dnscmd
All domain controllers in AD domain	Domain partition	<domain name>/System/ MicrosoftDNS/	DNS console, dnscmd, AD Users and Computers
All domain controllers specified in the scope of the following application directory partition	Application partition	NameOfYourChoice.<domain name> (in this case the application partition must first be created using dnscmd)	DNS console, dnscmd

Try locating a person's telephone number in your address book, which is kept in alphabetical order by last name, when you do not know what that last name is. Similar difficulties apply to DNS, where each record would have to be compared to the query parameters to issue a reply. Hostnames are also indexed in alphabetical order; this is too inefficient for reverse name resolution. Reverse lookup zones are effectively the second address book with the same addressing information, ordered by "telephone numbers" (IP addresses) and grouped by local telephone exchange codes (network addresses).

There is no direct dependency of in-addr.arpa records and forward lookup zone records, which means you can create records in one zone without regard for what was created in the other one. As Figure 2-7 illustrated earlier, when you create a reverse resource record, you indicate in which IP subnet this resource is located. The last octet in the host's IP address is used as its hostname in a PTR record; hence the uniqueness of records in the in-addr.arpa zone is observed due to the uniqueness of IP addresses. Windows Server 2003 now allows using classless reverse lookup zones, based on classless IP addressing. (This DNS feature is described in more detail in RFC 2317.)

on the
job

If you want to look up an FQDN address based on a known IP address, use ping with the −a switch. The operating system will detect which is being queried based on the first character of the requested resource. This is one reason why domain names cannot begin with a numeric character.

Zone Transfers

To provide reliable and highly available service, you need to maintain at least two copies of each zone. The integrity of information contained in these two zones and the state of synchronization make the difference between a service that works and a service that does not. Replication mechanisms used for this synchronization are getting consistently better in terms of network traffic they generate and the security of exchanges they conduct. The latest improvement in these areas is possible thanks to Active Directory integration.

Full Transfers, Incremental Transfers

Standard zone replication can be classified in two types of transfers: full transfer (AXFR transfer messages) and incremental transfer (IXFR transfer messages). Incremental transfer communicates only those records in the primary zone that have changed since the last replication cycle. It assumes that secondary servers already have some version of the zone file with its own serial number. Primary servers keep track of all changes and serial number increments. Servers exchange their serial numbers, and the primary server can compile all changes not yet submitted to the secondary server based on the change history. Windows Server 2003 defaults to incremental transfers because it greatly reduces the amount of traffic generated by DNS replication.

AXFR transfers, or transfers of entire copies of the zone, may still be necessary under the following circumstances:

- A new secondary zone is configured, and servers need to exchange zone information since the secondary zone in question is empty.

- IXFR transfers are supported, but the change history file on the primary zone server is damaged or other problems exist, preventing the primary server from submitting changes.

- One of the servers participating in the transfer does not support IXFR transfers (these are BIND servers prior to version 4.9.4 and Windows NT 4.0 DNS servers).

If you are dealing with environments described in the final item in the preceding list and you have old secondary servers, you may need to configure the BIND Secondaries option, as shown earlier in Figure 2-14. This will ensure that legacy secondary servers understand incoming transfer requests and force primary Windows Server 2003 to use AXFRs exclusively.

Active Directory Integrated Replication

Zone replication between AD Integrated zones does not need to be configured separately. Since in AD Integrated zones, DNS records are LDAP objects, they will be replicated to other domain controllers as if they were plain AD objects. This replication is based on AD sites, which will be covered in Chapter 3 in more detail. For the purpose of this discussion, *sites* are areas of the network connected using high-speed, reliable media such as Ethernet.

In addition, there is intrasite replication between domain controllers in one site, and intersite replication between bridgehead domain controllers located in different sites and possibly connected by a slow WAN link. Intrasite replication happens automatically every 5 to 15 minutes, whereas intersite replication is a fairly flexible process that can be configured based on available bandwidth, preferable replication schedule, replication transport, and other factors.

on the
job

When you raise the domain functional level in Windows Server 2003, the intrasite replication interval is decreased to 15 seconds.

With AD Integrated zones you do not need to worry about DNS zone replication separately from AD replication, and you do not need to plan, test, deploy, and maintain two distinct replication schemes. Perhaps one of the greatest things about AD replication is that IXFR transfers are further split, allowing property-based updates. This means when one field in a resource record changes, AD servers will exchange just that field information and will not be sending entire records around the network.

As you can see, AXFR, IXFR, and AD replication are progressively more advanced forms of replication, saving more and more bandwidth. If the IP address of a record changes, AXFR transfers the entire zone, IXFR transfers the entire host resource record, and AD replication transfers just the new IP address. And since the introduction of application partitions in Windows Server 2003, you can even specify precisely to which servers this IP address will get replicated. (If you have ten AD domain controllers and only three of them are also DNS servers, you only need to replicate this IP address to three DNS servers.)

EXERCISE 2-2

CertCam & MasterSim ON THE CD

Working with DNS Application Partitions

In this exercise, you use the DNSCMD utility to view and manipulate application partitions on your DNS server. Then, using the DNS management console in MMC, you will place your AD Integrated DNS zone into this new application partition and define the scope of replication.

To perform this exercise, you will need access to a domain controller running a DNS server, configured with a zone. To access DNSCMD, you will first need to install Support Tools by running the SUPTOOLS.MSI package from the Windows Server 2003 CD, \SUPPORT\TOOLS\ directory.

1. Select Start | Run, type **cmd,** and press ENTER.

2. At the command prompt, type **dnscmd <*your server name*> / EnumDirectoryPartitions**. This will display existing application partitions. If you get a "program could not be found" error, you may need to switch to the directory where you installed Support Tools.

3. At the command prompt, type **dnscmd <*your server name*> / CreateDirectoryPartition newdnsscope.<*your domain name*>.com**. This will create a new application partition named newdnsscope.<*your domain name*>.com.

4. Launch the DNS management console from the Administrative Tools folder either in the Control Panel or by choosing Start | Programs | Administrative Tools. Select a forward lookup zone, go to the General tab, and click the Change button (opposite Replication).

5. Select "To all domain controllers specified in the scope of the following application directory partition," and choose newdnsscope.<*your domain name*>.com. DNS information for this zone will now be stored in this new application partition.

6. Using the DNSCMD utility with the **/EnlistDirectoryPartition** and **/ UnenlistDirectoryPartition** commands, you can specify which domain controllers should be included in the scope of this application partition.

Delegation of Zones

A DNS server configured with one zone and a domain can self-sufficiently serve all requests for records contained in the subdomain, providing that the subdomain has also been created. You can create resource records in the subdomain exactly as you would in the parent domain. However, if your domain name contains a large amount of records or you simply want to have someone else administer the subdomain, you could also delegate authority for the subdomain to a separate DNS server. Formally, delegation was designed to distribute query loads between several DNS servers.

Let's consider an example where this delegation is necessary not just for load-balancing. A mid-to-large-sized company has presence throughout the country and a similarly distributed administrative structure. The main planning decisions are being made in the central office, but actual administration is delegated to four or five different IT divisions responsible for their branch offices (say, New England, West Coast, Midwest, Southwest, and Southeast). Companies like this may need their own namespace, while still being part of the larger company namespace.

The best way to set this up is to have your company domain name as the parent domain for all five regions, then create five delegated subdomains, such as newengland.<*company domain*>.com. Practically, this would entail using the DNS management console, selecting the parent domain in question, and clicking New Delegation in the Action menu. You would have to provide the name of the subdomain you want to delegate and a list of NS servers that will assume authority for this subdomain.

DNS Security

DNS servers maintain critical two-way name resolution links between private networks and the Internet, and as such, they are exposed to external access. This in turn means that they are likely targets for external attacks. DNS security is a two-sided coin: first you need to make sure that Windows Server 2003 is secure as a platform for the service, and then you can secure service-specific functionality.

It is not uncommon for organizations to have demilitarized zone (DMZ) networks, or in other words, segments of the private network designated for public access. If the company is hosting their own public DNS service in-house, a publicly accessible namespace must be presented on a DNS server in the DMZ. However, this runs a risk of the DNS server being hacked; so private portions of the namespace that must only be accessible internally should not be placed on the same server in the DMZ. For this reason, companies usually maintain either two separate namespaces, or a separate subdomain for Active Directory, internal addressing, and further domain delegations.

In either case, usually two or more DNS servers are used; at least one is placed in the DMZ network, and the other one in the internal subnet, not accessible from outside. Firewalls are used to block all types of traffic between the servers in the DMZ and nodes in either outside or inside networks, except those necessary to maintain network services provided by the DMZ servers.

When you configure a DNS server located in a DMZ network, it is recommended that all services and features be removed and disabled except those necessary to support name resolution. This is called reducing the attack surface. Services such as

WWW, NetBIOS, Server, Computer Browser, Task Scheduler, and numerous others increase the likelihood that someone will manage to find a flaw in one of them, potentially gaining control of the server. (Buffer overflows in so many different components of Microsoft operating systems are famous for this.)

All unnecessary network ports not involved in DNS resolution should be disabled using a variety of software and hardware methods, in addition to being blocked on the firewall (which also may be compromised in some rare cases). DNS servers exposed to the Internet should not contain any internal records and most certainly should not participate in the domain structure. Simple but necessary rules such as password complexity and account lockout should be instituted. Using the hisecws.inf security template as the basis for your configuration might not be a bad idea. This list goes on and on, far beyond the scope of this book.

Typical DNS-related attacks are summarized here.

- **DNS footprinting**   Theft of zone information allows attackers to learn about internal addressing and services.

- **Denial of service (DoS)**   A massive amount of fake recursive queries are submitted to the server, making it too busy to service legitimate requests.

- **IP spoofing**   A fake IP address obtained through DNS footprinting is used to make it appear that the attacker is inside the network.

- **Man in the middle, or redirection**   Interception of DNS traffic allows attackers to take over communication between the nodes. This attack can be combined with DNS cache polluting, which results in compromised NS records added to the DNS cache.

Some of these attacks may be prevented; others may be contained. Cache polluting attacks may be prevented by setting the Secure Cache Against Pollution option in the Advanced settings of DNS server properties (shown in Figure 2-14). This results in discarding records from the cache, where the authoritative server and requested resource appear to be in different domains. These are very likely to be a result of unwanted interference by third parties trying to cache their NS record on your DNS server.

DoS attacks based on recursive queries may be eliminated altogether by rejecting recursive queries. The option Disable Recursion controls this setting (as shown in Figure 2-14). However, it may not always be desirable to do this. Other methods outside the scope of DNS may be used to eliminate numerous attempts to establish TCP or UDP connections if they appear to come in large quantities from the same source. Also, Windows Server 2003 may be optimized to drop TCP/UDP sockets faster and not wait for the default time-out period.

Hosts that are allowed to request DNS transfers are controlled through the zone properties, on the Zone Transfers tab, and this helps to mitigate footprinting attacks. In addition to this, Windows Server 2003 allows disabling automatic NS record creation in AD Integrated zones. The **Dnscmd /Config/DisableNSRecordsAutoCreation 0x1** command enables this option on a per-DNS-server basis. The **Dnscmd /Config /DisableNSRecordsAutoCreation 0x0** command returns this functionality to its default state.

Dynamic DNS functionality should never be permitted on externally accessible servers. However, in the internal portion of the network, this feature has joined the ranks of must-haves. To better control dynamic updates in internal networks, secure dynamic DNS updates are used (available in Active Directory Integrated zones). This guarantees that unauthenticated computers would not be permitted to register their hostnames automatically. In addition to this, in Windows 2000 Server and later versions, you can set permissions based on individual records, which can be used to lock down write access to critical records supporting the infrastructure (see Figure 2-20).

FIGURE 2-20

Zone security and access control lists

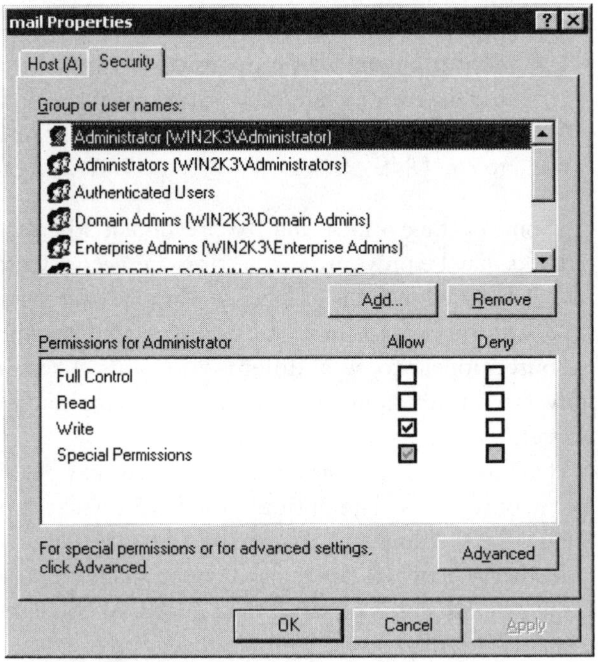

Besides setting permissions at the resource record or domain/subdomain level, consider setting permissions on two other key areas supporting DNS service:

- Registry key HKEY_LOCAL_MACHINE\System\CurrentControlSet\ Services\DNS\
- Content of %systemroot%\system32\DNS\ directory

If necessary, access auditing may be turned on as well, although administrators are advised to exercise caution using this feature because it may result in excessive logging and lead to poor performance.

Public cryptography is the only method presently known to provide an extremely high degree of security. It ensures that communications were not tampered with in transit, and guarantees the source of the transmission. DNS service in Windows Server 2003 now supports DNS security extension DNSSEC described in RFC 2535. Presently, Windows Server 2003 supports additional security zones compatible with the DNSSEC specification, which includes DNSSEC-specific resource records such as KEY, SIG, and NXT. Cryptographic operations (such as zone signatures) are not yet supported.

Dynamic DNS Updates

Dynamic name registration opened the door for DNS into local network environments. A local network environment usually contains many mobile devices, such as laptops, and equipment between departments or users flows in a more casual way than it normally would in the server rooms. This results in very high rates of name changes, additions, and deletions in the namespace. Windows 2000 Server introduced Dynamic DNS (DDNS), providing additional incentive for the push away from NetBIOS. DDNS allows hosts to register themselves with appropriate DNS zones every time they boot up or join the network. If a dynamic registration request is submitted to a secondary DNS server that maintains a read-only copy of the zone, the request is forwarded to the primary DNS server. Dynamic registration also occurs if the IP configuration changes on the client, if a hostname is modified on the client, or if you trigger the process manually using the **ipconfig /registerdns** or **ipconfig /renew** command.

Dynamic Host Configuration Protocol (DHCP) servers are used in most networks to configure IP addressing information on the clients dynamically. The DHCP server in Windows Server 2003 can be configured to register combinations of "A" and PTR records with DNS as they are being issued to the client computers. Default settings assume that clients will register "A" records themselves, and the DHCP server will register PTR records, but legacy and non-Windows clients may not support dynamic registration. DHCP service in Windows Server 2003 would normally ask the client if it knows how to register with the DNS, and if no reply is received, DHCP will create registrations for the client if so configured. Windows 2000 Professional and Windows XP Professional allow administrators to control whether they should register with DNS.

Dynamic DNS registrations can be secure and non-secure. Although non-secure registrations conform to the RFC 2136 standard, it has a major drawback of allowing anyone on the network—even those nodes never authenticated by domain controllers—to write to the zone file. This does not necessarily mean that they do not have write access to any other record in the zone file. Non-secure updates are suitable for smaller environments that are isolated from the outside world.

Secure updates involve a complicated process, key elements of which are listed here:

- Selecting an authentication protocol understood by both client and server. Usually this defaults to Kerberos.

- Using the selected protocol to establish the identity of client and server.

- Registration submission and receipt of signed confirmation of successful (or otherwise) registration.

Dynamic registration solves the problem of adding records to the zone on-the-fly, but as you might be thinking by now, this led to another problem of cleaning up these registrations once they are no longer associated with the client who registered them. Things like hard reset, blue screen, or freeze of a client computer are bound to leave behind registrations in the system. Besides taking up space and making the zones unnecessarily large, this also may result in incorrect replies issued by the DNS server. Microsoft provides a solution to this problem.

Removing Stale Records

Removal of stale records is done based on record timestamps. The Timestamp field contains the precise time when a record was added or refreshed using DDNS. The scavenging process attempts to locate stale records by comparing record timestamps with the refresh intervals, configured in the server or zone aging/scavenging properties (see Figure 2-21).

When working with scavenging, two intervals can be configured: no-refresh and refresh (both by default are set to 7 days). The no-refresh interval indicates how long

FIGURE 2-21

Aging/scavenging
properties

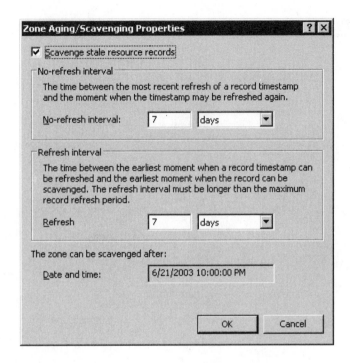

the DNS server should wait before refreshing a record. The refresh interval indicates how long the DNS server should wait after the timestamp refresh is allowed before it may attempt to scavenge a record. Clients coming online and regenerating their registrations automatically cause the timestamp to be updated as well; they more or less let DNS server know that they are still online. Combined with the DNS server's attempts to refresh these records after seven days (by default), chances that stale records will remain in the system for a long time are reduced to practically zero.

By default, records created prior to enabling scavenging, and static (manual) registrations, do not have timestamps, which excludes them from the scavenging process if it is enabled later on. To turn on scavenging for manually created records, you have to enable the "Delete this record when it becomes stale" option in "A" or PTR record properties. (Note that some options are only displayed when you select the Advanced submenu from the View menu in the DNS management console.) To enable scavenging, click the Aging button on the General tab in zone properties (this will open the property page shown in Figure 2-21), and choose Scavenge Stale Resource Records. Figure 2-22 shows the General tab of zone properties.

FIGURE 2-22

General tab of
zone properties

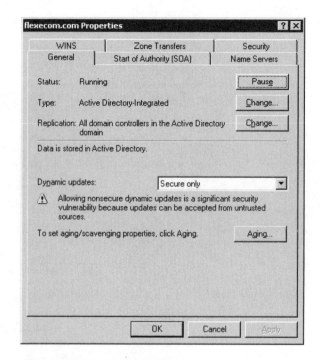

CERTIFICATION OBJECTIVE 2.02

Implementing DNS Services

Despite the apparently convenient and easy-to-use DNS management console,
implementing DNS server is a lot more complicated than it seems. A wise man once
pointed out: if you fail to plan, you plan to fail. Before you even launch DNS console
on your way to configuring DNS zones, you should carefully plan the namespace, how
DNS will interact with DHCP and WINS, whether this machine should be a domain
controller, and what the implications are of deploying Active Directory, if that is the
long-term goal.

Among the most basic requirements for installing and configuring a DNS service
on a server is a static IP address. If the server is dual- or multi-homed, you will need
to determine which interface(s) the service should be listening on.

Installing DNS Services

The DNS server may be installed either manually by someone with administrative rights on the system, or as part of the domain controller installation process. If you install DNS services manually, at the end of the installation process you will have a caching server that does not have any forward lookup zones yet. (It does install several reverse zones by default.) If you install the first DNS server as part of the domain controller installation process, you will have to install DNS services locally in order to add AD-specific zones and SRV records.

If you are installing the DNS server manually, go to Control Panel | Add/Remove Programs | Add/Remove Windows Components. Under Network Services, select DNS service. You may be prompted to choose which mode is used by Terminal Services so that Windows Server 2003 can configure internal parameters correctly. It will not be necessary to reboot after DNS installation; the service will be ready to be configured and used.

on the
()ob

You can test the DNS server's functionality by clicking the Test button in server properties on the Monitoring tab.

As Figure 2-23 illustrates, the DNS management console (found in Administrative Tools, or directly as a snap-in to MMC) displays reverse lookup, forward lookup, and cached zones in a familiar tree format. Windows 2000 Server administrators will also notice the Event Viewer shortcut placed right in the DNS management console. Be mindful that some of the options are not available unless you switch to Advanced mode in the View menu.

Configuring Forward and Reverse Lookup Zones

To create a forward or reverse lookup zone, switch to the respective zone type container (Forward Lookup Zones or Reverse Lookup Zones), and from the Action menu select New Zone. This will launch the New Zone Wizard, which takes you through the process. You will be asked to provide the following information:

1. What type of zone would you like to create (primary, secondary, or stub zone), and should it be stored in Active Directory?

2. What is the replication scope of this zone (if you chose to store it in Active Directory)?

FIGURE 2-23 The DNS management console

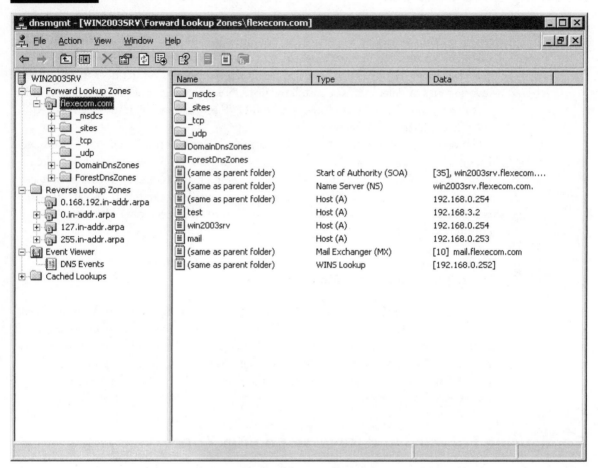

3. What is the zone name (for example, the sales subdomain in your company domain: sales.<domain name>.com)?

4. What types of dynamic updates will be permitted (in AD Integrated or primary zones only)?

5. What is the address of the master DNS server (for secondary zone only)?

6. What is the network ID to be used in the reverse lookup zone, if you are creating a new zone from the reverse lookup zone container?

Some clarifications should be made in regard to the preceding list. Secondary zones cannot be stored in Active Directory. Since AD is based on a multimaster replication model, all zones stored in AD are master copies (primary or stub zones).

If you do not want your zone to be stored in Active Directory, you will need to provide the filename (*.dns by default) where zone information should be stored. Records in *.dns files are considered to be portable to BIND servers; the opposite is also true. If you are making changes through the DNS console and you want to copy the text version of the record you just created, use the option Update Server Data File under All Tasks in the Action menu to write changes to the zone files immediately. For the reverse operation, when you add a record manually to the zone file and want this change to be parsed into the DNS console, use the Reload option from the same menu.

Configuring Clients

For the DNS service to be used in the name resolution process, clients must be configured accordingly, and at the very minimum they must be configured with the DNS server's IP address. This may be achieved using a variety of methods. In the order of increasing priority, these methods are as follows: DHCP assigned settings, locally configured settings, local policy assigned settings, and domain policy assigned settings (see Figures 2-24 and 2-25). These are discussed in more detail in the following chapters. For now, note that some methods will not be available for all clients—a significant portion of the group policy settings is designed to be used with the latest Windows clients such as Windows XP. Table 2-5 summarizes the domain policy settings.

Note that all local settings with the exception of Dynamic Update and Connection-Specific DNS Suffix are available on all Windows clients, including NT 4.0, 9x, Me, Windows 2000, and later. Support for dynamic updates and connection-specific DNS suffixes was introduced with Windows 2000.

In the DHCP column in Table 2-5, Dynamic Update and Register PTR Record are listed as "maybe." DHCP cannot force clients to configure these parameters in the system, since some of them simply may not know how to do that. However, if configured, the DHCP server can do both for the client, interacting directly with the DNS server. Figure 2-26 illustrates this setting in DHCP.

The following sections describe three main types of DNS client settings, applicable to Windows 2000/XP/2003 clients. These are DNS server addresses, DNS suffixes, and DNS registration.

FIGURE 2-24

Configuring DNS clients using domain policy

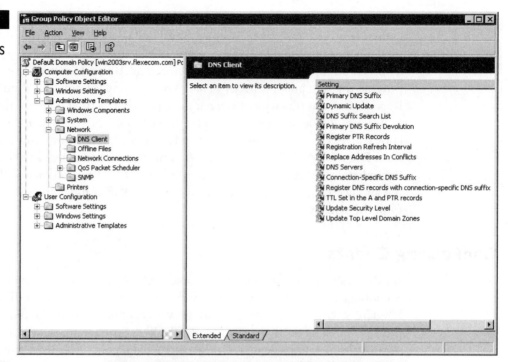

FIGURE 2-25

Configuring DNS clients using local settings

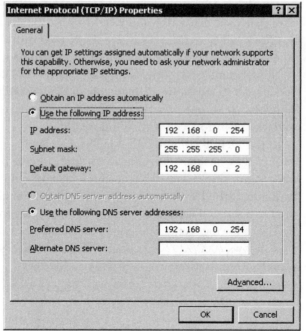

TABLE 2-5	Configuring DNS Clients Using Policy, Local Settings, or DHCP Server		
	Policy	**Local Setting**	**DHCP**
Primary DNS Suffix	2000/XP/2003	Yes	No
Dynamic Update	XP/2003	Yes	Maybe
DNS Suffix Search List	XP/2003	Yes	No
Primary DNS Suffix Devolution	XP/2003	No	No
Register PTR Record	XP/2003	No	Maybe
Registration Refresh Interval	XP/2003	No	No
Replace Addresses in Conflicts	XP	No	No
DNS Servers	XP	Yes	Yes, option 06
Connection-Specific DNS Suffix	XP	Yes	Yes, option 15
Register DNS Records with Connection-Specific DNS Suffix	XP/2003	Yes	No
TTL Set in the A and PTR Records	XP/2003	No	No
Update Security Level	XP/2003	No	No
Update Top Level Domain Zones	XP/2003	No	No

ⓦatch *When you install the first domain controller in the network, make sure that all DNS server IP addresses in the* *TCP/IP settings on all network interfaces of this controller point to its own IP address.*

DNS Server Addresses

It is possible to configure clients with several DNS server IP addresses. This does not imply that all of the configured servers will be queried simultaneously or in some random or round-robin fashion. The client attempts to contact the first server on the list first; then if this server is inaccessible, it goes on to the next server in the list. Usually, at least two DNS server addresses should be configured: a preferred and alternate DNS server.

FIGURE 2-26

Configuring
dynamic DNS
updates with
DHCP

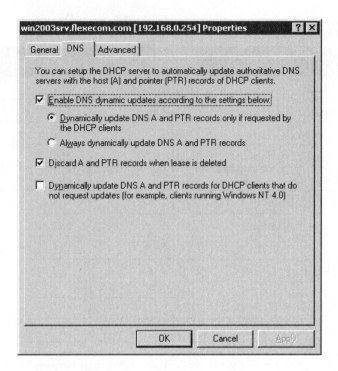

win2003srv.flexecom.com [192.168.0.254] Properties

General DNS | Advanced |

You can setup the DHCP server to automatically update authoritative DNS servers with the host (A) and pointer (PTR) records of DHCP clients.

☑ Enable DNS dynamic updates according to the settings below:

   ⦿ Dynamically update DNS A and PTR records only if requested by the DHCP clients

   ○ Always dynamically update DNS A and PTR records

☑ Discard A and PTR records when lease is deleted

☐ Dynamically update DNS A and PTR records for DHCP clients that do not request updates (for example, clients running Windows NT 4.0)

   OK   Cancel   Apply

on the
Job

If the preferred DNS server issues incorrect replies, the client will not be able to detect that there is something wrong with this DNS server and will continue to submit requests to this server. It will switch to the alternate DNS server only if the preferred server is down or if the order of the DNS server list is altered administratively.

If your client computers are participating in the AD environment, you should always configure them to use those DNS servers that have SRV records. Assigning an ISP-assigned external DNS server address will make it impossible for clients to participate in the domain and locate internal network resources.

DNS Suffix and Client DDNS Registration

Windows uses a DNS suffix to append parent domain names to DNS queries, thereby submitting FQDN name resolution requests, even though users may be providing only the hostname portion of it. This is especially useful if your domain name is lengthy. For example, instead of referring to server1.sales.newengland.flexecom.com, you may want to configure clients in the sales subdomain with the sales.newengland.flexecom.com suffix, which would allow referencing the resource simply by the hostname, "server1."

Two settings are available for this purpose: Primary DNS Suffix and Connection-Specific DNS Suffix. The former is located on the Computer Name tab in My Computer properties. Click Change, then More, to access this setting (see the following illlustration).

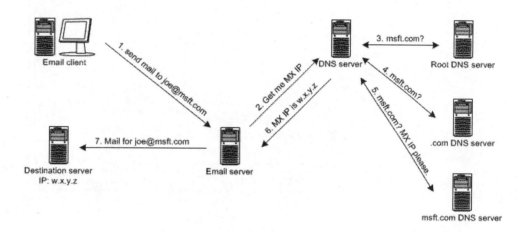

Connection-Specific DNS Suffix is configured on a per-network-interface basis. To access this setting, right-click the My Network Places icon on the desktop, go to Properties, then right-click any local area connection, and select Properties again. (If you do not have the icon on your desktop, go to Start | Settings | Network Connections.) In the "This connection uses the following items" list, choose Internet Protocol (TCP/IP), and click Properties. Then click Advanced and switch to the DNS tab. Figure 2-27 depicts this settings screen.

Using our example, the option "Append parent suffixes of the primary DNS suffixes" would cause server1 to be requested from the primary suffix domain first (sales.newengland.flexecom.com) and then from the parent domain newenglend.flexecom.com. If this does not satisfy your scenario, you may configure a custom list of suffixes for each connection, but be mindful that the parent suffix option configuration applies to all interfaces.

FIGURE 2-27

Connection-
Specific DNS
Suffix
configuration

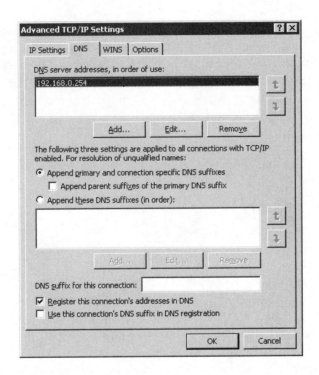

Automatic DNS Configuration with DHCP

Here's a situation: you are using domain policies to configure your client DNS settings, but to obtain the policy in the first place, clients must resolve the domain controller location and IP address, which is what DNS servers are used for. This obviously creates a disruptive loop.

The solution to this problem is still the DHCP service, which has been used to dynamically assign IP addresses to clients for years. Although Windows Server 2003 adds more options for configuring advanced DNS settings and overriding settings received from DHCP during the boot-up process using domain policies, DHCP still plays a pivotal role in assigning IP addresses during the start-up phase, along with other very basic parameters (options 06 and 15). DHCP assigns IP addresses, subnet masks, default gateways, and in our case, DNS server addresses and connection-specific DNS suffixes.

Configuring DNS Zone Transfers

Zone transfers are configured in the properties of the primary zones, and during secondary zone setup, as described in "Configuring Forward and Reverse Lookup Zones" earlier in the chapter. Figure 2-29 shows that zone transfers may be denied altogether, or allowed to any server, zone name servers, or other designated servers, which are not necessarily authoritative for the zone. Allowing transfers to any server is a pretty dangerous setting, except in cases where your zones do not contain any internal resources at all (a fairly rare case in corporate environments).

This concludes the technical overview of DNS and basic configuration steps that most administrators are likely to face. Let's turn now to DNS planning considerations in the context of Active Directory implementation.

CERTIFICATION OBJECTIVE 2.03

DNS Planning Considerations for Active Directory

DNS is one of the network services that form the basis for Active Directory operation; AD cannot function without DNS. Active Directory is a catalog of objects, all of which have names based on DNS naming conventions. This, in turn, allows accessing AD objects from different Active Directory domains and forests, and distinguishes between them.

Do not confuse DNS and AD domains when thinking about integrating two systems. They have many things in common, yet they are not the same entity. In DNS domains, hostnames that belong to one particular DNS domain have a common suffix appended after the hostname. All DNS FQDNs have the same root ("."). This unites independent installations of DNS into one distributed system that functions as a whole. Definitions of Active Directory domains are more complex. AD domains do not just serve the purpose of common addressing and namespace; they also contain a variety of objects that have nothing to do with DNS—users and printers, for example. DNS might reference a computer using "computername.<sld domain>.<tld domain>," whereas Active Directory might reference the same object using "<sld domain>.<tld domain>/Computers/ computername."

on the **job**

AD may also use GUIDs, or globally unique identifier strings, in its references.

The AD form signifies that the referenced object is stored in the Computers container. Hierarchical organization of individual resources in AD need not coincide with DNS hierarchy, although they do stay in touch on a larger scale. In the context of AD, <sld domain>.<tld domain> would serve as the root, and DNS may be used to set up namespaces for AD child domains such as <subdomain>.<sld domain>.<tld domain>. DNS therefore creates a common namespace structure for forests, trees, and domains in Active Directory, allowing users to reference resources organized in AD regardless of their location.

Other reasons why DNS is critical to Active Directory were reviewed earlier in the chapter. DNS is used to actually locate AD-related network services in the network.

SCENARIO & SOLUTION

Is it possible to switch from a standard primary to Active Directory Integrated primary zone after the zone has been created?	Yes. In the zone properties, on the General tab, click the Change button and select the Store The Zone In Active Directory check box. This setting is only available on those DNS servers that are also domain controllers. Note that it is also possible to change the zone from Active Directory Integrated to Standard.
Is it possible to configure AD Integrated zone replication to occur separately from the rest of AD object replication?	You may select the replication scope for your DNS objects, since DNS data may be stored in the application partition. It is possible to configure this scope in any one of the following ways: all domain controllers in the domain, all domain controllers in the forest, all DNS servers, or some other custom scope. It is not possible to replicate DNS information "separately" from the main replication process if you use AD Integrated zones, because these zones use the same replication infrastructure as the rest of AD. You cannot choose the replication transport type and replication timing for intrasite replication.
Is it possible to prevent stale record scavenging for certain resource records?	Yes. The "Delete this record when it becomes stale" option in the properties of the record(s) in question controls this behavior. Also, records created manually are not scavenged by default (this can be manually set to the opposite).

Namespace Considerations

AD uses the DNS namespace as the basis for naming AD domains. Careful planning of the namespace will invariably make it easier to expand AD into new trees and domains, and will also make it easier to access resources using intuitive names. Ease of adding child domains as your network grows will prove critical in the Active Directory namespace life cycle.

Choosing a naming structure most appropriate for your organization will undoubtedly be influenced by the business factors, which are covered in the next chapter. Obviously, domain names should somehow correspond to what the company is doing, and in many cases it will be necessary to work with existing domain names. It is likewise necessary to honor logical and physical business division needs, for ease of use, security, administrative, and other purposes. It will also help to know what the company plans are for the immediate and longer-term future, if it is growing (naturally or through acquisitions), if it is planning partnerships or subsidiary spin-offs, and so on.

Windows Server 2003 allows renaming domains—something that was not easily available with Windows 2000 Server. However, even though it is a built-in feature, domain restructuring on a larger scale is often not a trivial task. This feature is intended more for unplanned circumstances; architects and administrators are still strongly advised to plan ahead. Though this might take more time in the rollout phase, it will certainly pay off in the long run. AD hierarchy begins with the *forest root domain*, sometimes referred to as either forest domain or root domain. Its purpose is to initiate the AD namespace, and in practice, it is often left empty—that is, not used for storing actual user or application objects. Since every other domain in this forest will inherit the name of this parent container, this is the most critical part in creating the namespace. Table 2-6 summarizes the advantages and disadvantages of several namespace strategies.

It is recommended that you plan your AD structure first, and then create DNS subdomains to reflect your AD planning results. This may be somewhat difficult to accomplish in environments where the DNS structure is already in place. In this case, it is still recommended that you plan the AD structure first, and then either use a DNS subdomain or a completely separate namespace for the purpose of maintaining the AD infrastructure. Keep in mind that the external namespace should not collide with your internal namespace, or it may cause some name resolution problems for your users. This is why Microsoft recommends registering your DNS domain name to be used as the AD namespace, even though you might not be providing any network services to external clients.

| TABLE 2-6 | DNS and AD Namespace Strategies |

Naming Scheme	Advantages/Disadvantages
The AD root domain name is the subdomain of a publicly registered and externally accessible SLD DNS domain name.	All AD information is isolated from the Internet. The internal namespace is integrated with the external, in a consistent and logical fashion. The AD root domain requires extra hardware to support a dedicated AD domain controller and DNS service. It may not be necessary to restructure the existing DNS infrastructure. FQDN hostnames will be longer. It is not necessary to register additional domain names with ICANN; you just need to delegate subdomains.
The AD root domain name coincides with the publicly registered and externally accessible SLD DNS name.	Users will have shorter and easier names to work with. It is becoming more difficult to administer the DNS server, authoritative for the company domain name. Firewall configuration will have to be more secure, and therefore more difficult to set up. It is not necessary to register additional domain names with ICANN. You will have to synchronize internal and external DNS resource records selectively, exercising caution not to expose internal naming or service information to the outside world.
The AD root domain name has nothing in common with the publicly registered and externally accessible SLD DNS name.	Administration and security is easier to practice, since internal and external namespaces are created completely separately from each other. The internal namespace and its associated resources are inaccessible from the Internet. You may need to maintain two sets of records (one in the internal namespace and one in the external namespaces) for some resources. There is no need to keep internal and external namespaces synchronized. It may become more difficult to integrate internal and external namespaces so that users are able to access resources on the Internet using the external namespace internally. It is not necessary to restructure the existing DNS infrastructure. It is possible, however, that you will have to update existing DNS servers to support SRV records.

Replication and Performance Considerations

When you have two identical DNS systems (identical meaning they are at least properly planned and configured), it all comes down to how fast you can resolve names. Since

DNS name resolution is essentially what makes your network tick (in the absence of major problems elsewhere), DNS performance is paramount. DNS clients do not wait for a reply indefinitely; eventually, they time out. The crucial aspect in maintaining optimal performance is not the horsepower of your DNS machines, although holding all other things equal, this is important as well. More fundamental to maintaining adequate performance is, again, how well your structure is planned.

Windows Server 2003 is undoubtedly among the top performing network operating systems, and its DNS implementation features a number of performance-optimizing features. Among these are cache tuning, stub zones, multiple server load-balancing, and delegation of subdomains. A wise mix of these features allows you to attain any performance level that may feasibly be required by an organization.

In addition to performance-optimizing DNS features, Windows Server 2003 provides some 62 Performance Monitor counters related to DNS services, out of the box. These counters can be used to chart many aspects of DNS functionality, including the number of recursive and iterative queries received, WINS resolutions performed, percentage of requests fulfilled from the cache, and other detailed statistics, which helps in resolving service-related bottlenecks (see Figure 2-28).

Zone data synchronization is directly related to DNS performance. Outdated zone records may cause DNS servers to issue invalid or nonexistent addresses, and cause perceived disruption in services sought by clients. The result is wasted corporate productivity or even lost revenues due to an externally inaccessible e-commerce website. Proper replication planning should be designed to minimize the impact of changing resource records. For standard zones, this comes down to planning your TTLs and refresh/retry intervals in the SOA record.

At the same time, don't forget that excessive replication might not be desirable over WAN links, especially during business hours. To minimize this traffic, use DNS servers that support IXFR transfers, or store your zones in Active Directory. In corporate environments supported by Windows Server 2003 DNS servers, AD integrated replication is the most eligible candidate, since it takes full advantage of a well-thought-out and mature AD replication mechanism. This implements flexible intersite replication schedules and property-level replication.

Add to the list of helpful features, Windows Server 2003's application partitions, which you can use to define the scope of domain controllers designated as DNS servers, and replicate DNS information selectively to these controllers.

Finally, make the location of DNS servers in your distributed environment an integral part of your plan. Microsoft recommends placing a copy of the zone into each network segment, connected to the rest of the infrastructure via a slow and/or

FIGURE 2-28   DNS counters in Performance Monitor

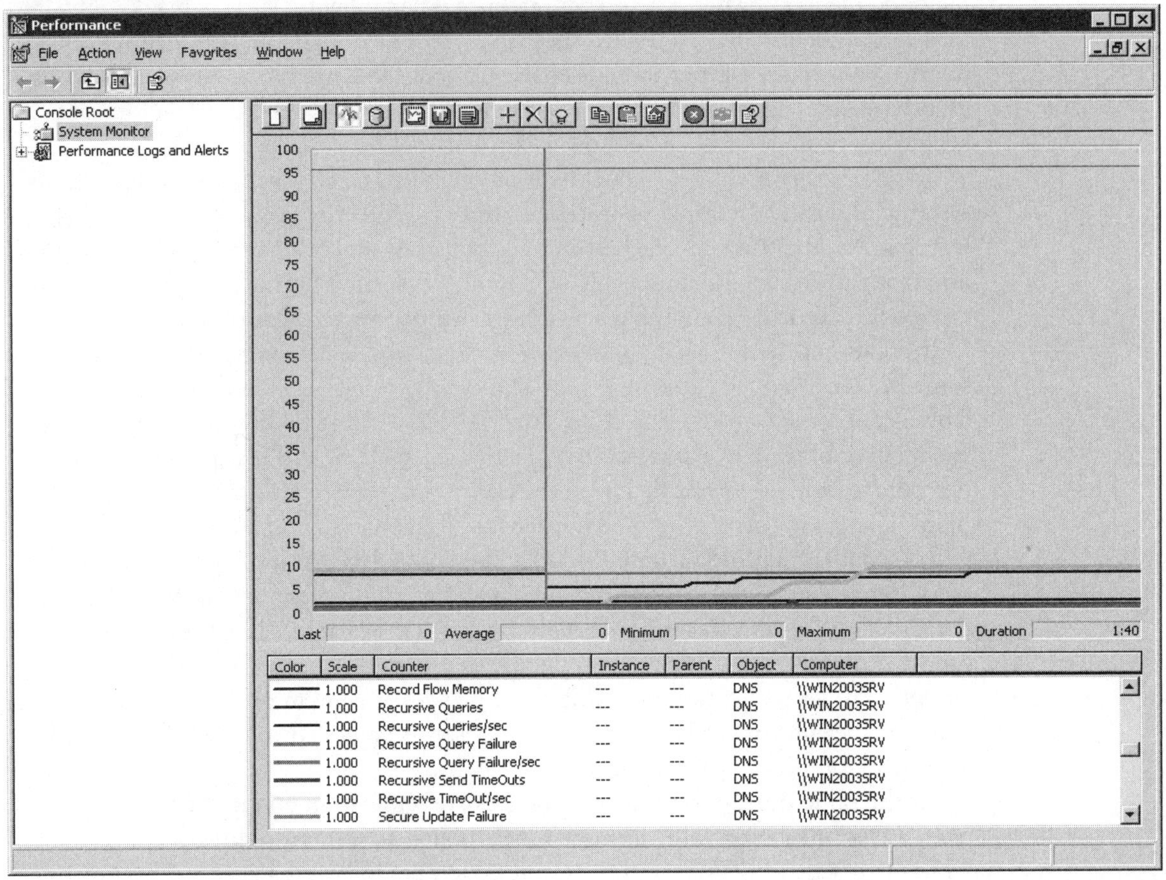

unreliable link. Placing secondary or AD Integrated zones on the server located in a remote network has two key implications. First, it optimizes query times by storing resource records locally in the network. Queries do not have to cross slow and saturated WAN links to resolve network services, which perhaps are located as close as the same (remote) network. Second, zone replication traffic results in a single transfer of the zone records and saves traffic resulting from subsequent requests, resolving them from a local copy of the zone. Depending on the size of your remote network, caching servers may provide the best compromise between the two—the WAN is used to request only those records requested by clients, and once those records are obtained, further requests are resolved from the local DNS server cache.

It is also important to note that the DNS server placement strategy should be coordinated with the AD server placement strategy. Clients need global catalog services in Active Directory to locate domain controllers and log on to the network. global catalog services, in turn, are resolved through the DNS, thanks to SRV records. We will go into more AD-related aspects in the next chapter.

Security Considerations

The need to keep your environment secure is obvious. DNS server attacks, or attacks involving DNS servers, are still quite widespread due to the core network role they play and the need to remain accessible externally. Unfortunately, some of those attacks still succeed due to ever-increasing knowledge and ability in the hacking community, new vulnerabilities being discovered in various DNS and OS implementations, and finally, inattentive or short-staffed DNS administrators.

The first step toward securing your DNS environment should be the definition of a secure environment in the context of the needs of your company. Hypothetically speaking, security levels may be identified as low, moderate, and high. A low security model may be acceptable in small networks, networks not connected to the Internet, and networks without nonemployee visitors. The default DNS security configuration in such environments is acceptable.

A moderate security model may be implemented using standard primary and secondary zones, without AD integration. Usually, the moderate security model assumes controlled access to the Internet. DNS security features described earlier in "DNS Security," should be carefully considered and implemented where appropriate.

To implement high security models, you will usually be required to restrict access to/from the Internet. AD Integrated zones are highly recommended, and in fact are the only acceptable types of zones in Windows Server 2003, where Kerberos is used to control access to the DNS records and dynamic DNS updates. Even though standard zones allow secure dynamic updates, there is no way to force this setting and exclude non-secure updates. This in turn means that record updates may be performed from a nonauthenticated source. Furthermore, AD integration allows administrators to institute DNS resource access auditing, which means that attempts to access resources without an appropriate level of permissions will not go unnoticed by the system.

CERTIFICATION SUMMARY

This chapter reviewed the purpose, elements, and implementation of the domain name system. The introduction described what the DNS system is trying to accomplish and how and why it was created. The elements of the DNS system include resource records, such as "A," PTR, MX, NS, SOA, and SRV records, and the domain namespace and the fully qualified domain name composition, including root, top level domains, and second level domains. The chapter went on to discuss the roles played by participants of the DNS system: resolvers and servers, types of queries (iterative, recursive, reverse, and inverse), and types of DNS servers (caching, slave, forwarder, primary, and secondary). In the overview of DNS, we also looked at zone types. In Windows Server 2003, available zone types are standard primary, standard secondary, standard stub, Active Directory Integrated primary and Active Directory Integrated stub. Security issues were touched on in the context of the DNS components as well as in planning considerations for Active Directory.

Several tools are available when it comes to managing DNS servers. The **dnscmd** command-line tool and the MMC-based DNS management console are used to perform administrative tasks. The DNS management console is used for the bulk of administrative duties. We wrapped up our discussion with some considerations that apply to how the DNS system should be planned and implemented in light of Active Directory rollout.

✓ TWO-MINUTE DRILL

Overview of DNS

❑ DNS is used to resolve FQDNs into IP addresses and vice versa.

❑ FQDNs include the hostname, all levels of domains, and the root.

❑ The TLD, or top level domain, must be registered to be used externally.

❑ SLDs (second level domains) and lower-level domains are maintained by individual companies.

❑ DNS uses resource records to set up hostname-to-IP mappings.

❑ Some resource record examples are "A," PTR, NS, SOA, MX, and SRV.

❑ SOA and NS records are used to define the DNS infrastructure and delegate authority for subdomains.

❑ DNS servers play different roles—primary, secondary, authoritative, caching, slave, forwarder.

❑ DNS implements "poor man's load balancing" with round robin.

❑ Recursive and iterative queries are used by DNS servers and clients.

❑ Reverse and inverse queries are two different ways of requesting a hostname based on the IP address.

❑ Several zone types exist in the DNS— the standard primary, secondary, and stub, and Active Directory Integrated primary and stub zones.

❑ Reverse lookup zones are used for reverse resolution and contain PTR resource records.

Implementing DNS Services

❑ DNS server in Windows Server 2003 implements DNS services and is considered to be a core network service.

❑ DNS namespace planning is the first step in implementing DNS services.

❑ The MMC-based DNS management console is used for the bulk of DNS administration; the **dnscmd** command-line tool must also be used for certain tasks.

❑ Secure dynamic updates and application partitions are supported only with Active Directory Integrated zones.

❑ Clients must be configured with DNS server addresses and other pertinent settings.

❑ DNS suffixes can be assigned on a per-computer and per-connection basis.

❑ DNS configuration can be assigned to clients using DHCP, manual configuration, or domain group policies.

DNS Planning Considerations for Active Directory

❑ DNS and AD namespaces are integrated to provide a consistent, logical object reference model.

❑ The DNS namespace begins with the root; the AD namespace begins with the TLD (most commonly).

❑ The AD namespace should be planned first, and the DNS namespace should be deployed according to the AD plan.

❑ To support AD, DNS services must support SRV records and should also support dynamic DNS updates (optional but recommended).

❑ AD Integrated zones are best for security and replication.

❑ A DNS server location in remote networks is highly recommended in order to optimize query performance.

SELF TEST

The following questions will help you measure your understanding of the material presented in this chapter. Read all the choices carefully because there might be more than one correct answer. Choose all correct answers for each question.

Overview of DNS

1. Secure services in your network require reverse name resolution to make it more difficult to launch successful attacks against the services. To set this up, you configure a reverse lookup zone and proceed to add records. Which record types do you need to create?
   - A. SOA
   - B. PTR
   - C. MX
   - D. SRV

2. What is the main purpose of a DNS server?
   - A. To resolve IPX addresses into NetBIOS names
   - B. To resolve IP addresses into NetBIOS names
   - C. To resolve IP addresses into FQDN names
   - D. To resolve FQDN names into NetBIOS names

3. SOA records must be included in every zone. What are they used for?
   - A. SOA records serve as a pointer to the forwarder server.
   - B. SOA records contain responsible-person information and ensure that all unresolved queries are forwarded to their address.
   - C. SOA records contain a TTL value, used by default in all resource records in the zone.
   - D. SOA records contain the email address of the person who is responsible for maintaining the zone.
   - E. SOA records contain the current serial number of the zone, which is used in zone transfers.

4. You are deploying an AD infrastructure in your organization and you would like to use an existing DNS infrastructure. Your organization is using the BIND implementation of the DNS server, which does not include support for SRV records. It is not an option to replace or upgrade the existing DNS server to Windows Server 2003 DNS. What will you have to do to ensure that your AD clients can locate and resolve network services provided by Windows 2003?
   - A. Delegate the following records from the BIND server to Windows Server 2003 DNS server: _tcp.<Active Directory domain name>, _udp.<Active Directory domain name>, _msdcs. <Active Directory domain name>, and _sites.<Active Directory domain name>

    B. It is not possible to deploy Active Directory in said circumstances.

    C. Delegate the following records from BIND server to Windows NT 4.0 DNS server: _tcp. <Active Directory domain name>, _udp.<Active Directory domain name>, _msdcs. <Active Directory domain name>, and _sites.<Active Directory domain name>

    D. Upgrade your BIND server version.

5. By default, if the name is not found in the cache or local hosts file, what is the first step the client takes to resolve the FQDN name into an IP address?

    A. Performs an iterative search through the root servers

    B. Performs an iterative search through the primary DNS server based on the network interface configuration

    C. Performs a recursive search through the root servers

    D. Performs a recursive search through the primary DNS server based on the network interface configuration

6. You are the administrative team leader in your company. To help promote the product line, you initiated a website project and assigned your site a simple and intuitive domain from the .biz TLD. You went through local testing of the site and opened it for access from outside your network. However, despite the fact that referring to this server using its IP address works, every time you try to access it using its FQDN, you end up on a site of a different company. In your local testing, this was not a problem. What is the most likely reason why external access does not function as expected?

    A. Prior to assigning your publicly referenced domain name, you needed to run it by an ICANN-accredited domain name registrar to make sure that it is not taken, and to make sure no one registers it later on.

    B. Check your Internet Explorer settings, or try using Netscape Navigator instead.

    C. Check that your SLD domain name does not contain "net," "com," or other reserved keywords.

    D. The .biz TLD domain is invalid on the Internet.

7. At some point during the name resolution process, the requesting party received an authoritative reply. Which further actions are likely to be taken after this reply?

    A. Request is submitted to the root server.

    B. Request is submitted to the closest caching server.

    C. After receiving the authoritative reply, the resolution process is effectively over.

    D. Requests are submitted to the remaining authoritative servers to verify the validity of the reply.

8. What is the main purpose of SRV records?

    A. FQDN resolution into IP addresses

    B. Domain controller NetBIOS name resolution into IP addresses

    C. SRV records are used to locate network services

    D. Using additional SRV records, you can define new domain controllers in the network

9. You are administering a network connected to the Internet. Your users complain that everything is slow. Preliminary research of the problem indicates that it takes a considerable amount of time to resolve names of resources on the Internet. What is the most likely reason for this?

    A. DNS servers are not caching replies.

    B. Local client computers are not caching replies.

    C. Users are referring to the resources using IP addresses.

    D. The cache.dns file may have been corrupted on the server.

10. You are a network administrator in your company. You implement Windows Server 2003 in your network, which spans three geographically dispersed locations (sites). Four thousand users are located in Chicago, another 3000 users are located in Seattle, and another 1500 users are based in Montreal. You are working out how you should deploy the DNS infrastructure. It has been determined that the Chicago and Seattle offices must employ secure dynamic updates. The Montreal office should not have a copy of the zone, which could be edited. How should you configure your DNS servers to satisfy the given conditions?

    A. Set up an AD Integrated zone in Chicago, another AD Integrated zone in Seattle, and a secondary zone in Montreal.

    B. Set up a secondary zone in Chicago, another secondary zone in Seattle, and an AD Integrated zone in Montreal.

    C. Set up a primary zone in Chicago, another primary zone in Seattle, and a secondary zone in Montreal.

    D. Set up a primary zone in Chicago, a secondary zone in Seattle, and a secondary zone in Montreal.

11. Employees of your company communicate with one of the company partners through their website portal extensively. To resolve their name, a local DNS server is used. You are trying to figure out a way to further optimize the process by placing NS servers for the domain in question on your local DNS server. However, you would like to avoid replicating the entire zone from the partner DNS servers due to security and bandwidth issues. Which of the following solutions seem to be suitable in this scenario?

    A. Create a secondary zone on your DNS server.

    B. Create a stub zone on your DNS server.

    C. Add NS records responsible for the partner's domain to the list of NS servers in your domain.

    D. Establish a trust relationship between the zones, maintained on your and your partner's DNS servers.

12. You are implementing a DNS infrastructure for a company. Active Directory was chosen as the network directory service. What should be the first thing you plan when it comes to DNS implementation?

   A. Begin with planning the AD structure and AD root domain name.
   B. Begin with planning a naming convention for your servers.
   C. Begin with planning a naming convention for your client computers.
   D. Begin with selecting an appropriate DNS server operating system and software that supports AD-specific records.

13. Which factors influence the process of assigning a name to the AD root domain?

   A. Security
   B. Business requirements
   C. NetBIOS names of legacy clients
   D. Existing DNS infrastructure

14. Your company uses ten domain controllers, three of which are also used as DNS servers. You have one companywide AD Integrated zone, which contains several thousand resource records. This zone also allows dynamic updates, and it is critical to keep this zone up-to-date. Replication between domain controllers takes up a significant amount of bandwidth. You are looking to cut bandwidth usage for the purpose of replication. What should you do?

   A. Change the replication scope to all DNS servers in the domain.
   B. Change zone storage from Active Directory Integrated to standard.
   C. Write a script that would copy *.dns files to all DNS servers based on configurable intervals.
   D. Create a separate replication schedule to force replication into off-peak hours.

15. You recently switched from configuring client nodes manually to dynamic IP addressing. To configure the DNS server list, you used group policies. You set out to install a new Windows 2000 Professional computer and attempted to add it to the domain, unsuccessfully. Upon checking IP configuration, you discovered that although IP addressing information appears to be correct, the DNS servers list is empty. What is the most likely cause of the DNS servers being unavailable?

   A. You did not configure the DNS server list on the DHCP server.
   B. When installing new clients, you should always assign IP addresses manually.
   C. The domain controller should be located in the same network segment where the client machine is being installed.
   D. Network connectivity issues are the most likely cause.

16. The next day after installing a new external DNS server located in an unprotected portion of the network, your IT department started getting calls with complaints that users attempting to connect to the company's news site are being forwarded to an underground site slandering the company. You attempted to clear the DNS cache and the service appeared to have been restored. However, after a few days the incident reoccurred. You suspect that your external DNS servers are being attacked and traffic gets redirected. What would be the first step in attempting to prevent this sort of behavior?

   A. Enable the Secure Cache Against Pollution option in the DNS server properties Advanced tab.

   B. Enable the BIND Secondaries option in the DNS server properties Advanced tab.

   C. Enable the Disable Recursion option in the DNS server properties Advanced tab.

   D. To prevent this type of attack, remove NS records from the zone serviced by the external DNS server.

17. Prior to launching a new DNS server, Joe tested it in a lab and confirmed that it works. Joe verified that the server resolves resource records, such as MX, PTR, and "A," from his zone. Confirming the functionality, Joe proceeded, thinking that test records will be deleted by the scavenging process because he enabled it on the zone level. After implementing the server in production, you notice that some records are redirected to the IPs that do not exist. You examine the content of the zone file and discover that Joe's test records have not been removed. How should this server have been configured to prevent this?

   A. For each resource record, you should have added another TIME record, which would provide timestamp information for the purposes of scavenging.

   B. To quickly get rid of those records, set the clock on the DNS server a month ahead and restart DNS service.

   C. You should delete test records manually.

   D. Records, created before aging and scavenging was enabled, do not contain timestamp information and hence fall outside the scope of the scavenging process.

18. Before installing your first domain controller in the network, you installed a DNS server and created a zone, naming it as you would name your AD domain. However, after the installation of the domain controller, you are unable to locate infrastructure SRV records anywhere in the zone. What is the most likely cause of this failure?

   A. The zone you created was not configured to allow dynamic updates.

   B. Local interface on the DNS server was not configured to allow dynamic updates.

   C. SRV records were created, but because these are system records, DNS management console does not display them.

   D. Networks with one domain controller rely on NetBIOS addressing and need WINS service instead of DNS to function properly.

19. Which of the following conditions must be satisfied to configure dynamic DNS updates for legacy clients?

   A. The zone to be used for dynamic updates must be configured to allow dynamic updates.

   B. The DHCP server must support, and be configured to allow, dynamic updates for legacy clients.

   C. Dynamic updates should be configured using domain group policies.

   D. Legacy clients cannot be registered dynamically with DNS because they still use NetBIOS names.

20. You are tasked with implementing Active Directory in your company. Your infrastructure is exposed to the Internet. As decided by your superiors, simple and short naming of resources should be key in both internal and external namespaces. Which AD naming strategies should you choose?

   A. Name your AD root domain using the same name that external clients will use to access company resources from the Internet. You should register this domain with ICANN.

   B. Use different names for your AD root domain and for externally accessible resources.

   C. Use the subdomain of the externally accessible DNS name in your AD root domain name.

   D. Register an additional domain name with ICANN and use a subdomain of this newly registered domain for your AD root domain.

LAB QUESTION

John is an administrator with a fast-growing company. Currently, there are about 30 network nodes and just one subnet. Within a year, the company is planning an expansion to perhaps 300 network nodes, with two new subnets. Presently, Windows 2000, Windows NT 4.0, and Windows ME are all represented in the network. One Linux server is used to provide access to the Internet and DNS server functionality, and this server is maintained by the ISP, which you are not allowed to reconfigure according to the terms of service. This DNS server supports SRV records, but does not support dynamic updates.

Management is planning to preserve the existing DNS infrastructure and to upgrade all outdated operating systems in use on the network. Consistently with the plan, John upgraded existing domain controllers to Windows Server 2003, using the Linux box as the DNS server. The way it stands now, John is installing new Windows workstations, assigning static IP addresses, assigning the DNS server an IP address, and creating a corresponding "A" record on the DNS server.

Upon segmenting a portion of the growing network into a new segment, many users, especially the ones using older client operating systems, started reporting problems in locating network resources. At one point, an unplanned outage of the Linux server due to hardware failure resulted in a stream of support calls. John is thinking that the existing infrastructure is becoming counterproductive.

In your opinion, what are the shortcomings of this expansion plan, and how do you think they should be addressed?

SELF TEST ANSWERS

Overview of DNS

1. ☑ **B.** PTR records are used for reverse name resolution.

☒ **A** is incorrect because SOA records are used to maintain the zone itself. **C** is incorrect because MX records are used for email service location and routing. **D** is incorrect because SRV records are used to locate network services.

2. ☑ **C.** DNS servers are used to resolve FQDN hostnames into IP addresses and vice versa.

☒ **A** is incorrect because IPX addresses are resolved using SAP broadcasts, not the DNS service. **B** is incorrect because NetBIOS names are resolved into IP addresses using WINS service. **D** is incorrect because resolution of FQDN names into NetBIOS names is not a basic network service; instead it is a more complicated procedure that may be implemented by some applications, where the DNS server would participate at some point in the process.

3. ☑ **C, D,** and **E** are correct statements about SOA records.

☒ **A** is incorrect because forwarder servers are configured on the DNS server level, not on the zone level. **B** is incorrect because if the DNS server cannot resolve a name from its local zones, it will redirect the query to another DNS server. If this DNS server is authoritative for the zone being queried and still cannot resolve the name, it will issue a reply, instructing the client that the requested hostname does not exist. There is no automatic interaction with a "responsible person" in the query resolution process.

4. ☑ **A.** You can delegate the zones containing records not supported by any given DNS server to a different DNS server, thereby preserving the existing DNS infrastructure. Microsoft recommends and supports this approach.

☒ **B** is incorrect because AD can be deployed as described in **A**. **C** is incorrect because Windows NT 4.0 DNS server does not support SRV records. **D** is incorrect because it contradicts the question (you are not allowed to interfere with an existing BIND server).

5. ☑ **D.** By default, the client submits a recursive query to the DNS server.

☒ **A** and **B** are incorrect because an iterative query is employed only if a recursive query fails first. **C** is incorrect because root servers do not support recursive queries; if that were the case, the root servers would have to know about every single network resource on the Internet and we would not have a distributed DNS infrastructure.

6. ☑ **A.** This is a mandatory practice when it comes to assigning a publicly accessible DNS domain name.

☒ **B** is incorrect because it does not matter which client browser you are using, the name resolution process should function regardless. **C** is incorrect because SLD domains have character and length restrictions, not the sequence of letters, and also SLDs must be unique. **D** does not describe such limitations.

7. ☑ **C.** An authoritative DNS server is given top priority when resolving domain names.
☒ **A** is incorrect because caching servers are given lower priority than authoritative servers. **B** is incorrect because root servers only help in finding an authoritative server, and they only contain pointers to SLD authoritative servers. **D** is incorrect because this sort of redundancy is usually not offered to regular DNS clients. Other methods are used to ensure that all servers, authoritative for the zone in question, have the same information in their locally stored zones.

8. ☑ **C.** SRV records are used in locating hosts that provide certain network services.
☒ **A** is incorrect because "A" records are used for this purpose. **B** is incorrect because the WINS service is used to resolve NetBIOS names. **D** is incorrect because new domain controllers are added to the domain using the utility specifically designed for that purpose—DCPROMO. It launches a fairly complicated process, which among other things adds its SRV records on the DNS server. The reverse is not true (adding SRV records by itself does not give you a new domain controller).

9. ☑ **A** and **B** are correct. Caching has a measurable impact on the DNS service quality. It is possible to switch off recursive query caching on the DNS server by changing the MaxCacheTtl value in the HKEY_LOCAL_MACHINE\SYSTEM\CurrentControlSet\Services\DNS\Parameters key to 0. Client computers likewise have a similar capability of not caching DNS server replies, except it is controlled through the MaxCacheEntryTtlLimit value in the HKEY_LOCAL_MACHINE\SYSTEM\CurrentControlSet\Services\Dnscache\Parameters key (0 will switch it off). When you browse any given website, your client browser requests innumerable pages, images, and other elements embedded on the page, using separate connections for each element. Without caching, all these connection requests would result in DNS queries submitted for the single IP address of the same server. You can turn off caching temporarily in cases where local domain name system restructuring is in process and you want to push changes to clients instantaneously. **D** is also correct because corruption in the cache.dns file often leads to unpredictable DNS functionality and sometimes even disrupts it completely. Cache.dns recovery procedures are described in Microsoft Knowledge Base article 249868.
☒ **C** is incorrect because referring to the resource using IP addresses only speeds up the process, taking the DNS resolution process out of the picture altogether.

10. ☑ **A.** AD Integrated zones enable multimaster zone configuration, and also support secure dynamic updates.
☒ **C** is incorrect because this does not satisfy the secure dynamic updates condition. In addition to that, if you use classic zones, you can only implement one primary zone. **B** and **D** are also incorrect.

11. ☑ **B.** Stub zones allow distribution of updated NS server information authoritative for various zones without actually transferring any resource records. This is designed to save replication traffic, usually associated with secondary zone maintenance.

☒ **A** is incorrect because if you implement secondary zone and configure replication, bandwidth usage will actually increase. **C** is incorrect because you can only add NS records to your zone that are pointing to authoritative servers for your zone. Adding an "alien" NS server will lead to occasional failures in resolving resource records contained in your local zone. **D** is incorrect because a "trust relationship" cannot be configured between DNS zones.

12. ☑ **A.** Before you proceed with DNS namespace planning, you should carefully consider the Active Directory namespace—most importantly, its root domain name. AD is the backbone of the Windows Server 2003 environment, and it is based on the DNS namespace. If you create the DNS namespace first, it may prove difficult to restructure it to accommodate different business requirements involved in AD planning. If you plan AD first and then create the DNS namespace accordingly, it will provide a convenient and logical structure for referencing directory objects such as users and computers.

☒ **B** and **C** are incorrect because server naming conventions are not considered critical in this scenario. Server naming is important, but secondary to namespace planning. Some sort of logical and easy-to-follow naming convention for your client computers is also important, but likewise is not critical. **D** is incorrect because operating system choice and hence DNS software selection are important but again are not critical in AD planning, so long as SRV records (and preferably DDNS updates) are supported.

13. ☑ **B.** Business requirements are by far the most important considerations for AD and DNS namespace planning. **D** is also correct because the existing DNS infrastructure may have an impact on namespace planning, should management decide that it is necessary to keep it.

☒ **C** is incorrect because NetBIOS names of legacy clients have no weight in choosing the namespace for AD/DNS. **A** is incorrect because security requirements have a potential impact on DNS configuration, but are unlikely to have an impact on namespace planning.

14. ☑ **A.** Application partitions allow replicating DNS data to a predefined scope of DNS servers, which are also domain controllers. In this scenario, you should configure replication to transfer DNS changes between the three domain controllers that have been configured as DNS servers.

☒ **B** is incorrect because replication of standard zones uses more bandwidth than AD Integrated zones, which have the ability to replicate properties of objects (fields of records in DNS terms). **C** is incorrect because replication mechanisms employed in Windows are more thought-out and advanced. **D** is incorrect because as it is stated in the question, it is very important to have the most up-to-date information in the DNS zones, and the suggested replication cycle is not likely to achieve this.

15. ☑ **A.** DNS server list should be configured on the DHCP server. It can only be configured through domain group policies for Windows XP clients, and only after at least one successful reference to a domain controller. For this to happen, if dynamic configuration is used, DNS servers should be assigned as part of dynamic configuration.

    ☒ **B** is incorrect because manual TCP/IP configuration only makes it more difficult to configure clients and keep their configuration updated. **C** is incorrect because clients and servers should be able to communicate cross-subnet, regardless of their physical location in the network, as long as their TCP/IP configuration is correct. DHCP servers should preferably be located in the same subnet, or otherwise the DHCP Relay Agent should be configured in the subnet in order to relay DHCP broadcasts across the router. **D** is incorrect because network connectivity seems to be in order, otherwise your client computer would automatically configure itself using an IP address from the 169.254.X.X range (APIPA).

16. ☑ **A** is correct because this setting prohibits caching of records, if the DNS server domain name and requested resource domain name do not coincide. This usually indicates that someone is attempting to intercept DNS query traffic.

    ☒ **C** is incorrect because the Disable Recursion option will not prevent someone from polluting your server's cache. **B** is incorrect because the BIND Secondaries option is necessary to support interoperability with older DNS servers. **D** is incorrect because this will render your server inoperable, or will require you to configure forwarder servers.

17. ☑ **C.** Test records should have been deleted manually along with the test zone, especially when there is a chance they could create a conflict with existing production zones or records. Aging and scavenging of stale records primarily serves the purpose of cleaning out those records, registered dynamically.

    ☒ **A, B,** and **D** are all incorrect because these records should have been deleted manually.

18. ☑ **A** and **B** are correct because for dynamic registration to work, the zones in question should be configured to allow dynamic registration. Local TCP/IP settings on the server's interface that will be used to submit dynamic registration requests to its DNS service should also allow dynamic updates.

    ☒ **C** is incorrect because SRV records are displayed in the DNS management console in the same way other records are. **D** is incorrect because DNS servers are always needed for domain controllers to function properly.

19. ☑ **A** is correct. The zone should be configured to accept dynamic registrations. This is true regardless of the client types. **B** is also correct. DHCP servers beginning with Windows 2000 Server and later have the ability to register "A" and PTR records for the clients, which do not yet support dynamic registration. DHCP servers should be configured accordingly to support this functionality.

☒   **C** is incorrect because domain policies do not affect the ability of older clients to register themselves with the zone. **D** is incorrect because older clients can be registered dynamically in the zone despite the fact that they still rely on NetBIOS names.

20. ☑   **B.** Using different namespaces for external and internal purposes simplifies administration of the DNS server infrastructure.

☒   **A** and **C** are incorrect because in either case you would have to manage integrated namespace and control security more strictly so that external users are not allowed to resolve internal resources. **D** is incorrect because this method only complicates administration and does not provide any benefits to the method described in **B**.

LAB ANSWER

1. John failed to plan the most basic aspect of name resolution: which resolution scheme to support in the future. If you plan to support both types of namespaces (hostnames and NetBIOS names, implemented by DNS and WINS, respectively), you must carefully plan how these systems will interact. First of all, based on the information provided in the lab question, both DNS and WINS must be employed for at least one year, the period identified as the timeframe for upgrade of the legacy operating systems. The fact that name resolution became a problem for some clients after the subnet was split in two tells us that WINS might not be used, and prior to the split all legacy clients used NetBIOS broadcasts to resolve the names of other machines. This is not an option in subnetted networks, and will also be a significant problem for environments experiencing growth. John might need to install a WINS service and configure all his clients with a WINS server IP address. However, since the push is on to migrate all clients to supported, modern operating systems, DNS should really be planned as the primary name resolution system. DNS and WINS integration assumes using DNS as the primary namespace and creating WINS and WINS-R records on the DNS server. John could also employ a DHCP server to dynamically register legacy clients in the DNS system.

2. Planned expansion of client computers to 300—a significant number if you manage DNS resource records manually—makes it a sound idea to switch on dynamic name registration in the DNS server and client settings. Since the terms of service with their current provider do not allow modification of Linux settings, John could install a dedicated Windows 2000 Server or Windows Server 2003 machine, enable and configure DNS service on it, and use it for client registration needs.

3. The fact that the network was effectively down when the Linux box had its problems, even for local network name resolution, tells us that the machine currently responsible for name resolution is the single point of failure in the network. There are several solutions John could consider

implementing in order to address this issue. He could go for primary/secondary zone setup in his network, or for implementing several Windows Server 2003 DNS servers and enabling AD Integrated zones. Client machines in this case would have to be configured with the secondary DNS server IP addresses, which can be achieved dynamically using DHCP server.

3

Planning and Implementing the Active Directory Infrastructure

CERTIFICATION OBJECTIVES

3.01   Plan a Strategy for Placing Global Catalog Servers

3.02   Plan for Flexible Placement of Operation Master Roles

3.03   Implement the AD Forest and Domain Structure

3.04   Implement the AD Site Topology

3.05   Plan a Strategy for Delegating Administrative Tasks

✓   Two-Minute Drill

Q&A   Self Test

Before any Active Directory rollout can take place, you must take the time to go through the planning stages and carefully evaluate every minor detail of the project. The price you might have to pay for planning mistakes is often quite high in later stages of the Active Directory life cycle. Windows Server 2003 delivers a few enhancements that make it possible to change things as fundamental as renaming the root domain—something that was very difficult to achieve in Active Directory on Windows 2000 Server. Nonetheless, lack of planning may result in higher maintenance costs (for instance, higher than necessary volumes of replication traffic over the WAN), administrative headaches, and in the worst-case scenario, reinstallation of Active Directory from scratch. Planning is far too important a process to be neglected, no matter how small or large your deplo`yment.

Active Directory consists of several forms of resource organization, such as domains, trees, and forests. AD infrastructure servers also play different roles—for example, a domain controller could also participate as a global catalog server, PDC Emulator, RID Master, Schema Master, and serve in some other capacities. Each of these components and organization mechanisms is discussed throughout this chapter. Understanding these concepts is crucial not only for the purposes of Exam 70-294 but also for your success as an Active Directory administrator.

CERTIFICATION OBJECTIVE 3.01

Plan a Strategy for Placing Global Catalog Servers

Planning placement of your global catalog servers will have a direct impact on users' experience working with Active Directory. Recall the DSA and DUA discussion from Chapter 1. *Domain controllers* (DCs) are one of the most fundamental elements of Active Directory. A domain controller is a server that stores Active Directory information and provides AD services on any given network, allowing users to interact with AD (searching for objects, logging on to the network, adding or modifying objects or attribute values, and so on). Most networks will have more than one DC for fault tolerance, load-balancing, and replication optimization purposes; so, if one server happens to go down, it will not affect users' ability to log on to the network.

Global catalog (GC) servers are used to store certain portions of directory information in specific locations as designated by an architect or an administrator. The GC is both a network service and an instance of physical storage of Active Directory objects. A

DC that also acts as a GC is called a global catalog server; all GC servers must be domain controllers, but the opposite need not be true.

Suppose we have a corporation with a head office in New York, several locations nationwide, a number of locations throughout Europe, and also a few offices in the Asia-Pacific (APAC) region. From an administrative perspective, it might make more sense to keep resources organized in domains based on a geographical dispersion of the company. If this were true, American users and computers would be stored in the American AD domain, the European domain would have information about European resources, and the APAC domain would hold information about Asia and Pacific resources.

It is reasonable to store frequently accessed information locally; problems arise when someone in the Edinburgh office in the United Kingdom attempts to find a telephone number for a user located in Rochester, New York. Most companies have slower and less reliable WAN connectivity between regional offices than on the campus of any given office. It is not unusual to have slower and less reliable links even between offices located as close as a few buildings apart.

Obviously, users in the UK have few reasons to be happy with the response times in this scenario. Global catalog servers were designed to solve this as well as a number of other problems common to highly distributed environments. The GC stores a partial replica, or copy, of all AD objects, regardless of their domain membership. This replica is partial because storing everything in one location may be technically challenging—AD now supports billions of objects, and all of them would need to be replicated between all GC servers. The closest GC server—in our scenario this would have to be in the Edinburgh office—would process the request instantaneously, returning the requested phone number to the user.

Now, what do you do if the closest GC server happens to be in Rochester, New York? Such a design would defeat one of the main benefits of having global catalog servers in your infrastructure. This is a fairly straightforward example of why you need to understand the concept of the global catalog, why it is important to plan how many catalogs to employ and where to place them, and why you need to set up the right balance between catalog replication traffic and quick response times.

Applications are no different from users when it comes to accessing directory information and searching for objects located in other domains. Client queries are addressed to GC servers via TCP port 3268, and if SSL transport security is used, via TCP port 3269.

Global Catalog Servers

The first domain controller in your infrastructure automatically becomes the first domain controller for the root domain in the AD forest. It is also configured as a global catalog server. Additional domain controllers joining AD are not promoted to global catalog roles by default, but administrators do have control over this. Administrators can promote or demote domain controllers to or from the global catalog role using the AD Sites and Services management snap-in, as you'll see shortly.

As a domain controller, the global catalog server contains a full copy of all objects defined in the domain to which this GC server belongs. It also contains a partial copy of all other objects located elsewhere in the AD forest. Figure 3-1 shows the global catalog's role in the infrastructure.

Physical storage in the Active Directory database on each DC is organized into several segments, called *partitions* (although in Windows Server 2003 they may also be referred to as *naming contexts*). In Windows Server 2003, there are four partitions: schema, configuration, domain, and application.

There can only be one version of the schema and configuration partitions in any given forest; they are stored on all DCs and are unique across the board. The domain partition stores domain-specific object information only; it is the same on all DCs that belong to the same domain. DCs are allowed to commit changes to this partition. GC-replicated data is a shortened compilation of domain partitions from all domains in any given forest. Figure 3-2 demonstrates this concept.

FIGURE 3-1

The global catalog's role in the infrastructure

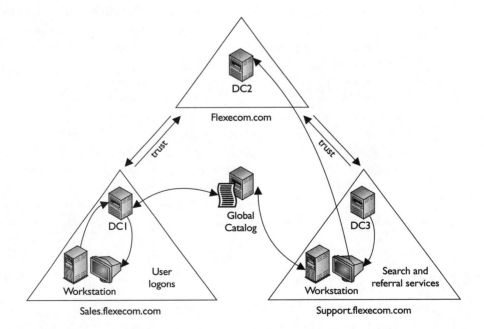

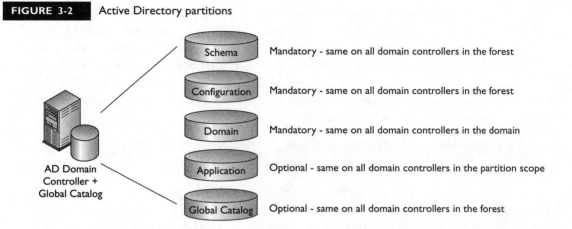

FIGURE 3-2   Active Directory partitions

In addition to acting as a global search facility, global catalogs also serve the following purposes:

- **User authentication**   Global catalog servers are used during the authentication process when a UPN (user principal name) is used as the logon name, and the local domain controller does not have information about the user in question. The UPN identifies the username and domain name, following the familiar format of an email address, such as username@company.com. For example, when Catherine travels from Denver (UPN catherine@americas.company.com) to Brisbane (domain name apac.company.com) and attempts to log on to the network using a workstation in the APAC domain (computer.apac.company.com), the domain controller for apac.company.com will not have any records needed to authenticate Catherine. It will have to query the global catalog in the APAC domain in order to complete the logon process.

- **Universal group membership information**   Global catalog servers also store universal group membership information, necessary to service authentication requests. Global catalog servers participate in logon processes by supplying global group information to local domain controllers authenticating users. Note that universal groups as a security mechanism are only available in the Windows Server 2003 AD environment when the domain functional level is set to at least native mode. The global catalog's role in the infrastructure groups as a distribution mechanism are available on other functional levels as well. (Domain functional levels are discussed later in this chapter, and group types are covered in later chapters.)

on the
job

Global catalog servers are required for a successful logon process in all cases, with the exception of administrative logon (in any situation), logon in an AD environment that has only one domain, and logon in a domain where the functional level is set to Windows 2000 mixed. Administrators can log on to the network whether the global catalog server is accessible or not. This exception allows administrators to do their troubleshooting work during unplanned GC server outages.

exam
watch

If a user attempts to log on while the global catalog server is down or otherwise inaccessible, the domain controller servicing the logon request will reject the logon attempt. If no domain controllers are available (and hence, no global catalog servers are available either), it may still be possible to log on to the domain using cached credentials stored from previous successful logons. This behavior depends on the policy setting and is enabled by default; it is not considered to be secure, but it is convenient (and oftentimes necessary) for laptop users who are using their computers on the road.

Now that we have established why you need a domain controller and a global catalog server in your domain, you will probably want to add additional DCs and then promote them to GCs in order to make sure your users can log on to the network, even if one DC or GC goes down. To promote (or demote) a domain controller to a GC server, follow these simple steps:

1. Launch the Active Directory Sites and Services MMC snap-in.

2. In the tree pane, expand the domain controller where you want to adjust GC settings, and right-click NTDS Site Settings. Click Properties.

3. The global catalog check box, shown in Figure 3-3, controls domain controller participation in the GC server pool.

Adding a DC to the GC pool effectively enables additional partition replication to the DC in question. From this moment on, your DC is added to the GC replication topology and will receive AD updates about objects not stored in the local domain.

As mentioned earlier, the GC contains only a partial replica of all directory objects, replicating only those attributes (or fields) that will most likely be searched by users. However, this default attribute selection can be adjusted administratively. In the Active Directory Schema console, you can set the option Replicate This Attribute to the global catalog (see Figure 3-4). But before making any GC-related changes, stop and

Designating
a domain
controller as
a global catalog
server

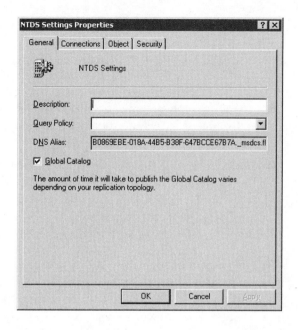

Customizing
global catalog
attribute
replication

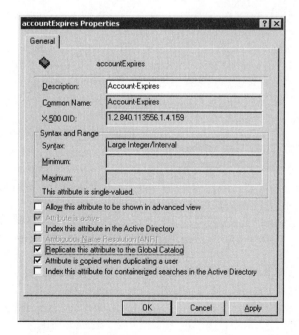

think about the big picture of AD replication, because even the smallest change, such as adding an extra attribute to GC replication, may significantly affect use of WAN bandwidth. When modifying attribute replication in GC topology, consider the following:

- Try not to replicate any attributes that are not absolutely critical to your environment. Attributes that are often looked up by users or applications are valid candidates.

- Consider how big the attribute value is and how often, on average, it changes. Keep in mind that replicated attributes in GC will be replicated to every GC server in the forest. If the attribute size is significant but rarely changes, it is a good candidate for inclusion because it will generate less replication traffic than a smaller attribute that changes more often.

Thus, administrators have the ability to replicate the most commonly searched attributes, as deemed necessary by a particular company.

When you modify attribute settings, you effectively modify the Active Directory schema, which should never be done casually. (Aspects of the directory schema and its modification are discussed in Chapter 1.) Windows Server 2003 still does not allow you to remove existing classes or attributes from Active Directory. However, if some attribute or class is no longer in use, or was created by mistake, administrators can deactivate it. Deactivated classes or attributes are considered defunct; they can no longer be used but can be reactivated if necessary. In Windows Server 2003 forests, you can reuse identifiers that were once used by deactivated schema elements. Also new to Windows Server 2003 is the ability to link auxiliary classes to individual objects, instead of entire object classes. Auxiliary classes can be attached and later detached from individual objects.

exam

watch

Keep in mind that in order to contain the fallout from modification of a partial attribute set, you need to run your forest in Windows Server 2003 functional mode.

Windows Server 2003 features a greatly improved AD replication engine. One of the more noticeable features introduced with this operating system is how additional attributes included in GC replication affect the existing state of GC replicas. In Windows 2000 Active Directory, the addition of a new attribute causes the GC replication state to be reset and invokes an entire replication cycle, forcing replication of those objects that may already have been replicated. Windows Server 2003 contains the effect of a new attribute inclusion by keeping existing replicas intact and simply replicating the attribute added by the administrator. The process of modifying a partial attribute set, therefore, no longer causes massive GC resynchronization.

New to Windows Server 2003 is the ability to save frequently used LDAP queries—the Saved Queries feature. Use the AD Users and Computers MMC snap-in, Saved queries container, to create saved queries.

To modify a partial replication attribute set, you must be a member of Schema Admins. Then follow these steps:

1. Click Start | Run, type in **regsvr32 schmmgmt.dll**, and press ENTER. Click OK in the dialog box that will inform you of a successful registration.

2. Click Start | Run, type in **mmc**, and press ENTER.

3. In the File menu, choose Add/Remove Snap-in.

4. In the dialog box that appears, click Add, select Active Directory Schema in the list of available snap-ins, and click Add. Click Close to close the Add Standalone Snap-in dialog box. Click OK to close the Add/Remove Snap-in dialog box. As an optional step here, you can click File and Save As to save this console in the Administrative Tools folder, which is useful if you plan on accessing this console on a regular basis.

5. In the console, expand the Active Directory Schema node in the tree pane, and select the Attributes container.

6. In the right-hand pane, find the attribute you would like to add, right-click it, and choose Properties. Replicate this attribute to the global catalog option controls, whether or not this attribute needs to be included in the partial attribute set.

If your forest is running at any functional level other than Windows Server 2003, these steps will cause full synchronization of the global catalog data.

Network Traffic Considerations

Placement of the global catalog server requires careful consideration of several factors—there is no "one size fits all" approach when it comes to GC placement. Naturally, users must be able to access at least one GC server in order to log on to the network, and, likewise naturally, local GC servers speed up AD queries submitted by users on the local segment of the network. Other applications may also be dependent on global catalog service availability—for instance, Microsoft Exchange server.

Central office must have at least one global catalog server; that is a given. In midsize to large branch offices where (or if) connectivity to the central location is reliable and not overly expensive, as defined by the company in question, global catalog servers should also be deployed, since this will improve overall logon and AD search processes and ensure that these functions are still available should the link go down. If you are dealing with a smaller branch office with up to 50 users, or if branch connectivity is unreliable, you should evaluate the advantages and disadvantages of two approaches, as outlined in Table 3-1.

TABLE 3-1   Pros and Cons of Two Global Catalog Placement Strategies

Approach	Advantages and Disadvantages
Remote networks connected over unreliable WAN links employ global catalog servers located in the central office.	*Advantages:* Global catalog servers are located in a central location. Technical personnel are available to resolve any difficulties that may arise. The company employs a smaller number of global catalog servers, which in turn results in hardware savings. Replication traffic is not crossing slow and unreliable WAN links. *Disadvantages:* All user logon requests and AD queries are submitted to central global catalog servers over unreliable and slow WAN links, which results in poor user experience. User requests saturate slow WAN links even further, and in many cases this added query traffic exceeds replication traffic. The global catalog may not be available at all times. Users may not be able to log on to the network when the link is down. The replication schedule can be adjusted to occur only during off-peak hours, such as at night when WAN links are not utilized to the same extent as during business hours. Without a local instance of the global catalog, user activity will generate a large amount of queries during normal business hours, which will put additional stress on WAN links.
Remote networks connected over unreliable WAN links employ locally placed global catalog servers.	*Advantages:* Remote networks have a global catalog server located on the local network segment. Client queries and logon requests are processed quickly; the global catalog server is available regardless of the WAN link status. Replication traffic, in many cases, will be less than the amount of traffic generated by clients (this largely depends on the amount of branch resources relative to the amount of resources in the organization). The replication schedule can be configured so that replication traffic is crossing WAN links during low-utilization, off-peak hours. *Disadvantages:* This approach requires more hardware. global catalog servers in branch networks must have enough horsepower and storage space to accommodate the needs of AD replication and to service user queries promptly. In addition, having only one global catalog server in any given local area network is not recommended, because this would make the GC a single point of failure. Remote offices may not have enough expertise to deal with service outages and repair global catalog servers; it may not always be possible to use Terminal Services or other means for remote troubleshooting.

In a simple case in which you have just one domain and a small network, it may seem as though a global catalog server is not needed at all, since every domain controller in the only domain knows about every resource in the forest. But this is not a good idea for two main reasons. First, certain applications could have been programmed to search for a GC server in the AD and request information from that server. And second, expanding such an environment into a more complex structure, perhaps with several domains, may not be possible.

In general though, when you are dealing with environments consisting of several domains, which may be further split into several sites, the best practice is to deploy a minimum of two GC servers in the central office, and an additional GC server in every site containing more than 50 users. Larger sites could also contain additional global catalog servers for fault tolerance and load-balancing purposes.

Universal Group Membership Caching

One of the new features introduced with Windows Server 2003 is the ability to cache universal group membership information on the domain controller servers. This feature mitigates problems associated with logon processes at a time when global catalog servers are unavailable. If one of your remote locations does not fit the bill for local global catalog installation, or you prefer not to install GC servers due to other technical or political reasons, WAN link availability becomes critical for basic network operations such as user logons. Instead of running the risk of relying on WAN links, you can enable the universal group caching feature on the local domain controller for users in the remote location.

To enable universal group caching, follow these steps:

1. Launch Active Directory Sites and Services from the Administrative Tools program group.

2. Expand the tree in the left-hand pane, and select the site you wish to adjust this setting for.

3. In the right-hand pane, right-click NTDS Site Settings and select Properties.

4. Ensure that the Enable Universal Group Membership Caching option is selected.

5. In the Refresh Cache From list, select the site where you want to cache group membership. If you leave this setting as the default, the cache will be refreshed from the closest site that is running the global catalog servers. Figure 3-5 shows this property page.

FIGURE 3-5

Setting
universal group
membership
caching

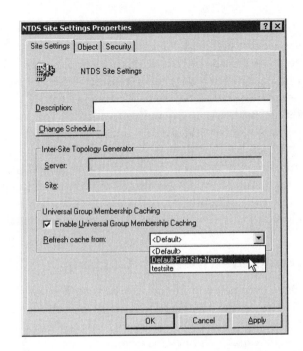

Note that only Domain Admins in the forest root domain and Enterprise Admins group members have sufficient privileges to adjust caching settings as outlined here.

After you enable universal group membership caching, the logon process is adjusted as follows: When a user logs on to the domain for the first time, the local domain controller, as usual, requests universal group membership information from the closest global catalog server. Following our example, this would be happening over a WAN link. Once the information is received from the global catalog server, it is cached on the domain controller servicing the logon request, and then from time to time it gets refreshed. From this point on, all subsequent logon requests generated by that particular user will be fulfilled by a local domain controller.

By default, universal group membership information is refreshed every eight hours. The local domain controller refreshes information from the global catalog server by submitting a universal group membership confirmation request.

Universal group membership caching is configured on the site level (sites are discussed in greater detail later in this chapter). To take advantage of this feature, you must ensure that all of the domain controllers in your remote site, or in other words, in a branch location where caching is configured, are running Windows Server 2003.

To summarize, the benefits of using universal group membership caching are as follows:

- Logon times improve due to authentication being fully contained on a local domain controller.

- Selected sites can now be implemented without deploying global catalog servers, which potentially saves hardware expenses without compromising logon functionality.

- Depending on how your domains are used, by reducing the total number of global catalog servers, you effectively reduce bandwidth requirements needed to ensure successful and timely GC data replication.

It is recommended that you use universal group membership caching whenever the remote location has a local domain controller but no locally maintained global catalog server, and only where all local domain controllers are running Windows Server 2003.

CERTIFICATION OBJECTIVE 3.02

Plan for Flexible Placement of Operation Master Roles

When working with Active Directory, a large portion of information stored on domain controllers can be modified on any domain controller. While creating a new user object, you can commit the object to any of the AD replicas in the domain in question, and this information will be propagated to other domain controllers. This is called *multimaster replication*. However, this is not a concept that applies universally to all aspects of domain operation. Certain domain functions must be performed by a single domain controller—this is termed *single master operation*. Single master operations must be performed on specially designated domain controller servers in the AD forest, and these are referred to as *operation masters*.

The concept is referred to as FSMO, or flexible single master operation; "flexible" stresses that single master roles can be transferred between domain controllers, but at the same time only one domain controller can play a given FSMO role at a time. At the same time, a single domain controller can play several FSMO roles. The following list outlines all five of the operation master roles, with the first two being forestwide roles (meaning only one master is allowed per forest) and the remaining three being domainwide roles (meaning each domain must contain one master for each of the roles).

- **Schema Master (one per forest)** Commits all Active Directory schema modifications

■ **Domain Naming Master (one per forest)**   Controls additions and removals of domains to and from the forest

■ **Infrastructure Master (one per domain)**   Keeps group-to-user references up-to-date as group membership changes, and replicates these references to other domain controllers in the domain

■ **Relative ID (RID) Master (one per domain)**   Assigns unique sequences of relative security ID numbers to domain controllers in the domain

■ **PDC Emulator (one per domain)**   Services logon requests submitted by older clients that are unaware of Active Directory; also replicates Active Directory information to NT 4.0 BDC domain controllers

Because you cannot configure more than one domain controller as a master for each of the roles in their respective areas of operation, you effectively have no fault tolerance solution for these critical domain and forest roles. Furthermore, the placement of these servers must be very carefully planned.

Operation Master Roles

The first domain controller you install in the forest automatically assumes all five operation master roles. Likewise, installation of the first domain controller for each additional domain in the forest makes that domain controller the master of all three domainwide operation master roles. When necessary, administrators can selectively transfer automatically assumed responsibilities to other domain controllers. This is also a quick solution to ensuring a fully functional infrastructure operation in cases when servers playing one of these crucial roles go down unexpectedly. Unfortunately, there is no automatic process of transferring operation master roles to healthy domain controllers; administrators must do this manually. Everyday domain functions depend heavily on operation master availability and how well you place them.

Let's look more closely at the five operation master roles.

Schema Master

Schema Master, as pointed out previously, is one of the two operation masters that can only exist on one domain controller per forest. This role manages access to the only read/write instance of the schema database. To make any sort of modifications to the Active Directory schema, you must connect to this server first.

In general, schema modifications are not something you do on a daily basis, although schema changes may happen more often in the very early stages of AD and application rollout and break-in periods. Applications such as Microsoft Exchange add roughly a thousand new object classes and attributes during installation. As an administrator, you may also need to make schema modifications—for example, if you want to add an asset tag attribute to your computer object class, or include a certain attribute in a partial replication set for global catalog replication. All of these changes are effectively schema modifications.

Keep in mind that some schema changes, such as additions of classes and attributes, cannot be undone. Hence, as noted earlier, changing the schema manually is not to be done casually. A careful approach involves testing of modified schema functionality before committing the change to the production environment. In the absence of a closely mirrored QA lab, you can install an additional domain controller in production, promote it to the Schema Master role, and take it offline. Then, all schema modifications should be committed to the database, and the functionality should be thoroughly tested. If no problems are discovered, this domain controller could be brought back into the production network, at which point schema modifications will be replicated to other domain controllers on the network.

Additional load placed on a domain controller that is performing as a Schema Master is minimal. You have to make sure that this machine is available to all administrators who must make changes to the schema.

Domain Naming Master

There can be only one Domain Naming Master per Active Directory forest. This domain controller must be accessible during addition and removal of domains to and from the forest, and also when you create trusts between domains located in different forests. When you create a new domain, the wizard uses the Remote Procedure Call (RPC) protocol to connect to the Domain Naming Master controller. You must be a member of Enterprise Admins group to add or remove domains from the forest (or have a comparable set of rights delegated to you). Since this group is physically located in the forest root domain (in other words, the first domain you install), it makes sense to keep the Domain Naming Master in the same domain.

Usually, administrators use the **dcpromo** command to promote the member server Windows Server 2003 to a domain controller. As part of the process, new domains, forests, and domain trees can be created. However, situations may emerge in which a remote branch administrator is installing a domain controller and adds a new domain for that branch, without having Enterprise Admins level permissions. If you do not wish to delegate Enterprise Admins rights to this individual, you can use the Ntdsutil tool from a central office location to execute the **precreate** command. This will create a new domain without running through the **dcpromo** process on a member server. Ntdsutil, running in the context of a user with Enterprise Admins level privileges, will create a domain object in Active Directory. Later on, the branch administrator runs **dcpromo** and assigns a name to this object, afterward creating the first domain controller object for the domain in question. This mechanism allows enterprise administrators to keep better track of who is adding or removing domains and when. Ntdsutil and other tools for managing the FSMO roles are discussed a little later in the chapter.

The Domain Naming Master is responsible for ensuring that all domain names in the forest are unique. When you attempt to create a new domain, the Domain Naming Master submits a request to a nearby global catalog server, asking for information on this domain. To ensure that the global catalog server is available at all times, it is recommended that you place the Domain Naming Master role on a domain controller also running as a global catalog. If it is not possible to place the Domain Naming Master controller on a global catalog server, there is a possibility that the link between the GC and the domain master will fail, resulting in a failed domain lookup process, which may lead to domain name duplication. With proper planning, of course, you will have prevented duplicate domain names from happening much earlier in the process.

Additional load placed by a Domain Naming Master role on a controller is very low, and only matters in the early stages when you roll out your Active Directory; however, the global catalog recommendation may significantly increase this load. It is very important that the Domain Naming Master remains accessible from any subnet in your network during implementation of Active Directory domains.

Infrastructure Master

There must be one Infrastructure Master in each domain in your infrastructure. The Infrastructure Master is responsible for group membership and SID-to-DN mapping between domains.

Objects stored on a given domain controller may reference other objects from other domains in the infrastructure. Such references are usually implemented as records that contain the GUID, SID, and DN of the referenced object. (SIDs are only used for security principal objects.) When you move objects within the infrastructure, GUID values stay the same and never change, but DNs may change, and SIDs also change if objects are moved between domains. The Infrastructure Master periodically checks such references stored in its local copy of the Active Directory database to make sure that they are still valid. It queries the global catalog to verify whether the DN and SID are still the same for a given GUID. If a change has been detected, the Infrastructure Master copies updated information to the local replica of Active Directory, and the changes are propagated to other domain controllers in the same domain during the next intradomain replication cycle.

Let's say you created a new domain group, Mobile Users, and included a User1 user account as one of the members for this new group. The Mobile Users group belongs to Domain A, and the User1 user account belongs to Domain B. Suppose you decided to rename the User1 account as Ninja, and modified the user account accordingly. This changes the DN of the object, leaving the SID and GUID the same as before. If the

Mobile Users group belonged to Domain B, the changes would become effective immediately; however, Mobile Users group is not part of the same domain, and it does not receive user account updates from Domain B. The Infrastructure Master comes to the rescue. The domain controller running as the Infrastructure Master in Domain A does not have information about user changes in Domain B, so it queries the global catalog to see if it still has the correct DN and SID values for the GUIDs of each object referenced outside of the domain it belongs to. If the Infrastructure Master finds an inconsistency, it updates group membership references in its local Active Directory replica. This update gets replicated to all domain controllers in Domain A.

Contrary to other operation master roles, the Infrastructure Master should never be placed on the same domain controller as the global catalog. If you do that, the Infrastructure Master will not function correctly, because the global catalog already contains a partial attribute set for all objects in the forest. Thus, the domain controller will not have references to objects outside of its database. If the Infrastructure Master is not forced to check the references, it simply will not do this, and hence the local copy of Active Directory will never get updated. There are two cases in which you do not necessarily need to observe this rule:

1. In cases when you only have one domain in your infrastructure. (You don't need an Infrastructure Master because there are no references to objects in other domains.)

2. In cases where all domain controllers in your infrastructure must also be global catalog servers.

In both cases, domain controllers have all of the infrastructure information in local replicas, and Infrastructure Masters are not really needed. Additional load placed on a domain controller participating as an Infrastructure Master is negligible. Administrators should feel free to place other operation masters on domain controllers running as Infrastructure Masters.

Relative ID Master (RID Master)

There should be one RID Master in each domain in your infrastructure. When security principals are created (Active Directory objects such as users, groups, or computers), they are assigned a security identifier, or SID. SIDs are made up of the domain SID, which is the same for all domain objects, and the RID, which must be unique within the domain. Since objects are created on a domain controller—any domain controller in the domain—each domain controller must have a pool, or sequence of RID numbers, that it can uniquely assign to domain objects created on the domain controller in question. Domain controllers must be able to contact the RID Master to obtain their RID sequences; the fact that only one server is assigning RID sequences ensures there is no overlap, which in turn guarantees that generated SIDs are unique.

RID sequences are assigned to domain controllers as they are added to the domain. As the domain controller operates and assigns SIDs, it eventually may deplete its RID pool. If at any time the number of available RIDs dips below 100, the domain controller locates the RID Master and contacts it to request more RID sequences. Even if the RID Master is temporarily unavailable, this should not affect the functionality of domain controllers because there is still some breathing room as far as available RIDs are concerned.

RID Masters are also used when you move objects between domains. The move originates on the RID Master in the domain where the object is being moved from. When you move an object from one domain to another, the distinguished name (DN) and SID parameters of this object change to reflect new domain membership. The globally unique identifier (GUID) remains unchanged. The RID Master participates in the process to ensure that there are no duplicate RID portions of the SID in the new domain.

Additional load placed on a domain controller running as the RID Master is fairly insignificant. Administrators should feel free to deploy other operation masters on the same domain controller if they wish. It makes more sense to place the RID Master and PDC Emulator on the same server if your infrastructure contains a fair amount of legacy workstations and domain controllers. If objects are created on those legacy machines, changes will be written to the PDC Emulator, and RIDs will be taken from the same server.

PDC Emulator

There must be one PDC Emulator in every domain. First of all, the PDC Emulator is used by older NT 4.0 era clients that may not be aware of the Active Directory environment. Those clients will treat the PDC Emulator as their PDC ("primary domain controller" in the Windows NT 4 days). The PDC Emulator also fulfills the NetBIOS computer browser master role for applications that may still rely on NetBIOS. In addition, if the Active Directory domain contains NT 4 BDCs, or "backup domain controllers" (running older SAM databases), the PDC Emulator replicates portions of Active Directory data to these legacy infrastructure servers. In other words, the primary task of the PDC Emulator is to ensure backward compatibility with legacy systems.

Don't assume that the PDC Emulator is not required in environments where no legacy systems exist. The PDC Emulator is responsible for replicating time-sensitive changes within Active Directory—changes such as user account lockout and administrative deactivation, password resets, and other sensitive events that may otherwise cause a security risk. When administrators disable someone's account, the change first gets replicated to the PDC Emulator, which immediately triggers replication to all other domain controllers. Also, group policy changes are committed to the PDC Emulator's replica of Active Directory before they are replicated to other domain controllers.

PDC Emulator availability is fairly important; without it, password changes would replicate slower, resulting in inconsistent user logon experience, depending on which domain controller the authentication request is submitted to. The PDC Emulator should be linked with other domain controllers in a reliable way so that the possibility of communication breakdowns is reduced. Just as with the Domain Naming Master, the PDC Emulator should have reliable access to a nearby global catalog server. Therefore, if possible, administrators should place a global catalog replica on the PDC Emulator as well.

Additional load placed on a domain controller running as the PDC Emulator is high, and this is especially true in large-scale domains. To achieve the best possible performance level, PDC Emulator servers should be located on dedicated domain controllers that do not have any other FSMO responsibilities.

Maintaining Business Continuity

Business continuity is paramount in any information system, and Active Directory is no exception. After all, the point of spending resources on implementation and support of the system is to save time and money in everyday business operations, allowing companies to become more efficient and more agile. The most frustrating part of implementing a system is when one crucial server goes out of service and a significant amount of downtime is incurred, grinding business to a halt; so instead of making a company more agile, the information system only increases the likelihood of failure. With several domain controllers supporting any given domain, this may not seem to be an issue with Active Directory; however, given the single point of failure in FSMO functionality, the following rules should always be observed when it comes to planning and placing your operation masters:

- Every domain controller that will assume operation master role(s) must have adequate hardware resources. Different operation master roles place various levels of stress on the system. In the next few chapters, we will review which additional responsibilities are assumed by servers when master operation roles are assigned to them. Administrators have to monitor domain controller health and transfer operation master roles depending on the circumstances. Hardware fault tolerance features such as RAID5, hot swappable drive bays, and redundant power supplies will never harm an operation master domain controller.

■ Equally important, operation masters must be available to all network nodes that participate in the domain in question. This means routing must be done correctly, and connectivity between domain controllers must be reliable—and better yet, redundant.

Reliable service provided by FSMO servers makes the difference between a network that works and one that does not. So what do you do if one of the master servers is at risk of going down and you want to transfer the role to another domain controller? Or, more important, what do you do if one of the master servers has already gone down? Chapter 4 deals with operation master failures and recovery procedures in greater detail. For the purposes of this discussion, we'll look at how to determine the state of FSMO servers and how to transfer roles to other domain controllers should that become necessary.

A set of tools and administrative consoles allows you to control and manage FSMO servers. The following sections provide a quick overview of the Dsquery, Netdom, Replication Monitor, and Ntdsutil tools, as well as the management consoles for transferring operation master roles.

Dsquery

A standard OS tool set includes Dsquery, which allows querying Active Directory for specific information. It is an LDAP query and modification tool, a typical example of command line LDAP client application. To find a specific FSMO server, type **dsquery server –hasfsmo <role>**, where <role> is the operation master you are looking for. This has to be one of the following: schema, name, infr, pdc, or rid. To find out which server in the forest is responsible for managing schema modifications, use **dsquery server –hasfsmo schema**. Note that schema and name command parameters will search the forest, and infr, pdc, and rid parameters will search the domain you are located in, unless you specify otherwise.

Netdom

The Netdom command line utility is installed as part of the Support Tools. It is effectively a shortcut to seeing all five FSMO servers at once, without having to type long and not easily remembered commands. This tool is limited to viewing Active Directory information. The command you want to use to view all five FSMO servers at once is **netdom query fsmo**.

Replication Monitor

Also a part of Support Tools, Replication Monitor allows you to verify connectivity to a given operation master server. You can use this tool to verify connectivity to FSMO servers from any domain controller anywhere within the same forest. Unlike Dsquery, Netdom, and Ntdsutil, Replication Monitor is a GUI-based tool, which does not allow transferring FSMO roles between servers.

Ntdsutil

The Ntdsutil command-line tool is part of the standard set of operating system tools. It allows you to perform a variety of modifications and operations in Active Directory. Among other things, Ntdsutil is the tool for performing authoritative restores of the AD database and transferring FSMO roles between servers. This powerful tool can cause plenty of damage if used by an inexperienced administrator; some may say it lacks user friendliness. It functions in a slightly different way from other typical command-line tools in that it has its own interactive command interface, similar to NSLOOKUP or Netsh. The following listing, which shows a sample dialogue between an administrator and Active Directory by means of Ntdsutil, demonstrates how to obtain a list of FSMO servers.

```
C:\Documents and Settings\Administrator.WIN2003SRV>ntdsutil
ntdsutil: roles
fsmo maintenance: select operation target
select operation target: connections
server connections: connect to domain flexecom.com
Binding to \\win2003srv.flexecom.com ...
Connected to \\win2003srv.flexecom.com using credentials of locally logged on user.
server connections: quit
select operation target: list roles for connected server
Server "\\win2003srv.flexecom.com" knows about 5 roles
Schema - CN=NTDS
Settings,CN=WIN2003SRV,CN=Servers,CN=Default-First-Site-Name,CN=Sites,CN=Configuration,DC=
flexecom,DC=com
Domain - CN=NTDS
Settings,CN=WIN2003SRV,CN=Servers,CN=Default-First-Site-Name,CN=Sites,CN=Configuration,DC=
flexecom,DC=com
PDC - CN=NTDS
Settings,CN=WIN2003SRV,CN=Servers,CN=Default-First-Site-Name,CN=Sites,CN=Configuration,DC=
flexecom,DC=com
RID - CN=NTDS
Settings,CN=WIN2003SRV,CN=Servers,CN=Default-First-Site-Name,CN=Sites,CN=Configuration,DC=
flexecom,DC=com
Infrastructure - CN=NTDS
Settings,CN=WIN2003SRV,CN=Servers,CN=Default-First-Site-Name,CN=Sites,CN=Configuration,DC=
flexecom,DC=com
```

Also note that Ntdsutil allows seizing FSMO roles from defunct domain controllers. This utility can be used to transfer FSMO roles from domain controllers irrespective of their current status.

Active Directory Domains and Trusts and Active Directory Schema Management Consoles

Administrators can look up and transfer forestwide FSMO servers, namely, Schema Master and Domain Naming Master, using the Active Directory Domains and Trusts and Active Directory Schema management consoles. The AD Domains and Trusts console allows transferring the Domain Naming Master role, and Active Directory Schema, the Schema Master role. Figure 3-6 illustrates the Schema Master properties and transfer page.

on the job

To use the Active Directory Schema console, you need to register it first. Use the regsvr32 schmmgmt.dll command to register the required dynamic link library. Then in the MMC console, add the Active Directory Schema console from the list of available consoles.

Active Directory Users and Computers Management Console

You use the Active Directory Users and Computers management console to look up and transfer domainwide FSMO servers—namely, the RID Master, PDC Emulator, and Infrastructure Master.

FIGURE 3-6

Schema Master properties in the AD schema console

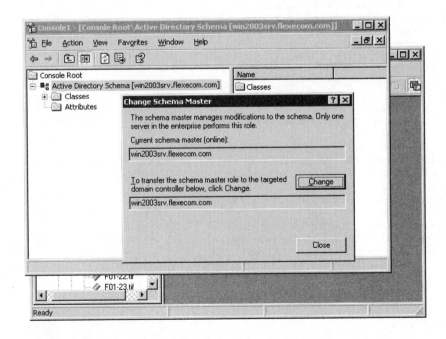

EXERCISE 3-1

Transferring the PDC Emulator Role to a Different Domain Controller

In this exercise, you use the Active Directory Users and Computers snap-in to transfer the PDC Emulator operation master role from one domain controller to another one. Ensure that you belong to either the Domain Admins or Enterprise Admins group, or have comparable permissions in the domain. Then log on to a domain controller.

1. Launch the Active Directory Users and Computers management console by clicking All Programs. Choose Administrative Tools, and then click Active Directory Users and Computers.

2. In the console tree pane, right-click Active Directory Users and Computers; then choose Connect to Domain Controller.

3. In the Enter The Name Of Another Domain Controller box, type in the name of the domain controller where you would like to transfer the PDC Emulator role, and then connect to the server.

4. In the console tree, right-click Active Directory Users and Computers again, point to All Tasks, and then click Operation Masters.

5. Switch to the PDC tab and click the Change button.

Operation Master Dependencies

Let's step back for a bit and summarize what we have learned so far. All of the factors outlined in this part of the chapter will influence your placement of the operation masters. Here is a review of common recommendations on how to place your operation masters:

■ If your infrastructure has only one domain controller, and hence, one domain, which also happens to be the forest root domain, it plays all five of the operation master roles.

■ Whenever possible, place the RID Master and PDC Emulator on the same domain controller. If they are located on different domain controllers, you must ensure that the link between the two is extremely reliable and fast enough to support replication and operation master interaction.

■ The PDC Emulator role places the largest amount of overhead on domain controllers.

■ The Infrastructure Master should not be placed on a domain controller running as a global catalog server. At the same time, the Infrastructure Master must have a reliable connection to a nearby global catalog server, preferably located in the same Active Directory site.

■ At the forest level, the Schema Master and Domain Naming Master should be placed on those controllers most likely to be accepting requests for their respective services. Qualified administrative personnel should have easy access to these critical servers.

■ It is a good practice to institute recurring checks of operation masters using the tools reviewed earlier. If your infrastructure is fairly reliable and has redundant domain controllers, keep in mind that operation master roles are not transferred from failing domain controllers on the fly; instead, this has to be done manually. Depending on the role, outages may not be spotted easily, while the infrastructure may suffer from "weird" problems.

Figure 3-7 illustrates a sample multidomain forest, indicating where operation masters could be placed. Remember that there is no "right" or "wrong" setup that will be everything to everyone.

FIGURE 3-7

Placement of operation master roles in a multidomain forest

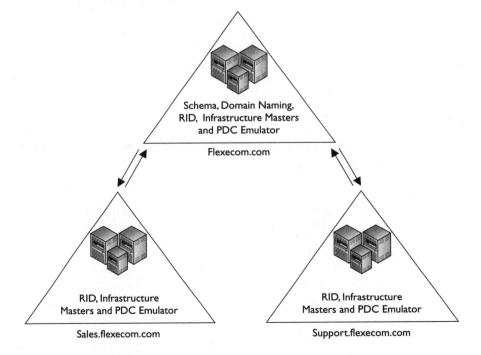

Schema, Domain Naming, RID, Infrastructure Masters and PDC Emulator

Flexecom.com

RID, Infrastructure Masters and PDC Emulator

Sales.flexecom.com

RID, Infrastructure Masters and PDC Emulator

Support.flexecom.com

CERTIFICATION OBJECTIVE 3.03

Implement the AD Forest and Domain Structure

The role of domains in Windows Server 2003 has not changed from what it used to be in previous versions—they still act as a common security and replication boundary. Users who belong to one domain, by default, inherit no privileges in other domains. Information about security principals (objects such as users, groups, and computers) is stored in Active Directory.

From the physical perspective, Active Directory information is stored in databases maintained on domain controllers. Domain controllers maintain Active Directory information, service queries, make sure that object hierarchy is in place, and ensure that changes committed to the local copies of the database are replicated to other domain controllers in the domain.

Domains may be grouped into domain trees. Domains participating in the same domain tree have a common portion in the DNS and Active Directory namespace. The domains within the tree are cascaded, similar to a typical DNS subdomain organization. All domains within any domain tree have automatic, two-way *transitive trust* relationships, meaning that users from any domain may access resources in any other domain, provided that administrators grant appropriate access privileges.

Domain trees, in their turn, may be organized into a common domain forest. The main purpose of domain forests is that they also act as common security mechanisms, although this time around, participating domains need not share the same DNS and hence, AD namespace. That is, any given forest may contain any number of trees, each of them having their own namespace. All domain trees within one domain forest are configured with two-way transitive trusts, which means every domain in the forest trusts any other domain in the forest. One element that must be common for all domains within a given forest is the Active Directory schema.

Automatic configuration of transitive trusts does not necessarily mean that domains and trees and forests lose their security boundaries. Trust relationships only make it technically possible to assign resource permissions to users located in domains other than where the resources are. Also new to Windows Server 2003 is the ability to configure a cross-forest trust, which makes it possible to make any domain in one forest trust any domain in another forest, using only one external trust relationship. In Windows 2000, you could set up external trusts between individual domains located in different forests, but in this case you would need to maintain multiple external trusts if you were to make all domains in one forest trust all domains in another forest.

The concept of Active Directory *sites* differs from security-related talk, which is centered on domains and various combinations thereof. Sites implement a common replication boundary used to better manage replication within and between domains. Changes within one domain will propagate to all domain controllers within that domain, but the mechanisms used to deliver these changes may differ based on how domain controllers are split between different sites. In other words, sites are used to control replication independently of domains. So one site may contain several domains, or vice versa—one domain may span several sites. Sites are discussed later on when we look at replication mechanisms.

Such an elaborate multilevel information system is flexible enough to fit practically any business scenario. It does not even matter if the system is implemented for one organization or for several organizations partnering or merging with each other.

Analyzing Business Requirements

Active Directory has come a long way since the days of SAM databases in Windows NT 4.0. These days, infrastructure planning is centered a lot more on business requirements and objectives, and not how they fit into technical possibilities and limitations of the Microsoft operating system. Active Directory uses a variety of mechanisms and industry-standard technologies that have made physical limitations of the system a non-problem, even for the largest of companies that exist today. Based on the definition of domain as a unit of resource organization into a common boundary, security considerations play a major role in choosing the right domain model.

Domain structure planning in basic terms comes down to two major strategies: upgrade and potential restructuring of an existing NT domain environment, or implementation of a new domain structure. Naturally, upgrade and restructuring of an existing NT 4.0 domain environment is more involved than starting fresh, primarily because an existing domain environment is way past the planning stages, and it may not be trivial to restructure mission-critical operations without significant disruption. That being said, regardless of the strategy, planning is the most vital part of the process.

One of the first things to consider is how many domains you should implement. A valid question is why consolidate existing NT 4.0 domains into one domain? It sounds easier just to upgrade everything to Windows Server 2003 and leave the structure intact. To better understand this, let's go back to the NT days. Back then, there were several reasons that could have forced you to use more than one domain. First of all, it was a technical limitation of SAM databases that could not handle more than approximately 40,000 directory objects in one domain. Windows 2000 and now Windows Server 2003 blow way past this limitation with a theoretical limit of 4 billion objects. Many organizations maintain several million objects in their Active Directory database and still provide outstanding performance.

A second reason for the multidomain model was lack of delegation of administrative rights in Windows NT 4.0. Windows 2000 and now Windows Server 2003 are based on LDAP directory technology, and as we saw in Chapter 1, these directories have standard features such as AAAs that allow delegation of administrative control based on organizational units (logical groupings of directory objects). Windows' implementation of LDAP technology goes farther to allow selective delegation of administrative tasks, such as resetting user passwords. So delegation of permissions is now as granular as current directory technology will allow.

A third reason was the numerous limitations in how Windows NT 4.0 replicated database information between PDCs and BDCs. Replication topology consisting of one primary domain controller and multiple secondary domain controllers, featuring practically no replication controls, was not suitable for implementation of large, geographically distributed domains. This problem has also been solved since the release of Windows 2000: now directory changes can be committed to any of the replicas on any domain controller, replication traffic is contained using sites, and intersite replication is flexible and features a number of customization options.

If you implemented a multidomain environment for one or more of these reasons, consider collapsing these domains into one Windows Server 2003 domain. Whether you create a company infrastructure from scratch or migrate an existing infrastructure to Windows Server 2003, the advantages of a single domain environment can be summarized as follows:

- **Ease of administration** Administration in a single domain deployment is centralized. One domain requires fewer servers; removes the need for many considerations such as where to place operation masters or how to configure trust relationships; and simplifies resource permission management, with only one domain where user objects are located. Users traveling between offices (and hence between domains) do not need to enter their logon names in UPN format, which includes their logon name and domain name where the user account is located. Authentication works faster in a single domain. It is not necessary to configure domain group policies several times. Users and computers operate in a single domain namespace, usually in a shorter and simpler form. Administrators need to maintain a smaller number of DNS zones. It is not necessary to delegate administrative permissions to administrators from other domains. Administrators do not need to worry about the cascaded structure of domains or their position in the forest. It also may be easier to integrate software into the Active Directory environment.

- **Ease of delegation** In a single domain model, you can create several organizational units (which will be discussed later on), distribute directory objects between these units, and delegate permissions to manipulate these objects to other administrators. In the multidomain model, this is a little more complicated.

- **Fewer administrative personnel** In a single domain model, there is no need to have separate administrators, or teams of administrators, responsible for each domain and its domain controllers. This flows from the centralized administration concept, and results in fewer "authority" issues that may arise in any organization.

- **Overall savings** This point is a result of easier administration and reduced administrative personnel to maintain a minimum quality level of the Active Directory infrastructure. TCO (total cost of ownership) is reduced.

Child Domains

Arguments in favor of the single domain model notwithstanding, in a number of situations this model may simply not be the right solution for the business case. If so, you may need to implement either separate domain trees (separate namespaces) or child domains. This section focuses on advantages provided by child domains. Remember that all child domains within the same forest automatically trust every other domain in the forest, which means that it is still possible to have centralized corporate applications such as workflow, email, ERP/CRM, and data warehousing; to set up a centralized file sharing structure; to search the entire Active Directory for objects; and so on.

The following are some business requirements that typically lend themselves to child domains rather than a single domain model:

- The company size is too large from an administrative perspective. Creating several domains may alleviate some of the problems usually associated with large companies. At a certain level, it may be difficult to manage resources of a company even with delegation and organizational units in place.

- The company prefers a decentralized administrative model. In some cases, centralized administration of company resources may be detrimental to growth, IT department usefulness, help desk response times, and so on. More often than not, separate units of the company will prefer to have their own IT departments with local control of the unit's resources.

- Perhaps a logical continuation from the preceding point, IT departments of separate units may prefer to eliminate interference from administrators of other units. Since a domain is a secure organizational unit, separate domains may be needed to contain authority of administrators who belong to separate units.

- Child domains may be necessary to reduce replication traffic. A domain is a replication boundary, in the sense that all domain controllers in the same domain must have the same Active Directory information about this domain. This is a questionable reason to implement separate domains, since sites can also be used to contain replication traffic regardless of domains. However, keep in mind that even when you use sites, if you have one domain controller on each side of a slow WAN, and both of them belong to the same domain, sooner or later replication traffic must cross the WAN. You may choose to schedule it to replicate after normal business hours, but if your office is located in New York, you have a domain controller in San Francisco, and another one in Tokyo, there are no nonbusiness hours as far as the WAN is concerned. In a multidomain environment, replication still occurs—the global catalog, schema, and forest settings still need to be propagated—but the amount of bandwidth used to replicate those portions of the Active Directory database is usually less significant.

- Geographical considerations may mandate separate domains. Continuing from the previous point, typically, offices in different countries will have to maintain their own domains for a number of other reasons, all of which point to geopolitical differences. Things like time zones, localized OS and application languages and settings, regional settings, and 128-bit digital encryption export restrictions may all require different and often incompatible domainwide settings. Geography is a key factor in having separate domains.

- Separate domain security policies may be required. Different security requirements should automatically be associated with separate domains. Account lockout policies, password policies, and Kerberos policies can only be applied at the domain level. Furthermore, formal definition of the domain itself has a lot to do with security. In a number of circumstances, even one branch may require separate domains—one for ordinary users, who don't want to be bothered remembering long and complicated passwords, and another one for users with access to classified information.

A child domain inherits the DNS domain name of the parent domain, and is effectively a subdomain of the parent domain. This allows reflecting either the geographic structure of the company or the area of commercial activity of a given company unit. Child domains may contain other child domains.

In addition to creating child domains, you can also create new domain trees. This strategy has no impact on trust relationships (comparing it to the child domain approach), and the same business requirements apply, with the only key difference being the distinguished namespace. If one of the new domains is for a separate business arm of the company, and it has its own Internet presence, you may want to create a separate domain tree for that arm, using their registered DNS domain name for AD namespace purposes.

Forest Root Domain

It is impossible to create new child domains or new domain trees without first creating a *forest root domain*. Every domain tree has a forest root domain—for example, the domain tree flexecom.com has its own forest root domain, which in many cases will bear the same name. We can add child domains to this forest root domain and name them secure.flexecom.com and dev.flexecom.com, for example.

The forest root domain is the single most important unit of infrastructure organization, and it is always the first domain created during the rollout of Active Directory. The first server promoted to domain controller effectively initiates the AD environment, and by default, it assumes all five FSMO roles plus the global catalog service. The forest root domain also maintains two important user groups: Enterprise Admins and Schema Admins. The Enterprise Admins group places the least amount of restrictions on its members, making them the most powerful group in the forest. It allows things such as controlling administrative group membership in any of the forest domains and adding domains to the forest.

This group is added automatically to all Domain Admins groups in the forest, effectively making members of the group administrators in every domain in the forest. The Schema Admins group is designed to assign necessary permissions for modifying the Active Directory schema. You should only consider adding qualified administrators who know what they are doing to either of these groups; membership in these two groups should be limited. If all of your domain controllers in the forest root domain were to break down and it was not possible to restore at least one of them, these two groups would be lost for good, and it would no longer be possible to modify the forest schema or domain membership in the forest.

Next, consider how to deploy your forest root domain. There are two classical approaches, as described in the following sections.

Configuring One of the Production Domains as a Forest Root Domain

After considering how many domains you should implement, evaluate whether you can use one of these domains as your forest root domain. Usually it makes more sense to pick the most important domain in your design and make it the forest root domain. This strategy makes it unlikely that administrators would ever need to remove this domain from the organization. Because this domain is the most important from your design perspective, chances are also pretty good that hardware fault tolerance will be in place and single points of failure would be eliminated (except for FSMO operation masters).

Using an Empty Root Domain

The empty root domain was briefly covered in Chapter 2. Using a dedicated forest root domain comes at a price of additional hardware, which must have enough redundancy built in, and yet these servers will be relatively idle. However, the expense may be justified if any of the following benefits apply to your particular design:

- By having a separate domain that contains Schema Admins and Enterprise Admins, you eliminate a situation in which regular domain administrators in one of your production domains have administrative rights for every other domain in your forest. In the separate forest root domain, you can limit membership in these groups to only those individuals who really need the privileges.

- Since the forest root domain is there only for infrastructure needs and will not contain many objects, the size of the database will be smaller than in other production domains, making it easier to devise a disaster recovery strategy that may include things like off-site domain controllers accepting replication traffic from the forest root domain.

- Any business restructuring involving additions or removals of domains is less likely to have a dramatic impact on the rest of the domains in the forest if you have a separate forest root domain. Imagine if you had to spin off one production domain from your forest, and it happened to be your forest root domain. This would require creating another forest root domain, effectively starting from scratch.

- The forest root domain forms your namespace. If you have to modify the domain tree structure, the fallout from renaming one domain lower in the structure is significantly less than renaming the forest root domain. Other namespace considerations also apply (these were discussed in Chapter 2).

on the
Job

While selecting hardware for your infrastructure servers, if you must find the best compromise between performance and fault tolerance/disaster recovery features, it is not recommended to give up fault tolerance features in favor of performance. The level of hardware performance does matter when it comes to Active Directory, but not at the expense of recoverability.

It is not unusual for administrators to create empty forest root domains when migrating a multimaster infrastructure from Windows NT 4.0—that is, a set of NT 4.0 domains where multiple domains were used to store user accounts, establishing trust relationships with resource domains. Moving thousands of objects from NT 4.0 to the

Windows Server 2003 domain, and thus changing how users access resources, may pose a problem. So instead of collapsing all resources into a single domain, administrators would create an empty forest root domain and simply upgrade Windows NT 4.0 master domains to Windows Server 2003. During the upgrade, domains are added as child domains to the forest. The new domain names are constructed to compromise between NetBIOS naming restrictions, but they do include the parent portion of the namespace from the forest root domain.

Let's look at an example to make this point a little clearer. Suppose you are migrating an infrastructure for a grocery chain. The company grew through acquisitions—it bought several smaller chains. The infrastructure consists of three domains: FoodCo, DrinkCo, and StuffCo. You are tasked to design the infrastructure in a way that will include a personalized domain namespace that must include the same parent domain to reflect the unity of business units. At a later date, the company may add more units, and your design must respect this requirement.

One of the better solutions here would be to create an empty forest root domain, such as "TheSuperStoreCo.com." (Make sure your name is still available for registration.) Then, upgrade NT 4.0 domains to Windows Server 2003 and name them "FoodCo.TheSuperStoreCo.com," "DrinkCo.TheSuperStoreCo.com," and "StuffCo.TheSuperStoreCo.com." This naming and domain structure strategy allows easy addition of business units later on and respects business naming requirements as well as NetBIOS restrictions.

Interaction between domains located in the same and in different forests will depend on domain functional levels, which are covered later in this chapter. Figure 3-8 demonstrates a sample infrastructure composition, including all elements discussed so far—domains, trees, and forests.

Application Data Partitions

Domain controllers running Windows 2000 and later, partition the Active Directory database into several segments. Prior to Windows Server 2003 we had the schema data partition (used to store the definition of the schema used in the forest), the configuration data partition (used to store infrastructure topology, all of the forest domains, and replication information), and finally, the domain data partition (used to store actual objects stored in the domain). Beginning with Windows Server 2003, application data partitions can be used to replicate application-specific information between designated domain controllers. In Chapter 2, DNS was used as an example to show how application partitions come in handy; here, application partitions are discussed in more detail.

FIGURE 3-8   Infrastructure elements

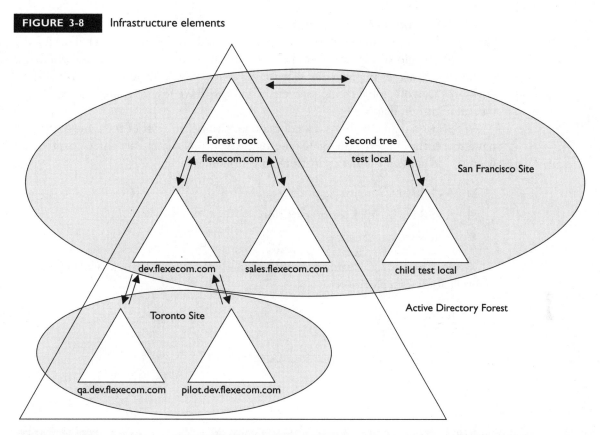

Flexecom.com domain tree

The application data partition can contain all types of objects except security principal objects (users, groups, computers). Data contained in the application partition does not replicate to all domain controllers—only those designated by administrators. Also, this data is not replicated to the global catalog. Application partitions can be assigned to any domain controllers anywhere in the forest; they do not necessarily have to be in the same domain. This is different from the domain data partition, which automatically replicates itself to all domain controllers within one domain. Application partitions serve as yet another vehicle to contain replication traffic, delivering application-specific information only to those locations that need this information.

It is technically possible to have application partitions and global catalog information on the same domain controller. However, global catalog requests directed to a domain controller running in this configuration will never return application partition data, even though both services are located on the same server. This is by design: the global catalog must always return the same result, no matter which global catalog server in particular is servicing that query. In general, there is no guarantee that all global catalog servers will always have the same application partition in their database.

Application data partitions, like domain partitions, are part of the same forest namespace; they observe the same naming conventions. There are three possible ways to add application data partitions to your namespace:

- A child of a domain partition
- A child of an application partition
- A new tree in the forest

Windows Server 2003 features several tools and mechanisms that allow manipulation of application data partitions:

- ntdsutil.exe
- ldp.exe
- Active Directory Service Interfaces (ADSI)

SCENARIO & SOLUTION

Which operation master is responsible for making sure that domain names are unique?	The Domain Naming Master.
When you use the universal group caching feature, are your domain controllers querying global catalogs during user authentication?	Yes, but only during the first logon of any given user. The result of the first request is cached and subsequently refreshed, and no further global catalog requests are made during the logon process.
Is the application data partition replicated to global catalog servers?	In general, no. Application data is only replicated to designated domain controllers.
What is the best way to separate the authority of two administrators over a set of resources?	Split up your organization resources in two domains and add the respective administrators to Domain Admins groups in their domains.

Domain Controllers

Domain controllers (DCs) are actual infrastructure servers that implement Active Directory service and a plethora of other network services, not necessarily related to AD. Domain controllers can also provide AD-integrated DFS services, certificate authority services, network services such as DHCP and DNS, and other services.

When you install your first domain controller, you create your first forest, first domain tree, first domain, and first site in your organization. Domain controllers store all AD-related database information, and they interact between domain users and applications on one side and the Active Directory on the other side. To promote a member server (any Windows Server 2003 server that is not running Active Directory services) to a domain controller, administrators run the Dcpromo utility after installation of a member server. Dcpromo takes you through several steps that you have to complete in accordance with your domain structure plan. The logical process is depicted in Figure 3-9.

FIGURE 3-9

The Dcpromo utility

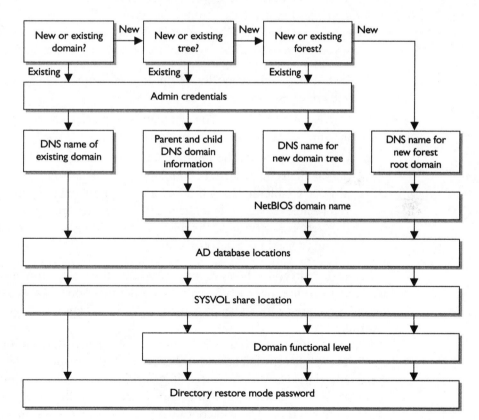

The Dcpromo Wizard collects administrative input as to whether this domain controller is going to initiate a new domain or participate in an existing one. If it is a new domain, you tell the wizard whether this domain is a forest root domain for a new forest, a child domain in an existing forest, or the first domain in a new domain tree, and so on. To answer these questions, your plan must be in place, you must have all the names of existing or planned domains, and you must know the enterprise administrator's username and password.

Dcpromo also needs to know where it should place the Active Directory database and transaction log files. All database file placement strategies apply to the Active Directory database. Ideally, administrators should place these files on a separate set of (preferably) hardware RAID disks, such as RAID1 or RAID5.

Dcpromo attempts to register service records on the first DNS server, configured in the TCP/IP settings on the domain controller you are installing. If you are adding a domain controller to an existing infrastructure and DNS settings are not configured properly (in other words, the server you are promoting is unable to find other Active Directory servers in the infrastructure), the process will not succeed. If the DNS server settings are correct but the DNS server itself does not accept dynamic registration requests, you will have to choose one of the following three options:

- **Install DNS server locally**   Dcpromo will launch a DNS setup wizard and will create the necessary zones.

- **Correct the problem**   You can manually check the zone settings and adjust dynamic update properties, then retry.

- **Continue, ignoring the problem**   In this case, you will have to manually add netlogon.dns file records to your DNS zone. This is not a trivial exercise, and is not advisable. If your DNS server is experiencing temporary difficulties and will be able to accept dynamic registrations later on, you could simply restart the Netlogon service on the newly installed domain controller, and it will attempt to add DNS records again.

Before domain controllers are introduced into the production environment, it is necessary to ensure that each domain controller functions reliably as a unit and that the infrastructure has redundancy and does not depend entirely on any given domain controller.

In small businesses, two domain controllers in a single domain infrastructure are usually enough; if one domain controller goes offline, it will not affect users' ability to log on and use network resources. If your organization has satellite offices, it is advisable to place at least one additional domain controller on a local network in each remote location. (Domain controller placement follows a similar logical pattern used to decide where to place global catalog servers; it may be optimal to add global catalog services to remotely placed domain controllers.) If one of the satellite domain controllers goes down but the WAN link is still available, users would be able to authenticate with a domain controller located in the headquarters.

Should the WAN link go down, there is still one domain controller (and global catalog server) available to users in the satellite office. In the unlikely event that both the satellite domain controller *and* WAN link go down at the same time, only then would user workflow be disrupted. Depending on specific business requirements, this may have to be prevented as well, in which case you would need more than one domain controller in each of the satellite offices, as depicted in Figure 3-10.

As usual, administrators have to weigh the need for reliable operation against minimization of replication traffic. Good solutions usually provide both; but there is no single strategy that will fit all companies. We look more into replication strategies in Chapter 4.

FIGURE 3-10 Domain controllers in satellite offices

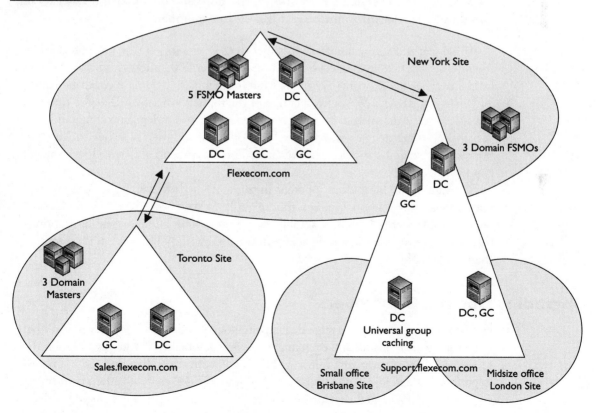

Having several domain controllers allows a fair degree of flexibility when it comes to unexpected outages. If one of the redundant domain controllers goes down and you are unable to restore it, it is not really a big deal, since other domain controllers in a given domain have exact replicas of the domain partition. The only inconvenience might be in transferring FSMO roles, if one of the operation masters was on the downed server. You may also need to designate the remaining domain controllers as global catalogs and/or participants in application partitions to replace the machine that is having problems.

on the
job

Having redundant domain controllers should not substitute for a solid backup and disaster recovery strategy. At least one domain controller in each geographical location should be backed up. If you use the NTBACKUP utility provided with Windows Server 2003, make sure to back up the system state on every domain controller. This will back up Active Directory databases (including all AD partitions), system files, the Registry, COM+ objects, the SYSVOL directory, the CA certificate database if the domain controller is also a CA server, DNS service information if the domain controller is a DNS server, and finally, cluster information if it is a cluster member.

When you add a new domain controller to the domain, AD data is replicated to the new server. Like its predecessor, Windows Server 2003 allows restoring AD data from a backup file, averting live replication from an active domain controller that may take place over a WAN irrespective of the replication schedule at the time you run Dcpromo. Administrators can use a new feature of the **dcpromo** command—the /adv switch—that toggles on advanced user options, and then specify a backup file from which Dcpromo should copy AD data. This can potentially save a lot of valuable bandwidth.

Be aware of two limitations inherent in this method, however. First, Dcpromo will not create any application partitions that might have been backed up from the "donor" domain controller (which may actually be rather helpful). The second limitation is that you have to make sure the backup file created with NTBACKUP is no more than 60 days old.

Upgrading Domain Controllers

How do you decide when to upgrade from an older Windows NT 4.0 server and when to perform a clean install and then migrate existing domains? If your organization runs some specialized software on Windows NT 4.0 domain controllers and there is no way to perform a clean install and phase out Windows NT 4.0 gradually, then performing an in-place upgrade might seem appropriate. However, it is generally recommended to perform clean installs to ensure optimum performance and reliability. Regardless of the upgrade path you choose, you must make sure that current domain controller servers have enough hardware to support Windows Server 2003 and this hardware is compatible with the new operating system.

If you must perform an in-place upgrade, it is recommended to upgrade Windows NT 4.0 PDC to Windows Server 2003 first, leaving existing BDCs on the network. The PDC Emulator service will ensure that BDCs and legacy clients will interact with the Windows Server 2003 in much the same way as if it was still a Windows NT 4.0 PDC. You can upgrade Windows NT 4.0 computers running Service Pack 5 and later; Windows NT 3.51 servers cannot be upgraded directly to Windows Server 2003. If you run into a situation where one of your BDCs is more powerful in terms of hardware, but the existing Windows NT PDC is not powerful enough to support Windows Server 2003, simply promote a more powerful BDC to PDC and perform an in-place upgrade on that server.

Some organizations may prefer not to perform an upgrade on a PDC server. In this case, you could demote a PDC to BDC and take it offline, and promote another BDC to PDC and upgrade that server instead. If the process does not go as planned and you have to revert to the previous setup, you can always bring the spare BDC online and promote it to the PDC role. After you are done upgrading the PDC, you can either upgrade the remaining BDCs, or simply install new servers and add them to the Windows Server 2003 domain, gradually removing Windows NT machines from the network. (This is recommended if existing BDCs are not powerful enough to run Windows Server 2003.)

When you upgrade your first PDC, configure the functional level of your forest as Windows Server 2003 interim whenever possible. This functional level delivers all benefits of Windows Server 2003 domain operation, but it is not available if your forest root domain is configured with the Windows 2000 functional level. The Windows Server 2003 interim functional level should only be used during the transition from NT domains, and should be raised to Windows Server 2003 after the last BDC goes offline or gets upgraded. Only when all of your NT 4.0 domain controllers have been upgraded to Windows Server 2003 can you take full advantage of the multimaster architecture.

Upgrading Windows 2000 Server domain controllers is a lot easier than upgrading Windows NT 4.0 because hardware requirements have not changed much, and more importantly, because Windows 2000 Active Directory technologies and infrastructures, on a bigger scale, remain the same in Windows Server 2003. Administrators will have to prepare the AD schema for migration, which is done by using the Adprep utility located in the I386 directory on the Windows Server 2003 CD. Run **adprep /forestprep** first on the Schema Master domain controller in the forest root domain, and then **adprep /domainprep** on the Infrastructure Master.

Domain Functional Levels

By default, when you install Windows Server 2003, the vast majority of AD features become available at once. Some advanced features may require all domain controllers in the domain to be updated to Windows Server 2003.

Beginning with Windows 2000, domains could be configured to operate in two modes: mixed mode and native mode. Mixed mode ensures that new features delivered with Windows 2000 will not cause compatibility issues with existing Windows NT 4.0 domain controllers. This concept was taken a step further with Windows Server 2003 and what is now called a *domain functional level*. A domain functional level tells participating Windows Server 2003 domain controllers what legacy systems still operate on the network; this setting is domainwide, as the name implies, and it has no impact on other domains in the forest.

There are now four domain functional levels: Windows 2000 mixed, Windows 2000 native (same as in Windows 2000 Server), Windows Server 2003 interim, and Windows Server 2003. By default, when you install your first Windows Server 2003 domain controller, domains are configured with Windows 2000 mixed level. You can raise this level, if necessary, with the AD Users and Computers snap-in.

Table 3-2 lists all available functional levels and types of domain controllers supported on each level.

Raising domain functional levels is a one-way process. If you change the Windows Server 2003 interim domain to Windows Server 2003, you will no longer be able to run Windows NT 4.0 domain controllers in that domain, and you won't be able to revert back to the interim level. Table 3-3 gives you an idea of what functionality you are forfeiting by running Windows Server 2003 on lower functional levels.

TABLE 3-2	Domain Functional Level	Domain Controllers
Systems Supported on Windows Server 2003 Domain Functional Levels	Windows 2000 mixed (default)	Windows NT 4.0 Windows 2000 Windows Server 2003 family
	Windows 2000 native	Windows 2000 Windows Server 2003 family
	Windows Server 2003 interim	Windows NT 4.0 Windows Server 2003 family
	Windows Server 2003	Windows Server 2003 family

TABLE 3-3	Limitations of Domain Functional Levels		
Active Directory Feature	**Windows 2000 Mixed**	**Windows 2000 Native**	**Windows Server 2003**
Renaming and restructuring of domains	Disabled	Disabled	Enabled
Time stamp of most recent logon (lastLogonTimestamp)	Disabled	Disabled	Enabled
InetOrgPerson class	Disabled	Disabled	Enabled
Universal groups	Enabled for distribution groups Disabled for security groups	Enabled (security and distribution groups)	Enabled (security and distribution groups)
Global group nesting	Enabled for distribution groups Disabled for security groups	Enabled	Enabled
Group conversions	Disabled	Enabled	Enabled
SID history (interdomain security principal migration)	Disabled	Enabled	Enabled

Let's review some of the features listed in Table 3-3 as they apply to the Windows Server 2003 domain functional level. The LastLogonTimestamp allows you to keep track of the most recent domain authentication performed by a user or computer. You can query this attribute using any of the LDAP query tools.

The new object class InetOrgPerson allows more seamless migration and interaction with other LDAP and X.500-based directories. This class inherits the user class and hence has all the attributes usually associated with regular user objects. InetOrgPerson is also a security principal.

Windows Server 2003 allows renaming domains. Hopefully, administrators will have done all their homework and this will not be necessary, but if business requirements change during the life cycle of Windows Server 2003 deployment, at least there are some options that allow you to deal with this change. Renaming and restructuring functionality accomplishes the following two things:

- It changes DNS and NetBIOS names of any domain in the forest, including the forest root domain.
- It changes the location of a domain within the forest, with the exception of the forest root domain.

To perform renaming or restructuring of your domains, use the rendom.exe utility located in the Valueadd\Msft\Mgmt\Domren directory on the Windows Server 2003 distribution CD.

Renaming domains, although now possible, is a rather tedious exercise that you want to avoid by proper planning. It should always be done as a last resort, but if you must rename a domain, keep in mind that the process is not instant and involves several steps. You will have to reboot all domain controllers in the domain in question and reboot all Windows workstations participating in this domain. If your network contains any Windows NT 4.0 clients, they will have to be removed from the domain and then added to the renamed domain.

on the **job**

The current version of the rendom.exe utility does not support renaming of domains running Exchange Server 2000.

Forest Functional Levels

The purpose of forest functional levels is much the same as domain functional levels, except the scope of this functional level is the entire AD forest, not just one domain. Forest functional levels affect AD schema features more than anything else, whereas domain functional levels enable domain controller-specific features.

Use the AD Domains and Trusts snap-in to modify forest functional levels. Table 3-4 lists all available forest functional levels and the minimum respective domain controller versions.

Next, Table 3-5 summarizes forest-level features enabled by switching to the Windows Server 2003 forest functional level.

TABLE 3-4	Forest Functional Level	Domain Controllers
Systems Supported on Windows Server 2003 Forest Functional Levels	Windows 2000 (default)	Windows NT 4.0 Windows 2000 Windows Server 2003 family
	Windows Server 2003 interim	Windows NT 4.0 Windows Server 2003 family
	Windows Server 2003	Windows Server 2003 family

TABLE 3-5   Limitations of Forest Functional Levels

Feature	Windows 2000 Level	Windows Server 2003 Level
Global catalog replication improvements	Enabled if both replication partners are Windows Server 2003	Enabled
Marking schema objects as defunct	Disabled	Enabled
Setting up forest trusts	Disabled	Enabled
Linked value replication	Disabled	Enabled
Renaming domains	Disabled	Enabled
Improved Active Directory replication and topology calculation algorithms	Disabled	Enabled
Dynamic auxiliary classes	Disabled	Enabled
InetOrgPerson object class	Disabled	Enabled

Trust Relationships

When a trust relationship is configured between two domains, users authenticated in one domain are technically able to access resources located in the other domain, subject to ACL permissions defined on each resource. Trust management operations are only available to enterprise administrators.

Trust relationships in Windows Server 2003 are bidirectional and transitive. This has been changed since Windows NT 4.0, in which trust relationships were characterized as one-way, nontransitive. The updated trust relationship means that if domain A is your forest root domain and it has two child domains, B and C, and there is a transitive trust relationship defined between domains A and B, and then between A and C, then child domain B also trusts child domain C. Also, users in domain C can access resources in domain B and vice versa. Windows Server 2003 uses two trust relationships to implement this functionality. Furthermore, these trust relationships are configured automatically within one forest. Compare this to Windows NT 4.0: with the three domains A, B, and C, you would need to configure six trust relationships manually, two between each domain. Now imagine that you have 15 or more NT 4.0 domains, and you need to make sure that every domain trusts every other domain!

As you can infer from this description, trust relationships have directions. If domain A trusts domain B, it means that trust relationship was configured from domain A to domain B (notice the arrow from A to B in Figure 3-11), and users from domain B can access resources in domain A. Table 3-6 summarizes trust relationship features.

External Trusts

External trusts are used to set up nontransitive trust relationships between selected domains from different forests. This type of trust relationship can be either one-way or two-way. You can use external trusts to configure trust relationships between any type of domain, including Windows NT 4.0 domains. Both Enterprise Admins and Domain Admins have privileges necessary to configure this type of trust, and usually it is used for administrative purposes (giving administrators in one domain authority to manage resources in a different domain that is part of another forest), or as a "Band-Aid" trust solution for companies merging two distinct forests. (Windows Server 2003 improves this with transitive forest trusts.)

FIGURE 3-11

Trust relationships in Windows Server 2003

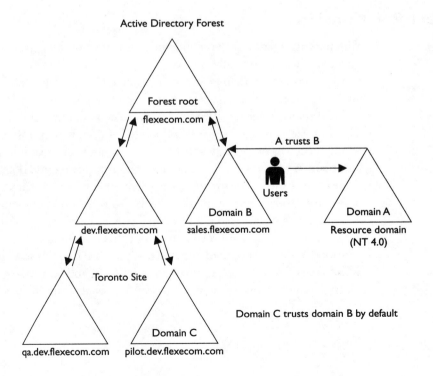

TABLE 3-6	Windows Server 2003 Trust Summary

Trust Property	Variations	Comments
Trust direction	One-way or two-way (sometimes called bidirectional)	In a one-way setup, one domain A trusts domain B. Domain A is the trusting domain (outgoing trust), and domain B is the trusted domain (incoming trust). Users from the trusted domain can use resources in the trusting domain. A two-way setup effectively mirrors the one-way setup in the opposite direction.
Authentication protocol	NTLM or Kerberos	NTLM is used to set up trusts with Windows NT 4.0 domains and in all other cases where Kerberos authentication is not supported by trust partners. Kerberos is an industry-standard, secure, better-performing authentication protocol supported by many operating systems, including Windows Server 2003. Windows Server 2003 trusts default to Kerberos.
Objects with which trust relationships can be established	NT 4.0 domains, Windows 2000 and 2003 domains, Windows Server 2003 forests, and UNIX realms	Trusts between Windows Server 2003 and Windows NT 4.0 are one-way, nontransitive, and based on NTLM. Transitive trusts between forests enable administrators to set up one trust relationship, making all domains in one forest trust all of the domains in another forest. This is something new to Windows Server 2003, and you must raise your forest functional levels to Windows Server 2003 to take advantage of this feature. Kerberos also allows setting up trust relationships with UNIX realms, which are analogous to domains in Windows terminology.
Transitive	Transitive trusts or nontransitive trusts	Transitive trusts are standard within Active Directory since Windows 2000. Transitive trusts minimize the number of trust relationships necessary to ensure that all domains in one forest trust each other. Within any given forest, trust relationships are transitive and bidirectional.

New to Windows Server 2003 is the ability to designate authentication domains selectively in environments where external trusts or forest trusts are used. This is called the *scope of authentication*. When users authenticate through the trust with Selective Authentication enabled, the SID of the trusted domain is added to user authentication parameters. This SID is verified when users from the trusted domain attempt to access resources in the trusting domain.

Using Selective Authentication, you can designate either domain scope or forest scope. For example, if you use an external trust between two domains from different forests, you want to select domainwide scope for your trust, enabling users from the external (trusted) domain to access resources in the local (trusting) domain. If you are working with forest root domains, setting up an external trust between two forests, you might prefer forestwide scope, so that all of the external forest users can access all of your resources in the local forest. As usual, trust relationships have no impact on resource permissions, which must be set separately on a per-resource basis or through existing user group membership. Figure 3-12 depicts the external trust concept.

Shortcut Trusts

Shortcut trusts, or cross-link trusts as they are sometimes called, are used to optimize authentication paths in more complex Active Directory structures consisting of many levels of child domains. When you authenticate from, let's say, it.north.us.flexecom.com to mfg.south.arg.flexecom.com, or when you attempt to access resources between these

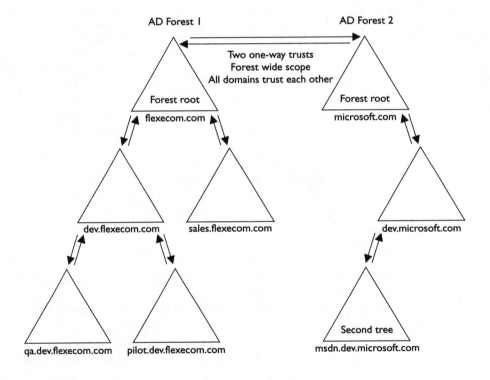

FIGURE 3-12

External trusts in Windows Server 2003

two domains, the authentication path, by default, takes you from one domain to another through every single domain in between, for example:

```
it.north.us.flexecom.com ? north.us.flexecom.com ?
us.flexecom.com ? flexecom.com ? arg.flexecom.com ?
south.arg.flexecom.com ? mfg.south.arg.flexecom.com
```

At least one domain controller must be accessible in each domain for this traversal to happen; plus it takes a considerable amount of time for the request to go through each of the domains. Instead, you can configure a shortcut trust between two deeply nested domains where you know users will access resources and authenticate very often. This will cut the traversal from six to just one instance and will speed up Active Directory response times as perceived by end users.

Cross-Forest Trusts

A subtype of external trusts, cross-forest trusts in Windows Server 2003 allow setting up transitive trusts on the forest level. Administrators must ensure that forest functional levels are brought up to Windows Server 2003 in all forests to be linked with a trust relationship. Cross-forest trust relationships effectively establish a trust between every domain in one forest with every domain in the other forest using just one link definition.

on the job *If one or more of the forests you are preparing for a cross-forest trust setup use a private namespace for addressing purposes (not Internet-registered and externally resolvable names), you may have to make sure that DNS zones are configured for transfer between DNS servers for two forests, or configure DNS Conditional Forwarding instead. Refer to Chapter 2 for more information on conditional forwarding.*

Let's look at an example of a cross-domain authentication mechanism in Windows Server 2003 using Kerberos trusts, as illustrated in Figure 3-13.

1. User Steve logs on to a workstation, providing credentials registered in the sales.flexecom.com domain. Steve wants to access the FCSRV1 file server in support.flexecom.com.

2. The workstation submits a request to the Key Distribution Center (KDC) domain controller (DC1) in its local domain and obtains a service ticket for the SPN (service principal name), FCSRV1.

3. DC1 may not be able to locate the requested SPN in its local replica of domain information. It then submits a global catalog request for the SPN in question. Since the global catalog does not contain all of the attributes of forest objects, it also may not find the requested SPN. In this case, it will check the trust relationship portion of its database to determine which of the domains have trust relationships. Of particular interest is the domain with the same domain name suffix, as provided in the initial user request. If this domain is found in the trust configuration, the global catalog returns the authentication path to DC1.

4. DC1 issues a response to the workstation.

5. The workstation submits a request for information to domain controller DC2 in the flexecom.com forest root domain. The workstation needs to locate a domain controller for the support.flexecom.com domain. DC2 returns a link to the DC3 domain controller in the target domain.

6. The workstation then submits another request to KDC running on DC3 and provides Steve's Kerberos ticket received in step 2.

7. Now that the workstation received a service ticket from KDC on DC3, it submits another server service ticket directly to the FCSRV1 file server in the support.flexecom.com domain. FCSRV1 reads the ticket and determines Steve's access level.

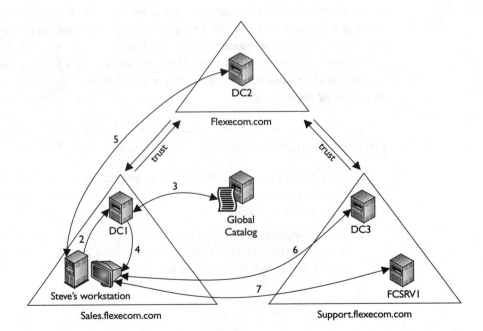

CERTIFICATION OBJECTIVE 3.04

Implement the AD Site Topology

Active Directory sites are used to define network segments that are connected using a high-bandwidth, reliable network medium, which distinguishes them from the rest of the network. As mentioned earlier in the chapter, whereas AD domains serve the purpose of logical and geographical segmentation of resources and the security organization of the company's IT infrastructure, sites break up intradomain replication topologies. The concepts of site and domain are completely distinct; you can configure multiple domains within the same site, and multiple sites within one domain.

Sites allow more controlled use of scarce WAN bandwidth, providing additional traffic control features to administrators. Factors such as reliability, throughput, and utilization should all be considered when planning sites and configuring replication schedules. In addition to giving you control over replication priority and schedules, implementing sites brings these benefits:

- **Traffic generated by domain clients is localized**   Workstations give preference to domain controllers local to their sites when deciding where to submit user logon requests.

- **File Replication Service (FRS) traffic is localized**   FRS is used to replicate group policies, logon scripts, and other elements, and it also considers AD replication topology. Sites optimize FRS traffic flow over WAN links.

- **Distributed File System (DFS) topology relies on sites**   If there is more than one replica of the same resource that was made available through the DFS, preference will be given to the replica located in the local site.

- **Active Directory Integrated applications may rely on site topology**   They may do this to put as little WAN traffic on the wire as possible. One example is application partitions and their replication.

When planning site topology, administrators use Ethernet as a benchmark for configuration. If you have several TCP/IP segments configured on the same local area network, which is operating at 10 Mbps or faster, they should be configured into one site. In theory though, other factors should be considered as well. You should know how many users are planned to be implemented in each site, how often the head count changes, and how often new computers are added and old computers are removed from the domain, to name just a few. All of these add traffic to the WAN link, where bandwidth is limited and transfers may be costly.

If at any time during the workday, replication of changes will fit into a few minutes worth of WAN transfer, deploying this branch as a separate site may be a moot point. Think of a small satellite office of about ten users, all users work with mostly local resources, and the branch is connected to the headquarters using a 128 Kbit dedicated line. Separate sites for this configuration may add administrative burden without bringing significant improvements, therefore defeating the purpose. And the opposite is also true: if your satellite branch is growing or changes fairly rapidly, and if most of the users work with external resources most of the time, a separate site may produce a significant improvement even on a higher-bandwidth WAN pipe.

Now let's consider intrasite and intersite replication. When you configure a separate site for your remote office and put one or more dedicated domain controllers in that site, replication topology within the domain gets adjusted. Changes within one site are replicated to all domain controllers for the domain in question quite promptly, whereas replication to other domain controllers outside of the site is scheduled for the next replication window. Replication between domain controllers within one site is called intrasite replication. Replication between the sites is called intersite replication.

Each server maintains connection objects, which effectively define the list of all replication partners participating in the replication topology. These objects also have schedules associated with them, and replication transport domain controllers must use them to communicate. Connections are initiated whenever a change occurs in the case of intrasite replication, and at preconfigured intervals in the case of intersite replication. By default, the replication interval between sites is 180 minutes. This can be adjusted in NTDS Settings using the AD Sites and Services snap-in.

In a multimaster replication scheme such as in Windows Server 2003, changes may be committed to any of the domain controllers. Domain controllers use USN serial numbers to distinguish which of the objects is newer when replicating changes (similarly to DNS replication). In conflicting cases, when two or more changes were made to the same object around the same time, one of the changes may be discarded based on its time stamp. The domain controller that recorded a change to its local database sends out a notification to its intrasite replication partners informing them of the fact. Domain controllers that have this originating server in their list of replication partners then request the change and update their local databases.

Next, these domain controllers that just received an update may in turn send a notification to their replication partners, and so on. The Knowledge Consistency

Checker (KCC) is a component of the operating system that calculates replication topology within the site. It constructs the topology so that a single domain controller has more than one replication partner, which improves reliability of the topology and makes a single domain controller outage relatively unimportant in terms of replication on a larger scale. KCC also makes sure that there are no more than three iterations of notification forwarding per change; so between any two domain controllers in one site there can be no more than three hops in the replication topology.

Replication latency is a lag between the time that the change is committed to the first replica of the Active Directory database and the moment when this change reaches the last domain controller for this domain. Intrasite replication latency has been reduced from minutes to seconds in Windows Server 2003—it is 15 seconds from the first change to the first notification. This lag is introduced to ensure that if an administrator is working on an object, and makes some changes that he or she immediately realizes are erroneous, there is time to correct the problem and communicate only the latest change, not both of them.

Replication partners receiving this update also wait 15 seconds before forwarding the update. Since KCC limits the number of retransmissions to three, the maximum latency in intrasite replication can be no greater than 45 seconds. Urgent replication of security-related changes such as password resets and account lockouts happens immediately. Due to the fact that intersite replication schedules are customizable by administrators and depend on specific implementation, it is not feasible to estimate cross-site replication latency.

Replication topology in Windows 2000 is effectively the same as in Windows Server 2003, but things were quite different in the Windows NT 4.0 days. Back then, we had one read/write domain controller, and replication was basically all about copying one version of the database to all read-only domain controllers. Windows 2000 and later implement multimaster replication technology.

Optimal replication topology is defined as an array of connections within the site that allows speedy replication changes without overutilizing the underlying network. This demands a compromise, because in many cases speed and utilization conflict. The KCC process runs every 15 minutes—it generates replication topology so that the number of connection objects per server is kept to a minimum, and yet there are no more than three hops between any two domain controllers. From this we can infer that if the number of domain controllers is less than seven, the topology will simply take the form of a ring. Should one of the domain controllers fail, this will not affect the ability to replicate data, but may impact the time it takes to replicate, albeit only by a few seconds. Next time the KCC runs, it will take the failed controller out of the replication loop.

As your infrastructure grows, along with the number of domain controllers, it takes increasingly more time to generate a more complex replication topology. Connection objects, created and maintained by the KCC, only concern the domain controller where the KCC runs, and are incoming, in relation to the server. However, the KCC runs on every domain controller, and having the same information about the domain, all KCC processes calculate the same topology on all domain controllers. As a result, you have bidirectional replication partner connection objects on each domain controller, and these domain controllers only know about their neighboring replication partners in the topology, not all of the domain controllers in the site.

By design, KCC does its work automatically, creating and deleting connection objects, and appending "automatically generated" to their names. Administrators can create connection objects manually, but this is only recommended in very complex network environments, and only for the purpose of taking some load off the recurring KCC process. Figure 3-14 shows properties of a connection object.

Connection
object properties

Site Links

In order to expand your replication topology beyond a single site, you should first define site links between the sites. Only after site links have been created can connection objects for domain controllers in different sites be generated. In contrast to intrasite replication, intersite replication needs more administrative intervention before things start working smoothly. When you define site links, you must assign link cost, or a relative number that takes into account actual bandwidth cost, bandwidth availability, and other factors if they apply.

The topology is generated based on site link costs, so if you define a cost of 10 to one link and 100 to another link, for example, there really must be a tenfold difference when you account for available bandwidth and link cost. If not, topology generation may not fully reflect the actual costs of the replicating information. Administrators also define replication intervals and duration in site link properties. Replication notifications are not submitted outside the site during hours not specifically configured as available for replication. Figure 3-15 shows site link properties.

FIGURE 3-15

Site link
properties

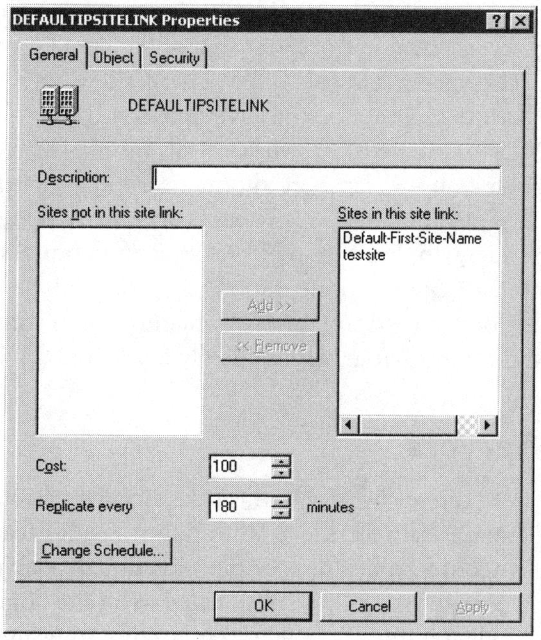

Intersite topology is generated by a domain controller fulfilling the functions of an intersite topology generator (ISTG). The ISTG knows about site links from the AD configuration partition, which means that all ISTG controllers in the forest have the same information on which they base their decisions. Any two sites do not have to have direct site links between them; they may have site link definitions to intermediary sites. When choosing a replication path between any two sites, the ISTG adds site link costs for all of the possible paths between the sites in question, and selects the one with the lowest cost.

In Windows Server 2003, the topology calculation algorithm has been improved, and it now scales to about 3000 sites per domain (compared to about ten times less in Windows 2000). Its algorithm also covers the entire forest area.

Another planning point administrators have to consider is which transport to select for each site link in their organization. Intrasite replication always uses RPC over IP without applying any compression (the RPC option in the connection object), knowing that there is enough bandwidth. In intersite replication, you can choose between RPC over IP with compression (the IP option in the connection object), or SMTP. The SMTP protocol is only used for intersite replication; domain controllers must be running the SMTP Service, and there should be a Certificate Authority server installed in the forest that will be used for message signing.

The main advantage of SMTP over IP is its reliability. An SMTP message either gets through or it does not, whereas the IP communication stream may be broken. Of course, there is a downside to using SMTP: it delivers 80 percent more overhead, which is all the transport information and formatting used to encapsulate and deliver AD replication packets. There is another reason why SMTP may not be suitable for intradomain, intersite replication: its functionality is limited to replicating schema, application, and configuration partitions only; SMTP cannot be used to replicate the domain partition, or the domain naming context. Use SMTP over unreliable WAN links that may sporadically lose connectivity.

Bridgehead Servers

As you can see by now, intrasite replication and intersite replication have plenty of differences between them. Within the same site, each server communicates with several neighboring replication partners. Eventually, one random change committed to any of the domain controllers is replicated to all site domain controllers in a matter of 45 seconds and three hops. Contrary to this, intersite replication is performed through so-called *bridgehead servers*. There can be only one domain controller that participates as a bridgehead server in each site at any given time, and by default it is selected automatically. In cases when the company uses public network segments for replication and firewalls in their network, administrators can override the automatic selection by punching in local IP addresses that are allowed to be reached from outside.

Other considerations in selecting a bridgehead server manually should be server "proximity" to the outside world (in terms of internal network hops over routers), overall network link and server hardware fault tolerance, and the horsepower of the server. If your domain controller hardware is not standardized and does not maintain the same performance level, you may want to designate one of your more powerful servers to handle bridgehead replication due to traffic compression and excessive CPU load associated with this role.

If you opt to select a bridgehead server manually, be aware that the KCC will not be able to recover from a situation if this manually selected bridgehead server goes down. Because of this, it is recommended that you designate at least two bridgehead servers in each site.

The big picture of a replication process that spans two sites may be described as follows:

- A change is made and is committed to a local domain controller.

- In 15 seconds, the local domain controller sends a notification to neighboring replication partners in the local site.

- Replication partners request the information upon receiving the notification, then wait for 15 seconds, and submit their own notifications to their respective replication partners. This reaches all domain controllers within one site in no more than three hops.

- At some point, this change reaches the domain controller designated as a bridgehead server. It waits for the next replication window and submits a notification to its bridgehead server counterpart in the second site.

- The second site's bridgehead server pulls the information via a site link, waits for 15 seconds, and sends local notification to its own replication partners in the second site.

- From this point on, the process of notifications and 15-second cool-offs repeats up to three times, replicating the change to all domain controllers in the second site.

Figure 3-16 depicts this process.

FIGURE 3-16

Intrasite
and intersite
replication
process

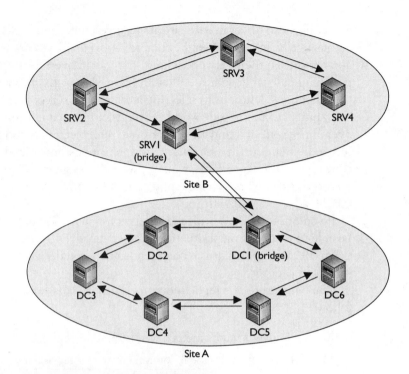

CERTIFICATION OBJECTIVE 3.05

Plan a Strategy for Delegating Administrative Tasks

At this point, it is obvious that Windows Server 2003 has sufficiently elaborate technology for building infrastructures of practically any size, spanning offices and companies on a global scale. Also, the more complex the infrastructure, the more crucial planning becomes and the more work must be performed by knowledgeable administrators. In large networks, it is not feasible to focus management of the entire infrastructure in the hands of a few administrators and expect them to know and remember every minute detail of network infrastructures.

Companies can dramatically reduce TCO of the infrastructure by reducing the areas of authority and dedicating administrators to these authorities, while keeping a few persons who can override any of the configuration settings from a single location.

So it is important to have this capability of distilling groups of objects into a common administrative area and assigning appropriate permissions to local administrators. AAAs (Autonomous Administrative Areas) and delegation are integral to any directory service that is based on X.500/LDAP.

Analyzing Requirements

To delegate permissions, including those necessary to perform administrative tasks, Active Directory uses organizational units (OUs). An OU is nothing more than a container in the AD domain, used to organize objects logically. You can move all pertinent objects into an OU (or a branch of nested OUs) and delegate administrative permissions to the OU in question. This allows a great deal of flexibility in terms of how granular you want to get when delegating permissions.

However, in keeping with everything to do with AD, the OU structure and delegation strategy requires thorough planning in advance of implementation. Likewise, it is important to distribute objects between OUs in a way that is consistent with your plan. Any single AD object can be located only in a single OU container, and in most cases this would mean they can be managed by a limited number of people.

Let's take a look at some ground rules that administrators observe when planning OU structure:

- **Always account for expansion**   OU structure should be chosen to make sense now and in the future, keeping in mind that company size now and in the future may not be the same.

- **Use a single rule for creation of first-level OUs**   First-level OUs in all domains within the same forest should be created based on a single rule (for example, departments, business units, or geography). If you do not follow the same pattern in all of your domains, things may become illogical and overcomplicated.

- **Refrain from unnecessary deep nesting of OUs**   Deep nesting not only affects navigation, but eventually will also impact LDAP and Group Policy Object (GPO) performance. Anywhere between three and five OU levels should suffice in 95 percent of scenarios.

- **Make your OU hierarchy intuitive**   The OU hierarchy should make sense—think of end users and administrators who will have to navigate and administer this structure.

■ **Manage group policies using OUs**   The OU is the lowest unit in the Active Directory structure to which you can apply a group policy. Unless configured otherwise, group policy settings will flow from higher-level structures such as top-level OUs and sites or domains.

■ **Use OUs for logical grouping of objects within one domain**   Since domains are used to establish the security boundary, and sites are used to establish the replication boundary, OUs are used for logical grouping of objects within one domain. It is best to keep your OU structure mapped to your business units, or departments (or nest the two). Thus, if one user or computer has to be transferred between departments, administrative change is basically a mirror of the political change, and it keeps things simple.

OU Structure

Keeping in mind all the basic OU planning rules outlined in the previous section, administrators will arrive at one of the following OU hierarchies: geographical, organizational, or object. In the next few sections, we consider each of these in more detail.

Geographical Hierarchy

If company operations are dispersed around the world, a logical choice is the geographical hierarchy, which forms the basis of the OU structure, or the top level. Each geographical location corresponds to one OU. They can be grouped by region and then narrowed down to cities, or each office may be represented by its own top-level OU. This will ultimately depend on the size and preferences of the organization.

An advantage of this structure is that both users and administrators can visualize the actual location of resources; although it might not matter in all situations, it keeps things consistent and logical. The OUs can be adjusted according to political changes without incurring changes to the entire structure—simply rename, delete, or add the respective OU.

One disadvantage of this approach is that it does not reflect the business model/operation.

Organizational Hierarchy

An organizational hierarchy reflects the business units and model of the company, eliminating a disadvantage of the geographical hierarchy. You map OUs to business units or departments and move objects that belong to these departments to the respective OUs. An obvious advantage of this model is that based on the name of the object, you can easily determine what jurisdiction within the company it falls into.

One of the more significant disadvantages of this model is the relative difficulty in changing the OU structure during major company restructuring. You may have to move departments around, or re-create the structure from scratch and move objects again. Furthermore, if one of the company units requires its own domain for security purposes, the integrity of the OU structure is broken, meaning it does not represent all departments in a consistent way (some departments will be missing). That being said, the organizational hierarchy is Microsoft's preferred choice.

Object Hierarchy

A separate OU container for each of the object classes—users, computers, printers, and all other types of objects—is established in the object hierarchy. The advantage of this hierarchy is ease of resource management; it is easier to delegate administrative permissions based on object types.

The disadvantage of this strategy is its lack of scalability. It will do more harm than good in mid- to large-scale AD deployments. This hierarchy is more useful as a second-level organization of resources under either geographical or organizational hierarchies.

All things considered, administrators can mix and match these three basic types of hierarchies, as long as things are kept consistent. It is still recommended to keep the same strategy for all top-level OUs within the same forest, or even organization. When you are done planning your OU structure, the next step is creating it. This is accomplished by using the Active Directory Users and Computer snap-in.

EXERCISE 3-2

CertCam & MasterSim ON THE CD

Creating an Organizational Unit

In this exercise, you create an organizational unit. Before you begin, make sure that you have Domain Admins or Enterprise Admins level privileges.

1. Launch the Active Directory Users and Computers snap-in. It is located in the Administrative Tools folder in the Control Panel.

2. In the console tree, select the domain you are about to manage. If you wish to create an OU within another OU, select the OU that will become the parent container.

3. Right-click the parent container and click New, then Organizational Unit (see Figure 3-17).

FIGURE 3-17

Creating a new
organizational
unit

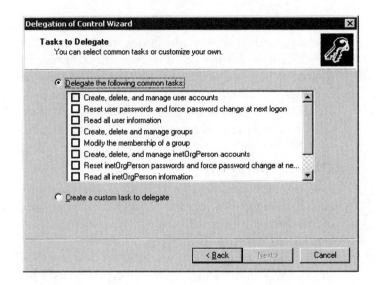

4. In the New Object | Organizational Unit dialog box, type in the name of the OU you wish to create.

5. Commit the changes and make sure the new container is displayed in the console tree.

Delegation and Security Issues

You have two methods for transferring administrative permissions to selected users: you can use the Delegation of Control Wizard, or you can add access control entries (ACEs) to discretionary access control lists (DACLs) of individual OUs. The Delegation of Control Wizard appears to be easier to use (but this depends on your personal definition of "easier"). This wizard takes you step by step through the delegation process; whereas manual configuration is more susceptible to human error and may take more time.

To delegate permissions, take the following steps:

1. Open the Active Directory Users and Computers snap-in.

2. In the console tree, expand your domain and right-click the OU to which you want to delegate permissions.

3. Select Delegate Control from the context menu.

4. The Delegation of Control Wizard will appear and take you through the rest of the process.

When working with the wizard, be prepared to answer questions about who you want to delegate permissions to (user or group) and which groups of permissions, or selective permissions, you wish to delegate. Figure 3-18 shows the step of the wizard where you have to select permissions for the users.

Security Groups

Securing the infrastructure is perhaps one of the most crucial administrative tasks in companies of any size, and this topic alone is worthy of a separate set of books. A vital part of planning the Active Directory implementation is how you will secure internal resources while making sure that resources are still accessible and access is easily manageable. For the sake of convenience and logical organization, users with common

FIGURE 3-18

Delegating permissions using the Delegation of Control Wizard

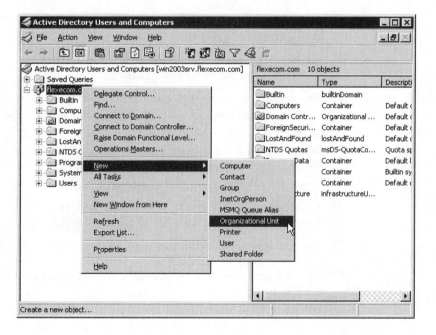

parameters or functions are added to common user groups. Groups can have different scopes: universal, global, and domain local.

- Universal groups can contain other groups or users from any domain located in the same forest. Likewise, universal groups can be used to define ACL entries on resources located anywhere in the forest.

- Global groups can contain groups or users from the same domain where global groups are defined. Global groups can be used to define ACL entries on resources located anywhere in the forest.

- With the domain functional level set to Windows 2000 native and later, domain local groups can include universal groups, global groups, and other domain local groups or users, where the last two are defined in the same domain. Domain local groups may be used to define ACL entries on resources located anywhere in the same domain.

Generally recommended group nesting and permission planning strategies can be summarized as follows:

- Users based on common parameters such as job functions should be added to common global groups.

- Create universal groups for use as forestwide global groups. Add global groups as members of the universal groups.

- Because universal group membership information is replicated to all global catalog servers, you want to keep the membership in these groups to a minimum, hence the recommendation to add global groups to universal groups, not individual users. If you add or remove individual users to/from the universal group, it will trigger global catalog replication. This will not occur if you add a user to a global group that is already a member of the universal group.

- Create domain local groups in a domain, and use these groups to define resource-level permissions. Add global or universal groups to domain local groups.

- If necessary, make individual users members in domain local groups.

Overall, the long-standing Microsoft mantra has changed from AGLP in the Windows NT 4.0 days to AGDLP, which simply reflects the name change of the local group to domain local group. The strategy in its fundamental principle has not changed since day one. This approach makes the most sense from the administrative and management perspective.

SCENARIO & SOLUTION

What do all domains within the same forest have in common?	All domains from the same forest have the same schema and global catalog. All domains within the same forest have two-way, transitive trust relationships to all other domains in the forest. All domains within the same forest can be managed by a group of people who are members of the Enterprise Admins group.
What is the main benefit of storing application data in application data partitions?	The main benefit of application data partitions is in how this data gets replicated within the AD forest. Administrators can designate to which specific domain controllers this information should be replicated.
What is a bridgehead server in the context of AD replication?	Bridgehead servers are used in the replication topology to transfer replication information between different sites. By default, the bridgehead server is selected automatically by the KCC, but this can be overridden.
In what circumstances should you use OUs as opposed to domains?	Organizational units are used to separate objects into a common administrative area and delegate administrative control over it to someone else. They also achieve logical grouping of company resources within one domain. OUs are better suited for resource management than domains, if there is no specific security policy requirement for the administrative area in which objects are grouped. If security policy is an issue, domains should be used instead.

Assigning permissions in this manner allows you to keep things consistent as your organization grows. Adding new users to a few select global groups based on their role achieves all permissions work in an instant. Furthermore, assigning 100 users to one folder may noticeably reduce resource access times compared to adding one group containing all of those users. As the size of the ACL grows, so does the complexity involved in maintaining this ACL, and the system eventually slows down when it has to enumerate long ACLs just to find a matching record that will either authorize or deny access in response to a user request.

When you manage workstations or standalone resource servers (servers not promoted to domain controller roles), you can only create local groups. These local groups are local to the computer in question, unlike "domain local" groups, and you can only add these local groups to resources on the single computer where they are defined.

Windows Server 2003 features the ability to convert certain types of groups if your forest functionality is raised to either Windows 2000 native or Windows Server 2003.

- **Global groups can be converted to universal groups**   This is only possible if the group you want to convert is not a member of other global groups (that is, the global groups are not nested).

- **Domain local groups can be converted to universal groups**   This is only possible if the group you want to convert does not contain other domain local groups.

- **Universal groups can be converted to global groups**   This is only possible if the group you want to convert does not contain other universal groups.

- **Universal groups can be converted to domain local groups**   This is not subject to any nesting limitations.

CERTIFICATION SUMMARY

Discussion in this chapter centered around Active Directory concepts and planning. We reviewed elements such as the global catalog, domain controllers, domains, sites, forests, and what each of them is used for, as well as the concepts of FSMO and replication. Armed with the conceptual knowledge, and after a bit of practice, you will be able to turn this powerful planning and administration foundation into a tool for troubleshooting advanced problems in Active Directory.

Based on the definition of domain as a common security boundary, this chapter provided an overview of the domain models that administrators can use in planning their infrastructure. It was established that the forest root domain is by far the most important Active Directory area and administrators should pay special attention to it. Several types of trust relationships were also reviewed. In basic terms, most of the Active Directory functionality is available in Windows Server 2003 out of the box; however, features that were introduced with Windows Server 2003 require domain functional levels to be raised to Windows Server 2003 in order to take full advantage of them.

The chapter defined sites, connection objects, site links, and bridgehead servers, and described how replication works in detail. Intrasite and intersite replication are similar, but the latter requires more administrative control, whereas replication within one site is configured automatically.

The final sections touched on some of the basic planning principles of organizational units and different types of security groups, along with how to delegate administrative duties. These concepts will be revisited as our discussion unfolds.

TWO-MINUTE DRILL

Plan a Strategy for Placing Global Catalog Servers

- ❏ global catalog servers answer AD search requests and in certain cases may get involved in logon requests.
- ❏ The global catalog stores the most commonly requested partial attribute set of all objects in the same forest.
- ❏ It is desirable to have at least one global catalog server in each site.
- ❏ You can use universal group caching to reduce the number of requests directed to global catalog servers during authentication.

Plan for Flexible Placement of Operation Master Roles

- ❏ There are five different FSMO roles, each of which can only belong to one domain controller at a time (within the scope of each role).
- ❏ The Schema Master and Domain Naming Master have forest scope; the PDC Emulator, Infrastructure Master, and RID Master have domain scope.
- ❏ If your forest has at least two domains, the Infrastructure Master and global catalog servers should not be placed on the same server.
- ❏ You can use the Ntdsutil tool to seize FSMO roles from defunct servers and assign them to other domain controllers.

Implementing the AD Forest and Domain Structure

- ❏ Only the forest root domain contains Schema Admins and Enterprise Admins groups of significant importance.
- ❏ The application data partition in AD can contain any custom data, but can never include SPNs (security principals).
- ❏ The vast majority of Active Directory features introduced with Windows Server 2003 become available after you raise the domain functional level to Windows Server 2003.
- ❏ All domains within the same forest are automatically configured with two-way, transitive trusts to their parent domains, effectively establishing universal trust within the forest.

Implementing the AD Site Topology

❏ Sites are areas of the network that are grouped together when the network's underlying medium is highly available and fast performing in nature.

❏ Sites allow administrators to manage replication and intradomain traffic such as requests to the global catalog and domain controllers.

❏ Each domain controller only accepts replication information from servers that have a corresponding connection object defined in the first server's configuration.

❏ Replication topology between sites (intersite) is calculated based on the cost of all site links between each two sites where transfers take place.

❏ Intersite replication is conducted through bridgehead servers only.

Plan a Strategy for Delegating Administrative Tasks

❏ Set permissions using domain local groups; add users to global groups.

❏ Objects that must be delegated for administrative control between different groups of people must be located in different OUs.

❏ Any given object can be located in only one OU at a time.

❏ Administrative rights for OUs are delegated using the Delegation of Control Wizard.

SELF TEST

The following questions will help you measure your understanding of the material presented in this chapter. Read all the choices carefully because there might be more than one correct answer. Choose all correct answers for each question.

1. Which of the following FSMO roles have domain scope? (Choose all that apply.)

   A. Infrastructure Master

   B. PDC Emulator

   C. Schema Master

   D. RID Master

   E. Domain Naming Master

   F. Application Master

2. Your domain includes controllers based on Windows NT 4.0, Windows 2000 Server, and Windows Server 2003. One of the domain controllers running Windows Server 2003 went down a week ago, and you decided not to deal with the problem at the time. Yesterday, the company hired a new employee, and you created a corresponding Active Directory account. She reports that occasionally she is not able to log on to the network. What is the most likely reason for this problem?

   A. You need to enable universal group caching.

   B. Windows NT 4.0 and Windows 2003 cannot function in the same domain.

   C. The server that went down had the PDC Emulator role.

   D. The server that went down had the RID Master role.

3. Your domain consists of two sites. One site has three domain controllers running Windows 2000 Server; the other site has one domain controller running Windows 2000 Server. You are installing the second domain controller in the second site, running Windows Server 2003. You want to use universal group caching in the second site. What should you do to accomplish this?

   A. Enable universal group caching on the new domain controller running Windows Server 2003.

   B. Enable universal group caching on all domain controllers in the second site.

   C. Enable universal group caching on all domain controllers in the domain.

   D. It is not possible to use universal group caching in this configuration because the second site runs a mix of Windows 2000 and Windows Server 2003.

4. You are an administrator for a large company, administering one of their domains, dev.flexecom.com. You decided to install Exchange 2000 for users of your domain. When you

go through the setup process on one of your domain controllers, you get an error. What is the most likely cause of this problem?

A. You do not belong to the Enterprise Admins group.

B. The Schema Master is unavailable.

C. The Infrastructure Master is unavailable.

D. You do not belong to the Domain Admins group in your domain.

5. You are an administrator with a large organization. Your forest functional level was raised to Windows Server 2003. You want to publish a new user object class attribute in your schema configuration. You are also aware that some of the WAN links in your organization connecting some sites are very busy at the moment. You are afraid that high volume replication of global catalog data will put too much stress on these WAN links. What should you do to optimize this process?

A. Publish the new attribute at night, when WAN utilization is at its minimum.

B. Turn off global catalog servers on all domain controllers in remote sites.

C. No further optimizations are necessary because you are only replicating one attribute.

D. You cannot perform the addition of an attribute to a standard user class.

6. Which of the following objects can be stored in application data partitions?

A. Users

B. Computers

C. Accounting application information

D. None of the above

7. You are administering a domain. All domain controllers are running Windows Server 2003. As a result of an IP address configuration error, communication between sites was disrupted on one of the domain controllers. One of the sites does not have a local global catalog. What should you do in order to be able to log on and correct the issue?

A. Use the administrator account.

B. Take the server to another site that has connectivity to the main site.

C. Use a dial-up service to connect to the global catalog.

D. Global catalogs are not used in the authentication process.

8. Which one of the following will require its own child domain? (Choose all that apply.)

A. Delegation of administrative permissions

B. Reduced replication traffic

C. The domain will contain over 100,000 user accounts.

D. Different geographical offices should have their own domains.

9. What applications use port 3268?

    A. DNS

    B. Global catalog LDAP

    C. FSMO

    D. Global catalog LDAP over SSL

10. What is the minimum number of global catalog servers that the organization should have in one forest, consisting of five domains, distributed over three separate sites?

    A. One

    B. Two

    C. Three

    D. Four

11. You are an administrator with a company that develops AD-integrated software for the tourism industry. Specifics of the industry and your application mandate the need to use Linked Value Replication and other features of Windows Server 2003 AD. Since your developers often modify forest schemas, you want to minimize potentially negative fallout on other users. What is the most appropriate course of action?

    A. Move all users to a separate domain.

    B. Move all users to a separate forest.

    C. Remove developers from the Schema Admins group.

    D. Move all developers to a separate site.

12. Your company has elaborate security controls involving many levels. You are using VPN, RRAS, DNS, and ISA servers in the DMZ segment. To simplify management and improve security on these servers, you put them into a separate domain and implemented a more rigorous password security policy. You want to ensure that if someone manages to brute-force a password from that domain, it would not compromise security on the internal network. At the same time, you would like to administer DMZ servers using accounts from the internal network. How should you configure a trust relationship between internal and DMZ domains?

    A. Make the DMZ domain trust the internal domain.

    B. Make the internal domain trust the DMZ domain.

    C. Do not configure a trust relationship.

    D. Configure a shortcut trust between the DMZ domain and the internal domain.

13. Your company decided to migrate to Windows Server 2003 AD. One of the key requirements set forth is that the company should have centralized administration and the same security policy for all users. The central office is connected to three satellite offices with 256-Kbit links.

Ninety percent of the time these links are utilized at 10 percent or more. You are planning site locations. What should you do to optimize WAN usage?

A. Configure three sites and one domain.

B. Configure four sites and one domain.

C. Configure three sites and three domains.

D. Configure one site and four domains.

14. The company you are with is acquiring a competitor. Both companies already have Active Directory with many domains. After the acquisition, users of all domains should have access to resources in most of the domains, irrespective of the forest. You decide to implement a cross-forest trust and migrate both forests to Windows Server 2003. However, your attempt to configure the trust did not complete successfully. What is the likely cause of this problem?

A. You do not have Enterprise Admins level permissions.

B. In addition to converting your forests to Windows Server 2003, you must also make sure that all PDC Emulators in all domains are running Windows Server 2003.

C. All domain controllers must be running Windows Server 2003, and the domain functional level should be raised to Windows Server 2003.

D. Before you can proceed to set up trust relationships between forests, you must ensure that all domains are configured to trust each other as well.

15. Which of the following statements about SMTP is correct? (Choose all that apply.)

A. SMTP is used for interdomain replication.

B. SMTP is used for intradomain replication.

C. SMTP is used for intersite replication.

D. SMTP is used for intrasite replication.

16. What must be done before delegating permissions to administer an OU to someone who is not a member of the administrators group?

A. Add the user in question to the Power Users group.

B. Add the user in question to the OU Admins group.

C. Configure the user to have administrative authority over all objects contained in the organizational unit.

D. Use the Delegation of Control Wizard and delegate permissions for this user.

17. Which of the following correctly describes the intersite replication process?

A. Transmission originates from several servers in parallel, but only the bridgehead server accepts communication on the receiving end.

B. Transmission originates from one bridgehead server and is received by another bridgehead server.

C. Transmission originates from one bridgehead server, but several servers are able to accept communication on the receiving end.

D. Transmission is conducted by several servers on both transmitting and receiving ends at the same time.

18. Which of the following methods of upgrading Windows NT 4.0 domains to Windows Server 2003 domains is suggested as optimal?

A. Reinstall everything; you cannot perform an upgrade of NT 4.0 domains.

B. Upgrade gradually from NT 4.0 PDC using the Windows 2003 interim functional level; then after all NT 4.0 domain controllers have been decommissioned, raise the domain functional level to Windows Server 2003.

C. Upgrade gradually from NT 4.0 PDC using the Windows 2000 mixed functional level; then after all NT 4.0 domain controllers have been decommissioned, raise the domain functional level to Windows Server 2003.

D. Upgrade gradually all NT 4.0 BDCs to Windows Server 2003; seize the PDC Emulator role and transfer it to Windows Server 2003; raise the domain functional level to Windows Server 2003.

19. Which of the following statements about universal groups is correct?

A. Universal groups can include any type of user or group account from anywhere in the forest, and they can be used to define permissions anywhere in the forest.

B. Universal groups can include only group accounts from anywhere in the forest, and they can be used to define permissions anywhere in the forest.

C. Universal groups can include any type of user or group account from anywhere in the forest, but they are not used in defining permissions on resources.

D. Universal groups can include group accounts from anywhere in the forest, and they can be added to domain local groups within domains.

20. While installing Active Directory, you placed AD files in a directory provided by default. After a brief period of time, you installed a service pack and a few applications, and discovered that there is not enough free disk space on the system partition. You need to transfer AD files to a different partition. Which of the following steps should be performed to achieve this?

A. Restart the domain controller in directory services restore mode.

B. Use Ntdsutil to transfer databases to another partition.

C. Use MOVETREE to transfer databases to another partition.

D. Remove system and hidden attributes from the ntds.dit file and move the file to the new partition. In the AD Users and Computers snap-in, set up a new pointer to the file that was moved.

LAB QUESTION

George is the administrative team leader in a rapidly growing company. He has been with the same company since inception, when only about a dozen people were involved in operations. Back then, George registered a DNS domain, thebestcoever.com, and installed a domain running Windows 2000 Server. To mail-enable the organization, George installed Exchange Server 2000. After a while, the company grew to 60 employees and opened another office on the outskirts of the city. The connectivity between offices was provided by a local ISP using dedicated lines. When the central office head count increased to about 80 employees and the satellite office increased to about 30 employees, George noticed that network logon performance was nowhere near its former benchmark and took too long. In addition, some of the users in the second office started complaining that searching for contact information in the global address book took too much time.

George decided that the existing domain controller, DC1.thebestcoever.com, is no longer capable of handling the increased load, and he purchased two additional servers. One domain controller, DC2.thebestcoever.com, was added to the main location. Since this server was more powerful than the existing DC1 machine, and George thought that the PDC Emulator role delivered too much processing overhead, he moved the PDC Emulator to the DC2 server, also adding global catalog services. The other purchase went to the second office, and he installed an additional domain controller, DC3.thebestcoever.com, also installing global catalog service on this server. Finally, George separated the domain into two sites.

These modifications led to a significant increase in performance.

The company continued to grow, and shortly after, they opened up another office. Using his previous experience as a benchmark, George installed the DC4.thebestcoever.com domain controller to that location right away, despite the fact that initially the company hired only six employees to maintain that office. Around the same time, George migrated all existing Windows 2000 Server domain controllers to Windows Server 2003, and raised the functional level to Windows Server 2003. The third office was connected to the central location using a poor-quality WAN link, and the company was liable for transfers based on volume. To avoid unnecessary replication, they decided not to place a global catalog server in the third office, but they did turn on universal group caching.

Business was so successful that after a while they decided to purchase another company. To preserve administrative control of existing administrators in the acquired company and to fit the new unit of the organization into the existing structure, George created a separate child domain for the acquired company, acq.thebestcoever.com, and pre-created this domain using Ntdsutil. He then sent a notification to his colleague in the new office with instructions on how to join the corporate domain. He also instructed fellow administrators to install Windows Server 2003 on the two existing controllers, and name them DC1.acq.thebestcoever.com and DC2.acq.thebestcoever.com, respectively. All other settings were left up to the administrators in the new domain.

Before long, one of the ACQ domain administrators started reporting inconsistent problems when their users tried to access resources located in corporate headquarters. After long troubleshooting hours, George established that the only resources that they were having trouble connecting to were those located on DC4.thebestcoever.com.

What, in your opinion, might be the reason for this inconsistent behavior in connecting to one domain controller in particular? Why are users able to access resources on other domain controllers without any problems?

SELF TEST ANSWERS

1. ☑ **A, B,** and **D** are correct. Out of five FSMO roles, two have forest scope and three, domain scope. The RID Master, Infrastructure Master, and PDC Emulator have domain scope.
☒ **C** and **E** are incorrect because these roles have forest scope. **F** is incorrect because this role does not exist.

2. ☑ **C** is correct. Because the domain contains some Windows NT 4.0 controllers, they should still be able to receive SAM database copies from the PDC Emulator. If the PDC Emulator is unavailable, changes will not be replicated to the BDCs, and requests submitted to the BDCs will be unsuccessful.
☒ **A** is incorrect. Universal group caching would have no impact in this scenario because sites are not used. **B** is incorrect because Windows NT 4.0 and Windows Server 2003 can coexist. **D** is incorrect because there is no likelihood of unavailability of RIDs, as the domain controllers contact the RID Master as soon as the available RIDs go below 100.

3. ☑ **D** is correct. To implement universal group caching, all of the domain controllers in the site where you want to deploy this feature should be running Windows Server 2003.
☒ **A, B,** and **C** are incorrect because one site contains a mix of Windows Server 2003 and Windows 2000 Server domain controllers.

4. ☑ **A** is correct. Most likely, if you work as administrator of one of the domains in a large enterprise, you will not have Enterprise Admins permissions.
☒ **B** may be correct, but **A** is more likely to be the problem in this case. **C** is incorrect because the Infrastructure Master is not involved in this scenario. **D** is incorrect because you are a member of the local Domain Admins group, since you are responsible for administering this domain.

5. ☑ **C** is correct. In Windows Server 2003, the global catalog replication state is not reset in this case, as it used to be in versions prior to Windows Server 2003. Only the newly added attribute will be replicated.
☒ **A** is incorrect. Replication at night is always a preferable choice, but because of the reasons outlined in **C**, this is not necessary. **B** is incorrect because this will cause a significant increase of traffic over the WAN link. **D** is incorrect because you can add an attribute as long as you are a member of the Schema Admins.

6. ☑ **C** is correct. The application partition may contain any type of objects except security principals.
☒ **A** and **B** are incorrect because these objects are security principals. **D** is incorrect because **C** is correct.

7. ☑ **A** is correct. An administrator can always log in to the network irrespective of the status of the global catalog.

☒ **B** and **C** are incorrect because you should use an administrator's account to log on to the network and correct the problem. **D** is incorrect because global catalog servers are used during the authentication process when the user principal name is used as the logon name, and the local domain controller does not have information about the user in question.

8. ☑ **A** and **B** are correct. Segmenting your environment into domains allows strict separation of administration and security control. This should also reduce replication traffic because domain data partition will not have to replicate between domains.

☒ **C** is incorrect. Beginning with Windows 2000 Server, you can store up to a theoretical limit of 4 billion objects. **D** is incorrect because even one domain can be split into several sites.

9. ☑ **B** is correct. Clients use port 3268 to submit global catalog requests using the LDAP protocol.

☒ **A** is incorrect because DNS queries use port 53. **C** is incorrect because FSMO does not use any ports—protocol RPC used for FSMO communication uses port 135 plus a range of dynamic ports. **D** is incorrect because the global catalog over SSL uses port 3269.

10. ☑ **A** is correct. Each forest contains the same information in all of its global catalog servers, irrespective of the domain.

☒ **B, C,** and **D** are incorrect because there is one set of information stored in the global catalog in all domains.

11. ☑ **B** is correct because one forest has the same schema in all domains. To isolate product development changes from possible AD meltdown in the production environment, you should seriously consider setting up a separate forest for R&D. Developers then would have the freedom to modify whatever they need and not be afraid of the potential impact. This holds true for any version of Active Directory.

☒ **A** is incorrect because any changes to the schema will be reflected in all domains within the same forest. **C** is incorrect because developers would not be able to test their changes to make sure the product works. **D** is incorrect because sites are not used to limit the scope of the schema, but rather the scope of replication.

12. ☑ **A** is correct. If you configure the DMZ domain to trust the internal domain, users in internal domains will be able to access the DMZ domain, but not the other way around. If the DMZ domain is compromised, this will not have an impact on the internal domain.

☒ **B** is incorrect because this trust relationship is the opposite of what the scenario is trying to achieve. **C** is incorrect because this will cause account duplication in the DMZ segment. **D** is incorrect because shortcut trusts are used for Active Directory optimization, not security configuration.

13. ☑ **B** is correct. A centralized administration and a single security policy give you enough hints that one domain should be used. Four sites should be deployed in the scenario—one for the central location and three others for each remote location.
    ☒ **A, C,** and **D** are incorrect because **B** is correct.

14. ☑ **C** is correct. Forest trusts are a lot easier to set up and maintain than separate trust relationships between each pair of domain controllers between forests. To achieve this functionality, both forests should be raised to Windows Server 2003 forest functional levels.
    ☒ **A** is incorrect because you would not be able to upgrade forest root domains. **B** is incorrect because **C** is correct. **D** is incorrect because transitive bidirectional trusts between domains are configured automatically within the same forest.

15. ☑ **A** and **C** are correct. SMTP is used in intersite and interdomain asynchronous replication.
    ☒ **B** and **D** are incorrect because intrasite replication always uses RPC without compression, and intersite but intradomain replication may use RPC with compression.

16. ☑ **D** is correct. This should be sufficient to delegate authority.
    ☒ **A** is incorrect because the Power Users group is a local computer group that has nothing in common with OUs. **B** is incorrect because this group does not exist. **C** is incorrect because a selective permissions assignment to existing objects will not grant administrators rights to create or delete new objects, and this is too complicated a structure to maintain.

17. ☑ **B** is correct. Transmission and receipt of intersite replication is done through one set of bridgehead servers.
    ☒ **A, C,** and **D** are incorrect. Replication traffic would not be controllable and would take too much bandwidth in the three cases listed in these answers.

18. ☑ **B** is correct. The Windows Server 2003 interim functional level is designed specifically for coexistence between Windows NT 4.0 domain controllers and the Windows Server 2003 environment. First, you need to make sure that existing hardware is compatible with Windows Server 2003, then upgrade the PDC.
    ☒ **A** is incorrect because it is possible to upgrade from the NT 4.0 domain infrastructure. **C** is incorrect because first migrating to Windows 2000 and then to Windows Server 2003, you will double the amount of work and chances that something will go wrong along the way. **D** is incorrect because the PDC should be upgraded first, and then you should either add Windows Server 2003 domain controllers or upgrade the remaining BDCs.

19. ☑ **A** is correct. **D** completes the strategy statement as to how you should use nested groups to minimize administrative effort and maximize Windows Server 2003 group management features.
    ☒ **B** and **C** are incorrect statements.

20. ☑ **A** and **B** are correct. If you back up your system and you are sure that the secondary domain controllers function well, you can start the domain controller in the AD restore mode and use Ntdsutil to move the files elsewhere on the disk.

☒ **C** is incorrect because MOVETREE is used to move objects within the AD infrastructure. **D** is incorrect because this will damage the domain controller.

LAB ANSWER

Despite the fact that it is the child domain that is having intermittent difficulties accessing resources in the central domain, the problem is most likely in the way George placed FSMO roles in the parent domain. George did not move the global catalog server off of the DC1.thebestcoever.com server, which also runs the Infrastructure Master role. This was not a problem until the company added a child domain. Prior to this addition, all domain controllers had the same domain data partition and had a full copy of all domain objects, hence the Infrastructure Master was not needed.

This has changed with the addition of the child domain. The DC1, DC2, and DC3 domain controllers still knew of all domain objects within their own domain, whereas the DC4 domain controller is not supposed to receive all changes made to objects in the parent domain. Because there is no global catalog information on the DC4 domain controller in the child site, and because the Infrastructure Master in the parent domain is located on the same controller as the global catalog server, DC4 was not receiving enough information about changes in the parent domain. This is the primary reason why users in the child domain had problems accessing resources in the parent domain.

George made a good decision not to place a global catalog server in the site with just six users, as replication traffic would outweigh the benefit of having local GC copy.

4

Managing and Maintaining an Active Directory Infrastructure

CERTIFICATION OBJECTIVES

A ctive Directory is the backbone of Windows networks, controlling practically every type of user and network interaction. Obviously, administrators have to know the inner workings and capabilities of Active Directory.

You already know that Active Directory is a complex structure, that an Active Directory forest may consist of several sites and domains, and that the domains within one forest have the same Active Directory schema, which in turn defines object classes and attributes. You also know that within the same forest there may be more than one unique namespace and that all domains within the same forest are automatically configured with two-way transitive trusts. Legacy Windows NT 4.0 domains can also be connected to the Active Directory forest using trusts that make it possible for users in the trusted domain to access resources in the trusting domain. Finally, the Active Directory domain structure represents a logical organization of the network and creates the common security boundary; whereas site structure has nothing to do with security or domains, and instead is used to handle replication traffic.

This chapter discusses several practical aspects of administering and maintaining the Active Directory environment, such as extending schemas, administering site and domain structure within the forest, and connecting domains located in different forests. Information presented here will help you to better understand how Active Directory works, hence, helping with day-to-day administration, and also helping to ensure that your Active Directory environment is fault tolerant and available. To better approach these topics, some of the basic directory topics discussed in Chapter 1 will be reviewed in the context of Active Directory in Windows Server 2003.

Last but not least, we will take a look at some troubleshooting and Active Directory restore operations.

CERTIFICATION OBJECTIVE 4.01

Manage an Active Directory Forest and Domain Structure

Certain functionality in Active Directory, such as user authentication or applications accessing optional attributes of Active Directory objects, is transparent to users. As far as users are concerned, they only need to know a few basic rules as they apply to the day-to-day interaction with Active Directory. However, this may not necessarily be true of Active Directory administrators.

This part of the chapter deals with interdomain authentication and schema modification. You may need to modify schemas if you're planning to install an enterprise-wide application that uses Active Directory to store certain pieces of information in objects that initially were not designed to store this information. As far as interdomain authentication is concerned, this may be driven by business requirements—for instance, when companies acquire or merge with other companies. Some of the business requirements also applicable to this situation were presented in Chapter 2.

Manage Schema Modifications

Every object stored in Active Directory, such as user, site, or security group, has a certain mandatory set of attributes that cannot be modified. For example, for user objects, these are attributes such as givenName, initials, and name; for site objects, these include siteName and gPlink (link to a group policy); and so on. All mandatory and optional attributes of a certain type of object collectively define this object, and are called the object class. Each Active Directory object is nothing but an instance of its corresponding object class. Attributes incorporated in this object class create a template, based on which all other objects of this type are created. In their day-to-day duties, administrators usually deal with instances of objects, not object classes. However, from time to time you will need to administer classes through schema modification. An Active Directory schema is a collection of all possible object classes and attributes that can be defined and used in the infrastructure.

A default Active Directory schema is installed when Active Directory is rolled out. Objects and attributes defined in this default schema are usually sufficient to provide the functionality needed in most of the networks. When you install an Active Directory integrated application that uses its own classes, extends existing classes, or you simply want to add a few custom fields to standard Active Directory objects, you will need to extend the schema. This is a fairly straightforward process from the technical perspective; however, it is very demanding in terms of planning for the following reasons:

■ Schema modifications are irreversible—new attributes defined in the schema cannot be removed using conventional methods. If this were possible, you would probably be wondering by now what happens to object instances that refer to attributes that do not exist anymore. Although it is not possible to delete classes or attributes, in Windows 2000 it is possible to deactivate them (marking as defunct) and, beginning with Windows Server 2003, to deactivate and then reuse the name of an existing but defunct schema element. Deactivating a class or an attribute does not remove this element from Active Directory, but prevents further operations involving deactivated elements, including modifications of defunct classes/attributes.

■ Since all domains within the same Active Directory forest must have a common schema, changes you make will replicate to all domain controllers forestwide. Depending on the quantity and types of changes you make, they may also impact replication traffic. For example, instead of replicating jpegPhoto attribute values that may contain pictures of employees, and making it available through the global catalog, you may choose to replicate a website URL, or a link to a SQL database, which may store these images.

■ Although highly unlikely, it is possible that there will be conflicts when you create objects or attributes. To create a new class or attribute, you have to indicate a unique X.500 object ID, or OID. The given ID must be unique for the attribute or class in the broadest of senses. OIDs are assigned by ISO, and uniqueness of these IDs helps ensure that interoperability is maintained between different directory services. If you're not developing an Active Directory integrated product, but are instead trying to make some Active Directory schema modifications to be used within your company, you may use the resource kit utility oidgen.exe. This utility generates a unique object identifier that belongs to the range of identifiers assigned to Microsoft. You can optionally request your generated numbers to be registered by contacting Microsoft.

Here is a sample listing generated by the oidgen.exe utility:

```
C:\Program Files\Resource Kit>oidgen.exe
Attribute Base OID: 1.2.840.113556.1.4.7000.233.28688.28684.8.274196.155554.825761.919990
   Class Base OID: 1.2.840.113556.1.5.7000.111.28688.28684.8.42340.259750.1425984.1043021
```

Oidgen.exe generates two base OIDs, one for an attribute and one for a class. These numbers are to be supplemented by administrative input, hence their name, Base OID. Using the listed OIDs as an example, the 1.2.840 range was issued and registered with ANSI, the American member of ISO, for distribution to the U.S.-based organization; 113556 belongs to Microsoft. The sequence that follows is up to Microsoft to assign. In this example, 1 identifies an Active Directory object. Continuing, number 4 identifies that this OID belongs to an attribute, and 5, to a class. What follows is a long sequence of randomly generated numbers that guarantees the uniqueness of any autogenerated OID. Finally, administrators should append their own ID number at the end of each OID, starting with a dot.

Based on the reasons just stated, any Active Directory schema extension should follow a test rollout in a separate test lab forest that closely resembles the production environment, running AD-integrated production and development applications.

Active Directory
Schema MMC
snap-in

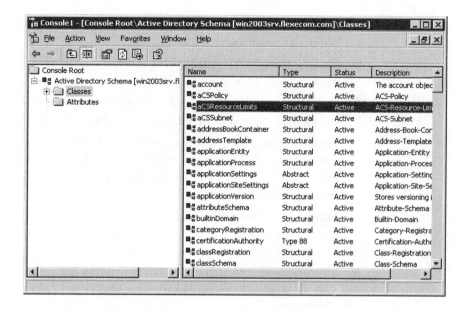

Two methods are available to help administrators with extending an Active Directory schema: using the Active Directory schema MMC snap-in, or programmatically. If this snap-in is not featured in the MMC snap-in list, you have to register it using the **regsvr32 schmmgmt.dll** command. Figure 4-1 shows this administrative console.

In this console, you can use the context menu to access certain features of the AD schema. Here, you can define who should be allowed to access and modify the schema (by default, only Schema Admins group members can modify schemas). Using this menu, you can also change the Schema Operations Master, or reload AD schemas if you perform some modifications programmatically and now wish to see them in the console. Expanding the Active Directory Schema container will expose two subcontainers: Attributes and Classes.

Attributes

As discussed in Chapter 1, attributes are used to describe objects. The same attribute can apply to more than one object class—for example, the managed By, description, and cN attributes are used by many object classes. Note that attributes are objects themselves, and when you create a new attribute, you need to describe this object to the system by providing values for the following fields:

- **Common Name**   This is how your attribute object name will be displayed.
- **LDAP Display Name**   This specifies the name of the attribute that will be used in LDAP queries. This value must honor LDAP syntax limitations—it

must contain only letters, numbers, and hyphens (no spaces) and must not begin with a number.

■ **Unique X.500 Object ID**   This is the object ID discussed earlier. The value must be globally unique.

■ **Description**   This provides a description for your attribute object. It can be the same as the common name or provide a longer description.

■ **Syntax**   Here you define acceptable values for your custom attributes. You can pick one of the 20+ value types, such as Unicode String, Case Sensitive or Insensitive String, Boolean, Integer, Octet String, and others. Syntax defines attribute value rules.

■ **Minimum, Maximum**   These properties can be used to define the minimum and maximum number of characters for string values, and minimum and maximum numbers for numeric values.

■ **Multi-Valued**   Each attribute can store either one or several values. Attributes such as memberOf and sIDHistory need to be able to maintain several values in a form of a list, and hence are multivalued. At this time, it is not possible to specify the sort order of these values, and if necessary, these functions can be implemented in the LDAP user interface tools.

Figure 4-2 shows the Create New Attribute dialog box.

Upon creating an attribute, you can find it in the attribute list and change some of its parameters—description, minimum and maximum allowed values—and also adjust its behavior in Active Directory. Figure 4-3 shows the property page of a custom

---

FIGURE 4-2

Creating a new attribute object in the Active Directory Schema MMC snap-in

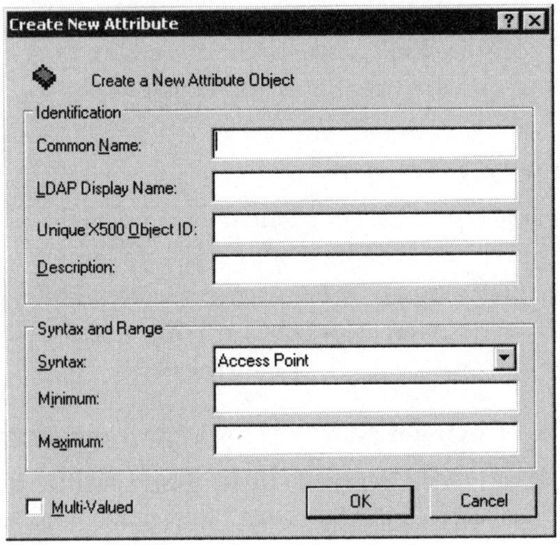

Modifying custom
attributes in the
Active Directory
Schema MMC
snap-in

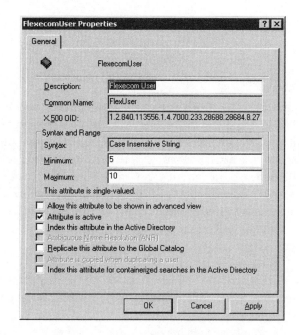

attribute. Chapter 3 described the use of the Replicate This Attribute to the global
catalog setting. If you choose Index This Attribute In Active Directory, this will speed
up searches for objects based on the value of this attribute. This functionality is similar
to that of a typical database (AD data, incidentally, is stored in a database), and should
be enabled if your application or users plan to use this attribute extensively. For example,
indexing phone numbers and last names might not be a bad idea.

Also note that this property screen is where you set the attribute state to defunct
(Attribute Is Active setting). It is not possible to control the state of attributes created
by the system; it is possible to defunct only those attributes created by administrators.

Classes

Classes are sets of attributes that fully describe a certain type of object. There are three
class types in Windows Server 2003:

- **Structural classes**   This is the only class type that can have object instances
  in Active Directory. Structural classes can inherit attributes from other structural
  or abstract classes.

- **Abstract classes**   These are very basic classes that form the foundation for all
  other structural classes. There are only about a dozen abstract classes.

■ **Auxiliary classes** These are more like an attribute list that can extend other structural class definitions. When extending existing structural classes, it is recommended that you implement custom auxiliary classes and then use these clustered attributes, instead of modifying structural classes directly.

When you create a new class, you have to provide Common Name, LDAP Display Name, Unique X.500 Object ID, and Description field values much the same way as if you were creating an attribute. Figure 4-4 demonstrates the difference: instead of specifying attribute syntax, you have to provide inheritance and type information. If you leave the Parent Class value blank, Active Directory will assume that this is a child of the Top class. If the Parent Class value is provided, the class inherits all attributes from the parent class. The inetOrgPerson class is a child in relation to the User class and, as such, contains User class attributes. On this screen, you must also pick the class type.

You can extend a structural class with a new set of attributes using either separately created attribute objects or by adding auxiliary classes. Adding auxiliary classes is the recommended approach because it minimizes the chances of mixing up custom and system attributes.

Administrators can add attributes to their classes either as part of the class creation process (see Figure 4-5) or later on, using class properties (see Figure 4-6). Figure 4-5 shows a dialog box where you can specify mandatory and optional attributes for the class.

Note that it is not possible to modify the list of mandatory attributes after the class has been added to the schema, but you can still modify optional attributes, as shown in Figure 4-6, and add auxiliary classes, as shown in Figure 4-7.

FIGURE 4-4

Create New
Schema Class
dialog box in the
Active Directory
Schema MMC
snap-in

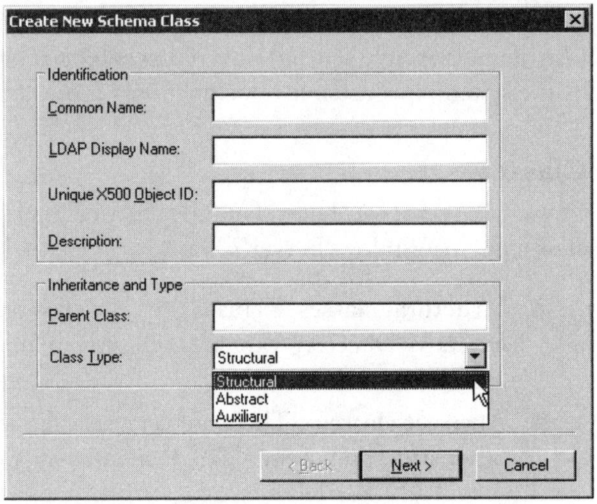

FIGURE 4-5

Assigning
mandatory
and optional
attributes to
an object class

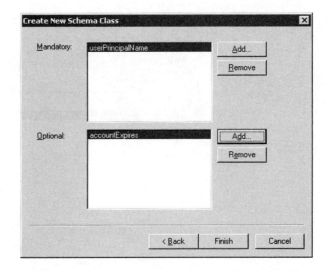

Including mandatory attributes in your attribute set will make it impossible to create an instance of any given object class without first assigning acceptable values to all mandatory attributes. You should only designate those attributes as mandatory which, if left without a value, will make it impossible to use a given object class instance. If you compare this to a user class, for example, its object instances would be pretty useless without meaningful objectSID and name attributes. The system automatically

FIGURE 4-6

Class properties:
modifying
optional
attributes

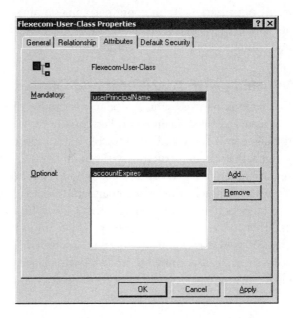

FIGURE 4-7

Class properties:
adding auxiliary
classes

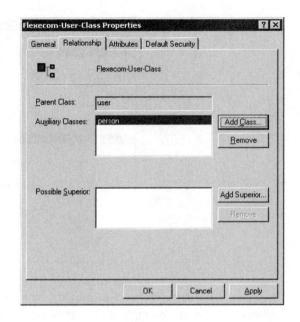

generates an SID for each user you create, and administrators must supply an account name value; otherwise, the object will not be created. As shown in Figure 4-7, new auxiliary classes can be linked to existing classes on the Relationship tab in class properties. The Possible Superior field is used to define which container classes, such as the organizationalUnit container, can contain child object instances of the class you are configuring. Finally, Figure 4-8 shows the General tab of a custom object class, where you can mark this object as defunct.

Working with Attributes and Classes

To create a new class or an attribute, you can use the Active Directory Schema snap-in connected to any domain controller. Since a copy of the forest schema is stored on each domain controller regardless of its role or location in the infrastructure, you will be able to view the schema structure without any difficulties (providing that you have the requisite Active Directory schema rights). You should also be mindful that this console allows manual selection of a domain controller (use the context menu of the Active Directory Schema container, and then select the Change Domain Controller option), and that connectivity to the Schema Master must be in place in order to commit schema changes. New classes and attributes can be created using context menus in their respective containers. So if you need to add a custom class, right-click the Classes container, and click Create Class. You will have no difficulties completing the rest of the process based on the steps described previously.

Class properties:
the General tab

The next step after creating new attributes and classes should probably be to provide some mechanism of interaction between these additions and the rest of your infrastructure: users, administrators, and applications. Active Directory snap-ins work with a predefined set of attributes and objects, and generally speaking, you will either need to customize existing tools or create new tools, perhaps using a web interface or a custom desktop application, so that new objects and properties can be created and configured. Let's say you created a new user attribute to store social security numbers. Applications using LDAP can start referencing this property right away, but it will not be available to administrators through the standard Windows management tools, unless these tools are customized.

Generally speaking, the burden of providing these tools is on the shoulders of developers and not administrators. However, there are a few resources available to administrators, namely, scripting, and customization of object property pages and context menus with Active Directory Display Specifiers.

Customizing administration tools is a topic worthy of its own book and goes beyond the scope of our discussion, but if you are interested, Microsoft's website has a few resources dedicated to this topic—one of them is a paper titled "Windows 2000 Active Directory Display Specifiers." The Windows Platform SDK also contains a wealth of information for developers.

Manage Trust Relationships

Chapter 3 discussed the benefits and purpose of using trust relationships in the Active Directory environment. A trust relationship between two domains makes it possible for users in the trusted domain to use resources in the trusting domain. Windows Server 2003 has several types of trusts developed for distinct purposes, and they may be configured automatically, without administrative input, or manually. The next few sections summarize features of each trust relationship and discuss what is involved in establishing trusts manually.

Trusts Configured Automatically

Trust relationships are configured automatically between any two domains in a parent-child relationship and between all tree root domains within the same Active Directory domain forest. The result of this configuration is that you have a single forest where all member domains trust each other implicitly, regardless of their location in the forest or within their own domain trees. Each time a new domain is added to the forest, it is configured with a two-way, transitive trust relationship with its parent domain. The fact that these automatic trusts are bidirectional and transitive helps ensure complete trust between all member domains, without having to maintain one-to-all trusts in each domain. (This is a feature of Windows NT 4.0–style domains.) Furthermore, automatic trust relationships cannot be reconfigured or removed; you can only view automatic trust properties in a read-only mode.

Automatic trusts are common to Windows 2000 and Windows Server 2003 domains on all functional levels. By default, the operating system uses Kerberos when authenticating cross-domain requests, and may also use NTLM as a fail-over mechanism.

Trusts Configured Manually

Trust relationships of any other type, or between any other domains not included in the preceding definition, must be configured manually using the Active Directory Domains and Trusts MMC snap-in, shown in Figure 4-9. Trusts configured manually may be either one- or two-way, depending on business requirements. Recall from Chapter 3 that users can access resources in the opposite direction of a trust link. So if domain A trusts domain B, users from domain B can access resources in domain A, providing that appropriate permissions have been set. Table 4-1 shows the trust types available in Windows Server 2003.

Before configuring trust relationships, you have to do a little planning in regard to how users in trusted domains will be resolving and interacting with resources in

FIGURE 4-9

Active Directory
Domains and
Trusts MMC
snap-in

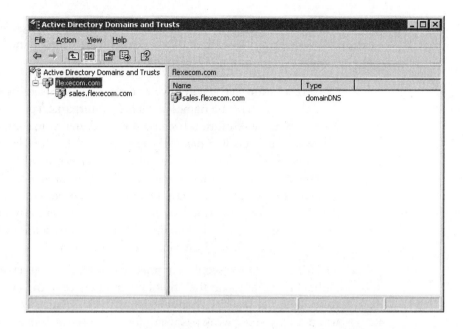

TABLE 4-1   Comparing Different Types of Trusts

Trust Type	Transitive?	Description
External trust	No.	Can establish with Windows NT 4.0 domains and Windows 2000/Windows Server 2003 domains located in another Active Directory forest.
Realm trusts	Configurable.	Can form a trust relationship with any non-Windows Kerberos realm that uses Kerberos version 5 as an authentication protocol. Kerberos realms are found in operating systems such as UNIX and Linux.
Forest trust	Yes, although it is transitive for any two forests. If you add a third forest and configure two trusts sequentially, the first forest will not trust the third forest.	You must have Windows Server 2003 forests running Windows Server 2003 functional levels to configure forest trusts.
Shortcut trust	Yes.	Can be configured between any two child domains to shorten LDAP referrals and reduce the extent and complexity of the authentication process.

trusting domains, and a few other considerations. It may not be possible to implement portions of your planning work until after trusts have been defined, but this should have no impact on planning of the following elements:

- **DNS resolution** You will have to configure DNS servers in each of the two domains to resolve the names of their counterparts. You should not rely on NetBIOS name resolution because several domains in different forests may have the same NetBIOS name. For example, a Sales third-level domain will have the same NetBIOS name by default, and this is consistent with Microsoft recommendations. In Windows Server 2003, you can use conditional forwarding or even stub zones to speed up DNS resolution between two deeply nested domains. You can also install another DNS server and use it for either delegation or zone transfers for both domains. There are quite a few options to consider when choosing what is best in a specific situation.

- **Trust password for secure channel (SC) setup** You have to communicate with administrators on the other end and negotiate the best password policy to apply to the security channel password. By default, Windows Server 2003 will not let you use weak passwords for a trust setup. Since this password is used on both ends of the secure channel, it must satisfy password policy requirements in both domains. Before a trust relationship can be used, it must be defined in both domains. (New to Windows Server 2003 is the ability to accomplish this from the same server.) To take advantage of this feature, you will need to know the username and password of an external domain account that has enough administrative authority to set up trust relationships.

- **Global groups** You have to define global groups (and universal, if necessary), which will be used to assign permissions to resources located in the external domain. Alternatively, you can use existing groups. If there is no plan to migrate users between domains (if that is not why you are setting up the relationship), there is no reason to choose one domain in favor of the other when deciding where global groups should be located. Otherwise, if you plan domain consolidation down the road, groups should be created in the domain that will remain after consolidation. This will help to avoid SID filtering complications.

- **Resource access permissions** You should define (or choose existing) local groups in the trusting domain where you will add your global groups with users from the trusted domain. Then you should ensure that these local groups have access to resources as required.

■ **Plan policy settings** By allowing or denying Logon Locally and Access This Computer From Network user rights, you can further restrict or enable users from the trusted domain to access resources in the trusting domain.

■ **Authentication type** When you configure an external trust relationship in Windows Server 2003, where both domains are running on the Windows Server 2003 functional level, two authentication types are available: domain-wide (standard option) and selective, which is a new feature in Windows Server 2003. When you select the Domain-wide option, it all comes down to assigning groups enough permissions to access specific resources. If selective authentication is chosen, the default behavior of the trust does not allow authentication across the trust link. You will get an "access denied" error message, even if appropriate permissions have been added to resources you are trying to access. The error message will attribute logon failure to a rejected authentication request by an authentication firewall. To allow access to a resource, you must also grant Allowed To Authenticate permission to the group in question on the server where the resource is located. This option was created to allow for the existence of external trusts between Windows Server 2003 domains on a long-term basis, where trusted and trusting domains need not be owned by the same company. Figure 4-10 shows this setting.

FIGURE 4-10

Allowed to
Authenticate
permission
in Windows
Server 2003

You can assign the Allowed To Authenticate right in Windows Server 2003 using the Active Directory Users and Computers MMC snap-in, in the properties of a computer object representing the server you are configuring access to. Don't forget that in order to make the Security tab available, you must enable Advanced Features in the View menu in the console toolbar.

After giving all of these considerations a bit of thought, you can now proceed to set up trust links. Use the Active Directory Domains and Trusts console shown in Figure 4-9. Expand the domain tree to a point where you see the domain you would like to set up a trust relationship for, right-click it, choose Properties, and then switch to the Trusts tab (shown in Figure 4-11). Note that this page has two sections, one for outgoing trusts and one for incoming trusts. Regardless of the trust direction, each trust relationship must be defined on each end of the relationship. The outgoing trust list contains all domains trusted by your domain, and the incoming trust list contains all domains trusting your domain.

FIGURE 4-11

Trusts tab
in domain
properties

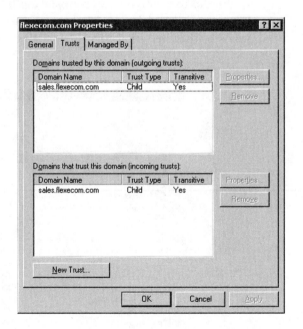

To set up a new trust, click the New Trust button. This will launch the New Trust Wizard, which will take you through a few steps. You will need to provide the following information in order to complete this wizard:

1. **Trust Name**   Supply the DNS name of the external domain. This should be an external forest root domain (if you are setting up a forest trust), the DNS name of a domain or a Kerberos realm, or in the worst-case scenario, the NetBIOS name of the domain.

2. **Trust Type**   Choices will depend on the domain and its relation to other domains in its own forest. Choices may be Realm, Forest, Shortcut, and External. In many cases, the wizard will detect the only possible type for a given situation and will not prompt for input.

3. **Transitivity of Trust**   Here you select whether your trust should be transitive. This information is only asked in the few cases when you are configuring a trust type that can technically be either nontransitive or transitive.

4. **Direction of Trust**   Choose outgoing, incoming, or two-way.

5. **Sides of Trust**   This screen allows you to select in which domains the wizard should attempt to configure trust relationships. As mentioned earlier, you need to configure trust on both ends. If it is a one-way, outgoing trust in the trusting domain, it should be configured as a one-way, incoming trust in the trusted domain. If you select This Domain Only, you will need to create a common password to be used later on for configuring the other side of the relationship. Should you choose Both This And The Specified Domain, you will be prompted for account credentials that have appropriate administrative access in the external domain.

6. **Trust Authentication Level (also known as scope of authentication)**   The wizard offers to configure whether this should be a domainwide authentication level or selective authentication. You will not be able to configure trust with selective authentication unless both forests are running on the Windows Server 2003 forest functional level.

7. **The last step in the process**   The wizard will display a summary of your trust settings and ask you to confirm the newly configured trust. (This might be a good idea if you configured trust on both sides as part of the same process, or if you are setting up the second side of the trust; otherwise, the wizard will certainly fail to confirm the new trust relationship.)

Once the trust relationship has been configured, you can access trust properties through the same property page (shown in Figure 4-11). You can also view the properties of each trust on the incoming or outgoing list, and for those trusts that you created manually, you can change the scope of authentication (domainwide or selective). For some types of trusts (such as realm trusts, where you have to select trust transitivity), you can also change transitivity. As shown in Figure 4-12, trust properties can be used to validate a trust relationship after it has been created on both ends. This is also a valuable troubleshooting tool. Last but not least, if the trust relationship is no longer needed, you can use the property page to remove it by selecting the trust and clicking the Remove button. Windows Server 2003 will prompt you whether this trust should be removed from the external domain as well, in which case you will have to provide an administrative username and password for the external domain.

A new built-in group was added to Windows Server 2003: Incoming Forest Trust Builders, that allows for granting rights to external root domain administrators to configure trust relationships with your domain, without giving administrative authority in your domain.

As usual with UI-based administration tools in Windows Server 2003, there is a command-line alternative for the Active Directory Domains and Trusts console: the Netdom.exe tool, provided as part of Support Tools. It has the same functionality as the console and more, also allowing you to reset secure channel passwords without

FIGURE 4-12

Parent-child trust properties

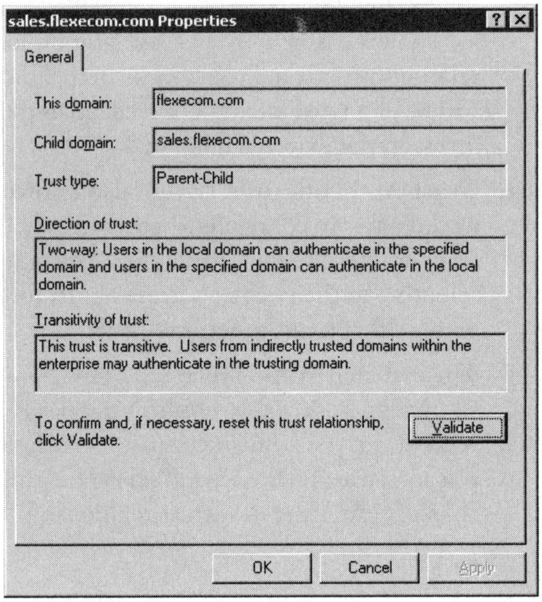

having to redo the trust. The following listing shows a portion of the Netdom.exe **trust /help** command, which demonstrates just how flexible this tool is.

```
C:\Documents and Settings\Administrator.WIN2003SRV> netdom trust |more
The syntax of this command is:
NETDOM TRUST trusting_domain_name /Domain:trusted_domain_name [/UserD:user]
       [/PasswordD:[password | *]] [UserO:user] [/PasswordO:[password | *]]
       [/Verify] [/RESEt] [/PasswordT:new_realm_trust_password]
       [/Add] [/REMove] [/Twoway] [/REAlm] [/Kerberos]
       [/Transitive[:{yes | no}]]
       [/OneSide:{trusted | trusting}] [/Force] [/Quarantine[:{yes | no}]]
       [/NameSuffixes:trust_name [/ToggleSuffix:#]]
       [/EnableSIDHistory[:{yes | no}]]
       [/ForestTRANsitive[:{yes | no}]]
       [/CrossORGanization[:{yes | no}]]
       [/AddTLN:TopLevelName]
       [/AddTLNEX:TopLevelNameExclusion]
       [/RemoveTLN:TopLevelName]
       [/RemoveTLNEX:TopLevelNameExclusion]
NETDOM TRUST Manages or verifies the trust relationship between domains
```

All of this is good, but so far, we have still not reviewed what practical implications these trust relationships have for users of the system. Two main functionalities come to mind: remote resource access, and local authentication (console logon) in the trusting domain.

- **Remote resource access** Providing that proper access permissions have been configured (this includes the Allowed To Authenticate right if selective authentication is used), remote resources can be accessed similarly to local resource access—using UNC names, such as \\Servername\sharename. These resources are also available through My Network Places (if NetBIOS browsing is supported by your network), and can be searched for in Active Directory (if they have been published). In addition to this, users must have the Access This Computer From Network right and NTFS permissions, if this resource is a file or folder located on the NTFS file system. If name resolution works as it is supposed to, remote network resource access is really no different from local network resource access.

- **Local logon in the trusting domain** After you configure the trust relationship from domain A to domain B, users with accounts in domain B will be able to log on locally on machines in domain A. To do this, they will need to choose domain B in the domain box on the Ctrl+Alt+Del screen, or use the UPN or <NetBIOS domain>\<username> format during the logon process. As demonstrated in Figure 4-13, a pre-Windows 2000 username is required for

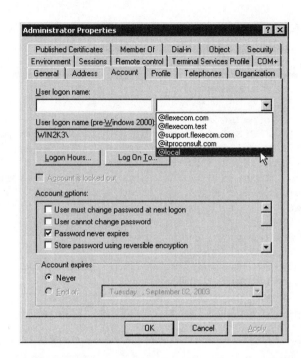

Adding a
Windows 2000–
style logon name
and UPN suffix

each account, but the Windows 2000 logon name and associated UPN suffix
can also be defined in user account properties.

*Note that you may not be able to use NetBIOS domains from the automatically
created domain list on the Ctrl+Alt+Del logon screen, if your enterprise has
forest trusts. Chances are pretty good that two enterprise forests will contain
identical NetBIOS domain names, such as Sales or North/South/East/West, in
which case DNS is the only way to refer to the domain.*

Manage the UPN Suffix

User principal names (UPNs) may be used to ease the process of console or network
logon in cases where users provide their logon names in the username@dns-domain
format. UPN logon names replace Windows NT 4.0–style logons, which used the
NetBIOS-domain\username format, primarily because of the lack of dependability
upon NetBIOS domains. UPN logon names resemble email addresses, and consist
of the logon name portion and UPN suffix portion, separated by the @ sign.

To keep things simple, a logon name in Windows 2000 and username in Windows
NT 4.0 may be the same, providing that the name satisfies both syntax requirements,

but this is not a requirement. By default, the dns-domain portion of the UPN logon name is assigned based on the domain where the user account is created, but this may or may not be desirable in cases of deeply nested domains; for example, you wouldn't want your UPN logon name to have a "research.ca.west.ad.thebestcoever.com" UPN suffix. When you create a new user account, you can manually choose the UPN suffix of any existing domain for your user account—the box, as shown in Figure 4-13, is populated automatically. To make it easier for users to enter their logon credentials, you can add your own UPN suffixes, in which case they will also show up in the list when you create a new account.

To add (or remove) a custom UPN suffix, you use the Active Directory Domains and Trusts console, right-click the root container in the tree pane (Active Directory Domains and Trusts node), and choose Properties in the context menu. After creating your UPN suffixes on the property page shown in Figure 4-14, you will be able to add these suffixes instead of those generated automatically based on the current and parent DNS domain names.

Let's go back to research.ca.west.ad.thebestcoever.com domain and take a look at the suffixes that are available to Research domain users by default. In this example, TheBestCoEver Corp has a DNS domain registered on the Internet: thebestcoever.com. But the forest root domain in Active Directory begins on the second level: ad.thebestcoever.com. This is done to keep external and internal namespaces separate, as per our discussion in Chapter 2. If we add the TheBestCoEver UPN suffix in the

FIGURE 4-14

Adding your own
UPN suffixes

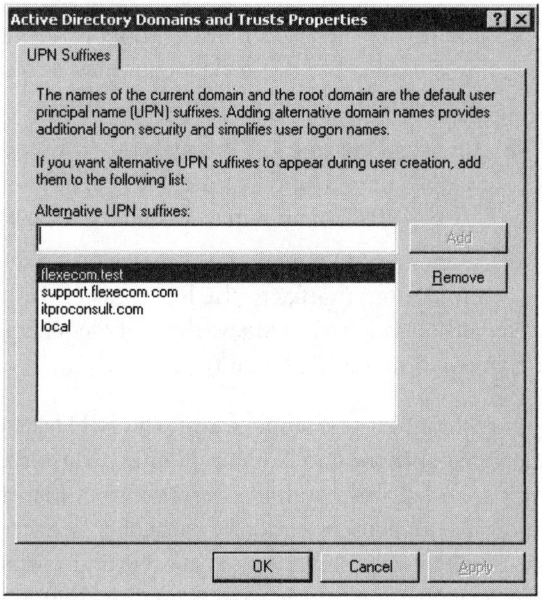

Active Directory Domains and Trusts console, the full listing of all available suffixes will be as follows:

- **research.ca.west.ad.thebestcoever.com** Research domain default suffix
- **ca.west.ad.thebestcoever.com** Parent domain suffix
- **west.ad.thebestcoever.com** Parent's parent domain suffix
- **ad.thebestcoever.com** Forest root domain suffix
- **TheBestCoEver** Custom UPN suffix added for user convenience

In addition to making things simple for users, UPN suffixes also fit into the Microsoft Exchange Server infrastructure and can be used to integrate the two if external email addresses do not use the same DNS domain names as the AD infrastructure.

Forest trusts complicate UPN management a bit. Within the same domain forest, UPN conflicts are eliminated, because all domain names are unique by design. When you set up a forest trust, because each of the forests was constructed and developed on its own, several types of UPN conflicts may arise:

- **Identical DNS names** If DNS domains weren't registered with the Internet authorities to ensure their uniqueness, it would be possible, although unlikely, that two distinct forests would opt to use the same private namespace, such as domain.local, in which case UPN suffixes would no longer uniquely identify a domain.

- **Identical NetBIOS names** Like DNS names, NetBIOS domain names used in Windows NT 4.0–style logons may no longer be unique, matching more than one domain name in several forests.

- **Identical custom UPN suffixes** If user naming conventions were identical in both forests, and by pure coincidence administrators added the same custom UPN suffix, logon names would no longer be unique.

- **Domain SID conflicts** When you have one forest, SID conflicts are eliminated thanks to the RID Master. In two separate forests, it is possible, although not very likely, that SID sequences used when creating new domains would no longer be unique.

In the context of a single forest, the RID Master makes sure that there are no SID sequence conflicts, the Domain Naming Master makes sure that domain names are unique, and global catalog servers redirect logon requests to domain controllers responsible for authentication of particular user accounts. When you have two separate forests, with two separate sets of masters and a separate global catalog, you lose track of what is happening in the other domain. There is no way to ensure uniqueness and collaboration between these elements when you have two distinct infrastructures that are growing and developing on their own, without being aware of each other.

A mechanism called name suffix routing can be used to avoid conflicts and configure UPN and SPN suffix routing if these conflicts are present. (SPN stands for service principal name.) You can access this mechanism using the Active Directory Domains and Trusts console, on the Trusts tab of your forest root domain node, then on the Name Suffix Routing tab in the forest trust properties (Figure 4-15 shows this tab).

Using name suffix routing, you can specify which forest root domain default or custom UPN suffixes should be routed to the external forest over the trust link. This will effectively limit the scope of authentication based on your UPN suffix. If you need to control routing of default UPN suffixes belonging to child domains in your forest, you can do that on the tab shown in Figure 4-16, which can be accessed by clicking the respective forest root suffix and then clicking the Edit button.

A UPN suffix routing list is compiled when you set up a forest trust relationship, and it is not updated automatically. All conflicting UPN suffixes will be automatically configured not to be routed between forests during the setup. There is one way to avoid manual configuration: use trust validation. Every time a new domain is added to the forest, or a new UPN suffix is assigned, go to the General tab of forest trust relationship properties, and click the Validate button. This process will verify the state of the trust relationship and refresh the list of suffixes configured on the Name Suffix Routing tab.

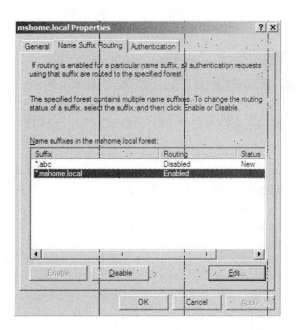

FIGURE 4-15

Name suffix routing between forests

FIGURE 4-16

Routing child
domain UPN
suffixes

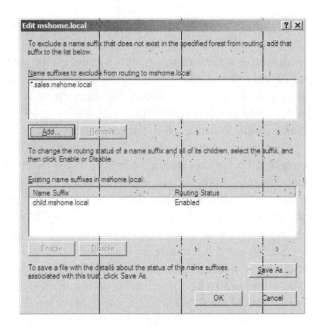

You may have to disable suffix routing manually in cases where conflicts still exist after running through the validation process, where conflicts cannot be identified automatically. In addition, security concerns may also be a good reason to disable a suffix; this must be done manually.

CERTIFICATION OBJECTIVE 4.02

Manage an Active Directory Site

Although an intrasite replication is configured automatically and does not require administrative input, configuring intersite replication requires a lot more Active Directory replication knowledge as well as knowledge about your network environment. Replication occurs based on replication topologies generated by the Knowledge Consistency Checker (KCC) and also replication schedules. KCC generates intrasite topology automatically, and also configures intersite topology in a semiautomatic way, but based on administratively defined settings. Administrators use the Active Directory Sites and Services console to define sites and configure replication transport and schedules. This console is shown in Figure 4-17.

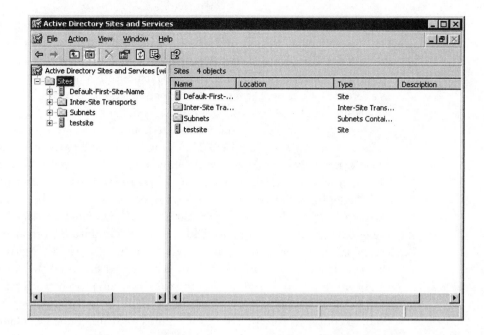

Active Directory
Sites and Services
MMC snap-in

Knowing how each of the parameters discussed in the following sections affects your replication topology is imperative not only for example purposes, but also for real-world administration of infrastructures that span more than one site. Replication settings are forestwide, and thus, only members of the Enterprise Admins or Domain Admins group in the forest root domain usually have access to all of the functions available through the Active Directory Sites and Services console.

Configure Site Boundaries

Before you commence configuring your replication objects, you have to plan and understand how many sites your infrastructure will need in order to implement the desired functionality. You also need to determine which of the networks or subnets will be added to which sites. Conceptual topics, such as what sites are needed for, were discussed in Chapter 2. Recall that sites are defined as common network areas that share fast and reliable connections, where plenty of inexpensive bandwidth is available at all times. In real-world scenarios, you will also have to account for link utilization; for example, even though dial-up is considered to be a slow and unreliable WAN connection, it should probably suffice for one or two workstations connected to a branch office.

Launching Active Directory Sites and Services (shown in Figure 4-17), you are presented with the Sites container that has existing definitions of all forest sites. By default, when you install your first Active Directory domain, a default site, Default-First-Site-Name, is created, and all infrastructure elements such as domain controllers are added to this common site. All other domain controllers that might be added later would also join this default site. Default-First-Site-Name must be present and is used as a temporary setting, because you cannot add a domain controller without specifying which site it belongs to—this site is used by default.

To create a new site, you simply need to come up with an intuitive name and select a site link, as shown in Figure 4-18. Using the Active Directory Sites and Services console, right-click the Sites container and choose New Site. You can rename your sites later without any measurable impact on the rest of the infrastructure.

In order for replication between sites to occur, there must be at least one site link associated with each site; otherwise, sites would be isolated. By default, the site link list presented in Figure 4-18 contains DEFAULTIPSITELINK, the origin and type of which can be inferred from its name. If you select this link as part of the site creation process, the default site will be linked to the newly created site using this default IP site link.

After you're done creating all of the sites, you can proceed with relocating domain controllers based on where they are supposed to be in the topology. Since all of the domain controllers are placed into Default-First-Site-Name by default, switch to the site and expand the Servers container. To move your server between sites, right-click the object that represents the server in question, select Move, and then in the window that pops up, pick a new site for your server.

Distributing your servers between sites manually is a fun process that may quickly grow unmanageable in infrastructures with many sites and a multitude of domain controllers. To automate the process, administrators can create subnets and associate them with the respective sites. When new subnets are created, additional domain

Creating a
new site

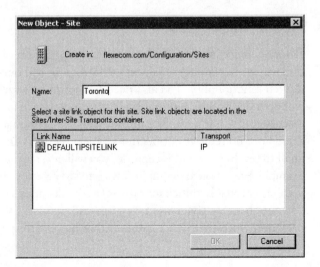

controllers joining the infrastructure will be assigned to their respective sites based on IP addresses. Note that DHCP functionality and subnets in the context of sites are totally unrelated, and administrators will have to ensure that all of the IP addresses assigned to the same subnet do indeed belong to the same site. To create a subnet and associate it with a site, follow these steps:

1. In the tree pane, right-click the Subnets container, and select New Subnet. A window, as shown in Figure 4-19, will appear.

2. In the Address box, type the network portion of the IP addresses you are assigning to the subnet; this is also called the subnet address.

3. In the Mask box, type the subnet mask corresponding to the subnet address typed in step 2. For example, to identify a range of IP addresses from 192.168.1.1 to 192.168.1.254, use 192.168.1.0 for the subnet address, and 255.255.255.0 for the subnet mask.

4. In the Select A Site Object For This Subnet list, pick a site you wish to associate with the newly created subnet, and click OK.

In addition to common site link settings, computers in the same site may be subjected to a common group policy, assigned on the site level. Administrators can define settings applicable to all computers in the same site using site-level group policies. A good example of settings that may apply specifically to all computers within the same site is the DNS server configuration. Indeed, if the site is large enough, Microsoft

FIGURE 4-19

Create a
new subnet

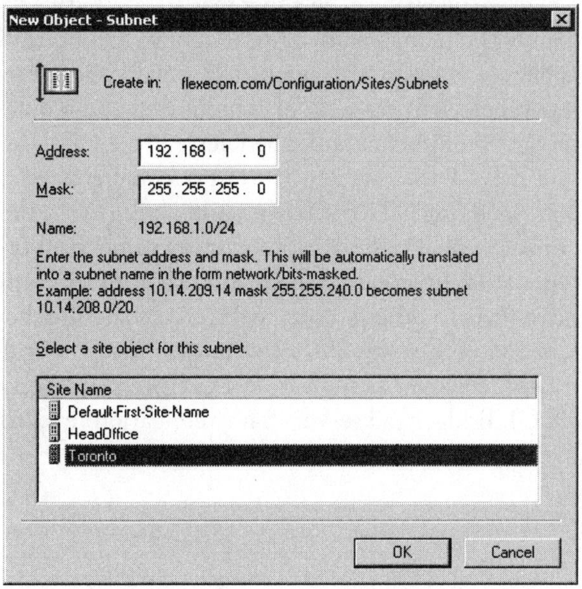

recommends that administrators place a local DNS server in that site to speed up name resolution requests and save network bandwidth using DNS caching. You would want all of your computers to be configured with the IP address of the local DNS server. These settings are located in the Computer Configuration\Administrative Templates\ Network\DNS Client section of group policy objects (GPOs are discussed in detail in Chapters 6 and 7).

Based on administrative requirements, it may be necessary to include many group policy settings not directly related to sites in a policy assigned on a site level, even if some computers within the site must have conflicting settings. You can always override site policy settings with domain and OU policies. Software Installation, Folder Redirection, Windows Update, Offline Files, and Group Policy Slow Link Detection settings are all good candidates for site-level policy inclusion because they may have a direct impact on site link utilization, depending on where your network servers and software repositories are located.

Another group policy setting of particular interest to site administrators is the Site Name configuration available in the Computer Configuration\Administrative Templates\System\Net Logon section. This setting can be used to assign all computers that fall under the scope of the policy to a site of your choice. If this setting is left unchanged, computers will attempt to learn of their site membership based on Active Directory configuration and their location within the OU structure.

Configure Replication Schedules

There are two basic events that may trigger Active Directory replication: changes being committed to a domain controller, or to the replication schedule. The first mechanism applies to intrasite replication, and as such, administrators need not worry about it. The second mechanism is more complicated and requires that administrators configure replication intervals and schedules.

Active Directory replication occurs between all server objects (they have a corresponding NTDS settings child object in the Active Directory Sites and Services console). NTDS settings consist of connection objects that represent incoming replication links established with other infrastructure servers. Generally, servers will have links to other servers within the same site, but some servers will have links to servers in other sites if they were designated as bridgehead servers by administrators or were selected as such by ISTG (Inter-Site Topology Generator, a component of KCC). Bridgehead servers have replication links to other bridgehead servers, located in other sites.

FIGURE 4-20

Default site
replication
schedule

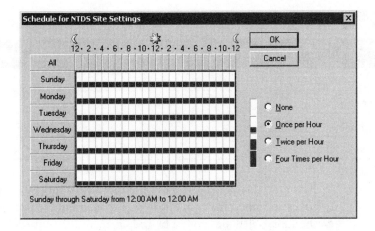

Connection object settings define replication schedules. A replication schedule is represented as a seven-day cycle, split in 15-minute intervals, as shown in Figure 4-20. During each of these 15-minute intervals, replication may either be allowed or disallowed. Although the exact moment when replication begins during each of these intervals is chosen at random (to distribute replication network load evenly), administrators can still edit this behavior on an interval basis using the ADSI editor. For each hour of the week, there are four settings: None, Once Per Hour, Twice Per Hour, and Four Times Per Hour.

Table 4-2 shows the effect of these settings on replication. The + signs indicate the 15-minute intervals during which replication occurs.

To configure the replication schedule for a specific connection object, follow these steps:

1. Using Active Directory Sites, locate the site container that has the server you wish to work with. (Connection objects belong to servers.)

2. Expand the server container, and then click the NTDS Settings object.

3. In the right-hand pane, right-click the connection you wish to configure, and select Properties. In the From Server column, you can see the name of the replication partner for each connection. The connection properties window will appear, as shown in Figure 4-21.

4. On the General tab, click the Change Schedule button. Using the settings from Table 4-2, configure your replication schedule as applicable, and click OK.

5. On the General tab, click OK to apply the new settings.

TABLE 4-2   Four Replication Interval Choices

Setting	00:00–14:59	15:00–29:59	30:00–44:59	45:00–59:59
None	-	-	-	-
One Per Hour	+	-	-	-
Twice Per Hour	+	-	+	-
Four Times Per Hour	+	+	+	+

Since our discussion is concerned more with intersite replication, we must digress to cover an important concept here. If you are modifying a replication schedule for a connection object generated by ISTG (meaning that this connection object defines the link between two bridgehead servers in different sites), your settings will be applied without a warning.

Automatically generated connection objects are created and maintained by KCC for intrasite replication, which means they link two servers within the same site. Automatically generated connections don't have a name; instead, they are marked as "<automatically generated>." If you attempt to modify such a connection, you will receive a warning, advising you that this connection is maintained by KCC, and

FIGURE 4-21

Connection
object properties

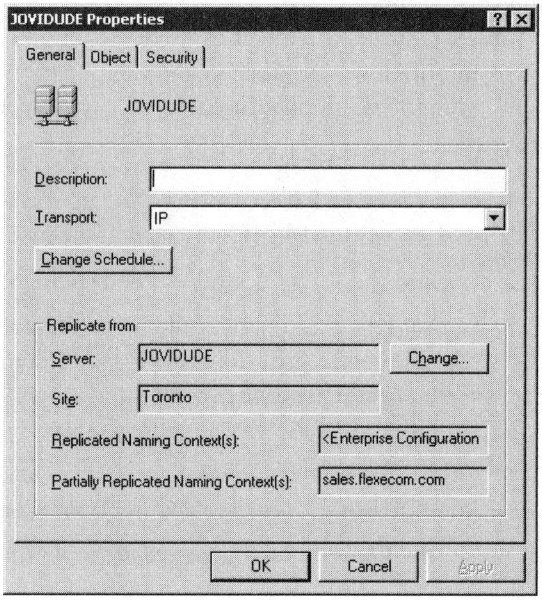

should you choose to proceed with manual configuration, the object will fall out of the scope of KCC. The general idea behind this is that if you have to adjust the default behavior of an automatically generated object, perhaps there is a business or technical requirement that is not met by default algorithms implemented with KCC; so it will stop managing this object altogether. Keep in mind that every time your topology changes (a new server is added, or an existing server is taken offline), you will need to review what impact this has on your static intrasite replication objects.

To deal with this situation, you can take advantage of the inheritance that takes place when KCC automatically generates new connection objects (intersite and intrasite). You can adjust parent NTDS settings to enforce your own replication schedule while allowing KCC to manage connection objects. Intrasite and intersite connection objects inherit connection object replication schedule settings from different parent objects.

Intrasite connection objects inherit replication schedules from the NTDS Settings object in each site. The process of assigning a custom replication schedule is largely the same for the NTDS Settings object as it is for individual connection objects, except you are modifying properties of a different object. After you modify NTDS settings, KCC will update the automatically generated connection objects during its next run, which happens at least once every 15 minutes. If necessary, you can force this process to happen immediately. First, you need to replicate your modified NTDS settings from the domain controller you are working on to other domain controllers. (Recall from Chapter 3 that this replication is performed every 15 seconds and results in changes propagating to all domain controllers within the same site in no more than 45 seconds.) If you have to trigger this part of the process manually, you can use the Replicate Now option in the connection object's context menu. This step is necessary to make sure that KCC uses updated NTDS settings when recalculating topology.

Optionally, before triggering replication manually, you may want to check the replication topology by launching the KCC process. To do this, use the NTDS Settings context menu in the server container you are working with, click All Tasks, and then Check Replication Topology. Figure 4-22 demonstrates this step. Going through this procedure does not guarantee immediate visible changes to the existing configuration; it may take a few minutes before all changes are calculated, committed, and replicated to all other domain controllers.

Getting back to intersite connection objects (which have names and can be found on bridgehead servers): they inherit replication schedules from SiteLink objects, defined in the Inter-Site Transports container. (Figure 4-23 illustrates the property page of a SiteLink object.) Administrators can use SiteLink objects to set replication schedules and replication intervals. Replication schedules, similar to NTDS settings, define

FIGURE 4-22

Triggering the
Knowledge
Consistency
Checker process

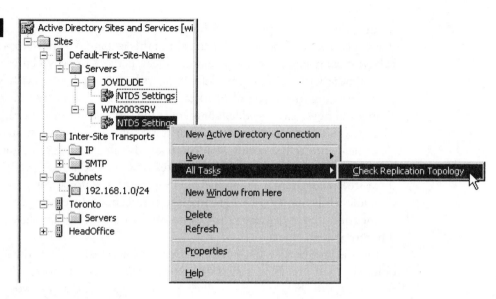

times of the day and week when the replication window is open. Replication intervals, however, define how often replication can occur after the replication window opens. This is different from intrasite replication, which is triggered by changes committed

FIGURE 4-23

Site link settings

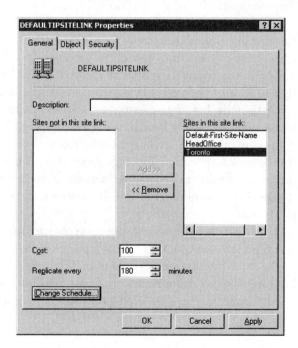

to domain controller databases. Intersite replication is triggered by interval settings. (To be technically correct, the replication interval controls replication frequency within the allowed replication window, but in practical terms, these statements mean the same thing.) In both cases, schedules determine the time of day and week when replication can take place.

The intersite replication interval is configured to 180 minutes by default, and it must be a multiple of 15 (this is to avoid two replication cycles in any one 15-minute stretch of time that can be defined in the schedule). Whenever the replication interval coincides with the 15-minute replication interval defined in the connection object representing the intersite connection between bridgehead servers, it is deemed replication enabled. The following illustration helps visualize this.

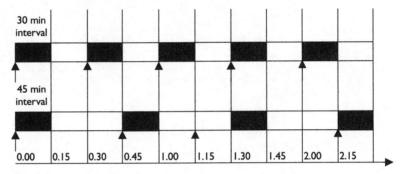

When your replication interval is not 15, 30, or 60 minutes, the replication schedule inherited by connection objects, viewable in connection object properties, does not let you see the big picture. Some of the replication windows allowed by the schedule may be omitted due to longer intervals.

To create a new SiteLink object, follow these steps:

1. Using the Active Directory Sites and Services console, expand the Sites container, then expand Inter-Site Transports, right-click the transport for which you wish to create a new link, and choose New Site Link.

2. In the Name box (see Figure 4-24), type the name you want to assign to the new SiteLink object.

3. Add two or more sites that you wish to connect using this link, and click Add.

The SiteLink object can connect two or more sites. Since you have to assign costs, schedules, and replication intervals on a link level, creating one link that connects more than two sites is generally not recommended, unless you plan to maintain the same cost, schedule, and intervals for all links between selected sites—in which case, using one SiteLink object to represent several links is better from the administration

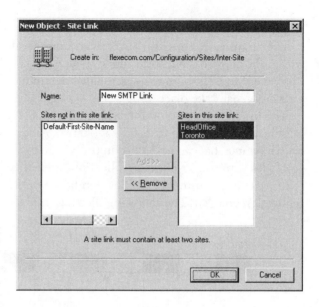

FIGURE 4-24

Add new site link

perspective. If all of your sites are connected to the same backbone, it may make sense to define one link object for all of the connections.

To adjust the site link replication schedule, follow these steps:

1. Using the Active Directory Sites and Services console, expand the Sites container, then Inter-Site Transports, and finally, the IP or SMTP container.

2. If you are configuring either an IP or SMTP SiteLink object, right-click the IP/SMTP container, and make sure that the Ignore Schedules option is turned off.

3. In the right-hand pane, right-click the site link you wish to configure, and select Properties. Figure 4-23 shows this property page.

4. In the Replicate Every box, select an appropriate replication interval setting. This must be a multiple of 15. (Setting this to 15, 30, or 60 will make it easier to manage in light of connection object replication schedules.)

5. Click Change Schedule, select a range of hours or days as applicable to your situation, and choose the appropriate replication settings, either Replication Available, or Replication Not Available.

Replication schedules and intervals become more obscured if you have to calculate overall replication topology in complex environments, where sites may connect to each other indirectly through other sites. In the worst-case scenario, inconsistent schedules may lead to missed replication windows and an overall feeling that replication is lagging. The following illustration depicts two situations reflecting this concern.

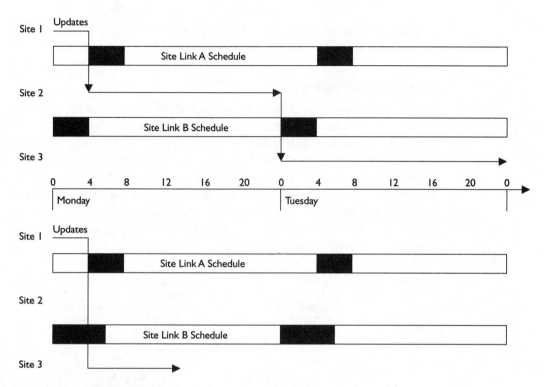

Configure Site Link Costs

SiteLink objects can be assigned a cost, which is an administrative setting that gives priority to one link over another. The lowest cost, intuitively enough, has the highest priority. When you assign costs to your links, consider available bandwidth, reliability, and costs charged by your ISP based on time or amount of data crossing the line. (This monetary cost suggestion is a relatively unimportant factor, but again, it depends on the organization.) If you leave the default link costs set to 100, or assign costs without proper planning, this may result in large replication streams being directed through unreliable or overutilized WAN links. Table 4-3 shows some cost link values suggested by Microsoft.

TABLE 4-3	Link	Cost	
Suggested Link Costs	LAN, backbone	1	
	T1 to backbone	200	
	56 Kbps	500	
	Branch office	100	
	International link	5000	

You can assign site link costs in the intersite transport link properties, on the same tab where you configure replication interval (as was shown in Figure 4-23).

Site Link Bridging

Site link cost configuration becomes more complicated as you factor in more sites, so by default, all site links are bridged. This means that if you have Site A, Site B, and Site C, and there is a site link X defined between Site A and Site B, and another site link Y defined between Site B and Site C, Active Directory assumes that there is a virtual link between Site A and Site C, with a combined cost of X + Y. Site link bridging allows you to maintain a smaller set of site links. You don't have to define all possible links involving all existing sites, but instead use just one link to connect each branch office to the corporate backbone. In fact, this is very similar to transitivity in trust relationships. The following illustration shows the benefits of this feature.

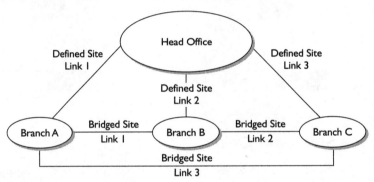

If bridging is used, administrators will only have to assign costs to three links; the rest will be taken care of by KCC. Otherwise, you need to define and calculate costs for six links; and if you don't, replication will not be transitive, and all branch site changes will not go farther than the central office site. Without bridging, the number of site links that must be defined manually increases progressively with the addition of new sites.

If Site A and Site C had a manual site link defined in addition to bridging, the replication path between Site A and Site B would depend on the costs of links between Site A and Site C (Z), and Site C and Site B (Y). If the cumulative cost of (Z + Y) is less than X (direct connection between Site A and Site B), then replication traffic takes a detour. So instead of replicating directly from Site A to Site B, it will replicate first to Site C, and then to Site B. If you have an infrastructure with many sites and some sites have more than one site link to other sites, ISTG will automatically calculate and choose the least-cost route from any site to any site. If one of the links goes down, traffic will be rerouted using other site links, if possible.

Be that as it may, bridging is not always helpful, as the next illustration demonstrates.

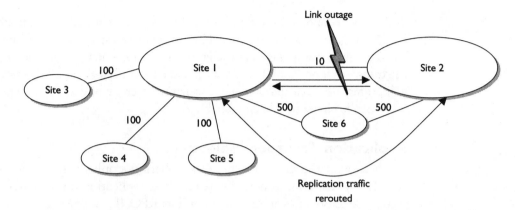

In this case, a problem with one of the links causes replication traffic to take a detour through a very slow and not very reliable 56 Kbit line. This line is not suitable for the kind of replication being attempted. Furthermore, that particular site may not even need the latest and most up-to-date global catalog information, and may function just fine without updates until the downed link is reinstituted. Finally, the link itself may not have enough routing capabilities for traffic to reach other sites. Any of these conditions may require site link bridging to be turned off. To do this, you need to turn off the Bridge All Site Links setting in the IP or SMTP container properties, as shown in Figure 4-25, and then define site link bridge groups manually.

FIGURE 4-25

Disabling default
site link bridging

After you configure the Site Link Bridge setting manually for individual links, the KCC will again be able to use these links to create automatic transitive site links, leaving out those links not included in the group. To create a new site link bridge, right-click the transport container (IP or SMTP), and choose New Site Link Bridge. A screen will prompt you to assign a name for the bridge group and add two or more site links for which bridging should be reenabled.

Replication Transport Selection

Connection objects created by the KCC inherit not only the replication schedule, but also the replication transport. There are three replication transports available in the Active Directory Sites and Services console: RPC, IP, and SMTP. What follows is a brief description of key differences between these three protocols.

- RPC is inherited if the connection object is created for intrasite replication. RPC uses synchronous remote procedure calls over TCP/IP and does not apply compression. It requires a reliable connection throughout the duration of the replication session and places no additional load on the CPU associated with taxing decompression operations.

- IP is inherited for intersite connection objects, if an IP-based SiteLink object is defined in the IP container (it is defined by default). IP transport uses the same calls as RPC and requires a reliable connection throughout the duration of the replication session. The difference between RPC and IP is that IP compresses RPC data, making it more suitable for WAN transfers, but requiring more processing power on both bridgehead servers.

- SMTP is inherited similarly to IP, when the connection object is created for intersite replication, and the SMTP Site Link has been configured in the SMTP container (it is not configured by default). For SMTP to function, you need to enable the Simple Mail Transfer Protocol service on both bridgehead servers. Since SMTP messages are vulnerable to interception and are traditionally submitted in open text, bridgehead servers require Enterprise Certificate Authority in order to encrypt replication messages. SMTP features a few major drawbacks: it does not support intradomain replication (in other words, it cannot be used to replicate domain partition, or naming context, as it is sometimes referred to). Another drawback is service overhead: it carries up to 80 percent more overhead than IP. By default, SMTP site link replication schedules are ignored, and only site link replication periods are used in conjunction with the connection object schedule. SMTP is the best choice when your domains are not separated among several sites (you have one remote site containing one separate child domain) and WAN connectivity is unreliable. SMTP guarantees delivery through session acknowledgments and retransmissions, and can be used to replicate Schema, Configuration, and Application partitions.

Monitor Active Directory Replication Failures

After you deploy an Active Directory environment, you need to ensure that domain controllers are still functioning and are able to accept user requests. Replication cycles must occur in a timely manner and without overloading the network.

In your daily administration tasks, you may encounter a few situations where domain controllers are not functioning as expected, at least as far as replication is concerned. Troubleshooting is always easier if you know what sort of problem you're dealing with. At first glance, problems can be obvious, hidden, or accumulated:

- **Obvious** Some examples of obvious problems that may be detected or even eliminated if the proper change management process is in place are changes in the site structure, replication schedule, Active Directory settings; the addition of new attributes and other schema modifications; the transfer of FSMO roles; and changes in password policies or authentication protocols.

- **Hidden** Some examples of these problems are physical network modifications, firewall setting changes, DNS setting changes, software installation or removal, hardware problems, and failures of auxiliary services in Active Directory, such as KDC, CA, IPSec, and so on. Although some of these changes can also be managed through the change management process, these are not directly related to Active Directory administration, and hence, may not be concentrated in the hands of one person or even one team of administrators. Most of the time, additional troubleshooting is needed to determine the cause.

- **Gradual accumulation of problems** Two main candidates here are replication and disk space. When you start out with your Active Directory environment, chances are, your replica of directory partitions will not be huge, but will grow over time. At some point, it may grow beyond the allowable replication window, resulting in inconsistent Active Directory information across sites for domains. Free disk space on domain controllers is also not used up overnight.

It follows that if you begin troubleshooting after a problem has emerged, the chances of finding the right cause in a timely way are significantly reduced. The situation may be further complicated by secondary problems that become pressing because they're more obvious or have greater impact on users. When Active Directory is not just an OS feature but an infrastructure backbone, administrators should institute recurring monitoring practices, establish performance and usage baselines, and compare daily or weekly results against this baseline. With a solid change management practice, the vast majority of obvious and hidden problems, as well as cumulative problems, will be prevented.

Monitor Active Directory Replication

To support the Active Directory infrastructure, you need to ensure that Active Directory controllers are functioning as expected. The Performance Logs and Alerts snap-in allows administrators to monitor server health. It features several hundred different counters, such as average disk queue length, CPU utilization, current queue length on a network interface, and memory paging, which you can use to diagnose hardware bottlenecks and problems. Although they have ranges of values that indicate whether the system is healthy or not, monitoring these settings in emergencies is not as helpful as monitoring them over a period of time in order to understand which value ranges are common for the system in question. Of course, if you suspect that a hardware component is about to fail, it should be replaced during the next maintenance window. Software applications and third-party processes not directly related to Active Directory should never be installed on domain controllers in the first place, but the focus in this chapter is not on software and hardware.

In addition to monitoring standard hardware performance counters, administrators should pay special attention to the following two performance counter categories:

- NTDS object counters
- Database object counters

NTDS performance object counters allow for monitoring the extent of activity in Active Directory. They present detailed replication stats and a wealth of LDAP and authentication counters.

Database performance object counters provide a wealth of performance information about the Active Directory database functionality and, more specifically, database cache performance and database file and table performance. The Active Directory database is implemented based on extensible storage engine (ESENT) technology, which is also used in products such as Microsoft Exchange Server. One caveat here: the database performance object is not installed by default, and administrators will have to manually register the esentprf.dll dynamic link library and restart the Performance Logs and Alerts console (formerly Performance Monitor) before they can use these counters.

on the **!** **ⓘ** o b

Database counter installation is more involved than just registering a dynamic link library. You can find more information on the process (actually, a script that will do everything for you) in Microsoft's Script Center at https://www .microsoft.com/technet/treeview/default.asp?url=/technet/scriptcenter/monitor /ScrMon08.asp.

But Windows Server 2003 monitoring capabilities go far beyond performance counters that are only good for providing statistical information, which in turn can be used to troubleshoot issues such as hardware or software bottlenecks. The Performance Logs and Alerts console can also be used to configure thresholds and alerts, which will be triggered if the thresholds are breached. You can also define time conditions for breaches. For instance, if CPU usage goes above 95 percent, it is normal for a spike; there is no need to send alerts. However, if it goes above 95 percent and stays there for over five minutes, it may indicate a problem that you want to know about.

Netdiag

Let's begin with a network connection. Successful replication, of course, is not possible without functioning network connectivity. Domain controllers must be able to resolve each other's names using DNS and establish a direct network connection using the TCP/IP protocol. Before troubleshooting each of the steps involved in this process in detail (running **ping, nslookup, tracert**, and so on), you should give Netdiag a try. Netdiag runs some two dozen connectivity and network services tests and displays the results according to the following switches:

- **/q**   Display only errors, that is, tests that have failed
- **/l**   Dump output into a netdiag.log file
- **/v**   Enable verbose mode
- **/fix**   Eliminate trivial problems if they are detected

Dcdiag

When you have established that network connectivity is not an issue, next you have to verify domain controller functionality. Dcdiag.exe runs a set of tests against a domain controller, similar to Netdiag. These tests include

- Connectivity
- Replication
- Topology Integrity
- NC Head Security Descriptors
- Net Logon Rights

- Locator Get Domain Controller
- Intersite Health
- Check Roles
- Trust Verification

Running Dcdiag without switches will launch a series of tests. It starts with a mandatory connectivity test, which verifies name resolution and pings the resolved IP address:

```
Doing initial required tests
   Testing server: Default-First-Site-Name\WIN2003SRV
    Starting test: Connectivity
       ........................ WIN2003SRV passed test Connectivity
```

After this initial test, Dcdiag performs over a dozen primary tests on the local domain controller. Results will be displayed similar to the following:

```
Doing primary tests
   Testing server: Default-First-Site-Name\WIN2003SRV
    Starting test: Replications
       ........................ WIN2003SRV passed test Replications
    Starting test: NetLogons
       ........................ WIN2003SRV passed test NetLogons
```

And so on… Once past these primary tests, Dcdiag proceeds to administer global tests, which apply to the Active Directory environment as a whole. Results pile up on the screen as shown in the preceding code. If you have to perform a single test, or perform a test that is not included in the standard set of tests launched with a simple **dcdiag** command, use the /test:<testname> switch.

Repadmin

The Repadmin utility is used to diagnose replication problems. In addition to the standard functionality accessible through MMC snap-ins, this tool can display some information not available elsewhere. This information includes the time stamp of the last successful replication cycle, error codes if this cycle was not successful, the history of all replication metadata and USNs, lookup of naming context replication parameters, SMTP replication settings, and much more. Repadmin allows digging as deep as it gets; UI tools expose some of this information in a more useful way.

The following code shows a sample of typical output in response to a **repadmin /showreps** command. In this example, you can see that our WIN2003SRV server in the default site replicated Configuration and Schema naming contexts with the Jovidude server located in the Toronto site. Both replications were successful.

```
C:\Documents and Settings\Administrator.WIN2003SRV>repadmin /showreps
Default-First-Site-Name\WIN2003SRV
DC Options: IS_GC
Site Options: (none)
DC object GUID: b0869ebe-018a-44b5-b38f-647bcce67b7a
DC invocationID: b0869ebe-018a-44b5-b38f-647bcce67b7a
==== INBOUND NEIGHBORS ======================================
CN=Configuration,DC=flexecom,DC=com
  Toronto\JOVIDUDE via RPC
    DC object GUID: daa1480f-5899-47cf-818a-933848b3e7db
    Last attempt @ 2003-08-04 22:59:06 was successful.
CN=Schema,CN=Configuration,DC=flexecom,DC=com
  Toronto\JOVIDUDE via RPC
    DC object GUID: daa1480f-5899-47cf-818a-933848b3e7db
    Last attempt @ 2003-08-04 22:59:06 was successful.
```

Monitor File Replication Service

File Replication Service (FRS) is used in Windows Server 2003 (and Windows 2000) to synchronize infrastructure files between domain controllers, and it also can be used to synchronize user data between member servers. SYSVOL folder content, such as group policy files, and DFS replicas are synchronized using FRS. To perform file copy operations between domain controllers and sites, FRS uses the same connection objects available to the replication mechanism of Active Directory.

Administrators should monitor FRS operations using two performance objects:

- **FileReplicaConn** Counters that collect performance stats of connections to DFS roots
- **FileReplicaSet** Counters that collect performance stats of replica sets

Keep in mind a few potential problem areas: First, FRS may stop if there is not enough space to stage replication. Other more obvious factors such as lack of free space on the destination server or network issues may prevent FRS from synchronizing content successfully. FRS network ports may get blocked by firewalls when replicating between sites.

There are three basic options available to administrators when troubleshooting FRS problems:

- Try creating a text file in the SYSVOL directory, wait for the next intersite replication window, and check the SYSVOL directory on domain controllers in other sites to see whether this test file was replicated. This does not diagnose the health or performance of FRS. It just checks whether it is functioning.
- Check the Event Log, File Replication Service. This log contains FRS-related errors, warnings, and informational messages.

■ Try using Ntfrsutl.exe (provided as part of Support Tools) to analyze the service. This utility is used to view FRS tables, memory, and thread information, and may be helpful in troubleshooting more complex FRS issues.

FRS logs can also be examined to expose some useful configuration changes and actual replication information. The Ntfrsapi.log file contains FRS configuration information and related changes, and Ntfrs_000X.log files show replication information. The X is a sequential number that increments when the existing log file fills up and a new log file is created. By default, these log files are located in the %systemroot%\ debug folder, and the maximum number of replication log files is set to 5. This can be adjusted in the HKEY_LOCAL_MACHINE\SYSTEM\CurrentControlSet\ Services\NtFrs\Parameters registry key. When all five replication log files fill up, the first log file is overwritten with newer events. After modifying Registry settings, you will need to restart FRS to make these changes effective.

Lines in FRS logs are quite long and not very convenient for viewing. Notepad may not be the best tool for viewing this information. Use logic to find what you're looking for—if you are looking for error messages, try searching on "fail," or if you suspect one replication partner is at fault, search on its computer name.

To avoid excessive logging, administrators can tweak the Debug Log Severity value in the FRS Registry settings. Try reducing this value to reduce the log message detail. This will cause only the more important messages such as errors and warnings to be logged. Finally, you can use event identifiers in the error messages and search http:// support.microsoft.com site. It is not uncommon for FRS replication to fail due to reasons such as failed RPC connections to the destination server (DNS resolution, slow network, firewall blocking), and lack of free space on the source server, necessary for staging. In addition, checking on whether the rest of Active Directory information is getting through might tell you if there is a problem with schedules (FRS uses the same replication topology and schedules as Active Directory).

Ntfrsutl

You can look up some FRS parameters without accessing the Registry or attributes in Active Directory by using Ntfrsutl. It can also display memory FRS stats and FRS process identifiers. All FRS transactions are stored in a %systemroot%\ntfrs\jet\ntfrs.jdb Microsoft Jet database. Five FRS tables store replica configurations on each computer: there is a dedicated table for connections, inbound and outbound log, version, and ID numbers. (The ID numbers table stores all files included in the replication process that FRS detected; the rest of the tables are self-explanatory.) Ntfrsutl is the only interface that administrators have to this database and table content. You cannot access this database using conventional tools such as Microsoft Access, due to its format.

Launching Ntfrsutl with DS <computername> parameters will display general service settings, subscriber information, replication partners, information about when the last replication attempt was made and what the outcome was, and even the replication partner schedule. Here is a sample replication schedule output:

```
Schedule
Day 1: 5555555555555555555555555
Day 2: 5555555555555555555555555
Day 3: 5555555555555555555555555
Day 4: 5555555555555555555555555
Day 5: 5555555555555555555555555
Day 6: 5555555555555555555555555
Day 7: 5555555555555555555555555
```

The Day column lists the days of the week, Sunday through Saturday. Schedules are stored, and displayed, in binary format. Each decimal number in this listing represents one hour and is made up of four bits (0000), with each bit representing one 15-minute interval. Bit values are, from right to left, 1, 2, 4, and 8. If your replication schedule is set to twice per hour, this would assign an 0101 value to each set of bits, and if you convert this to hex notation by adding 1 and 4, you get 5. Following this scheme, 1 means one replication per hour, 5 means twice every hour, 15 (F in hex) means four times per hour (1 + 2 + 4 + 8), and obviously, 0 means replication is not occurring during the hour in question.

Replication Monitor (Replmon)

Utilities and command-line tools are great when you have to dig deeper, or if you have an automated process running every so often that collects some data and acts accordingly. However, for day-to-day administration, this may not be the best approach. So Windows Server 2003 provides a few familiar graphical user interface tools that allow user-friendly administration, while providing many of the command-line capabilities. Some of the tools included in Windows Server 2003 were inherited from the Resource Kit, and they are not as user friendly as the MMC administration consoles. The Resource Kit was originally developed for administrators who were not satisfied with the functionality available with standard Windows management tools, so the user interface was not critical. The graphical interface tools, such as Replmon, are not included by default in Windows Server 2003, but are installed from Support Tools.

Replmon is the first such utility we look at. It allows you to view replication topology and a wealth of replication information and settings, and it is shown in Figure 4-26.

FIGURE 4-26

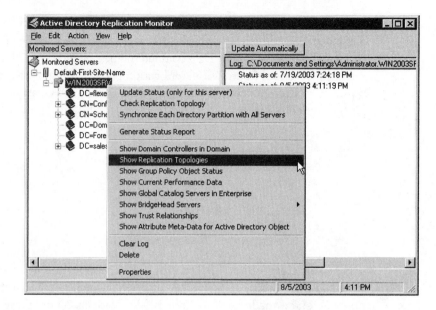

When you first open the Replmon tool, you have to add a server to be monitored. Property pages of the monitored server are accessible through the context menu (as shown in Figure 4-26) and allow you to perform basic troubleshooting. Figure 4-27 shows one of the tabs, FSMO Roles, where you can verify name resolution, connectivity, and binding for each of the five FSMO servers as applicable to the domain of the particular server that you are viewing. In addition to FSMO, other useful troubleshooting information is presented, such as:

- The TCP/IP configuration of the server
- Incoming connection object properties
- Whether the server is designated as a global catalog, if W32time and KDC services are running, and if writing to Active Directory is permitted on the server

One of the key functionalities of Replmon is its ability to generate detailed reports. You can customize the components that should be included every time you generate a status report. This customization page is shown in Figure 4-28.

The following list of steps guides you through the process of viewing replication topology using Replmon—a very useful representation of all intrasite/intersite connection objects in organizations with more than six domain controllers. (Recall

FIGURE 4-27

Server properties
in Replmon

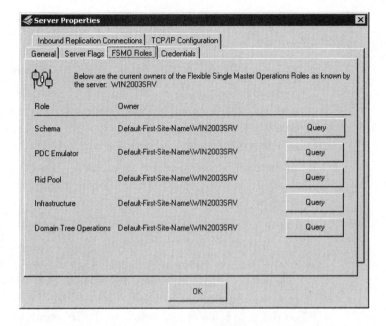

FIGURE 4-28

Customizing
status reports
in Replmon

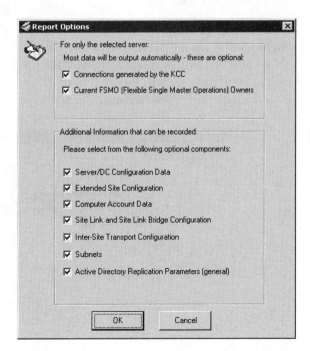

from Chapter 3 that if there are fewer than seven servers in one domain, topology is a simple ring.)

1. To launch Replmon, click Start | Run, type **replmon**, and press ENTER.

2. In the Edit menu, select Add Monitored Server. You will be presented with a wizard, which should help in locating the server you wish to add. Instead of typing in the name of the server, you might want to choose "Search the directory for the server to add" and pick a server from the list of sites and servers.

3. In the context menu of the added server (see Figure 4-26), click Show Replication Topologies. This will open an empty View Replication Topology window.

4. In the View menu of this window, select Connection Objects Only. This will display replication partner servers.

5. In the context menu of each server, as shown in Figure 4-29, you can pick intrasite incoming connection objects to be displayed. If you wish to view intersite connections, you will have to select Properties in the context menu on the server object and switch to the Inbound Replication Connections tab, shown in Figure 4-30.

Results will vary, but with just two servers, you can see that topology is a simple straight line, which is actually two one-way replication connections.

Note that Figure 4-29 shows intrasite connections between two servers when they were moved to the same site. Figure 4-30 shows the Inbound Replication Connections tab for intersite connections when the same two servers were located in different sites.

FIGURE 4-29

Intrasite replication topology in Replmon

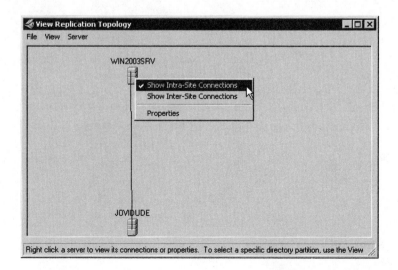

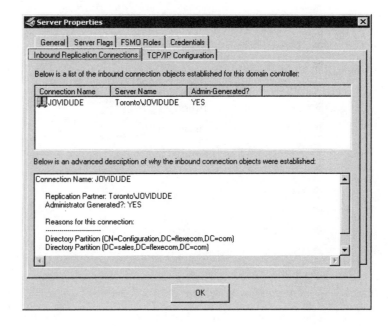

FIGURE 4-30

Inbound
Replication
Connections tab

Event Viewer

Most administrators start their troubleshooting work in Event Viewer. Indeed, the importance of this tool cannot be overstated. Event Viewer can be accessed using the Computer Manager console or as a standalone MMC snap-in in Administrative Tools. Event Log is a convenient display tool of a few *.evt files physically stored in the %systemroot%\system32\config\ directory. Since most of you reading this book will be familiar with Event Viewer, this section only mentions a few things as they relate to Active Directory troubleshooting.

The Directory Service log is present on domain controller computers, and all Active Directory–related information is logged here. By default, only critical errors and warnings are logged, as shown in Figure 4-31. However, you can adjust the level of detail using the HKEY_LOCAL_MACHINE\SYSTEM\CurrentControlSet\Services\NTDS\Diagnostics Registry key. Each of the values in this key is responsible for its own message category, which corresponds to Active Directory components. Available components are listed here:

- Knowledge Consistency Checker (KCC)
- Security events
- ExDS interface events
- MAPI interface events
- Replication events

- Garbage collection
- Internal configuration
- Directory access
- Internal processing
- Performance counters
- Initialization/termination
- Service control
- Name resolution
- Backup
- Field engineering
- LDAP interface events
- Setup
- global catalog
- Intersite messaging

The level of detail for all of these components can be set from 0 to 5, where 0 will only log critical events and errors, and 5 will enable logging of all events. The highest setting might limit the usefulness of the event log and place an unnecessary burden on the system, so detailed logging should not be used on a daily basis. For most Active Directory troubleshooting, the first two or three levels are sufficient, but if you have to raise the level, don't forget to throttle it back when troubleshooting is done.

FIGURE 4-31

Directory Service log in Event Viewer

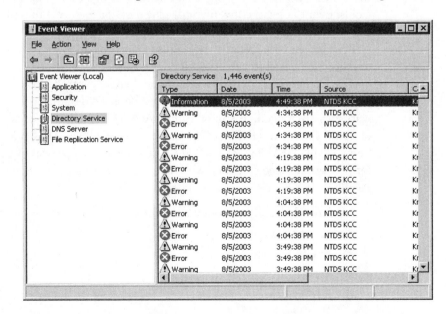

CERTIFICATION OBJECTIVE 4.04

Restore Active Directory Services

You may run into a situation in which administrative personnel made some Active Directory changes that later proved to be undesirable (for instance, if an object or two were deleted, or attribute values were overwritten and these changes were replicated to other domain controllers). You may experience hardware failures—such as the Active Directory database hard disk (or set of disks) going defunct as a result of a natural disaster or bad hardware—which add to the reasons why you should back up Active Directory data.

Hardware-related outages don't matter that much in environments that were built specifically to avoid single points of failure, that is, where systems are not affected by an outage of a single component—a domain controller in this case. If one of the many domain controllers fails and it does not provide any FSMO services, from the Active Directory perspective, the impact will be negligible. All you have to do to restore the server is to replace the bad hardware and **dcpromo** it back. If this server was used for FSMO roles, you move or seize FSMO roles to other domain controllers, and then follow the steps as if it were a plain domain controller.

However, some domains in your organization may not warrant more than one domain controller, and should a domain controller fail in a single-DC environment, you may need to recover AD data. Also, when a change is committed to a domain partition in Active Directory, it gets propagated to other domain controllers in this domain almost instantly; and if you later realize this change was made by mistake, it's too late to undo it.

One thing to keep in mind is that you cannot just reverse the impact of a deleted user account by re-creating it, giving it the same name, logon name, password, and the rest of the settings. The system will have assigned this "old" account a new SID, which will make it a completely different security principal from the permissions point of view. The same holds true about any security principal, be it a computer account, user account, or a security group. Deleting one account may not be a huge deal, depending on what impact it has on the system. (For example, deleting a user account that was used on a number of servers to schedule tasks and to run services may pose a big problem for administrators.) However, deleting a meaningful number of user accounts, or demoting the last domain controller from a child domain, is a more complicated matter.

So let's summarize. We have two major categories of problems that may warrant restoring Active Directory: total loss of Active Directory data, or accidental changes to objects or attributes that need to be undone. Microsoft has two distinct yet similar solutions to address these situations: authoritative and nonauthoritative restore of system state information. An *authoritative restore* performs a restore operation in a multi-DC environment and replicates the restored copy of objects to all other domain controllers, overwriting their copies of restored objects. A *nonauthoritative restore* performs a restore operation and accepts all Active Directory changes from other domain controllers—changes that were made after the backup operation was performed.

System State Backup

If one or more drives fails on a domain controller and Active Directory information is lost, you can either replace the server and reinstall the OS and then **dcpromo** to Active Directory, or you can attempt to recover Active Directory using a system state backup, if it exists. If you go with the **dcpromo** suggestion, it will copy the current Active Directory naming context onto the domain controller you are restoring. If you choose to go with system state backup, you will not have to worry about the following:

- Restoring from a system state backup does not interfere with FSMO roles; you do not have to move roles to other servers.
- You do not have to remove the failed domain controller from the Active Directory database. (You will have to remove the failed DC from Active Directory if you choose not to restore it.)
- When you restore the system state, additional information, such as the Registry, COM objects, and Certification Authority, is restored as well. This is not something that will happen by simply running **dcpromo** on a newly rebuilt box.

System state backup covers the following components:

- Boot and system files
- Registry
- Active Directory data
- SYSVOL directory
- COM+ Class Registration data
- Cluster service data (if the server was a cluster member)
- IIS data (if IIS was installed on the server)
- Certificate Services data (if a CA was installed on the server)

For various reasons, some files and Registry keys may not be needed for backup. These files and keys are defined in HKLM\System\CurrentControlSet\Control\BackupRestore\FilesNotToBackup and HKLM\System\CurrentControlSet\Control\BackupRestore\KeysNotToBackup Registry keys, respectively.

Active Directory–related files that are included in the system state backup are the main database and corresponding transaction log file (ntds.dit and edb.log), and the SYSVOL directory, which stores all group policies and logon script files. Note that it is not possible to restore these files without performing the entire system state backup— think of this as an all-or-nothing operation.

To perform a system state backup, you need to be a member of either the Backup Operators or Domain Admins group, but restoring from a system state backup is not allowed unless you have Domain or Enterprise Admins group membership. Administrators can take advantage of the built-in backup and restore utility, NTBACKUP, that has been there since the early NT days, or go with fancier enterprise backup solutions; but it will not be possible to back up system files manually or using scripts, because most of them have locks and are being used. There is no reason why NTBACKUP should not be used for system state backups.

NTBACKUP now starts in a wizard mode by default, but on the first wizard screen you can click Advanced Mode to get rid of the wizard and switch to the traditional NTBACKUP interface, shown in Figure 4-32.

On the Backup tab, shown in Figure 4-32, select System State. It is also recommended that you back up system and boot partitions to minimize potential file version conflicts in case you have to reinstall the system and recover the system state. The System State option will back up critical system files, but it will not back up the entire %systemroot%

FIGURE 4-32

Backing up system state data using NTBACKUP

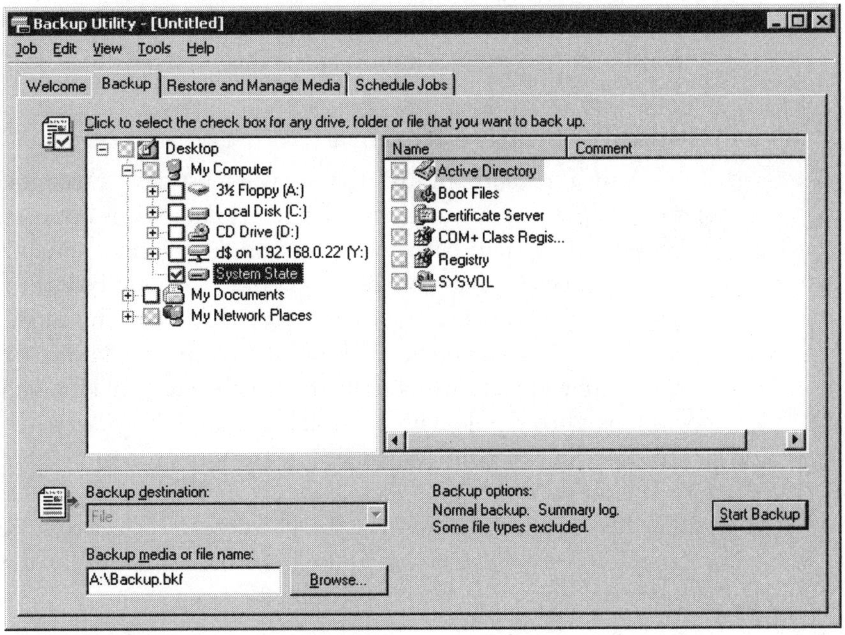

directory. When you are done selecting what needs to be backed up, you will then need to provide some information about where you want to locate the backup.

If you have a tape device attached to the system and ready for use, in the Backup Destination box you should be able to select either Tape or File. If no tape devices are found, File will remain the only option available. Here, you can use either local paths or UNC pathnames, and back up to a network share instead, where production backup systems may further back up individual system state backups to a centralized tape device. One problem with system state backups is that they cannot be performed over the network from a central network backup machine.

on the job

The total size of a system state backup will vary depending on the size of Active Directory partitions and installed services, but on average, on a newly installed domain controller without any Active Directory infrastructure implementation or object population, it can easily take half a gigabyte.

Some situations may make restoring undesirable; we review them later in this chapter. First, let's take a look at how to restore Active Directory on one of the domain controllers using authoritative and nonauthoritative restores. The tricky part here is when you restore a "good" copy from backup, in most cases it will be older than those copies sitting on other domain controllers. Depending on which of the two categories of catastrophic domain controller failures you are dealing with, you will need to decide how the postrestore replication should take place: from the restored domain controller out to all other domain controllers, or the other way around. Authoritative and nonauthoritative restores are the mechanisms you will need to use.

Nonauthoritative Restore

To perform a nonauthoritative restore, you must have a recent copy of the system state backup. Restoring an Active Directory database is not possible by simply using NTBACKUP or third-party tools. In order to perform a nonauthoritative restore, after fixing the root cause that took the server down, you must boot the failed domain controller in a special directory services restore mode (DSRM). This mode will force continued operation of a limited number of device drivers that are known to work reliably and will enable Active Directory functionality, which is required for database access and restore operations while the domain controller is online.

To boot your domain controller for a restore process, press F8 when you see a boot screen prompt, and choose Active Directory Restore Mode. Domain authentication will be disabled, so you must use the Directory Services Restore Mode Administrator account. You will have provided the password as part of the **dcpromo** process when this domain controller was first installed.

*DSRM passwords are worth including in disaster recovery documentation. In the absence of such documentation, administrators who forget this password and need to reset it should use the Ntdsutil command-line interface with the set dsrm password **command**. Ntdsutil is discussed in the next section and in the troubleshooting section.*

Upon logon, you should use NTBACKUP again, this time to restore Active Directory databases. To do this, click the Restore and Manage Media tab, (which is identical to the tab shown earlier in Figure 4-32,) expand the media that you want to use for your restore, click System State, and then the Start Restore button. The process is fairly straightforward, except that you first have to boot into DSRM and be mindful of potential system file conflicts: if you are restoring the system state over a new installation of Windows Server 2003, you may need to restore the boot partition first and then reboot the server. System state data will overwrite certain system files that may "break" a newly installed server if the server does not have corresponding versions of all other %systemroot% files, which are not included in the system state backup.

After the restore procedure, you can safely reboot your domain controller into normal mode. This completes the nonauthoritative restore process. Be aware that nonauthoritative restore does not adjust USNs of the objects it restores, which means that peer domain controllers will replicate all of the changes made to Active Directory objects since this backup was created. This is no help if you are working on restoring a group of user accounts that were deleted by accident; however, in the following cases, nonauthoritative restores are sufficient:

- When only one domain controller is used in the domain. This situation is conceivable only in small businesses or in remote branches, which have their own domains and having two domain controllers is not justified from the hardware expense perspective. Performing regular, timely system state backups is the only way to recover from a domain controller disaster in this case.

- When you simply need to restore a domain controller and bring it back online after a hardware failure, in which case replication of the most up-to-date changes from other domain controllers is a good thing.

Authoritative Restore

An authoritative restore differs from nonauthoritative in that the restored objects are assigned higher USNs than the respective USNs on other domain controllers, causing restored objects to be replicated to other domain controllers instead of being overwritten, as in nonauthoritative backups. Obviously, in addition to restoring objects, an authoritative restore needs to adjust some of their properties in the Active Directory database. Table 4-4 summarizes these changes.

TABLE 4-4	Type of Change	Attribute Change
Metadata Changes During Authoritative Restore	Domain controller changes	Highest-Committed-USN attribute USN-Changed attribute
	Object changes	When-Changed attribute USN-Changed attribute
	Attribute changes	Originating-DC-GUID attribute Originating-USN attribute Version attribute When-Changed attribute Property-USN attribute Is-Deleted attribute

When-Changed attributes are time-stamped with the current date/time reading, and USNs are set much higher than current USNs on other controllers to make sure that there is enough room to accommodate changes being committed on other domain controllers while the authoritative restore is taking place.

Authoritative restores are used only to recover from unplanned object state changes and attribute value changes in domain and configuration partitions. Authoritative restores cannot be used to recover from schema changes. This is why administrators are advised to exercise a great deal of caution when making changes to the schema—restoring schemas may cause data inconsistencies and loss, so schema partition is not subject to authoritative restores.

Within configuration and domain partitions, administrators can selectively restore certain data, or entire partitions. To perform an authoritative restore, you use Ntdsutil in addition to the steps covered in the "Nonauthoritative Restore" section earlier in this chapter.

The process is basically the same: boot the domain controller into DSRM, use NTBACKUP to restore system state data; but before a reboot can take place, you need to execute a few commands within Ntdsutil.

1. Click Start | Run, type **CMD**, and press ENTER. This will launch the command prompt.

2. Type **ntdsutil** and press ENTER. This will switch to the Ntdsutil command-line interface.

3. Next, type **authoritative restore** and press ENTER again to switch to the **authoritative restore** command context.

4. Now you need to set how you wish to restore Active Directory data. Use Table 4-5 to make an appropriate selection for your situation, and enter it in Ntdsutil.

5. This completes authoritative restore. Keep typing **quit** and pressing ENTER until you exit Ntdsutil, and reboot your domain controller.

on the
Job *You do not have to type full commands in Ntdsutil. It is sufficient to type just a few letters to make sure the input can be parsed into commands unambiguously. Authoritative restore, for example, can be shortened to au re.*

Table 4-5 describes four main command choices, one of which must be executed while in the **authoritative restore** command context, to make this restore authoritative.

Why would you want to specify the version increment manually? Well, it is conceivable that one authoritative restore was already performed and was not very successful. Now you want to use another domain controller to overwrite the previous authoritative restore with the new authoritative restore. This is where you need to jump ahead of USNs from the previous authoritative restore by a safe margin. Instead of the default 10,000, you might want to specify, say, 15,000.

Another important thing to keep in mind here is that you will want to minimize the extent of the authoritative restore in the partition, because restoring the entire configuration or domain partition may revert computer and trust passwords to their states at the time of backup on a larger scale, and you might have to do more work by resetting them manually after the restore.

Upon rebooting your domain controller, two things will happen. The restored Active Directory will receive and commit to its database the changes made from the time of backup, but only for those naming contexts (a.k.a., partitions), or portions of naming contexts, that were not marked as authoritative. Those naming contexts, or portions of naming contexts, that were marked as authoritative will replicate to other domain controllers in the organization (domain context to domain controllers in the same domain, and configuration context to all domain controllers in the forest).

TABLE 4-5	Authoritative Restore Commands

Command	Description
Restore database	This marks the entire configuration and domain partitions as authoritative. USNs are increased by 10,000.
Restore database verinc <number>	This marks the entire configuration and domain partitions as authoritative and increases USNs by <number> value.
Restore subtree <LDAP path>	This marks a portion of either configuration or domain data as authoritative, as specified in <LDAP path>. This must be an absolute, not relative, reference to an LDAP container. In practical terms, "container" here means OU. Note that this will restore all child objects in the OU, all of its subcontainers, and their respective child objects as well. USNs are increased by 10,000 by default.
Restore subtree <LDAP path> verinc <number>	This command is similar to the preceding one in what it will mark as authoritative. The difference here is that you have control over the default USN increment value.

Backup Age Issues

Restoring Active Directory databases that are more than 60 days old is generally not done and can lead to serious problems. When Active Directory objects are deleted, they are first marked as "tombstoned" (but are not removed from the AD database) and, after a configurable period of time (60 days by default), are deleted from the database during the garbage collection routine, which runs twice daily. Garbage collection removes all unnecessary records from the data and log file, and this freed-up space is later reclaimed by a defrag process. By restoring a backup that is older than 60 days, you risk creating phantom objects, that is, reinstating an active instance of a nonexistent object.

To avoid this conflict, you should always try to use the latest system state backup, or if you have to roll back more than 60 days, you can extend the delay between the time that objects are tombstoning and when they are removed from the database. Access this setting using the ADSI Edit MMC console, in the CN=Directory Service,CN=Windows NT,CN=Services,CN=Configuration,DC=<domain name>,DC=<tld> container. Right-click the Directory Service container and select Properties. This will display all available attributes. Find the tombstoneLifetime attribute in the list and set the desired value. Figure 4-33 shows this process.

Note, however, that you need to plan ahead and make this attribute modification before performing the system state backup. This strategy cannot be used as a quick-fix solution to the 60-day problem when disaster strikes.

FIGURE 4-33

Adjusting the default tombstoneLifetime value

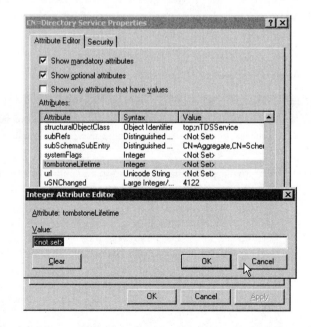

CERTIFICATION OBJECTIVE 4.05

Troubleshoot Active Directory

Active Directory will not function as expected without FSMO role server availability. Recall from Chapter 3 that there are five FSMO types, with two roles having forest scope and three, domain scope. Whenever there is a problem with FSMO servers—for example, if one of them becomes unavailable, malfunctions, or runs on more than one controller at a time—administrator intervention will be required.

FSMO role servers help manage domain and forest naming contexts. Naming contexts need to be stored on fault-tolerant hardware, and replication mechanisms must be reliable in order to maintain the same databases on many domain controllers regardless of the changes that are constantly being committed. Windows Server 2003 takes care of the latter with its replication engine, but there is no guarantee that you will not run into hardware issues on your domain controllers.

In this last part of the chapter, we will review what administrators can and should do to correct typical problems associated with FSMO server outages and other Active Directory–related problems.

Troubleshooting Failures of Operations Master Roles

Again, Active Directory has two FSMO roles with forest scope, and three with domain scope:

- Schema Master (forest)
- Domain Naming Master (forest)
- PDC Emulator (domain)
- RID Master (domain)
- Infrastructure Master (domain)

If you have three domains, a total of 11 FSMO roles will have to be maintained along with at least six domain controllers. (Remember that in this situation you do not want to place the Infrastructure Master and global catalog server together.) If one of the masters becomes unavailable, you may see some unusual behavior when performing certain domain or forest operations. Administrators will need to use MMC snap-ins such as Active Directory Users and Computers (for FSMOs with domain scope), Active

Directory Schema (Schema Master), and Active Directory Domains and Trusts (Domain Naming Master) to transfer FSMO roles to functional domain controllers. If transferring fails, you may need to seize the role from a server and make sure that the former owner of this role is taken offline permanently to avoid potential FSMO conflicts.

When FSMO domain controllers go offline, in addition to obvious domain controller functions being unavailable, other domain or forest functionality may be impacted indirectly, as described next.

Impact of Master Role Outages

In the case of a Schema Master outage:

- It will not be possible to create new attributes or classes, or perform any schema modifications for that matter.
- You will not be able to install applications that modify schemas—Exchange Server is a popular example.

An outage of the Domain Naming Master has the following impact:

- Any operations on domains, such as adding or removing domains from the forest, will be disabled.

An outage of the PDC Emulator will result in the following:

- The Windows NT 4.0 BDC domain controller will lose sight of the Windows Server 2003 environment. This is tantamount to taking the NT 4.0 PDC domain controller offline.
- Older client operating systems without Active Directory client software will not be able to log on to the network. If your network still has NT 4.0 BDCs, they will be able to pick up the slack and service logon requests for the duration of the PDC Emulator outage, but they will not be able to perform account modifications such as password changes.
- Rapid replication of security-sensitive changes in the domain will be disabled. The PDC Emulator implements one-to-all NT 4.0–style replication of changes, such as resetting passwords and changing account status to disabled.
- NetBIOS computer browsing may not work, if PDC Emulator was elected as the master browser.

A RID Master outage has the following impact:

■ In the early stages, a RID Master outage may go largely unnoticed. RID responsibility is to assign unique security identifier sequences within each domain, and it assigns a range of sequences. While this range lasts, you may be OK, but once it gets depleted, you will likely experience problems creating new security principals—user, computer, and group objects.

Finally, in the case of an Infrastructure Master outage:

■ User group membership changes may not be reflected in other domains in a multidomain environment.

Transferring and Seizing FSMO Roles

It is possible to transfer a role if the existing master is still available on the network—that is, if it is still up and running, you can connect to it and commit changes to its Active Directory partitions. This option is preferred. To transfer any of the three domain FSMOs, launch the Active Directory Users and Computers snap-in on a domain controller where you want to transfer these roles to, right-click the domain container in question, and choose Operations Masters in the context menu. Figure 4-34 shows the dialog box that will be presented.

FIGURE 4-34

Transferring
domain
FSMO roles

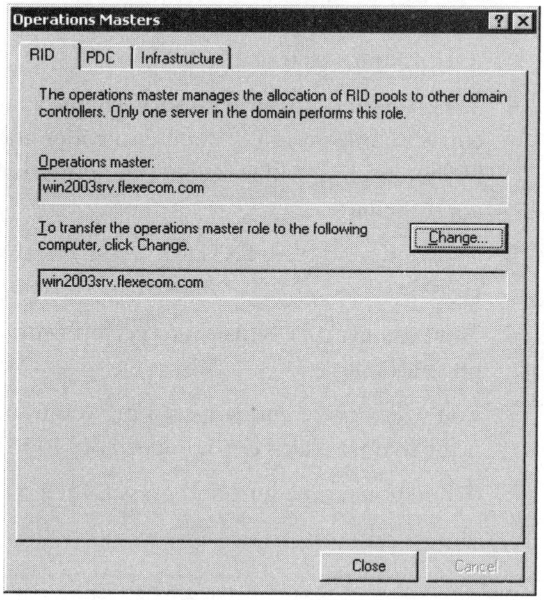

Here you can perform the transfer as necessary. Using this console you can also connect to any other domain controller in your infrastructure, so it is not entirely necessary to be physically logged on to a machine that will get FSMO roles. Transferring forest FSMO roles is very similar, except you use the Schema or Domains and Trusts snap-ins instead of Active Directory Users and Computers.

If the domain controller you are transferring from is not available anymore, you will have to use Ntdsutil to seize the FSMO role forcibly. Exercise 4-1 takes you through this process step-by-step.

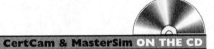

EXERCISE 4-1

CertCam & MasterSim ON THE CD

Using Ntdsutil to Seize an FSMO Role

In this exercise, you use Ntdsutil to forcibly reconfigure the Active Directory domain naming context to reflect an outage of a PDC Emulator role domain controller.

1. Click Start | Run, type **ntdsutil**, and press ENTER. This will launch the Ntdsutil command-line interface.

2. At the prompt, type **Roles** and press ENTER. This will switch the command context to FSMO Maintenance.

3. Next, type **Connections** and press ENTER again. Before you can seize the FSMO role, you need to establish a connection to a domain controller where you want to transfer this role.

4. Type **Connect to server <servername>**, and press ENTER. If you provide a correct name (it is a domain controller and the name can be resolved using DNS), binding will succeed, providing that local console user permissions are sufficient.

5. Type **quit** and press ENTER to return to the FSMO Maintenance command context.

6. Now you instruct Ntdsutil to perform the seize operation. Type **seize pdc** and press ENTER.

7. You will receive a message asking you to confirm that this is really what you want to do. Click Yes to proceed or No to cancel.

8. When done, type **quit** and press ENTER. (Do this twice to quit Ntdsutil altogether.)

When you seize a role, the Active Directory configuration partition is pointed to a new server for a given role, which completely ignores the fact that the former FSMO master is now unavailable. This may lead to a problem where you have more than one instance of the same FSMO role, should you decide to bring the former master online or restore it from backup. You will need to completely remove Active Directory from the former master server. If the regular Dcpromo process has failed for one reason or another, **dcpromo /forceremoval** will help to accomplish this.

Troubleshooting Replication Failures

Replication problems can be caused by a multitude of situations. To determine whether there is a replication problem, check Event Viewer, or use **repadmin /showreps** to view the status of inbound connections and the most recent replication information. Table 4-6 lists some of the possible error messages and potential causes that result in disrupted replication, but this list is not exhaustive.

TABLE 4-6	Repadmin /Showreps Status Error Messages

Error Message	Reason/Troubleshooting Steps
Access denied	This condition may be caused by outdated computer account passwords that correspond to domain controllers that are having this problem. There was probably a lengthy connectivity outage or a technical problem that forced a domain controller offline for a while. To correct this problem, you need to stop KDC service and use **netdom resetpwd** to reset the computer account password. Next, use **repadmin /add** to reestablish replication partner connections with other domain controllers, and then restart KDC services.
Authentication service is unknown	This error is likewise related to KDC service, so the first thing you need to do is to stop the service to reset Kerberos tickets. Next, depending on the status of connections, you will need to use **repadmin /sync** to synchronize naming contexts, or **repadmin /kcc** to regenerate replication topology. When finished, start KDC services.
Target account name is incorrect	This error may be caused by inconsistent sets of service principal names on domain controllers located in the same domain naming context, or a missing trustedDomain object between separate domain naming contexts. You can re-create the trustedDomain object by removing and reestablishing the existing trust relationship. If that does not work, you may want to look at SPNs for computer accounts using the ADSI Edit MMC snap-in.

TABLE 4-6   Repadmin /Showreps Status Error Messages *(continued)*

Error Message	Reason/Troubleshooting Steps
RPC server not available, DNS lookup failure	This is most likely a product of a network-related issue, and should be treated as such. You may want to start by testing DNS resolutions using NSLOOKUP, then try telnetting from one replication partner to the other on port 135 (RPC). If you can establish a connection using the DNS name in telnet, it is guaranteed not to be a network issue. Another step you may want to take is flushing the DNS cache locally and on the DNS server using **ipconfig /flushdns** and the Clear DNS Cache option on the context menu. Ping and Tracert tools may further be used to troubleshoot lower-level network problems. Check on whether the _msdcs.<forestname>. DNS zone is available and configured as it should be.
Directory service too busy	This condition may be caused by a duplicated connection object. You may have to use the LDP utility to search for duplication and delete it manually.
No more end-point	A fault in physical TCP/IP connectivity may cause this error. Incorrect DNS resolution of the name, which will give a wrong IP address, is another potential issue. Although unlikely, if the target replication partner is bogged down by a huge number of TCP/IP sessions—perhaps a denial-of-service attack is in progress, for example—it may result in this error.
Replication system encountered an internal error	One possible problem here may be an authoritative restore that was older than the tombstoneLifetime interval (60 days by default), which may have created phantom objects. You will first need to find globally unique identifiers (GUIDs) of these objects and then use tools such as LDP to search by GUID and remove all instances of these objects from Active Directory.
Time difference	You may receive error messages stating that a time synchronization window longer than allowed was detected. This is a rare issue—remember that Kerberos authentication is time sensitive. If, for any reason, the domain controller clock is out of sync with the rest of the domain (time zone settings are factored in), this may make this domain controller inaccessible for all other domain controllers and client machines. A time difference may result from a malfunctioning Windows Time service or, more likely, if someone manually adjusted the computer time. If this problem is on just one controller, give the **Net Time \\<PDCEmulatorName> /set** command a try. If the problem has been detected on more than one computer, this may be an indication of a more fundamental Windows Time service problem.

Troubleshooting Active Directory Database Failures

When you perform domain controller installation, the Dcpromo Wizard will ask you, among other things, where you wish to place the ntds.dit and edb.log data and transaction log files. By default, the %systemroot%\ntds directory is suggested, but this is far from ideal. You should always place your Active Directory files on a fault-tolerant set of hardware disks, and preferably on a drive that does not contain any system files or pagefile.sys. If your Active Directory domain controllers will be hit with a massive amount of production traffic (in other words, if your IT environment has hundreds of users or more) and you need to ensure both reliability and optimum performance, you might consider placing the data file on a separate RAID0 or RAID5 volume, and transaction logs on their own RAID1 volume.

Placing the main data file on RAID0 will ensure optimum read/write performance, but you must have a solid backup strategy in place because RAID0 provides no fault tolerance. RAID5, on the other hand, does provide fault tolerance but at a cost of write performance (it needs to calculate and write to disk additional parity information on the fly). So if most of your Active Directory operations are reads, RAID5 is a more sensible solution.

Table 4-7 shows Microsoft's estimates of what size your Active Directory database should be expected to grow to. Other factors such as the tombstoneLifetime period, garbage collection frequency, and database fragmentation state and defragmentation maintenance schedules will have an impact on the total size of the database. When your Active Directory is started, the database engine sets up two empty log files, res1.log and res2.log, each of which is 10MB in size. When the system runs down to less than 10 percent of free disk space on any volume, a warning is posted to the system log.

When Active Directory can no longer write data to the log due to space shortages, an error message will be posted to the system log again, but the Directory engine will be able to survive for a while using a reserved 20MB of space. Depending on overall database size and, more importantly, the amount of activity, it may go through 20MB rather quickly. Needless to say, administrators should institute daily checks or, better yet, automated monitoring and alerting of things like drive space to avoid the use of reserved log space. If it runs out of space, Active Directory will shut down.

As a side note, administrators should be aware of how the ESE database engine works. (This is true not only of Active Directory but of any Microsoft product implemented using this engine—sticking to our traditional example, Microsoft Exchange is one of them.) Log files (edb.log and all files such as edbNNNNN.log, where NNNNN is an incrementing sequence of numbers) are maintained for database transactions. Any database change, such as a modified attribute or added OU or object, is a transaction. Transactions are not written to log files immediately. First they are written to memory to ensure speedy response, and when the server becomes idle or when memory gets full, transactions are written to the log file.

TABLE 4-7	Object Type	Estimated Size in Database
Approximate Database Space Usage	User object	3.7KB
	Organizational unit container	1.1KB
	Attribute (10 byte value)	Approx. 100 bytes

on the
Job

Always try to shut down the domain controller gracefully. Some transactions may still be sitting in memory and will be lost if you pull the plug. These changes are usually the latest, and depending on the circumstances, they may not have been replicated to other domain controllers yet. It is important to ensure that production domain controllers have not only a redundant disk subsystem but also redundant power supplies from an uninterruptible power source.

Log files, again for faster performance, are allocated with 10MB each all at once (increasing the log file size is also taxing in terms of performance). When the first log file, edb.log, fills up, transactions are written to the next log file, edb00002.log, and so on. Remember that transactions are never written to the data file directly. Imagine what would happen to performance if you had to write hundreds of transactions per second to a file that is 20GB in size. Instead, 10MB log files keep accumulating and rolling over up to a certain point.

This "certain point" is system state backup. When system state backup is initiated, the database goes into backup mode, and a temporary transaction file is created that is used to write all transactions during the backup. Actual log files are frozen, and all transactions from those logs are committed to the database file (ntds.dit). After the transactions from log files are committed, logs are backed up as well and are removed from the disk. Note that committing logs to the database file does not mean a one-for-one data file increase.

The total size of the database plus logs will be less after the backup because logs usually contain plenty of changes that are overwriting each other if you reconstruct the events according to the timeline. Then, the temporary log file gets backed up as well, and the database is returned to the normal state, with only two live transaction log files—edb.log, and the second (empty) log, edb00002.log. Backups, therefore, do not shut down the database for the duration of the process.

From the preceding paragraphs, it follows that the data file (ntds.dit) stores the biggest chunk of data, except for the latest changes to Active Directory objects that were made after the latest backup. Therefore, administrators must treat log files as if they were actual data files (they sort of are data files). If you are wondering why your log files have filled up all the space you have thrown at them, it is probably due to a massive amount of current activity, and/or it has been a while since you performed a backup. Also note that it is not possible to perform a differential or incremental backup against an Active Directory database, so any type of backup that includes system state will produce the same result, as described.

Ntdsutil

If you are running out of space on the log volume, perhaps it's time to perform a backup. However, if your data file is on the same volume, you may need to move logs or data files to another volume. To perform this operation, you must boot your domain controller into directory service restore mode and use Ntdsutil to move files elsewhere:

1. Click Start | Run, type **ntdsutil**, and press ENTER. This will launch the Ntdsutil command-line interface.

2. Issue the Files command to switch to the file manipulation command context.

3. You have four choices: Move DB to <location>, Move Logs to <location>, Set Path DB <path>, and Set Path Logs <path>. The choices obviously suggest that you can either use Ntdsutil to move files and adjust Registry settings, or adjust the Registry settings and move files later manually. When you have files sitting on the disk and you want to move them, the Move command is the best choice. If you restored AD files from backup onto a drive that has more space, then the Set Path command makes more sense. <Location> and <path> are the same—the utility is expecting a full path, including the volume letter, where you wish to move the files or correct the Registry.

4. Type **quit** and press ENTER (repeat twice to quit Ntdsutil).

Those familiar with database technologies may be wondering by now if there is a way to check the integrity of an Active Directory database, and if it is possible to repair a database corruption. The answer is yes to both questions. Even healthy RAID arrays may throw occasional read or write errors under heavy stress, especially if your system uses a relatively new drive technology where system developers did not cover enough mileage to know of all possible performance-related issues. This was the case with some fiber HBAs and SCSI Ultra320 implementations in the early days.

If you suspect an AD database integrity problem, especially after read/write errors have been posted to the system log, you should research your hardware options and probably move database and log files to another volume. Then, using Ntdsutil, you can choose one of three options to perform database diagnostics and repair operations: Integrity, Recovery, and Repair. (Those familiar with ESEUTIL.EXE will recognize these options.)

■ **Integrity** This command is used to verify the integrity of the Active Directory database (data file). It will run a logical and physical inconsistency scan in an attempt to find any header or table inconsistencies or damage. The integrity check will read the entire data store, and thus if your database files are large, be sure to allow enough time to perform the integrity check.

■ **Recovery** The recovery process is your next step if integrity verification yielded some problems. This operation is also performed automatically if the last shutdown was not graceful. It scans the log files and attempts to replay them against the main data file. Every time an ESE database is started, it is automatically marked as "dirty shutdown." Unless you shut down the involved processes gracefully, this state will remain unchanged and will be detected the next time the database is initiated, and the recovery process will be attempted by the system automatically. If this process fails, your next best option is to restore from the latest backup and replay the transaction logs to "roll forward" all the changes that have occurred since the latest backup.

If you do not have a backup, or if transaction logs are damaged and cannot be replayed, the situation is getting interesting. If restoring from a backup is an option but log files are damaged, you may need to restore from backup and forget about rolling forward your transactions to the point of failure. (This is why it is recommended that you keep transaction logs on a mirrored volume, but it may not prevent all types of log problems.) If your environment has multiple domain controllers in each domain, this may not be a big issue because most of the changes will get replicated from other domain controllers. If backups do not exist, you may need to run a repair process.

■ **Repair** The repair process is used to perform a low-level physical repair of the main database file, without replaying logs. This may be used to address corruption problems; however, this should be your last resort because there is a high chance of losing some data, which may result in logical inconsistencies in the database.

All three database operations are performed using Ntdsutil, involving the ESENTUTL.exe tool that does the actual database work. This tool cannot work against the database while Active Directory is running, so you will have to restart the server and choose Directory Services Recovery Mode. Output from a help screen of the ESENTUTL tool is shown here:

```
DESCRIPTION: Maintenance utilities for Microsoft(R) Windows(R) databases.
MODES OF OPERATION:
    Defragmentation: ESENTUTL /d <database name> [options]
         Recovery: ESENTUTL /r <logfile base name> [options]
        Integrity: ESENTUTL /g <database name> [options]
```

```
   Checksum: ESENTUTL /k <database name> [options]
     Repair: ESENTUTL /p <database name> [options]
  File Dump: ESENTUTL /m[mode-modifier] <filename>
<<<<< Press a key for more help >>>>>
D=Defragmentation, R=Recovery, G=inteGrity, K=checKsum, P=rePair, M=file duMp
```

Note the defragmentation option. Active Directory will run the defragmentation process automatically; this is called online defragmentation. "Online" means that the Active Directory database will not be taken offline and will service user requests normally, maybe a bit slower due to higher than normal disk activity and memory usage. However, online defrags are usually not as effective as offline defrags. If you are running low on space, and there are no hardware upgrades on the horizon, you may want to try offline defrag first.

Generally speaking, offline defrags are not something you should do often, but running one once a month or a quarter may not be a bad idea. Ntdsutil is again used as an interface to the ESENTUTL tool. All database operations are performed from the Files context, and yes, you need to run in DSRM to perform any of these operations. Depending on how long and for what purpose Active Directory has been used up to this point, you may see some dramatic file size reductions.

The last Ntdsutil option to cover is Semantic Database Analysis. This will perform the logical scan of information specific to Active Directory, such as:

- Synchronization state of each naming context
- Presence of GUID numbers for each object
- Deleted objects' dates
- SID numbers of security principals

To run this analysis, go through the following steps (assuming the domain controller is in the directory services recovery mode):

1. Click Start | Run, type **ntdsutil**, and press ENTER. This will launch Ntdsutil.

2. Type **Semantic Database Analysis** and press ENTER. This will switch to the **semantic analysis** command context.

3. If you only wish to view analysis data, type **go** and press ENTER. Otherwise, to view the analysis and attempt to correct detected inconsistencies, type **go fixup** and press ENTER.

4. When done, type **quit** and press ENTER (repeat twice to quit Ntdsutil).

SCENARIO & SOLUTION

Is it possible to limit access to a few selected servers when using cross-forest trust relationships?	Yes. To achieve this, choose the Selective Authentication option when you create cross-forest trusts. Then assign Allowed to Authenticate permission to selected users on selected server objects in the Active Directory Users and Computers snap-in.
Is it possible to construct your own OID?	Even if you assign an OID string in a correct format, when constructing your own OIDs you run a risk of making the Active Directory schema incompatible with other Directory-enabled applications. In addition, it would not be possible to register such strings, if that becomes necessary. The answer is no, you should use oidgen.exe.
When creating a new class, do you have to assign system attributes such as uSN, createTime, and some other attributes necessary for successful replication?	No, these attributes are inherited from the parent of all classes, Top. This is the default behavior.
If you set up an intrasite replication schedule incorrectly, will this disrupt replication?	No, intrasite replication does not depend on schedules and replication intervals and instead uses update notifications as the primary replication trigger.
Why isn't it possible to use nonauthoritative restore in domains with multiple domain controllers when you want to restore objects from a certain subtree?	Nonauthoritative restore does not adjust restored object attributes, including USNs, which were up-to-date during the backup runtime. Since then, many objects would have increased their USNs, which will lead to newer data replicating on top of restored data. If you want restored data to overwrite current copies on other domain controllers, you need to perform an authoritative restore. It will increase USNs by a comfortable margin to make sure restored information is assigned a higher priority during replication.
Why isn't it possible to authoritatively restore the schema naming context?	This would cause some attributes and object classes, which exist in the current schema, to have no definitions in the restored version of the schema. Objects would exist but would not be defined; this would have serious consequences.

CERTIFICATION SUMMARY

This chapter discussed some of the main aspects of maintaining your Active Directory environment. After your main AD rollout is complete, you may need to adjust things like schemas, site structure, or trust relationships. This chapter took you through the processes and concepts associated with these tasks.

We reviewed the process of replication and site link and schedule management. When planning and managing replication, several things should be kept in mind: what transports are available for selection in which scenarios, what they can replicate and what they cannot replicate, how schedules and replication intervals work together to pick replication windows, and finally, what is involved in generating replication topology for intrasite and intersite replication.

Restoring AD services was discussed with an emphasis on directory services restore mode and benefits of using authoritative and nonauthoritative restores. The closing sections of the chapter examined some of the tools available to administrators for troubleshooting and monitoring the health of the Active Directory database and replication issues. Active Directory is a database, and it should be treated with care. You learned many practical applications of utilities such as Ntdsutil, which can be used to perform various operations against the database, and NTBACKUP, which can be used to back up AD databases. FSMO roles can also be moved between domain controllers when domain controllers running FSMO operations go down or become unavailable.

✓ TWO-MINUTE DRILL

Manage an Active Directory Forest and Domain Structure

❑ To set up a cross-forest trust, you either need to coordinate between two forest administrators, or use a shared password to set up a trust relationship from each side of the trust.

❑ All object instances in Active Directory are based on structural classes.

❑ The UPN suffix routing mechanism is used to detect and correct universal principal name uniqueness conflicts between forests.

Manage an Active Directory Site

❑ Replication link cost is specified in the site link properties. Costs are administrative values that assign priority to one link over another.

❑ You can assign replication schedules based on 15-minute intervals.

❑ Replication schedules for intersite replication are defined in the properties of SiteLink objects. Replication schedules consist of windows when replication is allowed, and intervals during which replication is preferred.

❑ By default, all site links are bridged. If you need to turn this off, you will need to explicitly create site links between all sites in a fully meshed scheme, or assign site links to site link bridges.

Monitor Active Directory Replication Failures

❑ The Replmon tool is unique in its ability to generate replication reports and display a graphical view of replication topology.

❑ Active Directory replication replicates AD objects, but the File Replication Service replicates files. AD and FRS replication use different engines but the same replication topology.

❑ Event Viewer contains a Directory Services log and File Replication Service log, which contain related errors and warnings.

Restore Active Directory Services

❑ When you have problems booting up your domain controller, you may need to use system state backups and nonauthoritative restore mode. System state backups include system files, Registry, COM+ registrations, and other information along with Active Directory databases.

❑ When you have to recover deleted Active Directory objects (tombstoned), you will need to use an authoritative restore.

❑ You can restore in authoritative mode from a system state backup that is less than 60 days old, unless the tombstoneLifetime setting was modified. You should minimize the scope of an authoritative restore by only restoring necessary subtrees.

Troubleshoot Active Directory

❑ The bulk of replication issues stem from connectivity outages and extended periods of domain controller downtime.

❑ You may need to seize an FSMO role forcibly if a transfer was unsuccessful, or if the former owner of the role is no longer online.

❑ Offline defragmentation, integrity checks, semantic analysis, and recovery and repair operations against Active Directory databases can be performed using the Ntdsutil command-line interface in directory services restore mode.

SELF TEST

The following questions will help you measure your understanding of the material presented in this chapter. Read all the choices carefully because there might be more than one correct answer. Choose all correct answers for each question.

Manage an Active Directory Forest and Domain Structure

1. The management of two different companies reached an agreement to include a complementary product of one in the product line of the other and take advantage of a popular brand name. You need to configure the IT environment to allow users of company A to access the resources of company B. You configure a trust relationship on your side and assign a complex password that satisfies your password policies. Then you send an encrypted email message to the administrators on the other end, letting them know what this password is. Next, you get a call from the other party, informing you of the fact that the administrators get the "password must meet complexity requirements" error message. What could the problem be?

   A. Email was intercepted and tampered with.

   B. The password must meet complexity requirements in both domains, not just one.

   C. There was not enough time to complete password synchronization.

   D. A trusted party password is generated automatically.

2. What class types are used to create object instances in Active Directory?

   A. Auxiliary classes

   B. Structural classes

   C. Abstract classes

   D. Top class

3. Why is it better to use UPN logon names instead of <domainname>\<username> when logging on to the network?

   A. UPN format usually coincides with the email address, and it is easy to remember.

   B. UPN format removes potential NetBIOS domain name conflicts.

   C. UPN is the only logon name format available with Windows Server 2003.

   D. Using UPNs allows you to take advantage of trust relationships.

4. You are working on extending schemas. You need to add the same five attributes to several new classes. How should you do this with the least amount of administrative effort?

   A. Add attributes to classes.

B. Create a new class for each attribute and add these classes to the structural classes you are going to use.

C. Add all attributes to the auxiliary class, and then add the auxiliary class to the structural classes to be used in Active Directory.

D. Use spare attributes in classes reserved by Microsoft for custom values.

Manage an Active Directory Site

5. Sites 1, 2, 3, and 4 are connected sequentially in a chain, and default bridging is switched off. The cost of Site Link A between Site 1 and Site 2 is 20, Site Link B between 2 and 3 is 30, and Site Link C between 3 and 4 is 40. Site Link A and Site Link B are added to Site Link Bridge AB. Site Link B and Site Link C are added to Site Link Bridge BC. What is the lowest total cost between Site 1 and Site 4?

   A. 90

   B. 60

   C. 120

   D. Not defined

6. Sites 1 and 3 are connected to Site 2. The replication window is defined as between 01:00 A.M. and 04:00 A.M. between sites 1 and 2, and from 02:00 A.M. till 05:00 A.M. between sites 2 and 3. The default replication interval is left unchanged at 180 minutes. What can you say about replication from Site 1 to Site 3, and about replication from Site 3 to Site 1?

   A. The replication schedule is adequate to perform replication from Site 1 to Site 3 and from Site 3 to Site 1 between 2:00 A.M. and 4:00 A.M. the same night.

   B. In both cases, replication information gets held up in Site 2 for about 24 hours.

   C. Replication from Site 1 to Site 3 is accomplished within one night's window, but the other way (from 3 to 1) gets held up in Site 2 for about 24 hours.

   D. Replication from Site 3 to Site 1 is accomplished within one night's window, but the other way (from 1 to 3) gets held up in Site 2 for about 24 hours.

7. What must be done in order to configure a replication schedule for intersite connection objects?

   A. You must configure the schedule and replication interval in SiteLink objects.

   B. You must configure the schedule and replication interval in NTDS Settings of the site.

   C. You must configure the schedule and replication interval in connection objects properties directly.

   D. Intersite replication schedules are generated automatically as part of KCC topology maintenance.

8. In addition to bandwidth, what else should be considered when assigning costs to site links?
   A. Reliability and availability of the link
   B. Traffic costs
   C. Physical media of the link
   D. Network protocol of the link

Monitor Active Directory Replication Failures

9. Which of the following utilities should you use to view a graphical representation of intrasite replication topology?
   A. Replview
   B. Repadmin
   C. AD Sites and Services
   D. Replmon

10. You decided to take a look at some Active Directory database performance statistics but could not find any Directory database-related counters in Performance Logs and Alerts. What could be wrong?
   A. To enable database performance counters, you must first install SQL Server.
   B. In order to view Active Directory database counters, you must first install them.
   C. You need to manually register the Active Directory Database MMC snap-in.
   D. You need to add database path strings to performance-related Registry keys.

11. Which of the following tools can be used when troubleshooting FRS issues?
   A. FRS logs
   B. Ntfrsutl tool
   C. FRS Administration MMC snap-in
   D. FRSUTL tool

12. Which of the following tools can be used to analyze Active Directory replication problems?
   A. Repadmin tool
   B. AD Sites and Services MMC snap-in
   C. Replmon tool
   D. Dcdiag tool

Restore Active Directory Services

13. If you restore a user account using an authoritative restore, what happens to the object's access privileges?

   A. Privileges within the same domain will be restored.

   B. All privileges are lost and must be reassigned.

   C. All privileges available prior to deletion are retained.

   D. All privileges available prior to deletion are retained, providing that the backup set is not older than 60 days.

14. You discovered some traces of a potentially harmful virus on one of the domain controllers. You launch antivirus software, and it reports successful cleanup, but you still observe some Registry keys that belong to the virus code. Which system state restore method is the most appropriate in this situation?

   A. Nonauthoritative restore

   B. Authoritative restore of the entire domain naming context

   C. Authoritative restore of a subtree in the domain naming context

   D. System restore using ERD (emergency repair disk)

15. For a number of reasons outside of your control, an authoritative restore failed to complete successfully. Circumstances suggest that another restore attempt from the same backup set might do the trick. Which Ntdsutil switches should you use to restore data from the same set authoritatively over the previous authoritative restore?

   A. Restore database

   B. Restore database, with verinc

   C. Restore subtree <LDAP tree>

   D. Restore subtree <LDAP tree>, with verinc

16. What is the default physical location of Active Directory data?

   A. ntds.dit file

   B. SAM file

   C. edb.log file

   D. Master File Table (MFT)

Troubleshoot Active Directory

17. You were troubleshooting Active Directory replication problems and found that automatically generated connection objects that would normally be displayed in the Active Directory Sites and Services MMC snap-in are missing. What should your next step be in diagnosing this issue?

   A. Run the **repadmin /kcc** command.

   B. Check KCC-related Registry values.

   C. Run the **repadmin /showreps** command.

   D. Run **net stop kcc**, then **net start kcc** commands.

18. One of the domain controllers in your environment has recently started to reboot itself sporadically. Last month alone it rebooted a few times, and the frequency appears to be on the increase. You decide to take the server offline for further investigation. You want to transfer FSMO roles to other servers, but it just so happens that triggering a transfer operation also causes it to reboot. You manage to transfer the Schema Master. What should you do to be able to take the server offline?

   A. Seize FSMO roles.

   B. Perform a restore on the malfunctioning server.

   C. Use Ntdsutil to move the ntds.dit database file to a functioning domain controller.

   D. Don't worry about FSMO roles because they are hardly used after AD rollout has been completed.

19. How do you move an Active Directory database to a different volume?

   A. Use the Move DB command in Ntdsutil, in the Files command context. You must boot into directory services restore mode first.

   B. Perform a system state backup, and then restore to a different location in directory services restore mode.

   C. Adjust the dbpath system variable to reflect the change.

   D. Use group policies to set the NTDS Files Path Registry key.

20. Which of the following may cause Active Directory replication to fail?

   A. DNS resolution problems

   B. Computer account synchronization problems

   C. Computer clock synchronization problems

   D. Incorrectly configured schedules

LAB QUESTION

Paul is administering a corporate network that consists of three Active Directory domains: central office w66.com and two production branches, stickytires.w66.com and bodykits.w66.com. The company is conducting business with another company that develops and markets a complementary product—custom rims. They have a Windows 2000 Active Directory domain, greatrims.com. Paul needs to make sure that greatrims.com employees can access some of the resources in w66.com. He configures an external trust relationship and access privileges accordingly.

Seeking to increase efficiency, not so long ago management made an executive decision to delegate some of the day-to-day IT duties from the central IT department to designated employees in each of the departments. As part of the plan, designated employees were delegated with User Create and Delete privileges. Paul conducted a training session on what should be done in order to create and delete user accounts, and which fields must be filled out when new employees are enrolled. One of the designated people from the sales department in w66.com decided to test this out and deleted a few user accounts, being sure that there was an easy way to restore this data, similarly to the function available in the Recycle Bin.

Paul had a two-week-old system state backup and decided to perform an authoritative restore. The process completed successfully, but, as it was found later on, a trust relationship between greatrims.com and stickytires.w66.com was damaged. Paul decided that another attempt at an authoritative restore might fix the issue, and scheduled some downtime for the next weekend. This time around, all trust relationships ended up damaged, and Paul lost his confidence in system state restore. What could be the reason for this failure? Was it possible to avoid this problem?

SELF TEST ANSWERS

Manage an Active Directory Forest and Domain Structure

1. ☑ **B.** It is possible that password policies in the other domain are stricter and require even more complex passwords—for example, passwords requiring more characters.
   ☒ **A** is incorrect because conventional email intercept methods fail to be effective when you use encryption. **C** is incorrect because a shared password is used to set up a secure channel in external trusts. **D** is incorrect because for the trust relationship to work, it must use the same trust password on both sides.

2. ☑ **B.** You can only create instances of classes using structural classes.
   ☒ **A** is incorrect because auxiliary classes are used to group attributes and extend existing structural classes with a batch of attributes all at once. **C** and **D** are incorrect because abstract and Top classes are used when creating new classes, but not object instances.

3. ☑ **A.** UPNs are often made the same as email addresses, and naturally for users, they are easier to remember. **B.** UPNs use DNS FQDNs after the @ sign, which uniquely identifies the domain in the organizational namespace regardless of its NetBIOS name.
   ☒ **C** is incorrect because it is possible to simply enter the username in the login box, or use conventional <domainname>\username logons. **D** is incorrect because UPNs are not required to take advantage of trust relationships.

4. ☑ **C.** This answer describes the easiest and most ideologically correct approach to assigning custom attributes; it ensures that odd attributes are not left out by mistake, and minimizes administrative effort.
   ☒ **A** is incorrect because it requires a lot more effort. **B** is incorrect because it requires too many classes for required changes, which can be implemented more effectively as described in C. **D** is incorrect because reserved attributes do not always satisfy custom requirements.

Manage an Active Directory Site

5. ☑ **D.** Bridging all links is turned off, and Sites 1 and 4 are not included in a common site links bridge, so it is not possible to calculate the total cost between Sites 1 and 4.
   ☒ **A, B,** and **C** are incorrect. **A** would be correct had we not turned off default bridging of all links.

6. ☑ **C.** A replication interval of 180 minutes means that there are three hours between each replication session. Replication from Site 1 to Site 3 will be accomplished within the same night: the first leg is triggered in the 01:00 A.M. to 01:15 A.M. interval, the second leg is triggered from 02:00 A.M. to 02:15 A.M. In the opposite direction, changes from Site 3 will get to Site 2

around 2:00 A.M. and will have to sit there till the following night when replication is triggered at 1:00 A.M. between Sites 1 and 2.

☒   **A, B,** and **D** are all incorrect because **C** is correct.

7. ☑   **A.** An automatically generated intersite connection object inherits scheduling configuration from the SiteLink object schedule and replication interval settings.

☒   **B** is correct for intrasite connection objects. **C** is incorrect because if you specify scheduling information directly in the properties of the connection object, KCC will stop managing it automatically and this may create manageability problems down the road. **D** is incorrect because KCC has nothing to do with setting up schedules; it simply generates topology and creates connection objects from a template.

8. ☑   **A** and **B.** Link costs are used to configure preferential treatment of certain links over other ones. Things such as traffic costs and, more importantly, reliability and availability of WAN connections are all valid factors to consider when assigning link costs.

☒   **C** and **D** are incorrect because the physical media and network protocol are irrelevant on the application layer.

Monitor Active Directory Replication Failures

9. ☑   **D.** Replmon is the tool that should be used here.

☒   **A** is incorrect because it does not exist. **B** and **C** are incorrect. In reality, you can use applications such as Visio to construct diagrams based on Active Directory topology, and even a clean sheet of paper and a pencil to jot down the topology based on command-line tool output, but the process gets increasingly complicated the more domain controllers you add to the mix.

10. ☑   **B.** By default, these performance counter objects are not registered; you will need to register them manually before you can achieve this.

☒   **A** is incorrect because installing SQL Server will install its own performance counters. **C** is incorrect because such a snap-in does not exist. **D** is incorrect because database file location has no impact on the ability to monitor performance and statistics.

11. ☑   **A** and **B.** You can use Ntfrsutl and FRS logs to diagnose and troubleshoot FRS issues.

☒   **C** and **D** are incorrect because these tools do not exist.

12. ☑   **A, B, C, D.** All of these tools can be used as described.

Restore Active Directory Services

13. ☑   **C.** The user account will have the same SID, GUID, and all other parameters that form the security principal.

☒   **A, B** and **D** are incorrect because these limitations do not apply.

14. ☑ **A.** Nonauthoritative restore can be used to restore system Registry and other system services, but not Active Directory data in a single domain with more than one domain controller.
    ☒ **B** and **C** are incorrect because this will restore older Active Directory data and assign it higher priority over replication. Even if the data is fresh, this operation will cause unnecessary replication traffic. **D** is incorrect because the ERD process cannot be used to restore the Registry.

15. ☑ **B** and **D.** Using these methods you can increase USNs by a comfortable margin to make sure they get higher priority over previously restored authoritative data.
    ☒ **A** and **C** are incorrect because you will need to use the verinc option.

16. ☑ **A.** The AD database is stored in ntds.dit.
    ☒ **B** is incorrect since a SAM file only stores a local user account database and is not used on a domain controller. **C** is incorrect because edb.log only contains transaction records. You may argue rather successfully that transaction log data *is* database data, but technically, the transaction log is a temporary storage of changes to data—the final destination is still the data file. **D** is incorrect because MFT does not store any user data, only system data necessary to maintain the file system.

Troubleshoot Active Directory

17. ☑ **C.** Repadmin with the /showreps switch will show the time of last synchronization and the reason for unsuccessful synchronizations for each of the replicated naming contexts.
    ☒ **A** and **B** are incorrect because these answers deal with KCC, and KCC is usually not the culprit in replication problems. **D** is incorrect because KCC is not a service, it is a system component, and this command would result in an error.

18. ☑ **A.** In this case, you may need to perform a seize operation against all FSMO roles still located on the server.
    ☒ **B** is incorrect since restoring may kill a significant amount of time and still prove useless, because at this point you do not know what is causing this behavior. **C** is incorrect because this will not let you transfer roles to other servers. **D** is incorrect because all FSMO masters must be functional during the life cycle of Active Directory.

19. ☑ **A.** The **Move DB** command in Ntdsutil is used to transfer database files to other volumes.
    ☒ **B** is incorrect because you cannot choose a location for system state restore. **C** and **D** are incorrect because these settings do not exist.

20. ☑ **A, B, C,** and **D.** Each of these methods is a valid candidate to cause Active Directory replication problems.

LAB ANSWER

It is recommended that you perform backups often and restore from the latest known copy, if that is necessary. If your backup is older than the tombstoneLifetime value, which defaults to 60 days, restores may partially reinstate deleted objects, causing problems. These objects would not be replicated, but garbage collection will not be able to remove them either. Next, computer account passwords are changed automatically every 30 days. This may cause authentication and replication problems on the domain controller where the restore is performed—you would have to reset the computer account password using either Active Directory Users and Computers or the Netdom utility.

A third scenario (which is probably what happened with Paul) is that automatically generated trust relationships of parent-child type change their passwords once every seven days. The system attempts to use the previous version of the password as well, which increases the password validity window to two weeks. You can use **netdom trust** with the /reset switch to reset passwords for any two domains. Paul made a mistake by rerunning the restore, because by the time they hit their scheduled maintenance window, the backup information was even older, and other trusts may have fallen victim to the same problem.

Paul did, however, select the right restore operation, but going with a subtree restore, as best practices suggest, may have been a better option to help avoid the problem. Using Ntdsutil, Paul might have decided not to tinker with naming contexts and just restore everything, using **Restore Database** versus **Restore Subtree OU=Sales,DC=w66,DC=COM**. This led to restoring the entire domain naming context, including trust and computer objects and passwords. Restoring outdated trust passwords was the main reason for this incident.

5

Planning and Implementing User, Computer, and Group Strategies

CERTIFICATION OBJECTIVES

The primary focus of most information system implementations is human interaction. It doesn't make a lot of sense to spend resources and invest in technology if the purpose is not to improve efficiency, productivity, and ease of use. Managing user and computer accounts therefore is a central administrative task in Active Directory infrastructure implementation.

As an administrator, you will have to manage resource permissions and ensure that the user environment is secure yet convenient, and that system design does not stand in the way of productivity. You will need to minimize security risks and make it, if not impossible, then at least very difficult to break into your environment. Several authentication policies and strategies can help in achieving this, and wherever necessary, you should consider using additional means to protect your infrastructure, including methods that provide a stronger degree of authentication protection, such as smart-card readers.

Depending on the size of infrastructures, they may contain a very large number of objects such as users and computers. This may mean a very real headache for administrators—organizational unit containers and user groups are the only ways to organize these objects into a consistent, logical structure, and still make it possible to have your environment in manageable shape after you have hit 10,000, 500,000, or several million objects in your Active Directory database. This chapter is dedicated to planning and implementing user groups, authentication strategies, and OU structure—the very essence of building scalable and manageable infrastructures.

CERTIFICATION OBJECTIVE 5.01

Plan a Security Group Strategy

We have to begin by getting familiar with fundamental object types that form the basis of user interaction with AD: user objects, computer objects, and group objects. Mastering day-to-day administration of these elements is not difficult to attain with the newest wizards and tools supplied with Windows Server 2003; what is a lot more complicated, and a lot more important, is to learn where to use each of these elements and how to plan an effective infrastructure that will adapt easily to change. This part of the chapter is devoted to user and group element planning and management, supplemented by a dose of practical recommendations and examples of how to use Windows Server 2003 tools to achieve the desired results.

The importance of strategy choice and planning cannot be overstated, and the larger the infrastructure, the more this holds true. Consequences of errors in the planning stages may prove to be show-stoppers in the medium- to long-term future of the infrastructure, potentially resulting in total loss of system scalability and negatively impacting factors such as productivity or security.

Active Directory User Accounts

User accounts (user objects, or instances of the user object class) serve the purpose of defining an element bearing its unique security identifier that will interact with Active Directory. User accounts do not necessarily represent just the users of the system; system processes also rely on user accounts because they are used to define the security context and assign privileges in the system. The most significant benefits provided by Active Directory in respect to user accounts are

- **Single sign-on (SSO)**   Directory standards discussed in Chapter 1 mandate that users need to authenticate to the system only once; in this process, their identity is established, and further access to resources does not require additional input of user credentials.

- **Centralized or distributed administration**   Administration tools and some side scripting can do wonders in the Active Directory environment. Administrators have a range of GUI and command-line tools at their disposal and can automate user account setup, mass migration, or imports, regardless of their physical location in the system.

- **Group objects**   Group objects are used to define users in groups that can be managed collectively as a single unit, which is especially valuable when it comes to assigning permissions and delegating system privileges.

When you create a new user account, Active Directory associates several identifiers with the newly created object instance:

- **Distinguished name (DN)**   This is used to uniquely identify the user among all other objects in the container and to define the position of this container in the LDAP directory. This DN is used when the system references this object for one reason or another. Recall from Chapter 1 that distinguished names follow a pattern similar to CN=Firstname Lastname/ CN=Users/OU= R&D/DC=company_name/DC=COM, where DC represents a reference to a domain element, OU to an organizational unit, and CN to a common name of a directory element. Distinguished names have to be unique directory-wide. An additional technical reference on these naming elements can be found in RFC1779. Distinguished names are derived from administrative input, and they change when you move objects between containers.

- **Relative distinguished name (RDN)**   Another type of directory name that administrators come across is the relative distinguished name, which is simply an object reference similar to CN=Firstname Lastname, and it must be unique within its own container. For a more detailed discussion on DN and RDN, please refer to Chapter 1. Like distinguished names, RDNs are derived from administrative input, and they do not change when you move objects between containers.

- **Globally unique identifier (GUID)**   GUIDs are 128-bit identifiers generated by the system automatically. "Globally unique" means no two identical sequences can be generated within the same AD forest. Unlike DNs, GUIDs never change regardless of move operations.

- **User principal name (UPN)**   The UPN is more user friendly than a DN and may be used to authenticate to the system as part of a set of credentials provided by users. UPNs are constructed from administrative input by adding a logon name (prefix) and an associated domain name (suffix), which may or may not match existing DNS names or even follow a DNS format. The prefix, in plain terms, is a username, and it is usually formed as an abbreviation of elements of the last name and first name, following a naming convention defined by administrators. The suffix, by default, is the DNS name of the forest root domain, but may be selected from a list of existing child domain names or from a list of additional UPN suffixes defined by administrators. The suffix and prefix are separated by the @ sign.

- **Pre-Windows 2000 logon name**   These logon names must be used instead of UPN names when users log on to the network from client machines that are running a pre-Windows 2000 operating system version. Pre-Windows 2000 logon names are also understood by Windows 2000 and Windows Server 2003. If you use this type of logon name, you must specify a NetBIOS domain name where the user account is located; otherwise, domain controllers will not be able to locate a matching user account. This may lead to problems where these NetBIOS domain names are not unique.

- **Security identifier (SID)**   This is the most important association from the security point of view. SIDs enable access control; objects without SIDs cannot be assigned permissions to resources or be restricted from accessing an Active

Directory element or another object. SIDs do not change when you move objects between containers in the same domain, and they are generated automatically by the system (with participation of the RID Master).

As you can infer, there are certain rules that govern naming of user objects in Windows Server 2003. User objects can be created locally on client computers and member servers, in which case they are not stored in Active Directory but instead in a local Security Accounts Manager (SAM) database on the computer in question. There is also a scope difference: objects created locally cannot be used to access resources on other machines. Local account logon names must be unique in the SAM database of the computer where they are being created.

In Windows 2000, user logon names must be unique domainwide, which also ensures that UPNs are unique forestwide, providing that administrators map logon names to their respective domain name suffixes and do not add custom UPN suffixes (the process and repercussions were described in Chapter 4). Beginning with Windows Server 2003, logon names you create are unique forestwide, which to a certain extent helps mitigate issues arising from adding custom UPN suffixes.

Note that domain controllers do not have local SAM databases. When you run Dcpromo, SAM is replaced by an instance of the Active Directory database, and all accounts you create on a domain controller have domain/forest scope.

Active Directory user account management is performed using the Active Directory Users and Computers MMC snap-in, shown in Figure 5-1. Figure 5-2 further demonstrates the first of the two input screens of the New Object/User Wizard, where administrators assign the most basic attributes of user accounts, such as first, last, and logon names. This wizard is invoked by right-clicking an organizational unit in the Active Directory Users and Computers console and choosing New | User from the context menu.

Administrators must further be aware that logon names (or more popularly, usernames) must not exceed 20 characters in length and that usernames are not case sensitive in standard Windows processes, including logon (although they may be sensitive to custom application lookups made against the LDAP directory). The 20-character restriction is actually a 20-byte restriction, and the actual number of characters will vary based on the OS character set; some languages may require more than one byte per character. Technically, logon names can be longer than 20 characters, but you can only log on using the first 20 characters. The OS does not restrict administrators from creating logons longer than 20 characters.

User principal names follow the same pattern as email addresses, and it makes perfect sense to assign them consistently with email addresses; to users it will appear

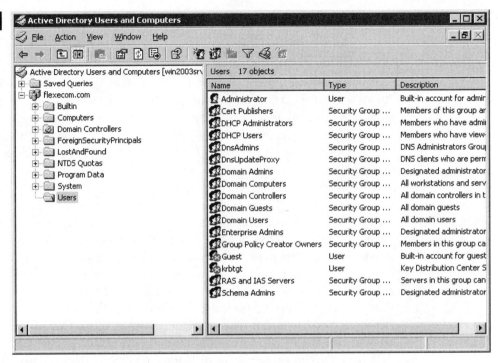

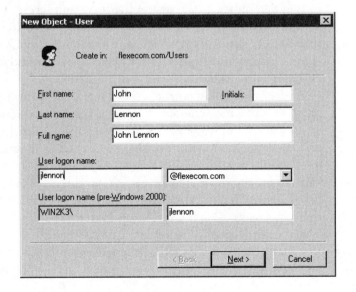

as if their email address and logon name are the same thing. This creates further naming convention restrictions, because in this case you should not use characters that are not acceptable for email addresses in the SMTP standard. Windows Server 2003 will not warn you of the fact. You can create a logon name with a space, for example, but you cannot use it in email addresses. The names of all LDAP objects can contain any Unicode characters, except leading or trailing spaces, number sign (#), comma (,), plus sign (+), quote ("), backslash (\ ), semicolon (;), and greater than and less than signs (> and <). SMTP restrictions are far stricter and will not be applied to usernames. If you wish to map the two, you will have to observe SMTP limitations without relying on Windows Server 2003 wizards.

User Account Passwords

When users log on to the network they need to identify themselves to the system using a pair of credentials: logon name and password. In addition to technical limitations that apply to logon names, administrators must also carefully craft their password-related restrictions. In this case, it works the opposite way. The longer the password, the less likely someone will guess it. Password restrictions are aimed at making passwords long and complex in nature, so system security and confidentiality of user data are enforced. When a new account is created, by default administrators must supply a temporary password for the user account, and they also may enable "User must change password at next logon," which will force users to reassign their password when they log on the first time. After that, users can change passwords anytime, and at least as frequently as configured by administrators. These default requirements for usernames can be cancelled by adjusting the appropriate policies, as you will see later in the chapter.

When assigning or changing a password, keep in mind that there should be the right balance between complexity and ease of remembering without having to write it down. Complex passwords are hard to break using brute-force methods and are next to impossible to guess, but the need to write these passwords down negates the effect, especially if users write them down and stick them on the monitor. Here are some recommendations that can be enforced by a password policy in the Group Policy Object Editor, which will be discussed later in the chapter:

- Avoid creating easily traceable associations between users and passwords: names, dates of birth, and names of children make bad passwords.

- Avoid using dictionary words.

- Despite being a pretty obvious recommendation, it is common to have blank passwords, "password" passwords, or logon names as passwords.

■ Passwords should be longer than six, or even eight, characters, should feature small and capital letters, numbers, and symbols.

■ When changing a password, change it—do not use the same one over and over again.

Other User Account Attributes

In addition to most vital associations such as GUIDs, DNs, and SIDs, user objects have dozens of attributes configurable after the account has been created. Most importantly, administrators can

■ Define logon hours. Users will be restricted from accessing network resources outside of their allowed hours.

■ Define a list of NetBIOS computer names to which local user logons should be restricted.

■ Define an account expiration date, after which the user account is disabled by the system.

■ Configure remote access properties (either through a remote access policy or on the account level).

■ Configure terminal services session settings.

■ Configure user profile settings such as profile paths, logon scripts, and applications that should be started upon logon.

■ Modify user group membership.

Account restrictions may be controlled individually or through the use of group policy objects, discussed later in this chapter and in Chapter 6. Figure 5-3 illustrates the Account tab of user object properties in the Active Directory Users and Computers console.

Using Automated Methods to Add Multiple User Accounts

If you need to configure quite a few attributes for each account you create, creating them manually, one-by-one, may prove to be one of the most boring and unnecessarily complicated tasks you can perform. Furthermore, in order for larger enterprises to keep their TCOs down, there must be a user import process that can be leveraged in migration or rollout projects. Automation has another key benefit: elimination of typos and errors associated with the human factor.

To address these issues, Windows Server 2003 ships with auxiliary tools that can be used to import or export user accounts between text files and Active Directory.

FIGURE 5-3

User Account
properties

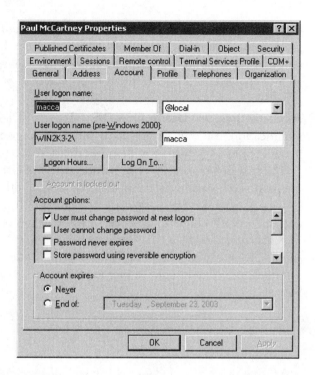

Two text formats are supported out of the box—comma-separated text files and LDAP-format text files. The tools are CSVDE (Comma Separated Value Directory Exchange) and LDIFDE (Lightweight Directory Interchange Format Directory Exchange). You can use these tools to copy objects such as user accounts, computer accounts, and group and printer objects from and to Active Directory in bulk as a single operation.

To use these tools, you must set up a source file that contains at least the information listed next for each user account:

- Distinguished name
- Object class
- User account logon name
- Username (full name, or display name)
- Whether the user account should be enabled (it is disabled by default)

Optionally, you can provide additional values for user account attributes. Passwords are left blank, and users will be required to change passwords at the first logon. If a person with malicious intent knows the format of usernames, this password situation presents a security issue, which is why accounts are disabled by default. If you know that user accounts are not going to be used immediately, it is recommended that they are not enabled until later in the rollout phase.

Account Import Using CSVDE   The CSVDE utility cannot be used for object modification. It is only employed to dump existing account information into a CSV file or create new objects based on information in a CSV file.

The first line of the CSV file is always a list of attributes that will be used in the import process. Attributes are separated from each other by a comma. This is followed by a carriage return (new line) and a number of lines, each representing a user account. Simply enough, these lines list the values of the attributes listed in the first line, also separated by a comma. Note that if the value of an attribute is missing, it should be left blank but still be followed by a comma. If one of your values contains a comma, the value should be provided in quotes. A few lines of code are shown here as an example:

```
objectClass, DN, userPrincipalName, sAMAccountName, displayName, userAccountControl
user, "cn=John Doe, ou=Sales, dc=flexecom, dc=com", JohnDoe@flexecom.com, JohnDoe,
 John Doe, 512
```

Most of this is self-evident, except the userAccountControl attribute, which is used to specify whether the account should be enabled or disabled. The number 512 enables an account; 514 is the default setting, which disables the account.

To import a text file, use **CSVDE -i -f <CSV file>**. The -i switch indicates that the tool should import the content into Active Directory, and -f provides the file to use. CSVDE will display status information in the command prompt and, optionally, can create a detailed log as it goes through the records. Logging is the best way to check if all of the records were imported successfully; you can simply click the container in question and see if any of the new objects actually exist. However, import problems on a small scale (say, a missing value in the file that resulted in one or two skipped records out of a hundred) cannot be detected this way.

Account Import Using LDIFDE   Microsoft's other tool for manipulating object information in Active Directory uses Lightweight Directory Interchange Format (LDIF) formatted files compatible with LDAP standards. Unlike CSVDE, LDIFDE can be used to edit or delete existing objects in Active Directory in addition to importing/adding new accounts.

LDIF files contain a series of lines that describe a new user account or provide modifications for the existing user account. Each line provides an attribute and a value for the attribute, which is quite different from the one-line/one-account format of CSVDE. The following rules should be observed when working with LDIF files:

- Lines that begin with a number (#) sign are used for comments and are ignored during import or edit operations.
- If an attribute value is missing, it should be indicated using AttributeDescr: FILL SEP, where AttributeDescr is the attribute of the object, and FILL SEP is an instruction to leave the value blank.

Here is an example of an LDIF file:

```
# This listing provides a sample of LDIFDE file that contains one record
objectClass: user
DN: cn=John Doe, ou=Sales, dc=flexecom, dc=com
userPrincipalName: JohnDoe@flexecom.com
sAMAccountName: John_Doe
displayName: John Doe
userAccountControl: 512
```

The import or modification process is launched by the LDIFDE tool. The command **LDIFDE -i -f <LDIF file>** triggers an import of the specified file. The -i switch indicates that the operation performed is an import, and -f indicates which file should be used. If the -i switch is not used, the default operation mode of this utility is export.

Other Automation Techniques

When you use either CSVDE or LDIFDE, other switches may be handy, depending on the situation (these switches apply to both tools), such as:

- **-v switch**   Enables verbose mode and shows diagnostic information.
- **-s <servername>**   Indicates which domain controller to use during the operation.
- **-j switch**   Provides a log file path.
- **-k switch**   Forces LDIFDE to ignore possible errors during the operation. Errors may be caused if you indicated attribute values that violate value types or constraints, if a nonexistent object class was specified, and if an attribute or object already existed when you performed an import operation.
- **-c <OldDN> <NewDN>**   Replaces strings in distinguished names (such as when you exported from one environment and now wish to import into a different domain and different container without modifying the file).

- ■ **-t switch** Specifies a custom port, if your directory does not use port 389 for LDAP.
- ■ **-u switch** Instructs the tools to use Unicode format.
- ■ **-?** Shows these switches: command-specific switches, and command syntax and examples.

CSVDE and LDIFDE tools use the Active Directory Service Interfaces (ADSI) to access and manipulate directory objects. ADSI can be used together with Windows Scripting Host (WSH) to automate any part of an Active Directory object's life cycle. Custom applications can use ADSI to create or modify objects programmatically, and administrators can write their own scripts to perform custom operations or work with custom data sources, such as text files that do not follow CSV or LDIF formats. It would be problematic to rearrange attributes and values within the file. It is a lot easier to write your own script and parse data in a custom fashion. Scripts also come in handy when you need to enumerate all user accounts, or user accounts with a specific value in one of their attributes, and change a portion of another attribute. For example, your branch office moves to a new location, and phone numbers change as a result; instead of modifying hundreds of user objects manually, you can script it.

Finally, scripting saves the day if you are delegating one-off user additions or other operations to less technical peers, and there are only a few attributes that they need to specify. Instead of letting them use Active Directory Users and Computers, you can create a very simple script that will collect the required parameters by interacting with the person, create the account based on user input, and maybe even notify administrators of the fact.

VBScript and JavaScript can be used with WSH to write ADSI scripts, and the ADSI is also accessible to any other coding language that can pass function calls to a system library.

on the
job

Scripting skills are not tested on the exam, but are lifesaving in the real world. You can find many samples of VBScripts for the Windows Server 2003 environment on Microsoft's Technet site in the ScriptCenter section at www.microsoft.com/technet/treeview/default.asp?url=/technet/scriptcenter/ default.asp. Also check out the ADSI Scriptomatic tool at www.microsoft .com/technet/treeview/default.asp?url=/technet/scriptcenter/tools/admatic.asp, which can be used to automate script writing, at least to a certain extent. This can be used to create a base version of the script that you can customize further.

Active Directory Computer Accounts

Active Directory requires every computer participating in the domain environment, be it Windows Server 2003, Windows XP Professional, Windows 2000, or Windows NT 4.0, to have a corresponding computer object (or account) associated with it. Windows 9x systems do not need a computer account to interact with the network, and are not assigned any SIDs. By default, computer accounts are created in the Computers container when you add them to the domain, but they can also be created manually in, or moved to, any organizational unit container, much like user accounts.

Active Directory Groups

In corporate environments, the number of user accounts may reach significant numbers, and administration of many thousands of users is not a trivial task. Facing this chore, administrators must have a way to deal with user configuration and user access restriction tasks in a collective, efficient way. Since the early days of Windows NT 4.0, Microsoft has provided user *groups* as a means to unite users based on certain criteria. The purpose of a group is to make it easy to administer user rights by assigning permissions to a single directory object, not a thousand. Groups are security principals, which means they have their own SIDs; which in turn makes it possible to add them to access control lists of resources.

Groups are not containers; containers are used to store leaf objects, and one object can only be stored in one container. Think of groups as a logical association of user objects regardless of their position within the OU or even the domain structure. This means one user object can be associated with many group objects at the same time. This allows you to group users based on several criteria at the same time. For instance, you could maintain groups based on office location and the roles people play in the company, and add technical personnel accounts to groups representing technical staff and to groups representing their geographical location.

Managing user access in Windows Server 2003 is not much different fundamentally: administrators add users to groups, then assign permissions to groups. This has three major effects. First of all, this approach makes it possible to keep user management logical and scalable no matter how many users you manage and how many resources they need to access. Second, the administrative task of assigning user permissions comes down to adding users to appropriate groups, which saves a lot of administrative effort and prevents inconsistent rights assignment (where two users with similar functions are assigned different rights). This also makes it easier to troubleshoot access problems. Third, adding groups to resource access control lists (as opposed to adding individual users) allows you to keep performance on acceptable levels. (Long access lists need more processing power and in extreme cases, result in performance degradation.)

What has evolved over time, as Windows technologies matured, is how these groups can be used in the Active Directory environment. Groups can be used to maintain a certain hierarchy when it comes to assigning permissions, that is, groups can be nested. Nesting makes organization of groups more flexible; nested groups inherit access permissions from their parent group.

Not all groups are created equal. Windows Server 2003 differentiates between groups based on their type and scope. There are two types of groups—distribution and security groups. To assign permissions to resources, you can only use security groups. In terms of group scopes, there are local groups, domain local groups, global groups, and universal groups. Types and scopes are discussed in more detail later in this section.

Depending on domain functional levels, some group type functionality may not always be available. Before we get to this, let's quickly review domain and forest functional levels as they relate to groups.

Windows Server 2003 Domain and Forest Functional Levels

As discussed in Chapter 3, Windows Server 2003 has four domain functional levels and three forest functional levels. Table 5-1 lists the levels for domains, and Table 5-2 lists the levels for forests.

While most of the forest functional level features deal with schema, interdomain, and interforest interaction, such as bidirectional transitive trust relationships, global catalog replication improvements, and deactivation of schema classes or attributes, some of the domain functional level features have a direct impact on groups. Table 5-3 compares three group features impacted by the domain functional level: group nesting, group conversion, and security groups with universal scope.

TABLE 5-1   Domain Functional Levels

Level	Supported Domain Controllers
Windows 2000 mixed (default)	Windows Server 2003, Windows 2000, Windows NT 4.0
Windows 2000 native	Windows Server 2003, Windows 2000
Windows Server 2003 interim	Windows Server 2003, Windows NT 4.0
Windows Server 2003	Windows Server 2003 only

TABLE 5-2	Forest Functional Levels

Level	Supported Domains
Windows 2000 mixed (default)	Windows Server 2003, Windows 2000, Windows NT 4.0
Windows Server 2003 interim	Windows Server 2003, Windows NT 4.0
Windows Server 2003	Windows Server 2003

on the job

Don't forget that raising domain functional levels is a one-way ride. Administrators should weigh the necessity to implement new features available in higher functional levels against the inability to add or maintain domain controllers running older Windows operating systems. Use the Active Directory Domains and Trusts or the Active Directory Users and Computers console to perform domain functional level changes. Right-click the domain container, and click the Raise Domain Functional Level context menu to raise domain functional levels. Use the General tab in the Properties context menu to view current functional levels for the domain and forest.

Windows 2000 native and Windows Server 2003 functional levels enable SID history. This makes migrating security principals between domains smoother, allowing users, computers, or groups to access resources in their original domains by retaining previously assigned SIDs.

TABLE 5-3	Domain Functional Level Impact on Groups

Group Functionality	Windows 2000 Mixed Level and Windows Server 2003 Interim Level	Windows 2000 Native Level	Windows 2003 Native
Group nesting	Allowed for distribution groups but not security groups, with the exception of adding global groups to domain local groups.	Allowed for both distribution and security groups.	Allowed for both distribution and security groups.
Group conversion	Groups cannot be converted.	Groups can be converted.	Groups can be converted.
Universal security groups	Allowed for distribution but not security groups.	Allowed for distribution and security groups.	Allowed for distribution and security groups.

Group Scope

Before we jump to creating and managing groups, we need to look at group types and scopes. Table 5-4 compares group scopes available in Windows Server 2003.

Do not confuse domain local groups with local groups on member servers and workstations in your network. Local groups on workstations and member servers have no relation to the domain functional level and will always have only local machine permissions scope. You cannot create any other group type locally. These "local" local groups are created in the SAM security database using the Computer Management snap-in, as opposed to domain local groups, which are created in Active Directory by means of the Active Directory Users and Computers snap-in.

Now that we see the big picture of users, computers, and groups, let's see what the specifics are of each group type and scope, how groups are used in assigning permissions to access resources, and how this impacts planning and group strategy.

TABLE 5-4 Comparing Group Scopes

Group	Domain Functional Level	Group Membership	Permissions Scope
Domain local group	Windows 2000 native and Windows Server 2003	Same as in local groups	Domain local groups can be used to assign permissions to resources in the domain where these groups are defined. Local groups are converted to domain local groups when you upgrade Windows NT 4.0 PDC to Windows Server 2003.
Global group	Any level	Global groups can only contain security principal members from the same domain where they are defined.	Global groups can be used to assign permissions to resources in the same domain where they are defined, and can be added to other groups in other domains where trust relations exist.
Universal group	Windows 2000 native or Windows Server 2003 (security type)	Universal groups can contain security principals from any domain in the forest, although adding members from domains running in Windows 2000 mixed mode is not recommended.	Universal groups can be used to assign permissions to resources anywhere in the forest and trusting domains.

Group Scope and Permissions

Domain local groups were designed primarily to be used in defining permissions in discretionary access control lists (DACLs), which are maintained for every object. The entries outline which security principal has what kind of access to the object in question. Domain local groups have domain scope, meaning they can be assigned to a DACL within the domain that they were created in.

When you need to add several people to a resource ACL, the recommended approach is to create a domain local group for this purpose and add accounts to the group; then use this domain local group to assign specific permissions to specific objects in the domain.

Unlike domain local groups, global groups have a wider scope. They can be added to domain local groups anywhere in the forest or trusting domains, much like universal groups. Global groups can contain security principals only from the domain where they were defined, and should contain users that require the same level of access to certain resources. Global groups cannot nest domain local groups, but can nest other global groups on Windows 2000 native or Windows Server 2003 functional levels.

Administrators in trusting domains can add global groups from trusted domains to domain local groups or directly into resource ACLs in their domains. To continue the preceding example, instead of adding users to the domain local group on an individual basis, the recommended practice suggests that you should add these users to a global group, then add the global group to a domain local group, and use this domain local group to define permissions in resource ACLs.

Universal groups can contain security principals from any domain and also be assigned permissions in any domain, providing there is a trust relationship between the domains in question. Infrastructures of small organizations can use universal groups to simplify their group nesting and strategy. Large organizations can leverage universal groups to simplify permissions management through more flexible user organization. Universal security groups can only be created in domains running on Windows 2000 native or Windows Server 2003 functional levels.

Group Type and Permissions

Distribution groups are designed more for communication purposes than for security. These groups can be used together with Active Directory integrated email applications, such as Microsoft Exchange, to maintain distribution lists. Group objects can have email addresses assigned to them, and when you send an email to a distribution group address, it will be expanded and delivered to every member of that group. Distribution groups are not security enabled and are not considered to be security principals—that is, they cannot be defined on a resource ACL. Microsoft recommends creating distribution groups whenever you do not plan to use them for security purposes.

Security groups fit more closely with the classic definition and use of groups: they can be used to assign permissions to security principals such as users and computers for purposes of accessing resources. You only have to define permissions using security groups once. Upon doing so, every user that is included as a member in the group automatically receives all permissions granted to this group. In addition, security-enabled groups can be used for group policy filtering, discussed separately in Chapter 6.

The notion of access tokens is central to how security groups affect users. The Local Security Authority (LSA) running on each Windows client or server is responsible for the local logon process and user interaction with the system as far as authentication goes. The LSA is also used to process authentication requests to Active Directory that are made through Kerberos or NTLM protocols. When a user logs on interactively, the LSA on the domain controller selected for this authentication request generates an access token for the user in question.

The access token contains the username and associated SID, and a list of all groups this user belongs to, along with their respective SIDs. Access tokens are always local; as the user proceeds with his or her work, this access token is used by the systems involved to verify the user's identity and determine which resources he or she is allowed to access. This is why changes in security group membership do not kick in until the user logs off and logs back on—security access tokens are generated when the user logs on interactively.

on the **!** **Job**

When a user connects to a server, the LSA on that server must build a local access token representing the user. The server does this by extracting SID data from the Privilege Access Certificate (PAC), which is located in the session ticket. (See "The Kerberos Authentication Protocol" section later in this chapter.)

Security groups can also be used for distribution purposes, since they can be assigned an email address, too. However, this is not recommended because security groups affect access control speeds, and excessive security group membership is bound to slow down the process. Distribution groups are not included in access tokens, and hence it affects the speed of token generation, token size, and subsequent token submission and processing to other systems.

If your distribution group strategy coincides with security group strategy, it may be better to mail-enable security groups, which will reduce the total number of groups you have to support and manage memberships for.

Figure 5-4 shows universal group properties for a security type group in the Windows Server 2003 functional level domain.

FIGURE 5-4

Universal group
properties

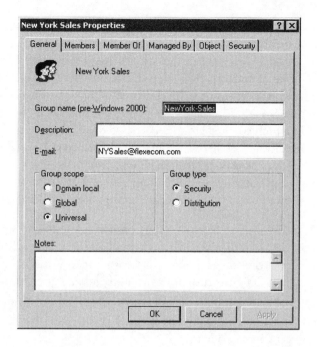

Group Nesting

Group nesting is not a new concept, but its usage has been extended with the introduction of Windows 2000. Prior to Windows 2000, global groups could not contain other global groups (that is, be nested). However, adding global groups to local groups was a standard feature—even, some might say, the purpose of global groups. (This also constitutes nesting, except it applies to groups of different types.) Now when you raise the functional level to Windows 2000 native or Windows Server 2003, you are allowed to nest groups of the same types. Global groups can contain other global groups.

Group nesting is one of the concepts that is central to group structure planning: it refers to adding groups with one scope into other groups of the same or different scope. Due to some limitations in the replication process, groups may not contain more than 5,000 members.

on the
job

The 5,000 group member limitation only affects Windows 2000 forests or Windows Server 2003 forests that haven't been raised to the Windows Server 2003 forest functional level. This level fixes the replication problems.

Nesting makes it possible to work around these limitations, and it quite significantly reduces network traffic associated with replication of group-related modifications, such as membership changes. Naturally, nesting was not designed to be a workaround; it provides the ability to group your users based on organizational roles, rank, departments, projects, or specific tasks they need to perform, either locally in their office or collectively with the folks in other offices, domains, or even forests. So it gives administrators the ability to manage permissions collectively, independently of domain or OU structure. Nesting comes in handy when you want to devise a strategy in which you first group users based on organizational roles and then add these groups to another group of the same scope that may be used to unite all organizational role groups based on geographical or business structure.

Nesting functionality depends on domain functional levels. Table 5-3 partially showed that on the Windows 2000 native or Windows Server 2003 functional level:

- Universal groups can contain as their members user and computer accounts, other universal groups from any domain with a trust association (providing that those domains also run in the Windows 2000 native or Windows Server 2003 functional level), and global groups from any trusted domain.

- Global groups can contain user accounts from the same domain where global groups are defined. Global groups can nest other global groups, also from the same domain.

- Domain local groups can contain user and computer accounts, global groups, and universal groups, no matter what domain these objects come from, providing there is a trust relationship. Domain local groups can also nest other domain local groups from the same domain.

Lower functional levels do not allow the same sort of functionality when it comes to nesting. Global groups cannot nest other global groups, only user and computer accounts; domain local groups cannot nest other domain local groups, only global groups and computer and user accounts; last but not least, security-enabled universal groups are not available at all.

To add nesting to groups, you use the Active Directory Users and Computers console. Switch to the container where the group in question is located, and on the group's context menu, click Properties. Then switch to the Members tab and choose which groups should be added to the members list (see Figure 5-5).

on the
job

Nesting does have a flip side: excessive nesting is probably not that great an idea because troubleshooting permissions becomes more difficult, and managing groups is less transparent. You will have to strike the balance that is right for your environment.

FIGURE 5-5

Adding nested
groups

Security Group Strategy

Creating new security groups involves making a decision about what scope to assign to
the group. There are a few standard strategies that administrators can take as a template
for their infrastructure and modify as necessary. One thing to keep in mind is that
there are no universally suitable solutions—one size does not fit all. That being said,
some of the fundamental security group principles apply to all organizations. What may
have an impact on the strategy is the size of the organization.

Strategy for Small Business

Small businesses with Windows 2000 native or Windows Server 2003 functional levels
and limited organizational structure (divisions and branch office counts are small in
terms of numbers) will most likely be inclined to employ universal groups for all their
needs, and rightly so. This strategy allows companies to add security principals from
anywhere in the organization and use the same groups anywhere in the information
system to assign permissions, without having to go into details and maintain in-house

expertise. This strategy won't last long in growth-oriented companies; so if growth is the ultimate goal, the following approaches may be employed:

- Begin by using universal groups; then convert them to global or domain local groups to stay consistent with medium and large-scale deployment recommendations (see the following section).

- Some organizations may choose to adopt the strategy recommended for the midsize and large companies from the outset. One disadvantage of using universal groups for everything in large infrastructures is that universal groups are replicated to the global catalog, and if membership in these groups changes often, it may have a measurable impact on the network through replication.

Strategy for Medium and Large Organizations

This is the area most affected by planning, as switching your strategy down the road when you have hundreds or thousands of users distributed between groups may prove to be a challenge. The larger the organization, the more intensive the information exchange and reliance on technology, and the more costly it is to restructure if downtime or work interruption is involved. The recommendations that follow aim to provide modularity and flexibility when it comes to security groups, while keeping in mind replication traffic and scalability issues that may arise.

- Use global groups to group user accounts based on a logical criterion. What this logical criterion is depends on the situation. In a geographically dispersed company, you may choose, for example, to have an IT-NYC global group and IT-Toronto global group in the respective offices. Information technology staff members would be added to these groups in their respective offices. Global groups are therefore called account groups.

- Put global groups (regardless of what domain they were created in) into domain local groups.

- Use domain local groups or standard local groups on member servers to assign permissions to individual resources. Domain local groups are called resource groups.

- Delegate authority to administer groups and permissions to managers or team leaders who are in charge of the departments or offices in question.

This approach was abbreviated AGLP in the Windows NT 4.0 environment: add *accounts* to *global* groups, then global groups to *local* groups, and finally, assign *permissions* to local groups. With the introduction of Windows 2000, local groups were renamed to domain local groups to avoid confusion between local groups on the domain controllers (which can be used to assign permissions to resources domainwide) and traditional local groups that can be created on individual workstations and member servers (which can only be used to assign permissions on local machines). This changes the abbreviation to AGDLP: *accounts -> global groups -> domain local groups -> permissions*.

Windows 2000 and Windows Server 2003 also may feature the AGULP strategy, which promotes adding *accounts* to *global* groups, global groups to *universal* groups, universal groups to *local* groups (domain local, of course), and finally, *permissions* are still assigned to domain local groups.

The main push behind this multitiered approach is to add modularity to your environment. Membership on every tier (domain local groups, global groups, universal groups), nested or not, can be easily modified by adding or removing a few groups, which translates into automatic permission changes for thousands of employees.

Group Conversion

Group conversion is a process of modifying group type or scope without changing group object identifiers, or group membership for that matter. You can convert any distribution group to a security group of corresponding scope (that is, convert a domain local security group to a domain local distribution group, or vice versa), and you can convert domain local groups or global groups to universal groups, or convert universal groups to global or domain local groups. Note that you cannot convert a global group to a domain local group, or a domain local group to a global group, without first converting it to a universal group. Also, when you convert the group type from security to distribution, existing permissions assigned to the group are lost.

In other words, group conversion is a handy feature if you have to regroup due to a shortcoming in initial planning and you don't want to spend days creating new groups and adding existing users all over again. Some restrictions do apply, however. For example, you cannot convert the scope of groups that have other groups nested in them, and you cannot convert groups on functional levels lower than Windows 2000 native.

To convert a group, simply open up group properties, as shown earlier in Figure 5-4, and choose a different scope or type for the group. Click the Apply button when done.

Note that it does not matter which functional level your domain is running on from the distribution group perspective. As established earlier, security groups are affected by functional levels, and your strategy will have to account for this. Newer security group functionalities are not compatible with older domain controllers.

Default Explicit and Implicit Groups

Windows Server 2003 delivers a basic skeleton of users and groups when you first install the operating system, and then some Active Directory–specific groups are added when Dcpromo is executed.

Users

By default, two local user accounts are created when the operating system is installed: Administrator and Guest. These accounts can be used to log on locally while Active Directory has not been deployed, or if the machine has not been added to the domain yet, or any time during its participation in Active Directory if someone needs to log on locally, without authenticating to the domain. When you run Dcpromo, the local account database is migrated to the Active Directory, and local accounts become unavailable.

The local (as well as Active Directory) Guest account is disabled by default, and for security reasons, it is generally recommended not to use it. Standard security practices suggest renaming it because it is most likely to be used in brute-force password attacks.

The Administrator user account is a member of the Administrators group (or Domain Admins, if the server is a domain controller) and has virtually no restrictions on what it can do in the system out of the box. Also, for security purposes, it is recommended that you make the following changes:

- Create another user account to be used for administrative purposes, preferably naming it in a way that does not give away its privileged system status (Superuser, Admin are obvious names, for example). Add this account to the Administrators local group on a domain member server or to Domain Admins on a domain controller.
- Disable the built-in Administrator user account.
- Revoke administrative rights from the built-in account by removing it from administrative groups.

It might be a good idea to make this one of the first steps on the path to implementing your account strategy, because as the system matures and new applications and services get installed, they may accidentally be configured to run in the context of this account, which sometimes creates unwanted dependencies; renaming the Administrator account or revoking its full privileges will affect these applications and services.

Default Explicit Security Groups

When Dcpromo completes its process, the Active Directory environment will have two pre-created containers—Builtin and Users—which will have a few groups and users defined. Group and user accounts that you (or the system) create as objects in Active Directory are termed "explicit." Table 5-5 provides an overview of explicit groups created by default in the Builtin and Users containers.

Note that some of these groups may not be installed in some cases. Builtin container groups will always be configured on any domain controller regardless of network services, but the Users container groups will depend in part on the network services deployed in the domain you work with.

TABLE 5-5   Default Explicit Security Groups

Explicit Default Group	Description
Account Operators	This group contains user accounts that are allowed to administer other user accounts. By default, this group is empty, and it is a built-in local group.
Administrators	This group has the least amount of restrictions imposed on its members. Members are allowed to perform reconfiguration and update of the local computer system, install applications, administer user accounts, and so on. This group is a built-in local group; it contains the Administrator user account, Enterprise Admins, and Domain Admins group accounts.
Backup Operators	This group contains user accounts of those who are allowed to perform backups and restores of the file system, regardless of file or folder permissions. Backup Operators is a built-in local group that contains no members by default.
Guests	This group contains all guest accounts—user accounts representing people with casual access to the system. This group is a built-in local group, and it contains the Guest account and Domain Guests group by default.
Incoming Forest Trust Builders	As the group name implies, user accounts included in this group have authority to establish incoming trusts to their own forest. This is a built-in local group, and it contains no members by default.
Network Configuration Operators	This group contains user accounts that can be permitted to perform certain network configuration tasks, as required. This is a built-in local group and contains no members by default.
Performance Log Users	This group allows its members to manipulate performance log settings remotely. This is also a built-in local group, but it contains an implicit Network Service user account by default.
Performance Monitor Users	This group is similar to Performance Log Users, except it contains no members by default and serves the purpose of allowing someone to monitor this machine from the network.

| TABLE 5-5 | Default Explicit Security Groups *(continued)* |

Explicit Default Group	Description
Pre-Windows 2000 Compatible Access	This built-in local group is used for backward compatibility purposes; it allows its members read access to all user accounts and groups. By default, it contains the PDC Emulator computer account and Authenticated Users implicit group.
Print Operators	This built-in local group is used to control access to domain printers. None of the user accounts are included by default.
Remote Desktop Users	Members of this group are allowed to log on to domain machines using the Remote Desktop Protocol terminal client (mstsc.exe). This is a built-in local group that contains no members by default.
Replicator	This group is used for the purposes of file synchronization between domain controllers. The type of this group is the same, built-in local, and by default this group contains no members.
Server Operators	Similarly to Backup Operators, this group is used to grant permissions to individuals to administer domain servers. This built-in local group is not populated with any user account members by default.
Users	The Users group enforces a number of system restrictions to user accounts added as its members. Users are not permitted to modify system settings. This built-in local group has a few members by default—the Domain Users explicit group and Authenticated Users and Interactive implicit groups.
Windows Authorization Access Group	This group can be used to grant access to the tokenGroupsGlobalAndUniversal attribute on User objects. By default, this built-in local group only lists the Enterprise Domain Controllers implicit group as its member.
Users\Cert Publishers	This group is used to grant permission to publish certificates in Active Directory. This domain local group is configured when you install a CA, and, by default, contains the CA server account as its member.
Users\DHCP Administrators	This group can be used to designate personnel as DHCP service administrators. The DHCP Administrators group is a domain local group by default, but it can be changed to universal and then to global, if necessary. It contains no members by default.
Users\DHCP Users	This group is used to grant read-only access to the DHCP administrative console. The scope of this group is the same as DHCP Administrators, and it also contains no members by default.
Users\DnsAdmins	This group is identical to DHCP Administrators, except the service in question is DNS. It is installed with DNS network service.
Users\DnsUpdateProxy	This group allows its members to perform DNS updates in place of DNS clients. This is useful when your older clients do not support dynamic DNS updates and a DHCP server is configured to perform updates on their behalf. It has global scope, by default, and contains no members.

TABLE 5-5	Default Explicit Security Groups *(continued)*

Explicit Default Group	Description
Users\RAS and IAS Servers	Computers added to this group will have access to dial-in attributes of user accounts. You would normally place your remote access servers into this group. It is of domain local scope (this cannot be changed) and contains no members by default.
Users\Telnet Clients	If the telnet remote access application is installed, the Telnet Clients group can be used to designate users who should be allowed to connect to telnet terminals.
Users\Domain Admins Users\Domain Computers Users\Domain Controllers Users\Domain Guests Users\Domain Users	This is perhaps the most commonly used set of groups. The names speak for themselves—the purpose of each group is to grant elevated system privileges (or restrictions, in the case of Guests and Users) to their respective members. Domain Admins has global scope and features the Administrator account as its member by default. Domain Computers has global scope, and all non-domain-controller computer accounts are members by default. Domain Controllers has global scope with domain controller members by default. Domain Guests and Domain Users are of global scope and contain the Guest account and all other user accounts, respectively.
Users\Group Policy Creator Owners	This global group contains the Administrator account by default. Members of this group are granted authority to create and administer domain group policy objects.
Users\Enterprise Admins	This group is arguably the most powerful and least specific group in Active Directory. Members of this group are automatically added to Domain Admins in each of the domains in Active Directory, thereby effectively making them administrators of all computers in all of the domains (the Domain Admins group is added to the local Administrators group on individual workstations). This is a universal group that contains the forest root domain Administrator account by default.
Users\Schema Admins	This is also a universal group that contains the forest root domain Administrator account by default. This group is used to grant Active Directory schema modification privileges to other individuals or computers.

When you add user accounts to the groups listed in Table 5-5, they are bestowed system privileges as shown in the table. IT professionals are strongly advised not to perform everyday work using accounts with administrative privileges—Domain Admins or Enterprise Admins even more so—unless your everyday work requires these elevated permissions. Obviously, even the most knowledgeable people can make accidental mistakes or be subject to virus outbreaks or hacker attacks. The high visibility of vital system accounts and exposure of these harmful processes to administrative privileges may wreak havoc of biblical proportions.

Similarly, you should also try to plan your structure so that the number of administrative accounts is limited. A large number of administrators makes it more difficult to keep track of changes, and potentially makes the system more vulnerable to malicious intent originating from within the organization—disgruntled administrators and espionage pose too great a threat to be ignored.

In summary, plan your users and groups so that the most restrictive system is in place, yet users can perform their tasks. Whatever users are not explicitly required to access, they should technically have no access to. Administrators should work on their network documentation using plain user accounts, and employ administrative accounts to configure or troubleshoot systems. A Power Users group allows a bit more freedom than a Domain Users group; it can allow for installing certain new applications, configuring a printer, or changing settings in the Control Panel.

Default Implicit Security Groups

The main concept behind implicit security groups (also known as special identities, or system groups) is that you cannot control their membership, and they cannot be reconfigured or defined manually. This is different from explicit groups, which, with a few exceptions, you have unrestricted ability to create, manage, and remove. Membership in implicit groups is assigned automatically based on what users of the system "do." Table 5-6 lists implicit Windows Server 2003 security groups along with brief descriptions.

Despite the fact that you cannot view or modify system group memberships using familiar Active Directory tools, you can take advantage of the concept by using identities as variables on your ACLs. (ACLs are discussed in detail in the next part of the chapter.) In other words, special identities can be used to assign explicit permissions to objects and the file system. The process of assigning permissions using special identities works by replacing SIDs in the ACL dynamically, based on which identity the user receives as a result of his or her actions. This adds flexibility to planning groups and permissions, but as you have probably noticed by now, flexibility comes at a price of additional planning requirements.

This list of system groups is not exhaustive. Other special identities exist in Windows Server 2003. They are Batch, Creator Owner, Dialup, Digest Authentication, NTLM Authentication, SChannel Authentication, Enterprise Domain Controllers, Local Service, Network Service, Other Organization, This Organization, Proxy, Remote Interactive Logon, Restricted, Self, and Terminal Server User. Although it is probably not worth going through them in detail, their names give you an idea of what they represent; for example, Dialup represents users who are accessing resources using a dial-up connection.

Thus far, we have been focusing on two distinct security elements, users and groups, and what role they play in the system. That does not explain how security controls

| TABLE 5-6 | Default Implicit Security Groups |

Implicit Default Group	Description
Anonymous Logon	All users and services accessing a Windows Server 2003 machine without explicit authentication (using a username and password) are automatically placed into this group. There seems to be a lot more focus on security these days, so Microsoft decided not to include the Anonymous Logon group as a member of the Everyone group in Windows Server 2003 (this used to be the case in earlier versions of the OS).
Everyone	This group assumes literally everyone except users who do not use credentials to authenticate to the system. If users enter their usernames and passwords, they are added to the Everyone group on the server in question regardless of how they access resources thereafter.
Interactive	This group automatically includes all users who access the resource in question while logged on locally; that is, the user must be logged on locally and must be accessing a resource on a local computer to be added to the Interactive group. Since the user has to authenticate in order to access a computer interactively, members of the Interactive group cannot at the same time belong to the Anonymous Logon group.
Network	This group is the opposite of the Interactive group. It will automatically include all users who are attempting to access a given resource using a network connection.
Authenticated Users	As the name implies, this group explicitly defines all users and processes who provide their logon information either by entering a username and password or using pass-through authentication.
Creator Group	The Creator Group identity, when used in permissions ACLs, will substitute itself with the primary group of the account that was used to create the object in question. In effect, Creator Group is not a group, it is just another special identity that can be used as a "variable" when defining ACL entries.
System	This special identity is used by the system to run system services, device drivers, and internal processes. Do not modify the default permissions of this identity. If you revoke access to system files, your server will stop working or even booting properly.

are implemented and maintained in Active Directory. Earlier chapters dealt with the process of authentication; this part looks into the workings of authorization—the process of establishing whether or not a user request for access to a resource should be allowed or rejected.

Each object stored in Active Directory has an access control list (ACL) associated with it. The purpose of these ACLs is to list elements that have been explicitly granted or denied access to the object. This security information is propagated down the LDAP structure, causing child containers and objects, depending on the settings, to inherit security settings of their parents. Let's review the basic concepts involved in the authorization process.

Security Principals and Descriptors

As mentioned previously, a security principal is a user, computer, or group account defined either in Active Directory, on a standalone (member) server, or a local computer. Security principals are the only security elements that can be added to ACLs. Every time you create a security principal in the system, a new SID is generated and associated with the principal. In all authorization processes, the system uses SIDs; SIDs are listed on the ACL (not user or group names). This is why when you create a principal, then delete it, and re-create exactly the same principal, it will never be the same from the security perspective.

A security descriptor is a binary data structure that contains information about access permissions and auditing of the object in question. More specifically, security descriptors consist of:

- **Headers**   A set of system flags used to indicate, among other things, which security descriptor elements are included in this descriptor.

- **Discretionary access control list (DACL)**   DACLs are access control lists that are made up of individual access control entries (ACEs). DACL is what most of us really mean when we say ACL—this is what effectively is used to define who gets what kind of access to this particular object.

- **System access control list (SACL)**   SACLs are also made up of ACEs, but they are used to define auditing rules for this particular object. Once object access auditing has been enabled domainwide, individual SACLs that state which access events should be recorded must be defined on each object that needs to be audited.

- **Owner of the object**   This is one of the key concepts. By default, owners and creators of the object are allowed to configure SACLs and DACLs. Administrators cannot change the creator attribute of the object, but they can revoke ownership of the object, if that is necessary to reassign permissions in cases where the creator has blocked everyone from accessing the object.

- **Primary group of the owner**   The primary group setting defines the primary user group when user accounts have memberships in more than one group.

Each access control entry also consists of specific parameters, such as a SID, header (Allow or Deny entry), binary access mask, a set of flags describing how permission inheritance has been configured, and ACE type (described in Table 5-7).

TABLE 5-7	Type	Description	Used In
	Deny Access	Used to deny access	DACL
ACE Types	Allow Access	Used to allow access	DACL
	System Audit	Used for audit configuration	SACL

To manage object access permissions, follow these steps:

1. Click Start | Administrative Tools | Active Directory Users and Computers to open the ADUC console.

2. In the View menu, click Advanced Features to turn on hidden containers and tabs.

3. Choose an object you want to restrict access to, right-click it, and choose Properties. Switch to the Security tab, as shown in Figure 5-6.

4. To add or remove permissions, use the Add or Remove buttons to create new ACEs or remove existing ones. To add a new ACE, click Add, type in the name of a user or group account, make sure it gets resolved (underlined), and then click OK.

5. Finally, check off types of access that you wish to allow or deny for this particular user or group.

If you click the Advanced button on the properties page shown in Figure 5-6, it will call up the Advanced Security Settings window, which is new to Windows Server 2003. Here, you can view an exhaustive list of inherited and explicitly defined permissions, the object auditing settings, which security principal is the owner of the object, and the effective permissions. This mini-tool helps you troubleshoot access permissions on the fly.

Figure 5-7 demonstrates that by choosing a security principal on this tab, you can quickly view the effective set of permissions for the chosen account. Note though that this tool only provides estimated permissions; actual permissions will depend in part on how the user accesses this object and what special identity it will be assigned.

Assigning Permissions

The mechanism described in the steps in the previous section can be used to assign permissions using one of the categories described in Table 5-8. Note that the table lists

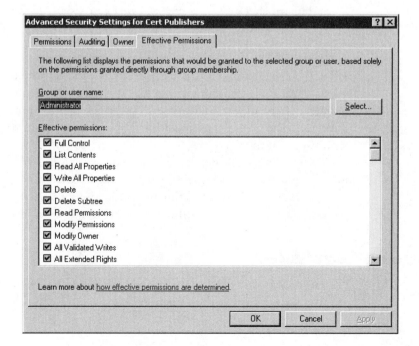

TABLE 5-8	Standard Permission Categories

Permission Category	Assumed Permissions
Full Control	Allows modifying ACLs and forcibly taking ownership of the object. In addition, it grants all other types of permissions assigned by other categories.
Read	Allows read-only access to object, owner, object attributes, and ACL.
Write	Allows everything that Read permission does, plus writing changes to attributes.
Create All Child Objects	Allows adding all types of objects to a container.
Delete All Child Objects	Allows deleting all types of objects from a container.
Special permissions	Assigns individual permissions from the balance of permissions not covered in the five categories above. If left unchecked, no specific permissions have been assigned in excess of the five categories.

only the standard permissions for generic objects such as containers. Overall, there are 15 permissions that you could assign to objects, and depending on how many attributes the object has, it may have in the neighborhood of 100 read and write permissions for each of its attributes.

To manage ACLs on a daily basis, it is very inconvenient to use special permissions and go through the list of dozens and dozens of object and attribute permissions. Special permissions should be used for fine-tuning only; use standard permissions whenever possible.

The six basic categories will appear in all ACLs regardless of the object type; that being said, some objects have their own object-specific standard permissions that more closely reflect their use in the system. For example, user objects also have permissions such as Change Password, Read/Write Group Membership, Read/Write Logon Information, and others.

If you wish to assign special permissions to your objects, follow these steps:

1. In the object's context menu, click Properties, and switch to the Security tab.

2. On the Security tab, click Advanced. The Advanced Security Settings box will appear.

3. On the Permissions tab, use the Add, Remove, and Edit buttons to modify special permissions as necessary. Figure 5-8 shows the Permissions tab.

Permissions tab
in Access Control
settings

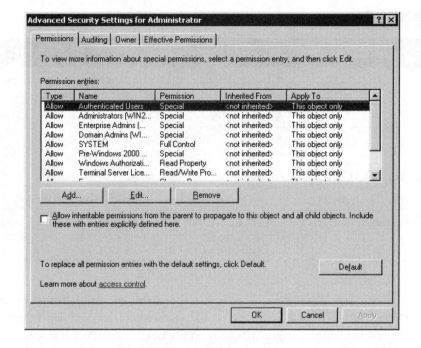

Be extremely careful when assigning special permissions. Make sure you test things after the changes have been committed. Giving insufficient permissions to object attributes may result in less than predictable object behavior.

Explicit, Implicit, and Inherited Permissions

It would be too difficult a task if administrators had to assign every type of permission for every object manually. Those rights assigned manually by administrators or automatically by the system appear on the DACLs, and they are explicit. By default, child objects inherit permissions from the parent container—all ACEs in the parent's DACL are copied to the child's DACL. If explicit Deny permission has been configured on the parent level, it is inherited by child objects; however, inherited permissions are overwritten by explicitly defined permissions. So if you assign explicit Allow permission to the child object, it will become effective over the inherited Deny.

In addition to this, the system makes a few assumptions about access rights; these fall under the implicit permissions category. Remember that there is always an implicit Deny at the end of each DACL: if a user account is not listed as an access control entry on a DACL, it will be implicitly denied access to that resource, although no explicit Deny permission for this user has been assigned.

Effective object access rights are calculated similar to the file system. In fact, it has been this way from the Windows NT 4.0 days. If one user account belongs to several groups, and each of them is present on the ACL, effective rights are accumulated from each group's settings, unless there is an explicit Deny that overrides all other settings. So if User A belongs to groups A and B, and group A has Full Control access and group B has Read access, User A will be assigned both sets of permissions, effectively granting Full Control permission. If User A belonged to group C, which has explicit Deny permission, User A would be restricted from accessing the object.

Managing Permission Inheritance

By default, permissions propagate down the LDAP structure. This is of help initially, but administrators may have to modify this behavior if necessary. When you assign permissions to a container, all containers and objects within that container inherit these permissions; this is referred to as multilevel inheritance. Single-level inheritance will only propagate the settings to child objects in the container, but not to subcontainers and their child objects. When setting up permissions, administrators have three options as to how these settings should be applied, as shown in Table 5-9.

Figure 5-9 further shows that security settings in Windows Server 2003 can also be propagated down to all specific object classes, such as Site Links, User, Group, Printer, or Trusted Domains objects. The standard schema contains upwards of 70 object classes, which you can use to configure security setting propagation.

In terms of technical implementation, inheritance works by transferring ACEs from a parent's security descriptor to the child's security descriptor. This transfer process has to happen when either of the following conditions occurs

- A new object is added to the container
- DACL or SACL of the parent object is modified

TABLE 5-9   Inheritance Settings

Inheritance Option	Description
This Object Only	Applies settings only to the object on which the operation is being performed. This effectively turns propagation off.
This Object and All Child Objects	Applies to the object where the operation is being performed and all child objects and containers down to the deepest level—multilevel inheritance (setting by default).
Child Objects Only	Applies to the object on which the operation is being performed and all child objects immediately below the object—single-level inheritance.

FIGURE 5-9

Configuring
inheritance

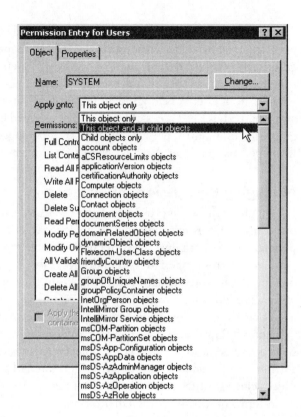

In theory, administrators benefit from this mechanism because they do not have to worry about assigning permissions manually to all child objects, and the process guarantees that permissions inherited are identical on every object they are propagated to. At the same time, explicitly defined permissions override inherited permissions, so flexibility is maintained. Administrators can easily tell if ACEs have been inherited—they appear with grayed-out check boxes that cannot be modified.

Blocking Security Inheritance

You do, however, have an option of blocking inheritance if that is needed. This may be useful in cases where you have an organizational unit container for sales or accounting personnel in a department, and you wish to provide stricter security and prevent other users from tampering with OU objects. In this case, you have to use the setting "Allow inheritable permissions from the parent to propagate to this object and all child objects," as shown in Figure 5-8. Unchecking this box and applying the change results in a pop-up shown in Figure 5-10, and then a warning, as shown in Figure 5-11.

FIGURE 5-10

Blocking
inheritance
permission
conflicts

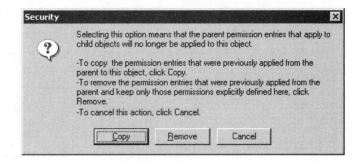

On the first pop-up, you will need to decide how inherited permissions should be
dealt with—if they are to be copied to the DACL permanently or removed from the
DACL. The second pop-up advises you of performance implications of removing
inheritance and reapplying it from a lower-level container. As can be inferred from
the message, the higher the object is in the structure, the bigger the performance hit
will be.

Object Ownership

Each object in Active Directory has its owner—the user account that was used to create
an object immediately becomes its owner. Owners have Full Control permissions on their
objects and therefore can make any changes they require, even lock out administrators
from accessing the object. By default, in Windows Server 2003, the Administrators
group initially assumes ownership of directory objects. Then, individual users become
owners as they create objects, with the exception of user accounts that are members of

FIGURE 5-11

Performance
degradation
warning

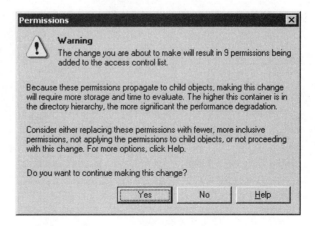

the Administrator and Domain Admins groups, in which case these groups become the owner. The Owner field in the security descriptor simply contains the SID of the administrative group instead of the user.

To view the current owner of an object, switch to the Owner tab of the Advanced Security Settings window. The Current Owner Of This Item field displays the owner of the object. Figure 5-12 shows the Owner tab.

Transferring Ownership

Using the Owner tab (shown in Figure 5-12), you can also forcibly take ownership of the object, if you have administrative privileges in the domain. Members of the Administrators group can take ownership regardless of their permissions on individual objects because they have the Take Ownership of Files or Other Objects system privilege. In addition, any user who has Full Control or Take Ownership rights can simply assign the ownership to their own account.

FIGURE 5-12

Owner tab in
Advanced
Security Settings

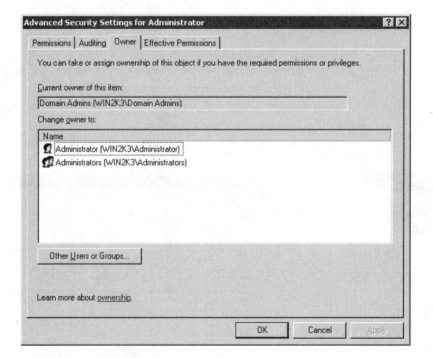

Note that the Change Permissions right enables users to reassign ACEs, and technically they can assign the Take Ownership right to themselves and then take ownership of the object without having membership in the administrative groups, or having the Take Ownership right in the first place.

on the
job

Note that ownership transfer is a two-step process. You cannot transfer ownership to someone else; you must assign Take Ownership rights, and then have the person in question take the ownership. (Administrators, again, are sort of exempt from this rule because they can take ownership, anyway.)

SCENARIO & SOLUTION

Is it necessary for all users in the forest to have the same UPN suffix, set to the forest root domain suffix by default?	Not really. Administrators can add custom UPN suffixes using the Active Directory Domains and Trusts console, and assign custom or existing child domain UPN suffixes when creating (or modifying) user accounts.
Is it possible to automate user account import from an external source?	Yes. To accomplish this, administrators should use CSVDE or LDIFDE tools. These tools can export and import directory objects from, and to, an LDAP directory service, using CSV or LDIF files for intermediary storage purposes.
What do you use distribution groups for?	Distribution groups are not considered to be security principals—that is, they do not have SIDs and are not participating in the Active Directory security scheme. They can be used by Active Directory-integrated email applications to maintain mailing groups while minimizing processing overhead associated with mail-enabled security groups.
How do you use implicit security groups, also known as special identities?	You really don't use them, although they can be assigned to an object DACL and serve as a SID variable. User actions in the system define which special identities they assume. If a user connects to a resource using a network connection, he or she is automatically added to the Network group.

Plan a User Authentication Strategy

The need for a strong authentication system in information systems goes without saying. As we approach a time when we will have practically paperless office environments, the value of information is often difficult to estimate. Theft of vital business information makes security the number one topic in information systems, and authentication is a point of entry into the protected network.

A proper authentication system is essential to both administrators and users. Administrators must ensure that the system makes it reasonably difficult for intruders to take advantage of potential security problems that will surface from time to time. Users, in turn, want to be certain that their information is safe, that there is no interception or misrepresentation going on, and yet it is still reasonably easy to interact with the system.

Remember from Chapter 1 that authentication is a process of establishing user identity, by comparing logon credentials supplied by users or processes with an LDAP or other database. Early chapters pointed out that an outstanding benefit of a directory-based system is its ability to organize user accounts in one place, making it possible to administer the system from a central location, using one tool or set of tools. Users are associated with a domain account, and if administrators change their password once, this setting becomes effective on all domain computers. The Single Sign-On concept also surfaced, effectively making users authenticate to the directory only once and then, based on this authentication, have their access controlled throughout the infrastructure.

The biggest threat to a highly distributed infrastructure, as common sense suggests, comes from the need to conduct authentication over the network; in some cases, this involves public segments of the network. You could place a restrictive firewall on the network perimeter, but this defeats the purpose of having the system, as it will presumably keep the bad guys out, but will also not let the good guys in. Hence, there is a need both to encrypt authentication information using reasonably secure protocols and to ensure, with a high degree of probability, the authenticity of the parties involved in communication. Note that you will not read terms like "prevent" or "eliminate" here—there are some very secure technologies available, but all of them are still created and managed by people and are subject to human error.

A successful authentication process establishes user or process identity, and either rejects or allows access to the system, also establishing the level of access if permitted.

In terms of Active Directory, a security token is generated that contains, among other characteristics, a user's group membership and account SID, which are used again and again for authorization purposes as the user interacts with the system. Although the combination of username and password is, by far, the most common way to authenticate to the system, it is, of course, not the only way.

Active Directory can also be integrated with devices such as smart cards and smart-card readers, proximity cards, smart tokens or magnetic keys, biometrics scanners (retina, fingerprints), and so on. They all serve a common purpose—to establish user identity by providing some personal identification, which is going to be critical as users engage in information exchange (source authenticity verification). Clearly, the username and password method is the cheapest, built-in, ready-to-go alternative to more expensive (but also more secure) ways of ensuring that authentication is not performed by an intruder. Fingerprints or eye scans, for example, would fit the bill here.

In the balance between two extremes, there is smart-card authentication. Users will need to know their passwords and have smart cards on them. This prevents someone with a stolen password or a stolen card from authenticating, but if both get leaked to the same person, the system is again compromised.

The following sections focus on Windows Server 2003 mechanisms that deal with authentication—Kerberos and smart cards are topics of particular interest. This section of the chapter touches on some topics of Chapter 6, especially when it comes to password policies and digital certificates.

Kerberos Authentication Protocol

Beginning with Windows 2000, Microsoft has been relying on Kerberos as the native Active Directory authentication protocol. The currently implemented version of this technology is version 5. Kerberos has a number of advantages over NTLM (NT LAN Manager), which has been used in the past in DOS-based network environments and Windows NT 3.5x and 4.0. These advantages are described here:

- When users attempt to access resources on a member server in a domain, the member server does not need to request authorization from a domain controller each time such a request is made. Servers can perform authorization based on the information provided by the client. This not only saves some network traffic and a bit of time, but also reduces the likelihood of successful interception and cracking of logon credentials by reducing the number of times this sensitive information must travel the network.

■ It is no longer safe to maintain infrastructures where clients assume that servers are always what they are supposed to be; that used to be the case in NTLM. Clients must likewise be sure that they are communicating with the real servers that are authorized to engage in such communication and share resources that may be. This reduces the likelihood of man-in-the-middle attacks and address spoofing, where attackers maliciously redirect client traffic to their own servers. Kerberos allows mutual authentication—that is, establishing the identity of the server and the client.

■ The delegated authentication principle is also made possible in Kerberos. In distributed systems, it is not uncommon for user actions to spawn other processes that will have to interact with the system on behalf of the user, indirectly. It is important to ensure that the risk of elevating privileges is very low, and that this intermediate process runs in the context of the user who triggered it, receiving the same level of access. This process also needs to authenticate.

■ Kerberos makes it easier to build trust relationships with other domains. It is Kerberos that made it possible to get rid of one-to-many trust relationships that existed in Windows NT 4.0. Two-way transitive trusts make Kerberos a clear leader in building large-scale enterprise systems with many domains. Within the same forest, administrators do not have to lift a finger to set up all necessary trusts.

■ Microsoft's implementation of Kerberos is based on an industry standard, originally developed at the Massachusetts Institute of Technology as part of the Athena project, which began in 1983 and was supported by IBM and DEC. Version 5 of this protocol was completed in the mid-1990s. Since this is an industry standard, Microsoft's Kerberos authentication can also work with any other UNIX-based system running Kerberos V5, making it possible to extend Single Sign-On across different platforms. RFCs 1510 and 1964, along with some others, describe the Kerberos standard in great detail.

exam
ⓦatch   *Shifting a domain to native functional level does not prevent down-level clients from operating. It disables replication to NT 4 BDCs. Unless policy settings are configured to disable NTLM, raising the functional level does not disable NTLM authentication.*

The scope and implementation details of Kerberos are extensive, so we will review the main concepts.

The purpose and objective of Kerberos can be summarized this way: how can you ensure the authenticity of two communicating parties so that both of the parties involved are certain that no misrepresentation is made? A possible solution would be to implement a shared secret, configure each system involved in communication to use this secret, and then implement a way of letting each system know that the party knows this secret. Sending the secret over the network to the other guy is not very safe. Imagine sending user passwords by open text email.

Kerberos solves the problem using cryptography and secret keys. It relies on a symmetric cryptography and trusted third-party authority, the Key Distribution Center (KDC). The KDC is installed on domain controllers and consists of two key services: AS (authentication service) and TGS (ticket granting service). The process works as follows:

1. A user authenticates to the KDC by sending a username and hashed password value (no actual password is submitted over the network).

2. KDC receives the information and uses the same password hash value stored in Active Directory to read the request and time stamp, to ensure that this is not a replay attack. The Kerberos protocol is time sensitive.

3. KDC generates the so-called TGT, or ticket granting ticket, encrypts it with its own secret encryption key, and then encrypts it with the user's password hash from Active Directory, also including a session key. The double-encrypted TGT travels to the user, and if the user is who she says she is, the hash value calculated from her password will be the same, and she will be able to open the KDC-encrypted TGT and get her session key, which will be used for all future ticket requests. The authentication service has completed its function.

4. Next, the user requests a service ticket from the KDC that will form the basis of authorization. The user must submit the once-decrypted TGT to KDC to confirm her identity. If KDC can read this encrypted TGT using its secret key, authentication completes successfully and the user's identity is established. KDC will then issue a service ticket, encrypting it with the session key. TGS generates a server ticket as well and returns it to the user. The TGT submission and service ticket request is made through the TGS portion of KDC.

5. Now all the user has to do is read her service ticket and send the server portion of the ticket to the server where the resources she wants to access are located.

6. The server decrypts its service ticket, still encrypted by TGS, using its key established with the KDC on a permanent basis. The server returns a time

stamp that is encrypted with a service ticket session key, which is also known to the user. If the user manages to decrypt the information and read the time stamp, this will automatically confirm the identities of both server and user to each of the parties. The server reads the service ticket, authenticates the user, and establishes a session.

Step 6 may need clarification. When the user submits the server portion of the service ticket to the server, it also sends its encrypted time stamp. If the server decrypts the time stamp successfully, it can safely assume that the client is who she says she is, and furthermore, it makes sure that this is not a replay attack by comparing the user time stamp with its own current time. If the time difference is greater than that allowed through Kerberos policy—five minutes by default—the request will be considered invalid and access will be rejected.

Then the server sends back a portion of this original request, also supplying the same client time stamp value it read from the client request. Because the session key is the same on the client and server, they must exchange a different set of information during the server-client portion of the exchange to generate a different encrypted value, because otherwise the client would have no assurances that the server is authentic. (Someone could have simply recorded the original request and sent it back to the client without decryption-encryption.)

The fact that the client receives only a portion of its initial encrypted request back tells the client that the server knows the same symmetric session key; it used it to decrypt the ticket, extract the time stamp, encrypt just the time stamp, and send it back. Both parties have the same secret key they use to encrypt authentication information.

Tickets have a lifetime value, after expiration of which they become invalid and have to be renewed. This happens without disruption of the user's work or the need to log in again, of course, unless the KDC is down. Also note that there is no direct communication between the server and the KDC on the domain controller in the authorization process. Once the service ticket has been received from the TGS, it remains valid for access to the server in question for the specified interval, which, by default, is ten hours. This saves network bandwidth, processor cycles (encryption is a taxing operation), and minimizes transmission of encrypted sensitive information.

All participants in this scheme trust the KDC. The KDC has access to Active Directory to retrieve user logon and password hash information; it stores all long-term cryptographic keys associated with participants such as servers. This key must be known only to the KDC and the participant in question. Physical KDC security therefore is paramount.

Service Tickets

Why use tickets and generate so much more traffic involved in setting up a session between the client and the server, when KDC could simply verify the client's identity, issue her a session key, and then submit the same session key to the server, encrypting it using the prenegotiated long-term key? Reality is a bit more complicated. First, session keys are temporary and must be stored in volatile memory; sessions expire for security reasons and must be renewed. Then, imagine what would happen if the client received its copy of the session key before the server gets its copy. The client would request communication using encrypted requests that the server would not yet be in a position to decrypt. Finally, with a many-to-many mapping between clients and servers that they may request access to, issuing session keys to servers would mean that servers must store these keys in memory on a temporary basis for all users—this is a scalability problem. Then, what happens if the server gets rebooted, and how would users and servers be able to establish a trust association?

KDC issues both portions of the service ticket to the client, and then the client submits the server copy to the server, along with the user copy. This ensures that there are no synchronization problems and no missing session keys involved in the process of establishing client-server sessions. The KDC server, on its part, does not care what happens to the service ticket once it has been issued. It can only be used for the purpose of accessing a specific server for a specified period of time.

Tickets and session keys are never written to the disk and are securely stored in volatile RAM, where they are difficult to access by unauthorized means. The server portion of the service ticket is stored on the client machine, still encrypted using a long-term KDC-server key, for the client stands no chance of getting this key to decrypt the ticket (nor does it really need to do this). Whenever access to the same server is required, this ticket is submitted along with the session request information, encrypted using the shared session key, and if the service ticket is still valid, the server accepts the request to establish a session. The server receives both copies of the service ticket. It uses its long-term secret key to decrypt its own portion and extract the shared session key, and then uses this shared session key to work with the client portion of the ticket. When the session is over, the session key and service tickets are discarded on the server side, but are still stored in the client credentials cache.

The lifetime of the default service and TGT is selected so that the user is not required to renew them throughout the same workday—ten hours leaves a bit of room for a standard eight-hour workday. When the user logs off, the credentials cache is purged and all negotiated Kerberos parameters are destroyed.

Local Logon Process

Kerberos is also used to log on users locally by authenticating them with Active Directory. The user logon process in Windows Server 2003 works as follows (this is effectively a zoomed-in version of the first two steps in the previous numbered list):

1. The user supplies his username, password, and domain name. The information is retrieved by the Local Security Authority (LSA) on the client machine.

2. The client LSA uses DNS to locate a nearby domain controller or, rather, a domain controller that is providing KDC service. Then a request is submitted to the AS portion of the KDC service on the chosen domain controller. Before the client is allowed to do anything on the network, he needs to get a ticket granting ticket.

3. The Kerberos system queries the global catalog server to get the details of universal group membership of the user. KDC generates and returns a ticket that contains the user's SID and membership information, which will be used in later stages of interaction with Kerberos.

4. LSA then contacts Kerberos again, this time to request another ticket, which will be used to establish access to the Workstation service on the local computer. LSA submits the first ticket received from the KDC.

5. KDC verifies the information contained in the original ticket and returns the second requested ticket to be used to access the Workstation service. This ticket will also contain the information extracted from the first ticket.

6. LSA decrypts the Workstation ticket, SID, and user domain local, global, and universal group membership information, and generates an access token.

7. The client computer spawns user processes, associating the access token with each of them. The access token will determine which resources this user has on local computers based on his SID and group membership.

Network Logon Process

A network logon occurs when a user who is logged on locally on a client machine tries to access a shared resource, such as a shared folder. The algorithm of network logons is similar to interactive logons described in the previous section.

The client computer requests a service ticket from the Kerberos (KDC service) on the domain controller that originally authenticated the interactive logon for this user. This ticket is received by the local LSA service on the client machine, and the server portion of the ticket is submitted to the server LSA. The LSA on the target server performs the necessary Kerberos operations and also generates an access token for the remote user. This token is used to authenticate client requests for resources located on this server.

Note that the SID and group information in this case is not refreshed—there are no global catalog lookups. Instead, the client uses a cached ticket with cached SID and group membership information from the interactive logon.

Smart Cards

Based on the preceding Kerberos description, most of us would agree that the algorithm is indeed strong. In fact, it was so strong (conceptually) that Microsoft had to abandon its own flawed NTLM/NTLMv2 protocol in favor of Kerberos V5. In the authentication process, Kerberos transfers minimal amounts of sensitive information over the network, and even if it is intercepted, hackers will have to work to decrypt the information, and then they are racing against time anyway. By default, they have five minutes to crack it.

Man-in-the-middle attacks against Kerberos seem very unlikely. But there is a weak link—the human factor of user interaction and passwords. If attackers find out a username and password, Kerberos becomes useless as a secure authentication protocol. (Usernames are less of a problem, but passwords may be easy to obtain from unsophisticated users by methods known as social engineering.) Hardware authentication devices attempt to solve this problem, or at least the social engineering part of it.

Smart cards, as most of you probably know, are credit-card-sized integrated circuit cards that have a connector, resembling SIM cards used in GSM mobile phones. They are used with USB or RS-232 card reader devices. Driver support for these devices comes right out of the box with Windows XP Professional and Windows Server 2003 operating systems. Smart cards are used to store private and public keys—X.509 V3 digital certificates that are used to authenticate users to the system (domain authentication). Now, you may wonder, why are digital certificates used with Kerberos, since they are based on asymmetric key cryptography, and Kerberos, up to this point at least, was symmetric and was based on a shared secret key? PKINIT is an extension to the Kerberos V5 protocol that enables the use of public key cryptography (asymmetric) for the purposes of Kerberos ticket exchange.

Using smart cards and readers offers the following advantages over traditional username/password systems:

- Even if cards are stolen, attackers cannot take advantage of them without knowing users' PIN codes. After three or five incorrect PIN code entries, the card is locked and administrative intervention will be required to unlock it.

- Smart cards are tamper resistant, meaning that forging or altering them is a fairly useless exercise, especially considering that they store digital certificates.

■ All operations involving sensitive authentication data are isolated from the rest of the client system, which makes it even more difficult for someone to tamper with the authentication process on the local machine.

■ Cards are the safest way to transfer user credentials between computers; you just have to take the card out of the reader (which would lock the workstation by default) and insert it into another reader on some other machine.

■ Smart cards offer a lot of application flexibility when it comes to developing new things. Already, Microsoft supports S/MIME, a digital signature in Outlook and Internet Explorer applications using the certificates from the smart-card reader; Windows VPN access and secure web access is also facilitated using smart cards. This API is available for anyone who wants to integrate their applications with smart-card technology.

Smart-Card Authentication

Smart cards store the private key and corresponding public key in the form of a digital certificate. The private key always remains on the card and is highly sensitive; if it leaks, the security is compromised. The public key should be distributed to anyone wishing to conduct encrypted communications with the user in question.

When the user inserts the smart card into the reader, this substitutes the CTRL+ ALT+DEL procedure and login information entry. The user is prompted for his or her PIN number, which is used by the LSA to access information stored on the card. LSA reads the public key (digital certificate) and submits it to the KDC for authentication purposes.

KDC, in its turn, verifies the digital certificate with Active Directory, extracts the public key, and encrypts the session key to this public key. Only the client can read this encrypted information using its asymmetric private key stored on the smart card. From this point onward, Kerberos works much the same way, using symmetric encryption in the form of the shared session key.

Network logons using smart cards are a lot less susceptible to attacks than password-based authentication. There is no password, so all dictionary attacks, brute-force attacks, and other password-guessing approaches are eliminated. Lost cards can be disabled administratively, and with only three to five attempts to enter a correct PIN code before a card is locked, attackers do not stand a chance of cracking them using conventional methods.

Smart cards do, however, require some tinkering on the part of implementers. First off, of course, you need a Certification Authority (CA) installed and configured on your domain controller(s). This is needed to implement the PKI infrastructure, necessary to issue certificates in the first place and then perform the public key exchange. This technology will be reviewed in more detail in Chapter 6.

You also need Active Directory, because smart cards do not work for the purposes of local authentication, only network-based authentication. Finally, you will need to acquire smart card components:

- **Smart cards** As noted earlier, these are credit-card-sized cards containing an integrated circuit and memory. Key exchange, digital signatures, and authentication can all be performed by this integrated logic.
- **Smart-card readers** USB, RS-232 (serial), PS/2, or PCMCIA devices provide the interface between the client computer and the card.
- **Smart-card software** Applications are used to write and lock/unlock smart cards, and perform other administrative functions such as PIN administration and card personalization. A standard API allows for writing custom applications.

Depending on the smart-card reader provider, you may get a solution that will work out of the box, without any extra driver installation or Windows infrastructure integration requirements. (Just to give those of you who are unfamiliar with this technology a rough idea of what the prices are, as of August 2003 smart cards are going for around $8, and USB readers are available for as low as $25, so pricing is no longer prohibitive. In addition, Windows Server 2003 ships with device drivers for ten manufacturers, so you have a choice, although Gemplus and Schlumberger stand out.)

To configure smart cards for access, administrators will have to enroll users for smart-card digital certificates through either automatic enrollment or, as Microsoft recommends, using a controlled process via a dedicated terminal. Administrators will have to install Enterprise Certificate Authority on a domain controller with a smart-card device. This will set up a Smart Card Enrollment station, which allows administrators to request smart-card certificates on behalf of users. The process involves requesting a signing certificate based on the Enrollment Agent certificate template. This is something that, by default, only administrators are allowed to do. Keep in mind that you will need vendor software installed on the CA if you want to personalize cards on the same station.

Once the certificate has been requested on behalf of the user and installed on the card, the card has been personalized, and smart-card readers have been installed on the user machines, no additional steps are required to begin logging on using smart cards. The process of working with the CA and associated digital certificate template operations and the user enrollment process is described in great detail in Chapter 6.

Password Policies

In Windows NT 4.0, password policies could be configured using the User Manager for Domains. With the introduction of Windows 2000, account and password policy settings are now configured using group policy objects and Active Directory. In short, the Group Policy Object Editor allows you to manage computer and user configurations based on their location in the Active Directory structure; you can apply anything from software, to logon scripts, to settings, to Registry keys, to file security settings using the GPO Editor. The next chapter discusses this technology more thoroughly. But for the purposes of this discussion, we will review just one of the groups of settings configurable through group policies.

Password policies are used to configure how passwords should behave in the system, and by default, Windows Server 2003 in Active Directory applies more restrictions than ever before. Some may say that for a system that, by default, relies solely on passwords, the default settings are still not enough due to the simple fact that password compromise in such a system means compromise of the entire system.

Figure 5-13 shows the Group Policy Object Editor MMC console with the default domain policy's Password Policy section displayed in the right-hand pane. Here you can configure the following:

- **Enforce Password History**   Twenty-four passwords remembered by default
- **Maximum Password Age**   Forty-two days by default
- **Minimum Password Age**   One day by default
- **Minimum Password Length**   Seven characters by default
- **Passwords Must Meet Complexity Requirements**   Enabled by default
- **Store Passwords Using Reversible Encryption**   Disabled by default

You may notice that these default settings mark a significant turnaround in the default security configuration strategy recently adopted by Microsoft. In Windows 2000 Active Directory out-of-the-box environments, for instance, the password complexity requirement was turned off, minimum password length was set to 0

FIGURE 5-13   Password policies in the Group Policy Object Editor

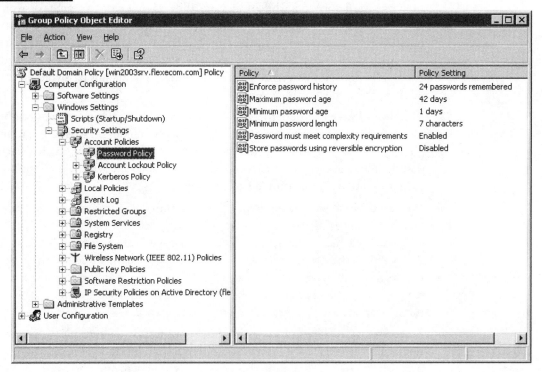

characters, and password history was set to remember just one password. Let's briefly review how these settings affect password strategy in Active Directory.

- **Maximum Password Age and Minimum Password Age**   These settings control how often users must, and can, change their passwords, respectively. In the case of maximum password age, passwords expire after the set number of days, and unless users change their passwords, they will not be able to access the system anymore. Passwords may be changed at any time though, unless the password age is less than the minimum setting. It is recommended that users be forced to change their passwords once a month, or more often in high-security environments.

You may have to override the maximum and minimum settings on individual accounts if you use special service accounts to run processes, such as SQL server or COM applications. An expired password for these accounts may require administrators to reset the password manually and then change it on all production servers in service settings, which may result in downtime.

- **Enforce Password History**   There is no real value in forcing users to change their password once in a while if they are allowed to retype the same password. The password history setting will force Active Directory to "remember" a set number of passwords used in the past, and will prevent them from being repeated. The default setting of 24 means users will have to go through 24 password changes before they can reuse passwords, and with a default password age of 42 days, this is nearly three years.

- **Minimum Password Length**   This setting guarantees passwords will not be too short for a given password policy. As Chapter 6 goes on to discuss group policies and passwords, the security implications of password length are clearly described in the context of password-cracking attacks. In short, the longer the password, the more difficult it is to guess.

- **Password Must Meet Complexity Requirements**   This is another setting aimed directly at preventing password-cracking attacks. Users are likely to use passwords that mean something to them—pet names, favorite songs, and so on. If the attacker knows the user well enough, these are the first password combinations the attacker will try. By forcing password complexity requirements, you restrict users to choosing passwords that use mixed case, numbers, and special characters all in one password.

- **Store Password Using Reversible Encryption**   By default, passwords are not stored in Active Directory; AD only stores a hashed value calculated using the password. Enabling this setting effectively means passwords will be stored in Active Directory instead of hashes, which is a very undesirable security risk. Microsoft suggests not using this option but provides it for application compatibility purposes.

on the *Job*

Note that enabling the reversible encryption setting will affect all users in the domain for which the policy is being configured. If there are only a few accounts that must use reversible encryption, instead of configuring the policy this way, set this attribute in individual user account properties.

An account lockout policy is effectively the flip side of the password coin, and it can be used in conjunction with password policies to ensure that attackers have no chance of brute-forcing a password using conventional techniques. Using account lockout threshold and duration settings, you can control how many attempts users have for entering a correct password before their accounts are locked out. Please refer to Chapter 6 for a more thorough discussion of account lockout and Kerberos policies.

CERTIFICATION OBJECTIVE 5.03

Plan an Organizational Unit Structure

The organizational unit (OU) is an Active Directory container that is used for intradomain object organization purposes. OU structures can be built separately in each domain, but they may follow the same logical scheme, such as mapping a business environment. OUs may contain any type of object: printers, shared folders, group accounts, user accounts, computer accounts, and so on. Functionally, OUs provide the following:

- **Delegation**   OUs can be used to delegate groups of permissions to certain people and enable them to perform specific operations on the objects, stored in OUs.

- **Group policy scope**   As mentioned in Chapter 3, group policies may be applied on the OU level. OUs provide the most specific scope, and therefore policies applied on this level override all other policies.

- **Ease of administration**   Obviously, storing thousands of files in the root directory on drive C: would not make any of us too productive; we use folders to organize resources on the disk. Likewise, OUs are used to organize resources in the Active Directory, to make it more manageable and structured, and to optimize resource location. All security settings assigned on the OU level by default are inherited by all child objects, which makes permissions management easier.

By far, the most important feature of OUs is their structural significance: OUs are used to implement a logical structure of resources that maps to the business organization and requirements. Users then may be delegated to manage their own resources in the same department or business unit, and by the same token others may be restricted from accessing resources in departments with sensitive information.

Microsoft recommends planning the Active Directory infrastructure bearing in mind group policies and their future application, and delegation. Using OUs within the domain structure for this purpose allows administrators to be less concerned with these recommendations during domain and forest planning and focus on it after the main structure is finalized.

Another OU planning consideration advises against using too deep a structure. OUs are active elements of the directory, and excessive nesting would cause unnecessarily intensive processing associated with maintenance of the structure—

calculating inheritance and ACLs due to object additions, movements, delegation, policy processing, and so on.

Deep nesting also affects LDAP performance, and when you create multilevel OU structures, it may become less than intuitive to navigate them, which may have a negative impact on user experience. Various sources propose different amounts of nested levels, but three to five levels normally should satisfy the needs of most enterprises.

Analyze Administrative Requirements

When it comes to OU structure planning, it is up to individual businesses to decide how they want to partition objects between different containers and what logic to use in coming up with a naming convention and overall structure. Different sources suggest various models: you can work from the centralized or decentralized administration/IT perspective, business division perspective, object/project, geographical, horizontal or vertical partitioning of organizational charts, and types of users (mobile, task, kiosks, and so on—see Chapter 3). The point is that no single approach fits all. Most successful implementations combine some or all of these ideas to get the best structure that fits the specific needs of a company. Keep in mind that, conceptually, OUs were conceived to represent the business structure of the company, much like sites are meant to split up replication areas, and domains to split up security areas.

Geographical Model

For large organizations that are widely dispersed geographically, the logical choice for the OU structure is a geographical model. The first-level OU could be set up based on countries or regions, such as Midwest or Asia & Pacific (that's if it is the same domain spread over a vast geographic area; some companies may prefer to deploy domains in separate regions instead). Second-level OUs could represent individual offices or business divisions within these regions, states/provinces, or cities. The main characteristic of this structure is that the parent levels are less likely to change during the lifetime of Active Directory. It also presents an intuitive structure to the users of the system, who have a clear understanding of where the objects are located simply by looking at the structure.

It is possible that the geographical and organizational models will coincide. For example, information technology administrators in one city will have their own geographical OU under their jurisdiction, instead of being managed by administrators from another OU. However, more often than not, the geographical model (assuming there are no second- or third-level business OUs) fails to capture the essence of business organization. For example, two distinct geographical units may have the same business units located in that office, requiring their own OU; or if a company is involved in costly research, it may opt to maintain one R&D department, which engineers from any geographical location should be able to access.

Organizational Model

As the name implies, the organizational model is used to build out the OU structure. This is really the main push behind the OU technology: to implement a structure based on the company's organizational chart, so to speak. For your first level, you could use business divisions; for the second, departments; and for the third, individual offices that report to the same managerial team within the corresponding department.

This is arguably the most intuitive design from the user perspective. It establishes a direct association between, the technical organization of objects in Active Directory domains and logical organizations of resources in the organization, making it easy for users to locate appropriate resources in the structure. This also makes it easier to mirror interdepartmental business processes in Active Directory—for instance, setting up department-based security policies, delegating OU administration to department team leads, or moving user objects between corresponding OUs when they are reassigned to another department or division. The latter automatically exposes users to the new OU administrator and new security policies in effect in the target OU.

Granted, by relying on the underlying business structure, you are exposing your OU structure to a shaky foundation. Every time there is an addition of a new product line (company division), decommissioning of an office, or some restructuring changes going on, this will require administrators to re-create the structure in an adequate way and move objects around. In the best-case scenario, you will simply have to rename OUs; in the worst, you may have to re-create your group policies and delegation to adjust to changes as well.

Object Model

The object model proposes to group objects of the same class in different OUs. So in effect, all printers in the organization would be placed in one OU, users in another one, groups in their own OU, and so forth. This model may provide some advantages in terms of group policy planning and administration of security settings. If your company has an administrator whose sole job is managing users, it will be easy to assign all necessary permissions for him or her to manage just that one user container. ACLs on domain containers would not be lengthy or complex.

Practically speaking though, this model has no chance of surviving on its own, even in small companies, if they are to grow at all. The number of objects may grow, and locating objects in the same OU may not be as transparent as it used to be when the structure was created. Nonetheless, when used in conjunction with geographical or organizational models, it may provide additional ideas on how to structure second or third OU levels.

Project Model

Basing the OU organization on projects is another alternative. For consulting companies involved in a project-based business, this organization may make sense. Each OU represents a different project and contains objects representing resources needed to develop the respective projects.

The biggest weakness of this strategy is the life span of projects and come-and-go OUs. Some projects may last for decades; others last a few days. Depending on the size and expected timeline of the project, creating and tearing down OU structures may prove to be a long-term pain. Since one object cannot be a child in more than one container, the constant moving and reallocating of resources may hike up the costs of owning an Active Directory infrastructure.

Distinguishing Groups from Organizational Units

This chapter has discussed two elements of internal structuring—organizational units and security groups. Recall that the two are distinctly different in composition and application.

- Groups are used to assign permissions to objects and file system resources and create distributions lists. OUs act as administrative containers; they are used to create a structure for the delegation of privileges to security group members, to implement group policy for a set of child objects, and to reflect the business structure of resources in the organization.

- Groups can contain only security principal members from different domains and even forests, depending on the group scope. OUs can only contain child objects (any objects, not just security principals) that belong to the same domain as the OU itself.

Analyzing Group Policy Requirements

Whichever model, or combination thereof, you choose for your organizational unit structure, always keep in mind that one of the purposes of implementing this structure is so that group policies can be assigned later on. A few recommendations have been put forth to alleviate the burden of group policy planning:

- *Separate user objects from computer objects into distinct OU containers.* This will help in group policy planning because you will be in a position to create object-specific policies. As Chapter 6 will show, group policies contain two major groups of settings—computer configuration and user configuration. Administrators can turn one of the sections off for a given group policy object altogether.

- *Create all-inclusive group policy objects that will apply necessary settings to large groups of objects.* If your users are subjected to a number of group policy objects, it will increase logon times and group policy processing overhead and will further obscure the planning and troubleshooting process. Likewise, computers will have to spend more time loading the operating system and finalizing settings.

- *Plan OU structure so that the fewest policies can satisfy configuration requirements of the most objects, and aim to apply these policies at the first OU level.* Remember that deeply nested OU elements will, by default, inherit all of the group policy objects from their parent containers. Granted, some of the containers will have to have their own configuration requirements; in this case, you might look into blocking policy inheritance or using security group filtering. (But be sure to read the next point.)

- *Plan your OU structure so that the need to use blocking, no override, and security group filtering is minimized.* Excessive usage of these features, as Chapter 6 further explains, could potentially create a group policy mess in an otherwise sound OU structure. Administration of such structures would make the lives of support personnel more difficult than they really should be.

CERTIFICATION OBJECTIVE 5.04

Implement an Organizational Unit Structure

Once you have an idea of what your OU structure is going to be, and you have given security groups and group policies some thought, it is time to create the structure and, perhaps, delegate a few permissions to support personnel.

Creating Organizational Units

The simplest way to add a new organizational unit container is to use the Active Directory Users and Computers MMC snap-in (shown in Figure 5-1). To add an OU, follow these steps:

1. In the Active Directory Users and Computers (ADUC) console, expand the domain container and click one of the existing containers that you wish to make the parent of the container you are about to create.

2. Right-click the container, and select New | Organizational Unit from the context menu.

3. In the window that appears (shown in Figure 5-14), type in the name of the new container and click OK.

on the job

Note that you will not be able to create new containers in most of the built-in groups.

Once the organizational unit structure has been put in place, you can use the OU property page to assign attribute values, manage security, assign group policies, and configure group policy, security inheritance, and blocking. Figure 5-15 shows the General tab of the property pages.

FIGURE 5-14

Creating a new organizational unit

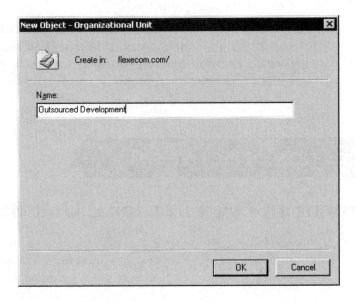

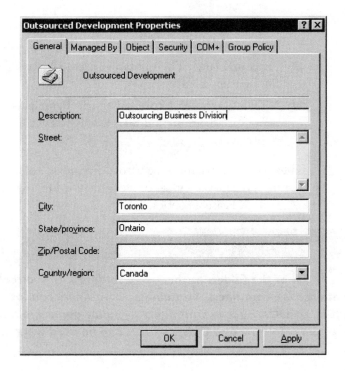

FIGURE 5-15

Managing
organizational
unit properties

Built-in Domain Containers

When you create a domain, it is automatically populated with a few containers (all of
which you can see by switching on the Advanced Features in the ADUC View menu):

- **Builtin**   All built-in groups and users go in this container.
- **Computers**   By default, all domain computers that are not maintaining the
  infrastructure (they are not domain controllers) are added here.
- **Domain Controllers**   This container holds all domain controller objects.
- **Users**   When you create a new user or group, Users is the default container
  for these objects.
- **LostAndFound**   This container holds orphaned objects. It is conceivable,
  although unlikely, that a new object could be added to a container that is
  being removed from the system on another domain controller. This object
  will be placed into the LostAndFound container when the deleted container
  state finally gets across to all of the domain controllers.

- **System**   This contains domain settings and configuration of some infrastructure services such as Active Directory–integrated DNS, domain DFS, and FRS.
- **Program Data**   This container is used by default for application partition information storage.
- **NTDS Quotas and ForeignSecurityPrincipals**   These two containers store quota specifications and SIDs associated with external trust links, respectively.

These containers cannot be used as first-level containers in your custom OU structure, and generally it is not recommended to expose them through the use of the Advanced Features option.

Delegating Permissions

You can create bulk permissions, delegating all the authority to administrative accounts, or you can delegate a very specific role to authorized people. A good example of using delegation is to assign user management rights to a team leader of a department, or to a help desk person responsible for user support in a decentralized administration model. The same effect can be achieved by assigning permissions to security principals manually; however, this would make delegation a tedious task that would be prone to human error. Using delegation, security group structures, and ACLs, administrators can assign permissions in a granular fashion to a single OU, OU subtree, an entire OU tree in a given domain, or the domain itself.

Using delegation, administrators can achieve the following:

- Delegate authority to modify values of container object attributes
- Delegate authority to create, manage, and delete child objects in an existing OU (such as adding user accounts and publishing printers)
- Delegate authority to modify values of child object attributes (such as resetting user password)

Here are some recommendations to consider when planning delegation: First, whenever possible, try to delegate control on the OU level in order to keep permissions inheritance and ACLs as plain as possible. Use the Delegation of Control Wizard whenever possible, basically for the same reason. Most of all, try to adhere as closely as possible to the delegation of business processes in the company. Following a similar pattern will make things more intuitive for users and ultimately will enhance their experience.

Delegation of Control Wizard

To delegate permissions, go through the following steps:

1. Start the ADUC console, and select an OU where you want to delegate permissions.

2. In the context menu of the container, click the Delegate Control menu item.

3. On the welcome screen, click Next.

4. On the Users and Groups screen, select the appropriate security principal using the Active Directory browser available through the Add button. When done, click Next.

5. On the Tasks To Delegate screen, you have two options: delegate a predefined common task, or create a custom task to delegate. For the purpose of the demo, let's click Delegate the Following Common Tasks (selected by default) and then choose Create, Delete, and Manage User Accounts from the list shown in Figure 5-16. Click Next when done.

6. The wizard now presents a summary of changes it is about to commit to the ACL of the container object. Click Finish to apply the changes.

If you choose to create a custom task, you will be presented with the screen shown in Figure 5-17. Here you should select what you wish to delegate permissions to—all of the objects in the OU, or specific classes of objects. To keep things as transparent as possible, it is recommended that you leave the default setting, which is "This folder, existing objects in this folder, and creation of new objects in this folder."

Next, on the Permissions page (see Figure 5-18), you can select categories of the permissions you wish to work with. Choices are General (Full Control, Read, Write, etc.), Property-Specific (read or write attribute values), and Creation/Deletion of Specific Child Objects (creating or deleting computer, group, user accounts, and so on).

FIGURE 5-16

Tasks to Delegate
page of the
Delegation of
Control Wizard

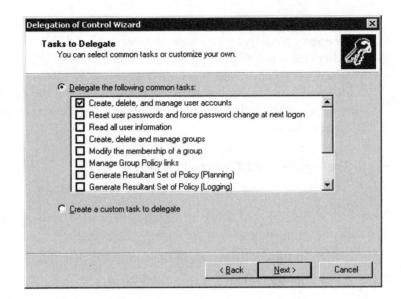

After you click Next, a familiar confirmation screen will be presented outlining forthcoming changes. Upon clicking the Finish button, these changes are applied to the container.

FIGURE 5-17

Active Directory
object type page
of the Delegation
of Control
Wizard

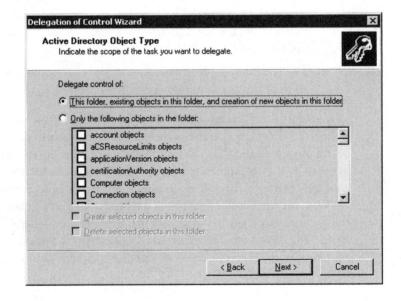

FIGURE 5-18

Permissions page
of the Delegation
of Control
Wizard

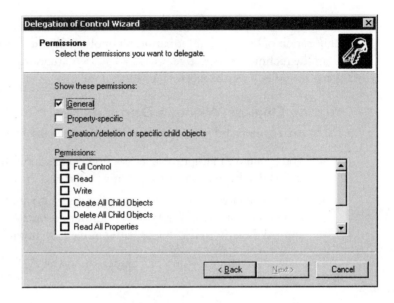

If you choose to employ common tasks, as suggested by the previous demo steps, the list of common tasks you are presented with is as follows:

- Create, delete, and manage user accounts
- Reset user passwords and force password change at next logon
- Read all user information
- Create, delete, and manage groups
- Modify the membership of a group
- Manage Group Policy links
- Generate Resultant Set of Policy (Planning)
- Generate Resultant Set of Policy (Logging)
- Create, delete, and manage inetOrgPerson accounts
- Reset inetOrgPerson person passwords and force password change at next logon
- Read all inetOrgPerson information

Moving Objects Within the Structure

You may have to move objects (regular object instances as well as containers) during the life cycle of your Active Directory environment. This chapter has already mentioned a few potential reasons for this, such as restructuring or organizational reallocation of human or information technology resources between departments. From the technical perspective, we'll look at two situations: moving objects within a domain, and moving objects to a different domain.

Moving Objects Within a Domain

This is a straightforward procedure, but the following might be helpful to keep in mind:

- You can move multiple objects as a single operation. This significantly improves the process by reducing administrative effort and the possibility of human error.

- When you move objects from one container into another one, security settings and group policies of the target container become effective. Security settings applied directly to the object being moved are not modified.

To move an object or group of objects, open the ADUC console and follow these steps:

1. Select one or more objects that are about to be moved. Use SHIFT and CTRL keys to select a batch of objects if necessary.

2. In the context menu, select the Move option. An OU browser will appear, as shown in Figure 5-19. Navigate to the target OU and double-click it.

A simpler way is to drag and drop objects or containers to the desired places within the structure.

FIGURE 5-19

Choosing a target
OU container

EXERCISE 5-1

Creating OUs, User Objects, and Moving Objects Between OUs

In this exercise, you will use the Active Directory Users and Computers console to create a few organizational units, then create a user object in each of these OUs, and finally, move one user account into another OU.

Creating an OU

1. Log on to the network using the Administrators group member account.
2. Click Start | Programs | Administrative Tools | Active Directory Users and Computers. The ADUC console will load.
3. Select a domain container, and using the context menu, click New | Organizational Unit.
4. In the window that pops up, type in the name of the container and click OK. Let's name it Sales.
5. Repeat the process and create another OU, Marketing.

Creating User Objects

6. In the context menu of the Sales OU, click New | User. In the window that pops up, type in the name of the fictitious user, and specify a logon name.
7. Click Next, and on the next screen, assign a password. Click Next again, and on the summary screen, click Finish.
8. Repeat steps 6 and 7 for the Marketing OU to create the second user account.

Moving Objects Between OUs

9. Click the Marketing container, and using the context menu of the user account, click Move.
10. In the window that pops up, navigate through your structure of OUs, and select the Sales OU. Click OK when done. Alternatively, you could have dragged this user account and dropped it into the Sales OU.

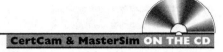

EXERCISE 5-2

CertCam & MasterSim ON THE CD

Delegating Permissions

In this exercise, you will use the Delegation of Control Wizard to assign user, group, computer, and printer object management rights to a user account that is not a member of the Administrators group. This exercise assumes you went through the steps in Exercise 5-1.

Using the Delegation of Control Wizard

1. Log on to the network using an account that is a member of the Administrators group.

2. Click Start | Programs | Administrative Tools | Active Directory Users and Computers. The ADUC console will load.

3. Switch to the Sales container context menu, and select Delegate Control. This will load the Delegation of Control Wizard.

4. Click Next, and on the Users and Group screen, use the Add button to select one of the two user accounts currently located in the Sales OU.

5. Click Next. On this screen, choose Create A Custom Task To Delegate, and click Next again.

6. Choose Only The Following Objects in the folder option, and check off the boxes corresponding to User Objects, Group Objects, Computer Objects, and Printer Objects.

7. Click Next. On the Permissions tab, select Full Control, and click Next again.

8. On the confirmation screen, click Finish.

Now let's take a look at how this process modified the ACL of the Sales OU. To view the ACL, right-click the Sales OU container and click Properties, then switch to the Security tab. Scroll through the list and find an ACE that corresponds to the account we were using in this exercise.

Moving Objects to a Different Domain

If you have to move objects between Active Directory domains, you cannot go dragging and dropping objects around. You will have to use either the Active Directory Migration

Tool version 2 (ADMTv2) or Active Directory Object Manager (MOVETREE.exe) from the Support Tools to complete this task. (ADMTv2 can be downloaded from Microsoft's website at http://www.microsoft.com/windows2003, in the Downloads section, under Tools and Feature Packs.) Microsoft recommends using ADMT whenever possible, only reverting to MOVETREE to move objects that are not currently handled by ADMT (contact objects is one example).

You may remember that when security principals are moved between domains, their SIDs are changed to prevent accidental duplication. However, GUIDs of all objects remain unchanged from birth to death. Since security settings rely on SIDs and not GUIDs, all security settings would be lost without exception—unless the SID History attribute is enabled. SIDHistory allows for recording previously assigned SID values to security principals, but this property is only available in Windows 2000 native or Windows Server 2003 domain functional levels.

There are other caveats to using the MOVETREE utility:

- Local and global groups get moved between domains without transferring users (due to the definition of what these groups may contain).
- Computer objects cannot be moved using MOVETREE. Use ADMT or Netdom instead.
- Group policy links to source domain/OU policy objects are retained. You will have to re-create these policies in the target domain, remove old links, and add links to the new GPOs.
- MOVETREE is a command-line tool that works with the Active Directory database; do not expect it to be user friendly. You will have to supply source and target DNS FQDNs, and source and target LDAP paths.
- MOVETREE will fail to move objects that are currently locked due to a competing process.
- Schema differences, although unlikely, will also cause problems, but that is not exclusive to MOVETREE. Rather, this applies to all object-moving programs. If their administrators are performing restructuring, and schema changes haven't had time to propagate yet, the schema configuration partition may not be the same on all domain controllers.
- Similar to the situation that creates orphans in the LostAndFound built-in container, MOVETREE will fail to move objects that have been deleted on one domain controller while the operation was in progress and the change is not yet in effect on all of the servers.

■ Other problems not necessarily related to MOVETREE are those stemming from network problems or an insufficient amount of disk space on the target domain controller.

The MOVETREE utility in Windows Server 2003 Support Tools does not have a limitation where you have to create a target OU before you can actually transfer the objects; it can do this on the fly. It can also rename the target OU if necessary.

To move a sample container without running a test, issue the following command:

```
Movetree /startnocheck /s <source server's FQDN> /d <destination's server FQDN>
/sdn <source DN, such as OU=Outsourced Development,DC=Sales,DC=Flexecom,DC=Com>
/ddn <destination DN, not necessarily using the same container name>
```

The ADMT tool, illustrated in Figure 5-20, is an MMC-based snap-in that does more than just move objects around. It can be used to migrate accounts between domains as old as Windows NT 4.0, all the way to Windows Server 2003.

After you install ADMTv2, start MMC and add the Active Directory Migration Tool snap-in from the list of available consoles. Let's go through a quick exercise of moving a user account between domains using ADMT.

FIGURE 5-20	
Active Directory Migration Tool MMC snap-in	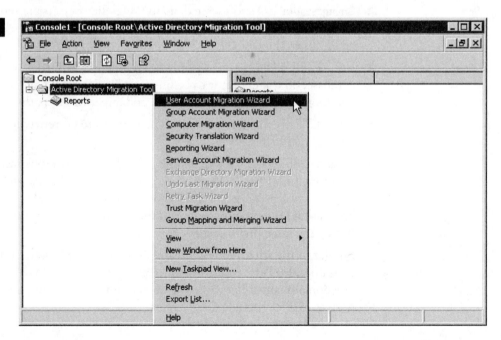

EXERCISE 5-3

Moving User Accounts Between Domains Using ADMTv2

In this exercise, you go through a simple process of moving one user account between two Windows Server 2003 functional level domains. To run this exercise yourself, you will need administrative access to a domain controller and at least two domains in your lab.

1. As shown in Figure 5-20, right-click the Active Directory Migration Tool container, and pick User Account Migration Wizard from the list. A welcome screen will appear. Click Next to continue.

2. On the Test or Make Changes screen, select Migrate Now to run the migration immediately without first simulating it. (Figure 5-21 shows this page.) Click Next.

3. On the Domain Selection page, select source and destination domains from the lists and click Next (see Figure 5-22).

4. On the User Selection page, select user account(s) to be migrated and click Next (see Figure 5-23).

FIGURE 5-21

Make Changes screen in the User Account Migration Wizard

User Account Migration Wizard ✕

Test or Make Changes
You can test your migration settings before actually making any changes.

Do you want to:

○ Test the migration settings and migrate later?

● Migrate now?

< Back | Next > | Cancel | Help

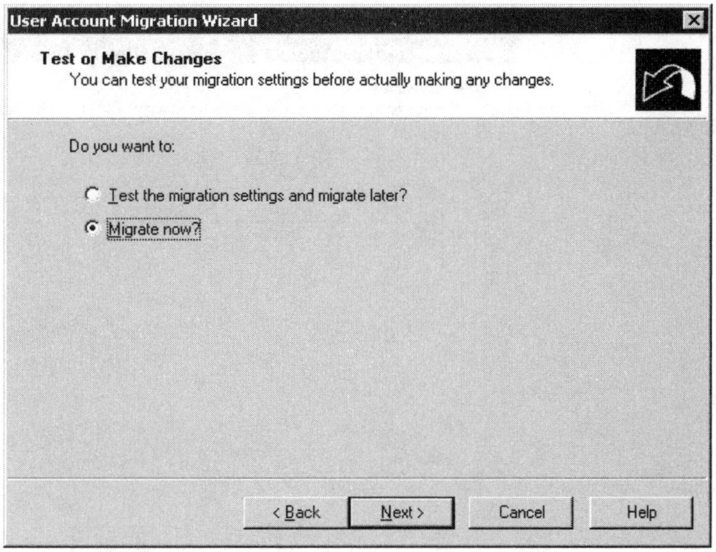

FIGURE 5-22

Domain Selection
screen

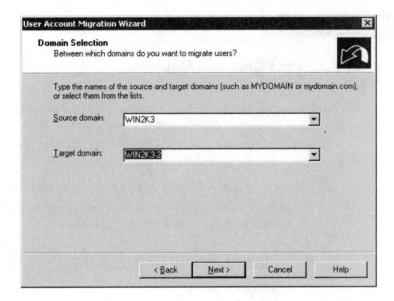

FIGURE 5-22

Domain Selection
screen

5. On the Organizational Unit Selection screen, shown in Figure 5-24, click Browse and select an appropriate target OU. You will be presented with a list of existing OUs for the target domain, similar to the one shown in Figure 5-19. When you pick your target, it will resolve into an LDAP DN reference. Click Next.

FIGURE 5-23

User Selection
screen

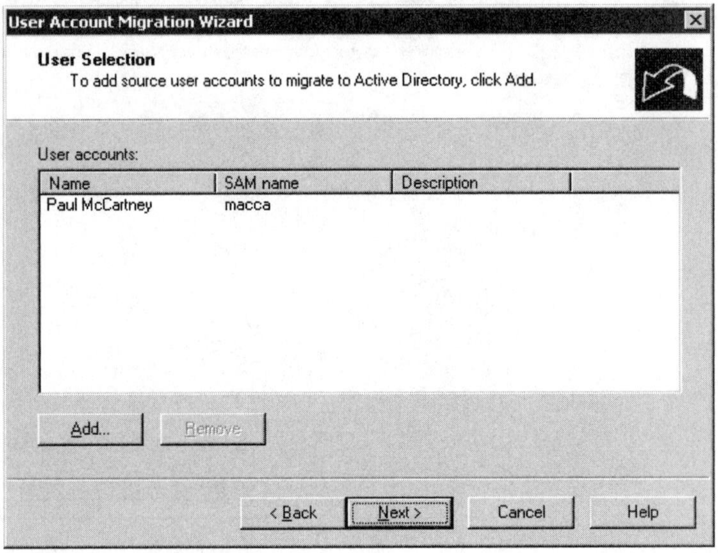

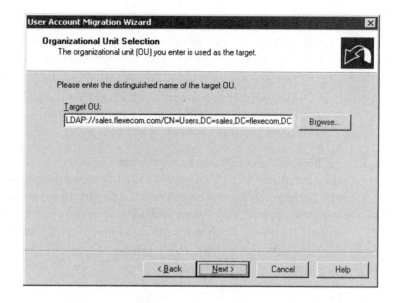

FIGURE 5-24

Organizational
Unit Selection
screen

6. On the User Options screen (shown in Figure 5-25), click Update User Rights if
   you wish to copy existing user rights to the destination OU. If you want to be
   sure that all groups in which these users may have membership are included,
   use the Migrate Associated User Groups option. Click Next when done.

FIGURE 5-25

User Options
screen

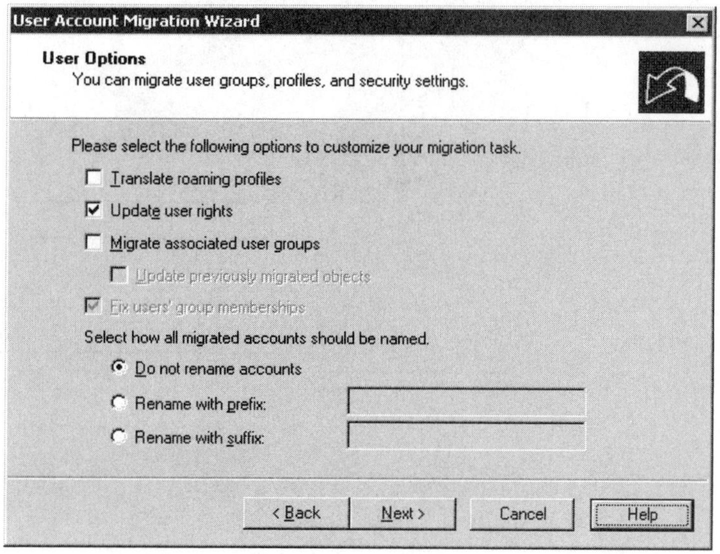

7. On the Naming Conflicts page, you can configure how name conflicts should be handled. Since this is a lab exercise, we know there are no conflicts in the target domain, so leave all default settings and click Next (see Figure 5-26).

8. After this, you will be presented with a standard confirmation screen from which you can launch the migration process you've just set up. Once the process is under way, you will receive a status page that you can refresh to monitor the process as it happens. It is shown in Figure 5-27.

This completes the user account migration exercise. To make use of HTML reporting available with this tool, you can invoke the Reporting Wizard from the step 1 context menu and go through a straightforward process of generating a report for all user migration operations. This will create a new report object in the Reports container. Figure 5-28 demonstrates a sample report from our migration.

FIGURE 5-26

Naming Conflicts
screen

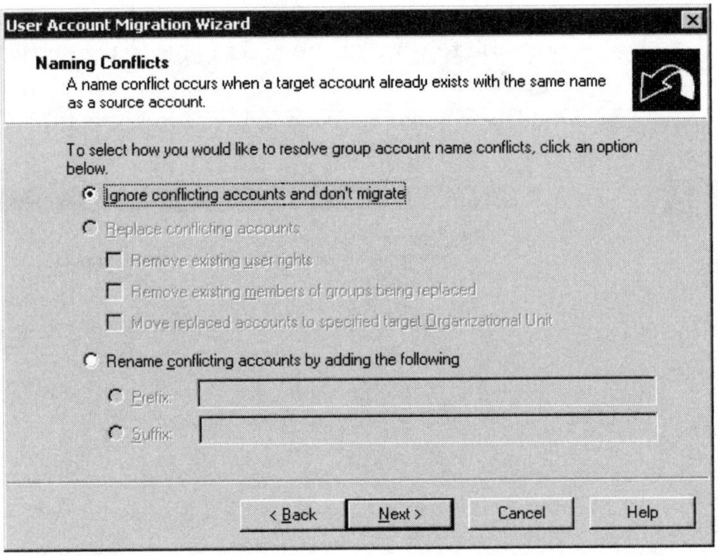

FIGURE 5-27

Migration
Progress screen

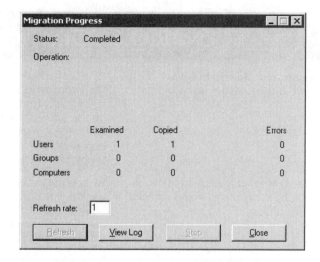

FIGURE 5-28 Migrated user and group accounts report

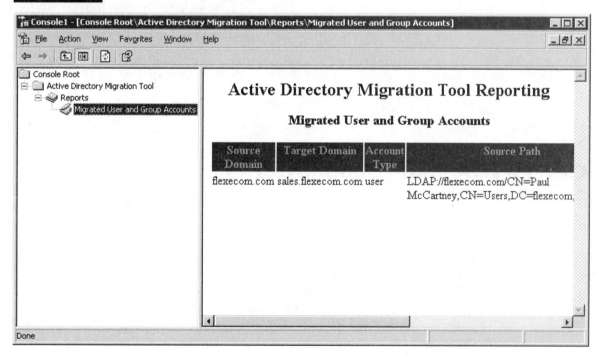

SCENARIO & SOLUTION

How can you summarize the idea of two-way authentication used in the Kerberos protocol?	In order for both parties to confirm the identities of their opponents, they employ a shared secret key, known only to them and a trusted third party. Based on the information being exchanged during session setup, the parties have to get a sign that their opponents have the same secret, although this secret is not transmitted on the wire in the clear.
Why is it safe to say that smart-card authentication is safer than traditional username/password schemes?	Even if the card is lost or stolen, it cannot be easily used. Smart cards use asymmetric encryption based on proven PKI algorithms. All certificate security calculations are performed on the card itself, which isolates it from potentially harmful system processes.
What are the main reasons for creating organizational units, and potential hazards of creating too many?	The main reason is to enable delegation of authority and application of group policies on a more specific level than domain or site. Creating too deeply nested OU structures negatively impacts system performance; creating too many OUs may reduce intuitiveness of the structure.
Why is it more difficult to move objects between domains than it is within domains?	Domains are security boundaries. When moving between domains, the GUID does not change but the SID (for security principals) does. It may be necessary to ensure that permissions are still effective after moving the object to the target domain.

CERTIFICATION SUMMARY

Creating the Active Directory structure, and implementing the organizational unit structure, then populating it with objects such as users, computers, and printers are the main tasks administrators should expect to face on a regular basis while working on implementing and, later on, supporting Active Directory.

Creating containers and objects in itself is not rocket science, although with the ADSI, administrators can get really creative if they have scripting skills. Planning this structure, however, is not a trivial task, and if left to chance, may make a difference between technology that does the trick and something that wastes resources and productivity.

This chapter reviewed security topics in a fair amount of detail, including the concepts of security groups, assigning permissions based on security group membership, delegation, and authentication schemes used in Windows Server 2003. We also looked at the functionality of the Kerberos V5 protocol, which is used for mutual authentication between client and server. Kerberos pays a lot of attention to the fact that the initial session setup occurs in an unprotected environment where packets could be intercepted and cracked, and that the identities of both client and servers cannot be assumed but must be proven. Kerberos V5 is ideally suited for inherently insecure network environments such as large, distributed corporate networks and the Internet.

✓ TWO-MINUTE DRILL

Plan a Security Group Strategy

❑ User accounts form the basis of security and authentication. Each user of the system should have his or her own corresponding user account.

❑ Administrators assign user and security group permissions to directory and file system objects.

❑ Security groups are used to simlify permissions management and reduce the number of ACEs listed on ACLs.

❑ Security groups have different scopes—local domain, global, and universal.

❑ Security group scope affects who you can add as members.

❑ Recommended security group strategies can be memorized using the abbreviations AGDLP and AGULP.

Plan a User Authentication Strategy

❑ Kerberos V5 is a default authentication protocol in Windows Server 2003 running in native mode (Windows 2000 and Windows Server 2003 controllers).

❑ The weakest link in any authentication scheme is users and their user account passwords.

❑ Using Password Policy in the Group Policy Object Editor, you can enforce the frequency with which users must change their passwords and configure required complexity levels.

❑ Using the PKI infrastructure and digital certificates can significantly increase your security by providing digital signatures and encryption services.

❑ Smart cards can also be used to boost security by minimizing the risks associated with social engineering and password cracking.

Plan an Organizational Unit Structure

❑ The organizational unit is an element of Active Directory that can be used to build intradomain object-organizing structures.

❑ The basic idea behind OUs is to map the organizational structure to the information technology and computer resources structure.

❑ OUs are containers, and as such, they can contain any type of child objects, including other OUs.

❑ OUs are also used to delegate authority to perform specific operations on child objects and to assign group policies.

❑ Deeply nested OU structures impact overall performance and reduce ease of use.

Implement an Organizational Unit Structure

❑ A properly planned OU structure is easy to implement using ADUC and scripting technologies.

❑ Moving objects between OUs and restructuring OUs are effective ways to keep up with organizational changes.

❑ When moving objects between OUs within the same domain, the objects you move automatically inherit all permissions and group policies from the target OU.

❑ When moving objects between OUs within the same domain, object permissions do not change if they were assigned explicitly.

❑ Moving objects between domains cannot be done using ADUC. Use tools like MOVETREE, Netdom, and ADMTv2 instead.

SELF TEST

The following questions will help you measure your understanding of the material presented in this chapter. Read all the choices carefully because there might be more than one correct answer. Choose all correct answers for each question.

Plan a Security Group Strategy

1. The user account is one of the basic elements of Active Directory and is also a security principal. Which of the following uniquely identifies a user account within the same forest?

   A. Distinguished name (DN)

   B. Email address

   C. Globally unique identifier (GUID)

   D. User principal name (UPN)

2. You are performing a restructuring of user groups and accounts, following all Microsoft recommendations and adding accounts to the global groups, then global groups to domain local groups, and finally, assigning permissions to the domain local groups. The next day, you receive calls from some of the users affected by the restructuring, complaining about "Access Denied" error messages on resources that they could access the day before. What is the most likely cause of the problem? (Choose all that apply.)

   A. While restructuring, you accidentally changed a few usernames or passwords.

   B. One of the global groups, now nested within domain local groups, still has Deny permission from the scheme you decommissioned.

   C. Resources that users are trying to access do not exist on the server in question.

   D. Users never logged off since the day before.

2. What is the difference between CSVDE and LDIFDE tools?

   A. LDIFDE allows creating, deleting, and modifying existing Active Directory objects, whereas CSVDE can only be used to create new objects.

   B. LDIFDE can work with any Active Directory objects, whereas CSVDE can only work with user objects.

   C. CSVDE can work with any Active Directory objects, whereas LDIFDE can only work with user objects.

   D. CSVDE is a command-line tool, whereas LDIFDE has a graphical interface.

3. In the previous year your, organization has enjoyed solid natural growth. New divisions and departments were formed as a result, and to keep up with expansion, new offices and computer resources are being acquired. Now you need to rearrange the OU structure, add user accounts, and review security group strategy. You created new global groups (Accountant Staff, Accountant Managers, and Accountants). Now on the same DC, you wish to nest the first two groups into the Accountants group, but for some reason they are not available in the list when you try to add them on the Members tab of the Accountants group. Likewise, these two groups cannot see the Accountants group on their Member Of tab. What is the most likely cause of this problem?

   A. The groups were just created, and you need to allow enough time for replication to propagate the change to all other domain controllers.

   B. The domain is running in a mode other than Windows 2000 native or Windows Server 2003, so global group nesting is not available.

   C. You do not have sufficient permissions to perform the operation in question.

   D. Groups are not listed by default. You have to use the lookup tool to query them out.

4. What is the difference between global and domain local groups?

   A. Global groups are visible forestwide, whereas domain local groups are only visible within the same domain.

   B. You can use global groups to assign permissions to any resources in the forest, whereas domain local groups can only be used to assign permissions in their own domain.

   C. Global groups cannot be used to assign permissions to resources.

   D. Global groups are used to assign permissions to resources, whereas domain local groups are used to maintain mailing lists.

5. You are managing a domain that has a DNS name of QQQbic.com, with a NetBIOS name set to QQQBIC. You have created a user account, configuring it as follows: First Name: Stevie; Last Name: Vaughan; Full Name: Stevie Vaughan; User Logon Name: StevieVaughan; User Logon Name (Pre-Windows 2000): svaughan. How do you have to instruct the user to log on to the network on a Windows XP Professional machine?

   A. Username svaughan; domain name QQQBIC

   B. Username StevieVaughan; domain name QQQBIC

   C. Username StevieVaughan@qqqbic.com; domain name not used

   D. Username svaughan@qqqbic; domain name not used

364 Chapter 5: Planning and Implementing User, Computer, and Group Strategies

Plan a User Authentication Strategy

6. Which of the following statements are true about the Kerberos version 5 authentication protocol?

    A. When a client is about to access a resource on a server, it has to request a service ticket from the KDC for every session with the server in question.

    B. The service ticket submitted to the client by the KDC is encrypted using a long-term key, which is established based on parameters such as user password hash. No one except the client and the KDC has access to this key.

    C. The service ticket is stored in the credentials cache on the client computer.

    D. The service ticket contains information that can only be decrypted by the server, access to which has been initially requested by the client.

7. Your network contains a few dozen computers and an Active Directory service. You have two domain controllers, with one of them providing KDC and time synchronization services to the network. You have implemented Kerberos authentication, and now some of the users are complaining that they cannot access resources on a few servers. What is the most likely cause of this problem?

    A. There is a problem with network hardware. You have to test the cables and check switches involved between the client and resource servers.

    B. Because of a large number of clients, the KDC service is experiencing a performance bottleneck. You have to upgrade the processor on the KDC server.

    C. It is possible that the network time service is experiencing a problem on the KDC server. Ensure that time settings on the KDC server and clients are synchronized.

    D. The KDC server cannot work properly on a secondary domain controller; move it to the primary domain controller.

8. What is a long-term key?

    A. It is a shared secret key that is known to all domain participants such as servers and workstations.

    B. It is a secret key, shared between domain controllers.

    C. It is a secret key for each user, known only to the user and the KDC.

    D. It is a secret key for each security principal, known only to the principal and the KDC.

9. What information is stored on a smart card when it is used for Windows Server 2003 authentication?

    A. A public key, which is used to encrypt the information to be sent to the user

    B. A private key, which is used to decrypt the information encrypted by the user's public key

    C. General user information, such as PIN and name

    D. Encrypted documents

10. Information in your organization is highly sensitive, and if it leaks, the company will very likely suffer a financial loss that may be too great to bear. You are researching new technologies to improve authentication. Which of the following benefits can you achieve by implementing a smart-card authentication system?

   A. User authentication is made safer. Chances of intruders preying on weak passwords and unsuspecting users are minimized.

   B. Electronic messages will be digitally signed using S/MIME. It ensures nonrepudiation, makes sure that the content has not been tampered with, and establishes the identity of the sender.

   C. Increased protection from information leaks—users will be less likely to employ sensitive information for their own purposes.

   D. File encryption will enable strong file security, allowing only authorized personnel to access the content of the file.

Plan an Organizational Unit Structure

11. Which of the following statements about organizational units are true?

   A. OU is a structure element with the most specific scope in terms of delegation of authority.

   B. OU is a structure element with the most specific scope in terms of assigning group policy.

   C. OU is a security principal, which means it can be assigned access permissions to domain resources, thereby granting access to all of its members.

   D. OU is a structure element that can be used to build a business-minded, logical organization of Active Directory objects within the same domain, and control replication between these units.

12. The management of the company is actively involved in planning to physically relocate parts of one of the offices. Marketing is moving to the new office and will be operating remotely from the rest of the users. You are tasked to devise a restructuring plan that will be used to adapt Active Directory to the change. Which of the following situations lend more support to restructuring OUs than restructuring domains (that is, segmenting the new office into its own domain)?

   A. The marketing department is remote but is connected to the same local area network.

   B. The marketing department is remote and is connected to the local area network using a reliable, fast WAN connection.

   C. The marketing department is remote and is connected to the local area network using a reliable but fairly slow WAN connection; replication traffic is fairly important, but the WAN connection provides satisfactory bandwidth.

   D. The marketing department is remote and is connected to the local area network using an unreliable and fairly slow WAN connection; replication traffic is fairly important, and the WAN connection is not suitable for replication.

13. What are the differences between organizational units and security groups? (Choose all that apply.)

    A. Security groups can contain users of the same domain where they are created; organizational units can contain users from any domain in the forest.

    B. Security groups can contain only user account objects; organizational units can contain any objects stored in Active Directory, such as computers and groups.

    C. Security groups are used to assign permissions to resources; organizational units are used to assign group policies and delegate authority to manage child objects.

    D. Security groups are used to maintain email distribution lists; organizational units are used to assign permissions to users and groups to access domain resources.

14. You are planning your Active Directory infrastructure. Which of the models could you use as the basis for the OU structure?

    A. Group Active Directory objects based on their business unit membership—organizational model

    B. Group Active Directory objects based on their geographical presence—geographical model

    C. Group Active Directory users with their respective computer objects and shared resources provided to the network

    D. Group Active Directory objects based on the group policy design or delegation requirements

15. Which Active Directory objects can be moved to organizational units? (Choose all that apply.)

    A. User accounts and computer accounts from the same domain

    B. Security and distribution groups from the same domain

    C. User accounts and computer accounts from trusted domains

    D. Printers and shared resources from the same domain

Implement an Organizational Unit Structure

16. Delegation of authority based on OU structure helps achieve which of the following?

    A. Assign administrative privileges to a user or group to manage objects within an OU.

    B. Assign ownership of OU objects to users or groups.

    C. Assign users or groups specific privileges to perform specific tasks or access specific properties of OU objects.

    D. Move objects to the OU in question.

17. Your organization is split into several departments, each having its own organizational unit in the Active Directory domain. It was decided that the sales department team leader, who coincidentally is technically savvy, should administer the sales department user accounts from

now on. How would you go about achieving this objective with the least amount of administrative effort, and without giving too much authority to the team leader?

A. Add her account to the Domain Admins group.

B. Add her account to the Enterprise Admins group.

C. Add her account to the local Administrators group on each computer in the sales department.

D. Delegate her rights to administer sales OU user accounts using the Delegation of Control Wizard.

18. Which of the following built-in containers are organizational units (that is, which can be assigned group policies and modified as necessary)?

A. Users

B. Computers

C. Builtin

D. Domain Controllers

19. Your company is made up of a few departments, with each of them having their corresponding OU in Active Directory. Which of the following actions can you take to reflect an organizational change, such as user reassignment from one department to a different one? (Choose all that apply.)

A. Move a corresponding user account between OU containers using the Move command in the context menu of the Active Directory Users and Computers console.

B. Move a corresponding user account between OU containers using drag and drop in the Active Directory Users and Computers console.

C. Delete a corresponding user account in the old OU container and create a new user account in the new OU container.

D. Use the MOVETREE utility to move a user account from one OU container to the other one.

20. The Active Directory Users and Computers console, with Advanced Features enabled, shows a LostAndFound container. What is the purpose of this built-in container?

A. All objects, deleted from Active Directory, are first put into this container, similar to the Recycle Bin on the desktop, in case you need to reverse the operation in the immediate future.

B. Objects that were created while their parent container was being deleted, and that change while being replicated to other domain controllers, are placed into this container.

C. LostAndFound receives copies of all objects from every move operation between OUs.

D. The Active Directory Users and Computers console does not have a LostAndFound container.

LAB QUESTION

The company you work for is in the business of renting ready-to-go offices to small companies and corporate clients wishing to establish a satellite office in the shortest of times, but on a temporary basis. The company assumes full responsibility for maintaining all office equipment and supplies, including but not limited to phone lines and equipment, copiers, and the computer network. The company is using Windows Server 2003 and has an existing Active Directory infrastructure in place.

A new tenant has signed an agreement to move in for a few months. Their requirements are as follows. Boris is a technical person, and he will need unconditional access to the tenant's computer resources. Senior management of the tenant company needs to access their confidential resources and restrict access to ordinary staff, which in turn will need secure access to a document store on a common network server.

One other concern expressed by the tenant is that users are accustomed to using email-address-like usernames to access the network, and these logon names must be the same as their externally accessible email addresses. Email addresses should obviously stay the same to avoid discarding the corporate identity and having to notify existing customers of an address change.

How would you suggest dealing with these requirements?

SELF TEST ANSWERS

Plan a Security Group Strategy

1. ☑ **A, C,** and **D** are correct. All of these can be used to uniquely identify a user account within the same forest.

   ☒ **B** is incorrect. Despite visual similarities with the UPN logon name, an email address is not a reliable way to uniquely identify a user.

2. ☑ **B** and **D** are likely causes of this problem. If, during user and group reorganization, it happens that a given user account gets assigned to several groups, where one of them has access to the resource and the other one has Deny permission to the same resource, Deny will be the effective permission. Likewise, users must log off and log back on for the group membership change to become effective.

   ☒ **A** and **C** are incorrect. If the target folder does not exist, users will be getting a "Network Path Not Found" error message instead of "Access Denied." Changing the user's username or password would result in an inability to log on for those users who logged off the night before.

3. ☑ **A** is the correct comparison of LDIFDE and CVSDE tools.

   ☒ **C, B,** and **D** are incorrect. **C** and **B** are incorrect because both tools can manipulate different types of Active Directory objects. **D** is incorrect because both tools are command-line tools.

4. ☑ **B** is a likely cause of the problem. In domain functional levels that can be used with older NT 4.0 domain controllers, you cannot nest global groups.

   ☒ **A, C,** and **D** are incorrect. **A** is incorrect because you are still working on the same DC, and replication to other domain controllers is necessary for consistent domain operation but not to perform this particular task. In addition, replication delay in the same domain has been significantly reduced in Windows Server 2003. **C** is incorrect because insufficient permissions by default are likely to prevent you from committing the change, but not view available groups. **D** is incorrect because searching for objects that do not exist (are not listed) will not yield any useful results.

5. ☑ **A** and **B** are correct comparisons of global and domain local groups.

   ☒ **C** and **D** are incorrect. **C** is incorrect because both groups technically can be used to assign permissions to resources. **D** is incorrect since it is advisable to use distribution groups for the purposes of maintaining mailing groups, because security mail-enabled groups add processing overhead.

6. ☑ **A and C** are correct. Using a pair made of a pre-Windows 2000 logon name and NetBIOS domain, or UPN name alone, will enable users to log on despite the fact that the logon is happening on a newer operating system. When you type in a UPN logon name, the domain box becomes disabled after the @ sign is typed in.

   ☒ **B and D** are incorrect. **B** is incorrect because the QQQBIC domain does not have a user account with the StevieVaughan username. **D** is incorrect because pre-Windows 2000 usernames are not used with UPN suffixes, although they can be assigned identically, in which case this would work.

Plan a User Authentication Strategy

7. ☑ **B, C, and D** are correct. Server tickets are stored in the client's cache to remove the burden of storing these tickets for all users on the server side. The fact that the ticket that came from a trusted KDC source, encrypted into the server's long-term key, which is only known to KDC and the server, tells the client that the server is indeed authentic, providing that the server successfully opens the ticket.

   ☒ **A** is incorrect. Tickets are stored in RAM throughout their validity period, defined in group policy and set to 10 hours by default. The client needs to request this ticket only once; after it is received, it is stored in memory and reused during subsequent requests for server resources.

8. ☑ **C** is correct. Time synchronization is critical for proper Kerberos functionality. If the time difference between server and client is more than allowed (five minutes by default), the Kerberos protocol will ignore authentication requests.

   ☒ **A, B, and D** are incorrect. **A** is incorrect because if the network was at fault, users would be having problems with all servers; or if the problem was on the server side, all users would have this problem with that particular server. **B** is incorrect because Kerberos is very scalable, and servicing a few dozen users is far from a test of its performance limitations. **D** is incorrect because the KDC service can serve Kerberos clients from any domain controller.

9. ☑ **D** is correct. A long-term key is created for each security principal and is known only to the principal in question and KDC.

   ☒ **A, B, and C** are incorrect answers.

10. ☑ **A, B, and C** are correct. Personalized settings and digital certificates and the private key are stored on the card. Digital certificates contain the public key.

    ☒ **D** is incorrect. Smart cards have a limited amount of memory (usually no more than 8KB). Smart cards do not store any user data in excess of what is covered by A, B, and C.

11. ☑ **A, B, and D** are correct. Implementation of smart-card authentication helps the overall security effort by minimizing the risk associated with traditional passwords.

☒ **C** is incorrect. Smart cards are used to secure the authentication process; how users take advantage of the privileges assigned to them is something that smart cards cannot control.

Plan an Organizational Unit Structure

12. ☑ **A** and **B** are correct. The OU is the smallest (most specific) element of the Active Directory structure that can be used to assign group policies and delegate authority.

    ☒ **C** and **D** are incorrect. **C** describes security groups and not organizational units. **D** describes Active Directory sites and not organizational units.

13. ☑ **A, B,** and **C** are correct. All of these scenarios suggest that it is not necessary to segment the remote office into its own domain to minimize replication traffic. OUs can be used with sites to achieve the desired outcome.

    ☒ **D** is incorrect. Going with OUs in this case would not be a sensible decision. Most likely, replication traffic will make matters associated with unreliable and slow WANs even worse. Consider using a separate domain.

14. ☑ **B** and **C** are correct answers.

    ☒ **A** and **D** are incorrect. **A** is incorrect because it describes the difference between domain local and global groups. **D** is incorrect because it describes the differences between security and distribution groups.

15. ☑ **A, B,** and **D** are correct. These are all valid criteria to be considered when implementing an OU structure. They can also be combined as necessary.

    ☒ **C** is incorrect. This strategy would mandate an unwarranted quantity of OU containers that would create a challenge for day-to-day management and may impact the overall perception of the processing speeds and capabilities of the infrastructure. Assigning group policies on an individual basis defeats the whole purpose of having group policies.

16. ☑ **A, B,** and **D** are correct answers. All of these Active Directory objects can be stored in organizational units.

    ☒ **C** is incorrect. Organizational units cannot contain objects that do not belong to the same domain as the OUs themselves.

Implement an Organizational Unit Structure

17. ☑ **C** is correct.

    ☒ **A, B,** and **D** are incorrect. **A** and **B** are incorrect because delegation can be used to assign more restrictive and more specific permissions rather than giving someone blanket administrative permissions or ownership. **D** is incorrect because it deals with moving objects, not delegating permissions.

18. ☑ **D** is correct.

    ☒ **A, B,** and **C** are incorrect. **A** and **B** are incorrect because they give too much authority to the user in question. (**A** will grant administrative rights in the entire domain, and **B**, administrative privileges in all of the domains in the same forest.) **C** is incorrect because it will not grant enough privileges to work with domain accounts and groups. The user will only be able to manipulate objects in the local SAM database on individual computers, which have no impact in the domain environment.

19. ☑ **D** is correct. The domain controller's Builtin container houses all domain controller objects; it is the organizational unit by default. This allows you to assign more restrictive group policies to domain controllers right out of the box, without creating your own OUs and then moving domain controllers. By no means must domain controllers stay in that container though.

    ☒ **A, B,** and **C** are incorrect. These containers are not organizational units and do not provide capabilities for assigning group policies and performing other operations common to OUs.

20. ☑ **A** and **B** are correct. These steps ensure minimal effort in achieving the desired results.

    ☒ **C** and **D** are incorrect. **C** is incorrect because this will destroy the existing user account, and the one you re-create will not have the same security identity (SID), so all permissions will have to be redefined and group membership will have to be re-created. You will also have to set a new password for this new user account and configure all desktop settings again, which adds to the inconvenience. **D** is incorrect because using MOVETREE here is far from being the easiest way to achieve this simple task.

21. ☑ **B** is correct. The object is moved to the LostAndFound built-in container when a child object is created in the parent container, which was deleted but not yet replicated to other domain controllers.

    ☒ **A, C,** and **D** are incorrect. **A** and **C** are incorrect because Active Directory does not have "recycle bin" functionality. Copying objects is not an option in Active Directory because all objects must have unique GUID, SID, and DN identifiers. **D** is incorrect because LostAndFound container does exist, although it is hidden by default. The Advanced Features menu is used to reverse this setting.

LAB ANSWER

The lab question does not suggest a single correct solution. There are several possible approaches that will probably work. To follow the strategies outlined in this chapter, however, you should deal with the situation in the following manner.

First, create an organizational unit that will represent the resources of the tenant company. To do this, you use the Active Directory Users and Computers console. Next, in this new OU, create global groups to represent the tenant managers and common tenant staff (say, <tenantID>-Managers and <tenantID>-Users). Next, create two domain local groups, again, one representing managers and one representing ordinary users. The two global groups should then be configured to have membership in their respective domain local groups.

Now you need to delegate permissions to ensure that the access requirements of the tenant company are met. Create a user account that will represent their tech Boris, and delegate authority to him to manage user, group, computer, and printer accounts in the tenant's organizational unit. To achieve this task, you use the Delegation of Control Wizard, again in the ADUC console. Then, on the shared file server, you need to create two shared folders, one for the tenant managers and the other one for the rest of the staff. Assign permissions using domain local groups, and make sure to cancel the effect of NTFS security setting inheritance. Remember that managers will need to have access to both of these folders and ordinary users only to the folder shared for them.

Finally, to accommodate the logon name and email address requirement, you need to take advantage of the UPN suffixes in the Active Directory Domains and Trusts console. You will need to create a custom UPN suffix that would be the same as the tenants' TLD DNS name, and then add this suffix to the user account on the Account tab of user object properties.

6

Planning and Implementing Group Policy

Group policy objects (GPOs) are used in Windows 2000 and Windows Server 2003 for workstation and server configuration, user environment configuration, and system rights restriction. Group policies are basically system policies that have evolved from the Windows NT 4.0 days. You also use them to enable software rollout and life cycle management, configure digital certificates, configure user profiles, modify Registry settings, and so on. Although GPOs can be used to configure standalone machines, this technology is a great deal handier when configured and used in the Active Directory environment.

Group policy in Windows Server 2003 can be applied on different infrastructure levels, and hence may have different scopes—these scopes are domain, site, and organizational unit. Different scopes help organizations to achieve different infrastructure management goals—for instance, you can implement a centralized or distributed administration model. Mechanisms such as filtering based on security group membership and Windows Management Instrumentation (WMI), policy inheritance, and blocking enable more flexible, granular, and at the same time, more efficient control of users and computers in your organization. However, this also means that as with any other Active Directory element, planning is essential.

Group policies in Windows Server 2003 introduced over 200 new settings, some of which only apply to Windows XP client operating systems. Group policy management was also changed by the addition of a few new tools. Microsoft now recommends using the Group Policy Management Console (GPMC) to administer GPOs. This management console is not shipped with Windows Server 2003, but is freely available from Microsoft's web site at http://go.microsoft.com/fwlink/?LinkId=12946. The GPMC improves navigation of group policy objects, which apply to any given object in your infrastructure. It also integrates the Resultant Set of Policy (RSoP) tool functionality, allows you to model and review effective policies, back up and restore GPOs, import, export, and copy policies between forests, and so on. In other words, the GPMC provides a unified interface to group policy management.

GPOs have the potential to reduce administrative time and costs involved in managing client computers and users, which also makes GPOs one of the most important areas on the exam. The purpose of this chapter is to review group policy concepts and planning considerations.

Analyze Your Environment

The main objective of group policy implementation is lowered total cost of ownership (TCO) through improved and streamlined management of the information system supported by Active Directory. Administrators benefit from this technology greatly by saving a lot of time and effort that they would otherwise expend in performing tedious tasks on a regular basis. However, you must still spend the time on careful planning and initial configuration of group policies.

Before you proceed with group policy deployment, the following must take place:

1. Analyze the existing computer equipment life cycle and user environment. Create a list that outlines how often, and based on what criteria, equipment maintenance and upgrades take place, and which tasks performed on a recurring basis consume the largest portion of time and effort.

2. Develop objectives for your implementation of group policies. Later in this chapter we review what they are and what they can be used for, but for now just bear in mind that knowing where you want to go is critical to figuring out the path you need to take. Define criteria for analyzing the success of your implementation. Outline which business requirements or administrative improvements you achieve by implementing each category of features.

3. Develop a detailed group policy implementation plan. This plan must honor business requirements, security requirements, and AD infrastructure specifics.

4. Test your proposed strategy in a lab or on a limited set of test users in production. Follow your plan as closely as possible and make adjustments as the test rollout unfolds, should that prove necessary.

Next, let's look at individual factors that should be considered when you work on creating this group policy implementation plan.

Group Policy Scope in Active Directory

A key feature of group policies is that they can be configured to have different application scope within the infrastructure. Users or computers that fall into the scope of any given policy can be grouped according to several criteria, such as domain or organizational unit membership. In all cases, you must have a clear understanding of which users or computers each individual group policy was configured for.

To better plan group policy scopes, you need a diagram or document that outlines the logical structure of Active Directory in your organization and the business functions that users perform in each of the logical divisions. You will need to know which users perform which tasks and where on the network they perform these tasks.

Different types of users will usually require specific computing environment configurations, and hence, configurations implemented by one particular group policy will not suit all of the users. From the group policy implementation point of view, it is more convenient to group these classes of users into their own organizational unit containers in Active Directory. In this case, administrators just need to place appropriate users into OUs and assign specific group policies to these OUs. If you are implementing a different OU structure, as described in Chapters 3 and 5, then you may need to implement a substructure, grouping users within geographical locations or business units.

If your OU structure cannot be modified, you may have to use security group or WMI filters to assign group policies (scopes and filtering are covered in more detail later in the chapter).

In addition to applying your group policies to organizational units, you can also apply them on the domain and site levels, which makes it possible to assign certain site-specific or domain-specific settings to all users in those segments. Local computer policies can also be featured in your strategy if necessary, but only in limited, perhaps server-side scenarios. Excessive reliance on locally configured policies will defeat the management benefits of implementing a collective configuration.

Group policies with site scope need to implement site-specific configuration settings, mapping users to the closest file servers, DNS servers, and so forth. It is important not to mix configuration categories between policies that you plan to assign on different levels. In this case, OU policies should not deal with assigning DNS servers and mapping drives to local file servers in the site, *unless* that particular OU group of users requires this specific configuration change. OU policies are applied last, and override all other settings by default.

Resource Location on the Network

Just as it is important to understand your logical topology, you should also understand where your network resources are concentrated. Note the following information:

- Site configuration and site links
- Presence or lack of roaming users (laptops and other wireless devices)
- Server placement (DNS, domain controllers, file servers)

This information is important to have handy when planning features such as Slow Link Detection. Based on whether actual link speed is faster or slower than the value configured in the Slow Link Speed setting, computers will consider connection to the domain controller to be either fast or slow, respectively. If the connection is determined to be slow, Software Installation, Scripts, Folder Redirection, and Internet Explorer Maintenance policy sections may not apply.

Security Requirements

You should carefully consider how much Internet exposure a particular managed network segment is expected to get. In addition to external security threats, you need to evaluate the risks associated with internal threats—for example, when perimeter security is breached and internal hosts are compromised. Internal risks also may come from disgruntled personnel, accidental or purposeful access to confidential resources, or excessive user curiosity in regard to technical aspects of the infrastructure. When you consider how much security a given server or network segment should be configured with, you may choose one of the security templates supplied with Windows Server 2003 as a foundation for further tweaks, or simply use this chosen policy for your group policy configuration.

Corporate Policies

Restricting user freedom in the system may be viewed as a positive thing from the IT department perspective, and at the same time as a negative thing from the management perspective. Corporate policies usually dictate the right balance between restricting users' ability to interfere with the system and assigning them the right amount of privileges to perform their duties effectively. Left unchecked, users may end up installing their own applications that impact productivity or compromise network security. Software restriction policies may be used to mitigate this risk. Depending on the type of business you are in, restricting everything that is not explicitly permitted might be a good idea (this would work best in schools, kiosks, libraries, and so on.). In addition to planning, administrators may have to do some negotiating and explaining to convince management that the chosen strategy is the best one for their business case.

Some corporate environments prefer to maintain a common desktop environment, with corporate wallpapers, menu items, Internet Explorer settings and bitmaps, and other elements of corporate propaganda. Group policies are used to achieve this.

Network and Storage Capacities

Available network bandwidth may affect your group policy strategy by introducing physical limitations on how many customizations and updates you can roll out. You need to have plenty of bandwidth between servers and clients to effectively implement features such as roaming profiles and offline folder synchronization. It is not uncommon for user profiles to be in tens if not hundreds of megabytes, which adds to logon and logoff traffic on the network. Likewise, if you are planning to use roaming profiles or folder redirection, ensure that your infrastructure servers have plenty of storage and sufficient backup capacity. You may need to decide which folders should be left out of profile synchronization with the server. In addition to Temporary Internet Files, you may have to leave Application Data, My Documents, or Desktop folders on user machines.

Ease of Administration

Group policy structure must remain manageable after implementation. Planning is needed to avoid situations in which "everything works fine," but no one really has enough courage to make a change. When the system works but is complicated to the point that you don't want to touch it, it is safe to say that it is not manageable. Here are some recommendations that may help in avoiding this situation:

- Name your policies using full, intuitive names that reflect the purpose and maybe even scope of the policy.

- Avoid using advanced group policy propagation features such as No Override, Block Policy Inheritance, and Loopback Processing. (Each of these is covered later in the chapter.) They may come in handy in a few situations, but if you have to use them on a regular basis, this may be an indication of mediocre planning.

- Avoid linking group policy objects defined in other domains; doing so may result in measurable group policy processing delays.

- Plan your strategy so that high-level policies (domain level) have to be changed as little as possible, and use lower-level policies (site and OU) to do most of the legwork. (If your sites span more than one domain, this would be the opposite: more generic policies on the site level, more specific policies on domain levels.)

- Get into the habit of using group policy planning tools such as RSoP.

- Limit the number of policies that have to be processed for any given user or computer. A large number of policies, especially if some of their settings are contradictory, are more complicated to administer and troubleshoot, and may also result in user logon slowdowns.

- Use security group filtering only when absolutely necessary.

- If you must deny the Apply Group Policy right when assigning permissions to group policy objects, see if you can also deny the Read Group Policy right. In most situations, reading group policies would make no sense if the client has no permission to apply them, and this saves time.

CERTIFICATION OBJECTIVE 6.01

Plan Group Policy Strategy

After you collect the necessary information about the network and Active Directory structure, the next step is to sit down and think about the business requirements that group policy could be used to address. As mentioned earlier, you also need to define criteria for measuring the effectiveness of your implementation down the road. For example, in the IT department this may be the number of daily help desk calls. The security department may want to enable auditing and user account lockout to institute resource access control and to prevent dictionary attacks or less sophisticated coworker password guessing. Managers may find themselves interested in increased productivity through automated software rollout. In some cases, these business requirements will conflict and administrators will either have to find a compromise or adjust AD structure or group policy strategy.

Based on business and administrative requirements, you choose a set of features that group policies need to implement. Then, you need to determine which groups of users and computers to apply these policies to. If your OU structure is not implemented yet, group policy design should be considered in OU planning. In addition, you may need to consider existing network capacity, and if necessary/possible, upgrade it to suit group policy needs.

Keep in mind that if you need to undo the changes implemented by group policies, it is usually enough simply to remove the group policy object link from the OU container, site, or domain. However, some settings may persist beyond this reverse assignment—settings like GPO-installed software, folder redirection, and some scripts. In this case, you may need a rollback plan, which is also a consideration in overall group policy strategy planning.

Finally, before you roll out group policies, test your strategy. You could use a testing lab, or in the absence of that, a set of test users who are not performing mission-critical work at the time. If you are testing group policies in a test lab, it should mimic your production environment as closely as possible. It should feature the same network configuration, slow links of the same speed as in production, as well as identical server and client hardware and configuration. If you encounter problems testing your strategy, analyze what may be causing it and make the necessary adjustments.

Analyze Requirements

As we established in the previous section, group policies simplify administration and allow configuration of operating system settings, application settings, and user interfaces. Group policies are not only useful in medium-sized organizations, where centralized administration makes sense, but also in small organizations. They can be used to apply the same settings on multiple machines with minimum effort, reliably and quickly, eliminating human errors and the need for administrative interference. Obviously, group policies are a lot more convenient to work with from one central location than on separate client machines, as is usually done in small networks.

To implement configuration standards in an organization, administrators create group policies that include several categories of settings, such as:

- Security settings
- Application packages to be deployed
- Computer system settings
- User environment settings
- Application-specific settings

We'll look at some of these in more detail later in the chapter. These categories may apply to distinct types of Active Directory objects. Most importantly, group policies can be configured for:

- Domain object (password or account policy)
- Domain controller objects
- Member server objects (application, file, and print servers)
- Client computer objects
- User objects

Table 6-1 demonstrates which categories of group policy settings can be applied to which objects.

When you install Active Directory and deploy your structure, two group policies are configured and applied by default: a default domain policy and default domain controllers policy. It is recommended not to remove links to these policies or even modify them because they deliver template configuration that enables secure domain operation in many scenarios.

Domain policies deliver domain security configuration to the domain in question, and as you may remember from Chapter 3, domains are used to form a common security boundary. Security-related settings such as the password complexity requirement, account lockout policies, and Kerberos policy settings are configured using domain policy (or a custom group policy applied on the domain level). You cannot define these settings on the site or OU level for domain users—these settings would apply to local security policies and would be enforced for users logged on using local accounts defined on desktop machines.

| TABLE 6-1 | Group Policy Settings and Objects | | | | |

Category	Domain	Domain Controller	Member Server	Client Computer	User
Security	Password, Account, Kerberos policy, PK trust list	User rights, file and Registry permissions, audit and event log settings, local settings	User rights, file and Registry permissions, audit and event log settings, local settings	User rights, file and Registry permissions, audit and event log settings, local settings	User public key policy
Application deployment	N/A	Administrative tools	Administrative tools	Mandatory applications (push)	Published optional applications (on demand)
Computer (hardware) settings	N/A	Disk quotas	Printer settings and disk quotas	Start-up scripts, logon scripts, disk quotas, and offline files	N/A
User settings	N/A	User desktop settings	User desktop settings	N/A	Logon scripts, Internet Explorer settings, remote access settings, folder redirection, desktop restrictions, network settings, system settings
Application settings	N/A	N/A	N/A	N/A	Microsoft Office and other application settings

The second default policy is applied to the domain controllers organizational unit container. This OU is similar in its functionalities to any other OU in the domain, except that you cannot delete it, and all domain controllers promoted within the same domain are added to it automatically. Because all users authenticating to the network communicate with domain controllers, domain controller policy deals specifically with logon events audit settings and allowed logon methods. Domain controller policies also set up controller-specific user rights, defining, for example, which groups are allowed to add computers to the domain. In contrast, file and print server policies may need to deal with things like disk quotas, printer publishing, and pruning settings.

Perhaps the most time-consuming task here is setting up policies for your users and computers. There may be companies that use all of their computer resources in the same way, but they are hard to come by in the real world. Most of the time, computers will be used to do different tasks by people with different needs—ranging from point-of-sale terminals to scientific research. In the past, this was a good enough reason to deploy different types of operating systems, designed to excel at performing that particular task and nothing else. Because the user environment and security level needed to be different for every industry, it was not a trivial task to come up with a standard, effective mechanism to configure the computer system and applications.

Microsoft came up with IntelliMirror technology and developed a basic solution to some aspects of this problem: group policies. Using group policies, you are effectively working with the standardized internal Windows APIs to create a managed environment, configuring things like the Registry, security settings, desktop appearance and functionality, Internet Explorer settings, folder redirection, assign or publish software, and so on. Third-party applications can be integrated to take advantage of this as well.

But before we go into configuring all of these features, you need to analyze what your computers are used for. Requirements that your policies need to address will depend on what functions these workstations must be able to perform, and which must be made unavailable. Microsoft offers their perspective on this by segmenting all possible scenarios into a few major categories. In the next few sections, we take a look at what these categories are.

These sample environments are provided just to give an idea of what can be achieved through group policies and to provide a starting point for planning and implementing GPOs. You don't have to follow these suggestions closely, but instead take one of the sample environments that is similar to your particular situation and do some tweaking.

Lightly Managed Environment

The first category, lightly managed environment, is best suited for "advanced" users and software developers, who may require full, or at the least restricted, access to computer configurations. This category also assumes scenarios in which regular users are entrusted with the same type of freedom due to a company preference or policy, or when tight control is either not feasible or unnecessary. This category may be characterized as follows:

- It requires the least amount of management.
- Users configure their settings themselves.
- Restrictions are minimal, but system settings are usually not available.
- Users access their data from multiple locations.

Table 6-2 shows suitable configuration options for this category.

TABLE 6-2	Configuration	Value or Comments
Recommended Setting Categories for Lightly Managed Environment	Number of users	No strict assignment, one machine may be used by several users
	Profile types	Roaming
	Do not delete roaming profiles	Roaming profiles are cached on the local machine
	Folder redirection	My Documents and Application Data
	Desktop settings	Users are free to modify their settings
	Assigned applications	Basic set of applications, installed automatically
	Published applications	Additional applications, installed on demand
	Security context template	User or power user
	Security template	Secure workstation

Highly Managed Environment

The highly managed environment implies significant restrictions and only authorized applications are allowed to run. This is a step above the lightly managed environment, and typical applications include customer service, help desk, and direct marketing activities. This category may be characterized as follows:

- Users can configure a limited amount of settings.
- Access to local folders is restricted.
- Users are allowed to access their data from multiple network locations.

Table 6-3 shows suitable configuration options for this category.

Mobile User Environment

Users "of no permanent address"—those who may or may not be located within the corporate network—are members of the mobile user environment. Mobile users usually work on a single computing device, such as a laptop, that is connected either using wired or wireless infrastructure. Some users may connect to the corporate network using dial-up connections, so slow network connection settings may be needed to optimize this environment. This category may be characterized as follows:

- Users should be able to access their data whether or not office connectivity is available at the time.
- Users should be able to store information locally as well as on network servers.

TABLE 6-3	Configuration	Value or Comments
Recommended Setting Categories for Highly Managed Environment	Number of users	No strict assignment, one machine may be used by several users
	Profile types	Roaming
	Do not delete roaming profiles	Roaming profiles are cached on the local machine
	Folder redirection	My Documents and Application Data
	Desktop settings	Only a limited number of settings is available
	Assigned applications	Limited set of basic applications
	Published applications	None
	Security context template	User
	Security template	Secure workstation

■ Users should be flexible when it comes to logging on and off the network. You may need to cache credentials so that laptops can validate their owners in the absence of domain controller connectivity.

■ When disconnecting from the network, files stored on your network servers should be synchronized with user files stored on laptop drives.

Table 6-4 shows suitable configuration options for this category.

Multiuser Environment

The multiuser environment is best suited for schools, universities, and libraries, where users are allowed to save personal settings and information, such as files and folders on their desktops, but they are not allowed to change hardware or network settings. This category may be characterized as follows:

■ Users may be set up to use their own accounts or a built-in guest account.

■ Users may not be allowed to write information to disks, with the exception of their user profile and redirected folders.

Table 6-5 shows suitable configuration options for this category.

Kiosk Environment

Kiosks are computer devices set up in public places such as airports or railway terminals. Passengers use these computers to look up current scheduling or ticket information or

TABLE 6-4	Recommended Setting Categories for Mobile User Environment
Configuration	**Value or Comments**
Number of users	Usually only one user per device.
Profile types	Could be roaming or local. To choose the best profile for your environment, consider the following: It may be better to use roaming profiles when fast connectivity is available between mobile users and the office network—at least once in a while. If your back office machines are being backed up, roaming profiles may be included in the backup plan. Roaming profiles are especially useful when users switch from mobile computers to office computers and back. It may make more sense to use local profiles when connectivity to the office is slow or expensive (dial-up is one example of slow). Also, some users may work from home on a regular basis, in which case roaming profiles may not be desirable.
Do not delete roaming profiles	Roaming profiles are cached on mobile devices; local profiles are stored on mobile devices.
Folder redirection	My Documents and Application Data.
Desktop settings	Most of the settings are available to mobile users, except those system settings you don't wish to be modified.
Assigned applications	Basic applications.
Published applications	Additional on-demand applications.
Security context template	User or power user.
Security template	Secure workstation.

to browse the Internet. Computing devices configured as kiosks do not prompt users for their login information and use one of the preconfigured accounts to go through the logon process automatically. Kiosk computers must have easy-to-use interfaces, and they must be secured as tightly as possible. Access to desktop and system settings is not allowed. Normally, users should not even be able to switch between applications. This environment may be characterized as follows:

- Maximum restrictions are applied on the computer system.
- Users are not allowed to modify environment or desktop settings.
- Users are not allowed to save information either locally or on a network drive.
- Depending on the application, computers may be configured for offline use, or for one-way communication from server to client only.

TABLE 6-5

Recommended
Setting
Categories
for Multiuser
Environment

Configuration	Value or Comments
Number of users	Multiple users work on the same machine
Profile types	Roaming profiles
Do not delete roaming profiles	Profiles are not cached locally
Folder redirection	My Documents and Application Data
Desktop settings	Users are allowed to modify a limited number of personal settings
Assigned applications	Basic applications, installed automatically
Published applications	Additional applications, installed on demand
Security context template	User
Security template	High-security workstation

- ■ Installation and removal of applications is not permitted.
- ■ Users are anonymous to the system, and they all use one account.

Table 6-6 shows suitable configuration options for this environment.

TABLE 6-6

Recommended
Setting
Categories
for Kiosk
Environment

Configuration	Value or Comments
Number of users	Only one user account.
Profile types	Local.
Do not delete roaming profiles	Roaming profiles are not used.
Folder redirection	My Documents and Application Data.
Desktop settings	Desktop settings are not available. The taskbar and Start menu are restricted and are not available on the system.
Assigned applications	One application.
Published applications	None.
Security context template	User.
Security template	High-security workstation.

Task Station Environment

Task stations are used when there is a need to perform one particular task, such as data entry, and nothing else. This situation is similar to kiosks in terms of system restrictions, except that you may want to use user profiles because task stations are most likely to be used in the office environment and not for public, anonymous access. This environment may be characterized as follows:

- Only one application is installed, which may be launched automatically upon logon.
- Several users may be using the same machine (shift work, for example).
- User data is stored on a network server and cannot be saved locally.

Table 6-7 shows suitable configuration options for this environment.

The Group Policy Management Tools

As our primary tool for group policy modification we will be using the Group Policy Object Editor snap-in, shown in Figure 6-1. Domain-level or OU-level policies can be invoked in the Group Policy Editor from the Active Directory Users and Computers snap-in.

TABLE 6-7	Configuration	Value or Comments
Recommended Setting Categories for Task Station Environment	Number of users	Multiple users work on the same machine.
	Profile types	Roaming.
	Do not delete roaming profiles	Profiles are deleted from machines upon logoff.
	Folder redirection	My Documents and Application Data.
	Desktop settings	Settings are restricted; the taskbar and Start menu are removed from the desktop.
	Assigned applications	One application.
	Published applications	None.
	Security context template	User.
	Security template	High-security workstation.

FIGURE 6-1   Group Policy Object Editor snap-in

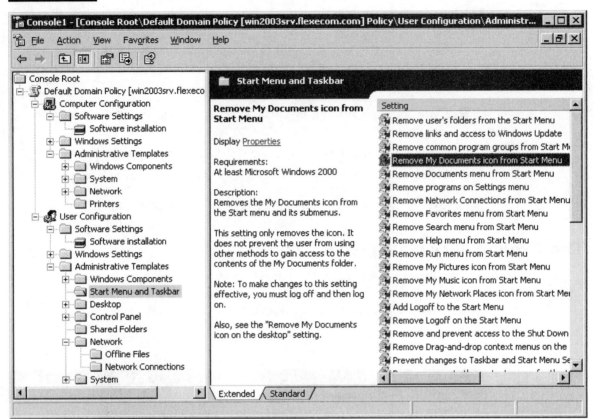

Within the domain or OU properties, select the Group Policy tab (shown in
Figure 6-2). Site-level policies can be accessed through the Group Policy tab in site
properties, using the Active Directory Sites and Services snap-in.

You manage local policies through the Local Security Policy snap-in in
Administrative Tools. However, we will not look at local policy settings in detail
for several reasons: First of all, local policies are applied first, and any setting
explicitly specified on the domain, site, or OU level will override the local settings.
Second, many computer settings can be configured locally on a machine without
using local policies. Third, local policies do not contain many of the settings
available through group policies, partly because local policies do not require Active
Directory in order to function. And last but not least, local policy cannot be applied

FIGURE 6-2

Accessing
domain-level or
OU-level group
policies

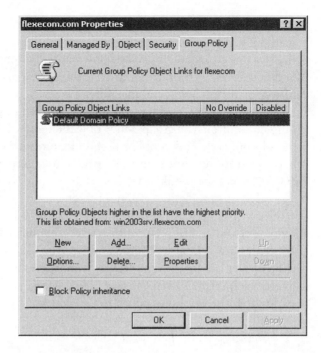

FIGURE 6-2

Accessing
domain-level or
OU-level group
policies

to domain controllers. So in effect, local policies are a limited version of group policies and are only good for standalone, perimeter servers that are not participating in a domain environment, or computers running in kiosk mode that are not hooked up to an infrastructure.

Before proceeding with the discussion of how group policies are applied, you need to understand that group policies are made up of two groups of settings: computer configuration and user configuration.

When users turn on their computers, but before they log on, computer policies are applied on the machine based on the location in the domain and the OU structure, and which policy objects were assigned to that particular segment. When users log on, the second set of group policy settings is applied based on where in the domain and OU structure this particular user account is located. So in effect, your policy consists of computer configuration taken from the policies applied to the computer object and user configuration taken from the policies applied to the user object.

The user logon and computer boot sequence are not the only conditions where group policy objects are retrieved and applied on the system. Group policy objects are also refreshed every 90 minutes without any disruption to users. This is not a strict interval; there is a 30-minute window during which refresh requests are submitted randomly. This is done purely for load-balancing purposes.

On the domain controllers, policy objects are refreshed a lot more often—every five minutes. These default settings will suit most environments, but if there is a need to force a policy update, it can be done manually using the **gpupdate** command on Windows Server 2003 or Windows XP Professional machines, or **secedit /refreshpolicy /enforce** on a Windows 2000 machine.

From time to time you may run into a situation in which you need to apply user configuration from the group policy object effective for the computer, not the user who is logging on. This could be useful in a terminal services or kiosk environment where you want to apply computer-specific user configuration and disallow certain privileges that users would otherwise get on a typical domain computer.

To solve this problem, you can set User Group Policy Loopback Processing Mode settings, available within the configuration of each group policy object, in the Computer Configuration\Administrative Templates\System\Group Policy section. Two modes are available: Merge and Replace. If you set the loopback setting to Replace, user configuration settings from the computer policy will replace user configuration settings from the user policy. Merge, as the name implies, will add user settings from the computer policy to user settings from the user policy. Figure 6-3 shows this setting.

If necessary, you may choose to disable either computer configuration settings or user configuration settings from the policy object altogether. This can be done through the properties of the policy object in the Group Policy snap-in, as demonstrated in Figure 6-4.

As mentioned earlier, group policies can be applied on four levels: locally, on a site level, domain level, and OU level. Remember also that policy processing is sequential, as follows:

1. (L) local policy
2. (S) site-level group policy
3. (D) domain-level group policy
4. (OU) OU-level group policy (top-level containers)
5. (OU) OU-level group policy (child-level containers)

The LSDOU abbreviation is a useful mnemonic device.

The group policy application algorithm ensures that conflicting settings are overwritten by those policies applied later in the process. So, for instance, if your site-level policy implements a setting and your domain-level policy implements the same setting but with a different value, the domain-level setting becomes effective.

FIGURE 6-3 User Group Policy Loopback Processing Mode settings

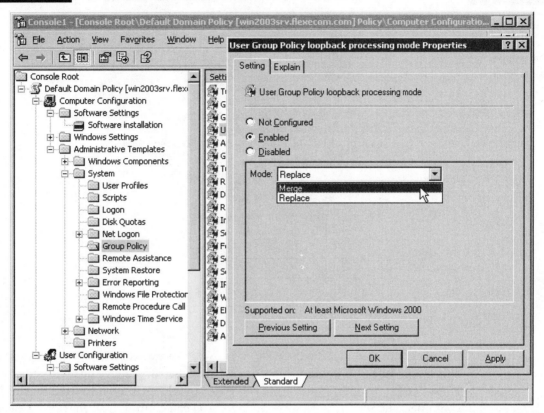

At the same time, if these two policies implement two different settings, the effective policy includes both of them: settings that do not conflict are accumulated. If a level has more than one policy applied to it, the policies are processed in the order they are listed in. As you can see, with proper planning it is possible to use all levels effectively to make sure that site-level settings deliver site-specific configuration without overlapping other levels, which would overwrite site settings, and the same holds true for local and domain policies.

This algorithm can be adjusted by group policy application options such as Block Policy Inheritance and Enforced (same as No Override). When you assign a group policy to the parent OU, this policy, by default, also applies to all child containers on all levels and all objects within those child containers. All group policy rules described earlier still apply. For example, if one of your child containers has its own policy,

FIGURE 6-4

Turning off user
or computer
configuration
settings for a
GPO

settings configured in that container policy will override the values for those settings
if they were set earlier by another policy on some other level higher up in the structure.
However, all remaining settings that do not overlap will be inherited by child
containers and objects in those containers. You can control this behavior for each
OU container in your domain. Inheritance can be blocked by enabling the Block
Policy Inheritance option in OU properties. (Figure 6-2 depicted this property page.)

Another way to achieve the same result is to use the Group Policy Management
Console (GPMC), shown in Figure 6-5.

This is where you select the OU you want to manage, and turn on Block Inheritance
in the context menu, as shown in Figure 6-6. This will remove all inherited policies
from the Policy Inheritance tab for the given OU in the GPMC.

Note, however, that the Enforced option will prevent Block Policy Inheritance
from becoming effective. This acts as a countermeasure to make sure that any given
policy becomes effective throughout your structure, even if regional administrators
with delegated privileges attempt to block centrally administered policy at some
point. Inherited policies will not be removed in the GPMC if they were enforced
(marked as No Override).

FIGURE 6-5   Group Policy Management Console

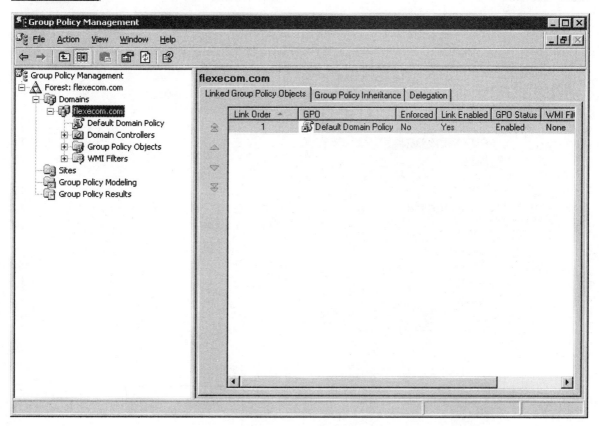

Local policy objects are processed even if Block Policy Inheritance is used to prevent domain, site, or OU policies from becoming effective on a machine or set of machines. This adds further flexibility in how you wish to use policies; however, it also adds considerations to planning. Remember that blocking inheritance (and No Override for that matter) should not be used on a regular basis; this will eventually make your environment unmanageable.

Blocking policy inheritance can be viewed as a double-edged sword: it adds flexibility to how group policy application is controlled and applied, but at the same time it leads to situations in which your domains are no longer centralized in terms of administration, potentially breaking up the integrity of your strategy. In this light,

FIGURE 6-6   Blocking policy inheritance using the GPMC

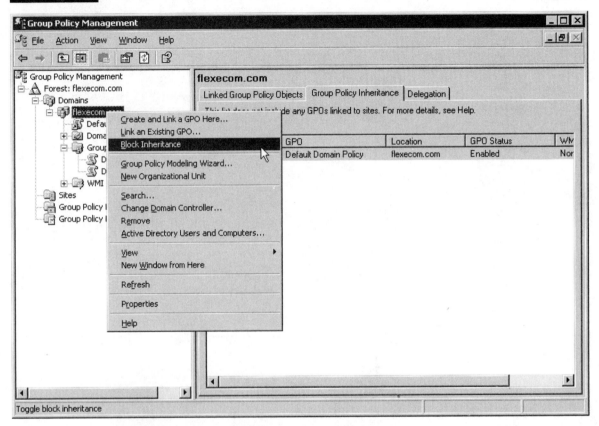

it is easy to see why enforcing (or No Override) takes precedence over blocking, and
forces policy application regardless of the configuration. Enforcing is directly opposite
to blocking, and it also ensures that parameters configured in the enforced policy do
not get overridden by policies applied on lower levels. Note that this is only true
about explicitly configured parameters and does not affect those left with default
values. You can configure No Override on the same property page as in Figure 6-2
(the Group Policy tab in domain, site, or OU properties), but you have to use the
group policy object's context menu (see Figure 6-7).

Enforcing policy settings may prove useful in situations where corporate standards
are very strict with respect to any given aspect of IT environment. Let's say that
management wants to enforce the same Internet Explorer start page for all users
in the company regardless of administrator or user preferences on the local level

FIGURE 6-7

Activating the No
Override option
for a group policy
object

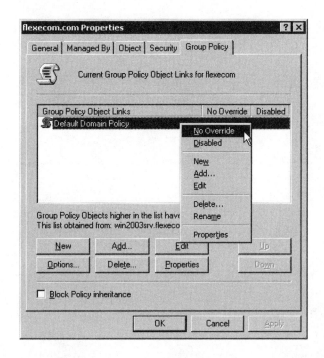

(in a remote branch, for instance). In Figure 6-8, you can see that even if your
default domain policy gets blocked at some level, the No Override option still
enforces the setting all the way to the workstation.

The illustration shows some possible situations when dealing with policy application,
blocking, and enforcing. All group policy values can be considered either enabled,
disabled, or not configured. The not configured state on lower levels leaves the setting
unchanged. If the setting is either disabled or enabled on a lower level, the state of
the setting will change depending on enforcing and blocking circumstances; in the
absence of either, the state applied by the policies lower down the structure becomes
effective.

Filtering

Blocking and enforcing are not the only options available to administrators in deciding
how group policies should be applied. Security group filtering can be used to limit the
effects of one or more policies on select users in one domain or OU. Group policies
can only be applied by those security principals that have the Apply Group Policy right
on the ACL of a group policy object. If you have several users in the same domain or
same organizational unit who you wish to block from receiving settings from a particular

FIGURE 6-8	Enforcing policy settings

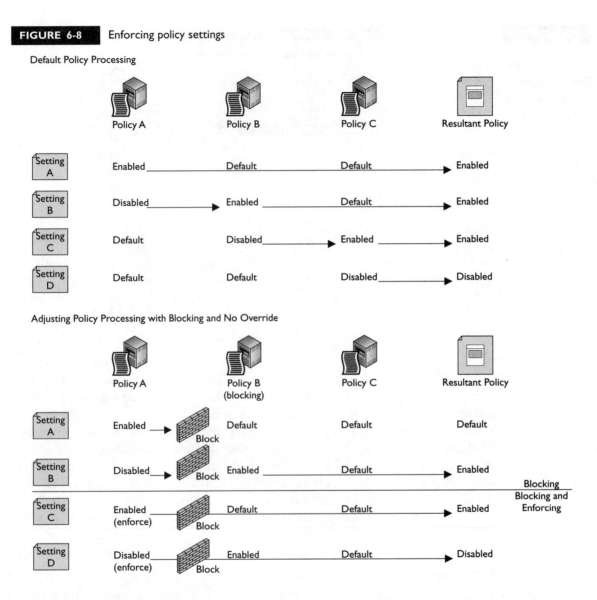

policy, you should organize these users and/or computers into a separate security group. Then, add this group to the ACL of the policy you wish to block, and subsequently deny Apply Group Policy permission.

As mentioned earlier, for optimal performance it is recommended that you deny Read rights as well, so that users won't even have to read the policy that is not meant for them. Now you can have several groups of users within the same group policy application area, such as an OU, yet have different group policies in effect for each group. Policy blocking cannot achieve this.

It is also possible to apply one group policy object to several domains or organizational units within the same forest. The essence of this technique is that group policy is just another Active Directory object, and when administrators configure a policy to be applied to a given AD entity, they simply set up a so-called link between that entity and the group policy object being applied. Using the GPMC, simply select a container to which you want to link an existing GPO, click the context menu option Link An Existing GPO, select the policy object, and click OK.

This will set up an association between a group policy object and an Active Directory element such as a domain or an OU. The beauty of this situation is that by making changes to one group policy object you make the changes effective in all of the entities to which this group policy object is linked. This achieves further flexibility, but as you can see by now, this does not make planning any less important.

As if all of the earlier was not enough, Microsoft went one step further in making sure their implementation is as flexible as possible. Windows Server 2003 introduces WMI filtering for group policy clients running Windows XP Professional or Windows Server 2003. WMI (Windows Management Instrumentation) is Microsoft's implementation of the Web Based Enterprise Management (WBEM) standard developed by the Distributed Management Task Force (DMTF). The purpose is to standardize information systems management by introducing SNMP-like technologies to desktop management. WMI has been around in Windows operating systems for years. It was introduced as an add-on feature for Windows NT 4.0 running Internet Explorer 5 or later, and has been an integral part of the OS ever since Windows 2000 was shipped.

In plain English, WMI sets up its object model and the interface, which administrators can use to query virtually any sort of operating system or hardware information, starting with BIOS versions, current motherboard voltage and fan speeds, predicted failure status of a hard drive, all the way through to current performance monitor values, Registry settings, and IP routing tables. Administrators can even set up their own event sinks and subscribe to certain system events, making it possible, for example, to institute a system reaction to a particularly evil system log event the instant it gets recorded to the log.

WMI supports enumeration of objects in collections (for instance, if you want to find a particular disk device on a system that has six disks), and it also implements WQL query language. (WQL resembles SQL, although it implements somewhat limited SQL features in its current implementation.) All this means is that you can query the same collection of six disks, specifying which characteristic you are looking for, and get only matching results from the system.

This is where group policy filtering kicks in—administrators can now filter group policies based on the result set returned in response to a WMI query. This makes it possible to do things like assigning the Microsoft Office suite only to computers that have at least 1GB of free space on their drives. Figure 6-9 shows the WMI Filter tab in a group policy object properties dialog box.

Figure 6-10 displays the WMI filter page, where you can write your own WMI filters.

Resultant Set of Policy (RSoP) Tool

Now that you have an understanding of what factors affect policy application and how the application process works, let's look at some of the tools provided with Windows Server 2003 that come in handy when planning group policies.

It may prove difficult to visualize the result of applying a number of policies, keeping in mind blocking, enforcing, and filtering, if any of these features are used. In Windows 2000, administrators needed to study all of the effective policies beginning from the site level on down to the last organizational unit in the structure. Gpresult (Group Policy Result tool) is a command line utility that Microsoft shipped with Windows 2000 to help address this situation, but its usefulness is fairly limited.

In Windows Server 2003, we now have the RSoP (Resultant Set of Policy) tool that allows modeling and viewing effective policy settings on any given object by

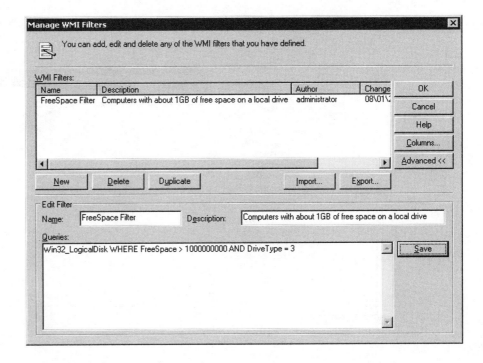

going through the same policy application steps as if this were part of a normal boot
and logon process. You can access this tool in at least three different ways: it is available
as a standalone snap-in for MMC (see Figure 6-11), but it is also integrated into the
GPMC, and the Active Directory Users and Computers and Active Directory Sites
and Services snap-in context menus. RSoP features an intuitive interface, and when
accessed from within the GPMC, it can also generate HTML reports.

After you install the GPMC, some of the group policy management tasks and
functionalities are taken over by GPMC, which aims at becoming the single point
of group policy configuration and management in your Active Directory structure.
Table 6-8 provides some comparisons between group policy management with, and
without, the Group Policy Management Console.

The RSoP tool can be used in two modes: planning mode (modeling in GPMC)
and logging mode (results in GPMC). Although the RSoP snap-in and GPMC have
different names for these two modes, the only difference between them is how the
information is presented to the user; in RSoP this is done in a right-hand pane
similarly to the Group Policy Editor (see Figure 6-12), and in the GPMC console,
users are presented with an HTML-based report (see Figure 6-13).

FIGURE 6-11

Resultant Set of
Policy MMC
snap-in

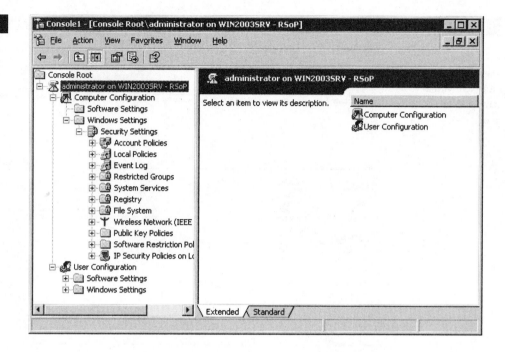

Modeling and results modes differ mostly in how the results are generated. In both modes, reports are generated based on the resultant set of group policy settings stored in the Common Information Model Object Management (CIMOM) database. In

TABLE 6-8   Comparing Group Policy Management Tools

Snap-in File Name	Full Name in MMC	Group Policy Admin Functions	Integration with Other Consoles and Snap-ins
dsa.msc	Active Directory Users and Computers	Navigate and manage domain and OU policies. If GPMC is not installed: set up and remove links to existing GPOs, manage blocking, enforcement, and security/WMI filtering; create and delete group policy objects; turn off computer or user configuration portions.	If GPMC is installed: the GPMC option is added to container context menus. If GPMC is not installed: the Group Policy Editor (GPEdit) can be invoked from the Group Policies tab in OU or domain properties, with blocking, enforcement, and filtering option configuration. RSoP can be invoked from the All Tasks submenu in the container context menu.

TABLE 6-8	Comparing Group Policy Management Tools *(continued)*

Snap-in File Name	Full Name in MMC	Group Policy Admin Functions	Integration with Other Consoles and Snap-ins
dssite.msc	Active Directory Sites and Services	Navigate site policies. If GPMC is not installed: set up and remove links to existing GPOs, manage blocking, enforcement, and security/WMI filtering; create and delete group policy objects; turn off computer or user configuration portions.	If GPMC is installed: GPMC can be invoked from the container properties, Group Policy tab. If GPMC is not installed: GPEdit can be invoked from the Group Policies tab in site properties, with blocking, enforcement, and filtering option configuration. RSoP can be invoked from the All Tasks submenu in the site container context menu.
gpmc.msc	Group Policy Management Console	Intuitive navigation of all policies in the forest, except local policies. View policy processing order. Manage processing order, blocking, enforcement. Create and delete group policy objects. Manage links between group policies and Active Directory elements. Create WMI filters and manage WMI and security filtering. Toggle computer and user configuration. Manage GPO security (ACLs). Back up and restore group policy objects. RSoP planning and modeling functions with HTML reports.	GPEdit can be launched using the policy context menu (Edit).
gpedit.msc	Group Policy Object Editor	Edit any policy object or template. Manage group policy object security, including Read and Apply rights. Add and remove ADM files (extends legacy Registry-based policies). Import and export security templates.	Security templates are viewed, edited, created, and deleted using the Security Templates snap-in, in MMC.
rsop.msc	Resultant Set of Policy	Navigate effective configuration delivered with group policies in either planning or modeling modes.	
Viewable through MMC (no separate MSC console file)	Security templates	Review standard security templates, make modifications, and create your own templates for further export to other GPO tools.	

FIGURE 6-12

Effective group
policy shown
in RSoP

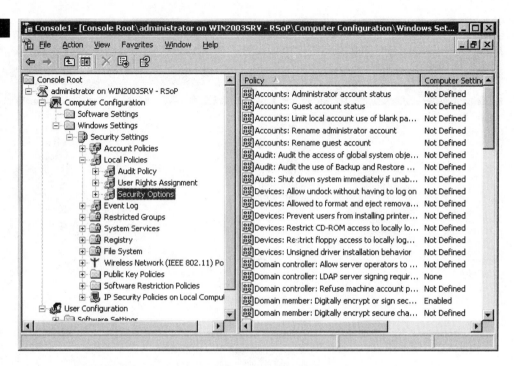

FIGURE 6-13

Effective group
policy shown
in GPMC

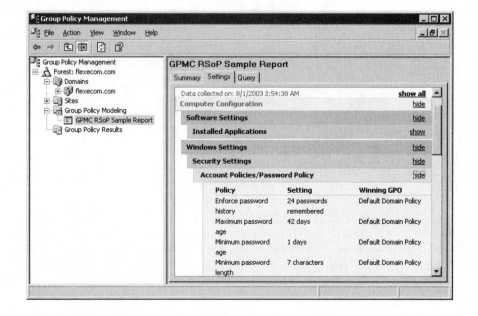

the results mode, the report is based on a CIMOM database located on a certain computer, with information that was formed as part of the boot, logon, and regular policy refresh processes—in other words, based on the actual, effective information. In the modeling mode, reports are generated based on the information in the same database—CIMOM—except this information is not actual and effective, but is generated on a domain controller by reading site, domain, and OU policies for a given computer and user.

The following chart illustrates the difference between the two processes. GPDAS stands for Group Policy Directory Access Service, and it is a component running on a domain controller that emulates group policy processing.

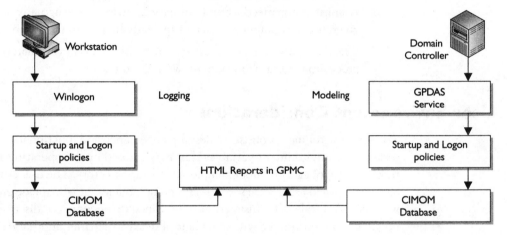

Results mode allows you to check which policy settings are effective when factors such as slow dial-up connections, user or computer security group membership, user or computer WMI filtering, or even GP-related problems come into play. Group policy results mode also takes into account local policies that are in effect on actual computers. Note that you need to run Windows XP Professional or Windows Server 2003 to query the client CIMOM database in the results mode.

In the group policy modeling mode, administrators need to select which factors in the following list should be accounted for when running a simulated application process, and which domain controller should be used to collect the results.

RSoP planning and modeling modes were created with a particular application difference in mind. Planning (or modeling) mode is helpful when any of the following applies:

- Administrators wish to model a new setting or a change in a policy and measure the effects in a certain domain, OU, or a site.

- Administrators wish to analyze a new policy and its effects in a new, not yet populated OU container.
- Administrators wish to see the effects of group policies when it comes to changing user or computer security group membership, or moving user or computer objects between sites or OUs.
- Administrators wish to evaluate the effects of slow network connections or loopback processing.

Logging (or results) mode is helpful in other situations, such as when:

- Administrators need to find out which settings were actually applied for any given user or computer. This is especially helpful in troubleshooting.
- Effective result sets may indicate which filter conditions matched during processing, if configuration allows ambiguity.

User Environment Considerations

The user environment consists of desktop appearance and functionality settings, and some of the environment variables that may be used by the operating system and third-party applications—for example, the Temp directory. The user environment can also be managed using local settings and group policies, in which case group policies will override locally administered settings. Since the focus of our discussion is group policy configuration, we will stay clear of desktop settings and hands-on desktop administration matters.

User environment configuration is delivered through the resultant set of all user configuration policy sections applied to the container where the user object is located. As you learned from the sections earlier in this chapter, all standard filtering, blocking, enforcing, loopback processing, and slow link detection rules apply in this case without exceptions.

Policy settings, configured in the user section of a group policy object, apply to users without regard to which computer they are logging on to (except for some situations where loopback processing is configured). What is important here is the operating system and service pack version running on the client computer: Windows XP Professional and Windows Server 2003 support all settings configurable in the Windows Server 2003 environment. Windows 2000, depending on the service pack level, supports most but not all of the settings configurable through the group policies. When you configure settings in the Group Policy Object Editor using extended view, client requirements are usually indicated in the comments section for each setting.

on the
job

If some of your client computers are running Windows 9x or Windows NT 4.0, you can configure a limited number of settings on those boxes using legacy system policies. System policies are based on the ADM files that apply changes using Registry settings.

The user environment can also be managed using scripts and Registry-based policies, defined in Administrative Templates. The following sections cover this in detail.

Logon and Logoff Scripts

Scripts can be used to automate virtually anything in the Windows environment. This of course includes administrative tasks and user environment settings, whenever users log on or off the system. Administrators have some flexibility when it comes to choosing which language to write these scripts in. VBScript (.vbs), JavaScript (.js), Perl, and DOS-based (.bat and .cmd) scripts are all supported by WSH (Windows Scripting Host). The User Configuration\Administrative Templates\System\Scripts section of a group policy object is used to control behavior of user scripts. You can choose whether or not you want scripts to be visible at runtime, which may be helpful in troubleshooting or if your logon scripts interact with users. You can also choose whether or not scripts should be executed synchronously or asynchronously.

If you select asynchronous processing, which is also the default value for this setting, the user interface (explorer.exe) will load without waiting for your scripts to finish; the synchronous setting produces the opposite effect. If scripted procedures must be fully executed before users are allowed to commence their work, synchronous processing may not be appropriate for your environment. Synchronous logon script execution settings are also available in the Computer Configuration section of the policy, and they have a higher priority over User Configuration settings. Note this behavior, because in most cases this works the opposite way, and there are very few exceptions.

Also note that there is a difference between logon/logoff scripts and start-up/shutdown scripts. Logon/logoff scripts are specific to a user object, whereas start-up/shutdown scripts are applied to a computer object, and both are configured using the Group Policy Object Editor. There is also a user object attribute accessible through Active Directory Users and Computers, where you can assign a logon script to selected users; however, this script will be stored in the file system, NETLOGON share, and not be part of a group policy object.

on the
job

By default, Windows XP does not wait for group policy objects (and scripts, for that matter) to be processed before it launches the user interface. Group policies are then processed in the background. You can control this behavior by setting "Always wait for the network at computer startup and logon" in the Computer Configuration\Administrative Templates\System\Logon section.

Internet Explorer Maintenance

Administrators can modify a number of IE settings, such as the homepage or Internet browser connection settings. IE maintenance settings are located in the Windows Settings section of User Configuration (a portion of the settings is shown in Figure 6-14).

Note that application of Internet Explorer policies does not involve modifying Registry settings.

Administrative Templates

The Windows operating system sets up the user environment based primarily on HKEY_CURRENT_USER (HKCU) Registry settings. This hive contains static settings configured locally as well as dynamic settings received from the group policy when the logon process occurs. The dynamic portion of these settings gets higher priority; it is located in two keys:

■ HKCU\Software\Policies

■ HKCU\Software\Microsoft\Windows\CurrentVersion\Policies

FIGURE 6-14

Internet Explorer maintenance, connection settings

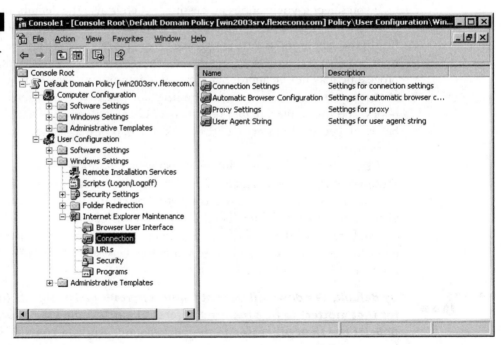

Users are restricted from making any changes to values stored in these keys. Let's briefly review user environment settings, which are configurable using group policy objects. In the Group Policy Object Editor, user environment settings in Administrative Templates are divided into seven sections, as follows:

- **Windows Components** This includes configuration of certain Windows applications and services that make up the user interface (Windows Explorer, Help, and Support Center); system applications and parameters (MMC, Task Scheduler, Windows Installer, Windows Update, Terminal Services, Application Compatibility); and add-on applications that have no direct impact on core system functionality (applications such as Windows Media Player, Windows Messenger, and NetMeeting). Windows Update settings allow administrators to control how updates available from the Software Update Service (SUS) should be applied on each system.

- **Start Menu and Taskbar** This may be used to modify the content of the Start menu and the appearance and functionality of the taskbar. This category features some 40 settings, including Turn Off Personalized Menus and Force Classic Start Menu, which can be used to turn off two of perhaps the most annoying Windows interface "improvements" ever.

- **Desktop** These settings affect desktop icons, the active desktop, and a few Active Directory interface features. Desktop settings allow you to remove icons and restrict context menus, the My Documents folder path, and some of the taskbar functions, such as toolbar modification.

- **Control Panel** Here you can restrict user access to the Control Panel, preventing users from modifying display settings, and adding or removing programs and printers. You can also adjust the Control Panel's appearance, switching it to the classic mode, if necessary.

- **Shared Folders** Two settings here specify whether or not users are allowed to publish shared folders or Distributed File System (DFS) roots in Active Directory.

- **Network** This category is divided into two distinct subcategories, one dealing with offline synchronization settings and the other one with network connection settings. Most of the settings are restrictive in nature and deal with how much access to standard functions is permitted.

- **System** This category contains script and group policy configuration settings, as well as user profile settings, a Ctrl+Alt+Del screen, and power management options.

The best way to familiarize yourself with a multitude of group policy settings is still hands-on experience. If you don't have access to a lab, at least open up the GPO Editor and spend some time browsing categories and reading through settings. To make it a little easier, Figure 6-15 shows the portion of the group policy settings structure containing the seven categories just discussed.

Registry-based template policies can easily be extended if standard Windows settings still somehow lack the functionality administrators are looking for. This allows developers to create applications, the behavior of which may also be controlled through group policy, thereby achieving close integration with Windows and allowing administrators to manage custom applications in a familiar way. All you have to do is create an ADM file, pre-populate it with appropriate settings, right-click the Administrative Templates container, and click Add/Remove Templates in the context menu. This will launch the Add/Remove Templates interface, as shown in Figure 6-16.

Although you can modify any Registry setting using custom administrative templates, applying custom settings outside of the two policy keys (HKCU\Software\Policies and HKCU\Software\Microsoft\Windows\CurrentVersion\Policies) is not

---

FIGURE 6-15

Group policy user configuration (Administrative Templates)

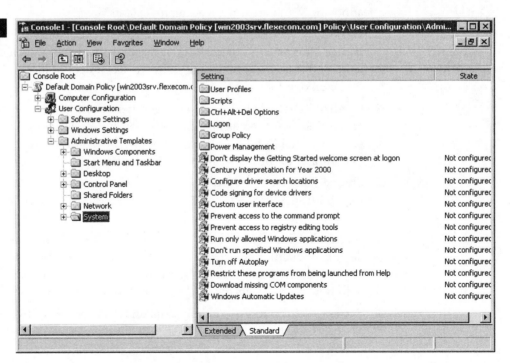

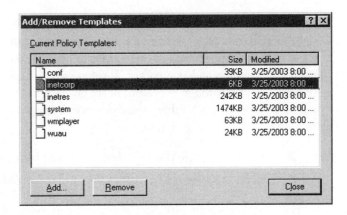

recommended, because settings in other locations are saved permanently until the next modification is performed, and thus are not dynamic.

Computer Environment Considerations

Computer environment configuration is very similar to user configuration in how settings are applied: computer objects receive resultant sets of computer configuration policy settings from all GPOs effective in the container where the computer objects are located. This resultant set affects computer settings and, indirectly, all users working on this computer. This may also have an impact on some functions associated with accessing this computer from the network, as opposed to being logged on to it interactively.

Similarly to user environment configuration, most of the settings related to operating system configuration that are not directly related to security will be configured through start-up scripts and Administrative Templates. Security-related settings are discussed later in the chapter, in "Computer Security Mechanisms."

Start-up Scripts

Start-up and shutdown scripts deliver functionality very similar to logon and logoff scripts, except that they are computer specific and are applied every time a computer system boots up or shuts down gracefully, regardless of whether or not a user logs on to the system.

Administrative Templates

The operating system configures the computer environment (which is computer specific and user neutral) based on the settings stored in the HKEY_LOCAL_MACHINE (HKLM)

Registry hive. This hive contains static settings configured manually by means of Control Panel applets and other system tools (usually only administrators are allowed to make these changes), application settings added as part of software installation, system services and device settings added as part of Windows installation, and last but not least, dynamic settings received through the resultant set of computer policies. If dynamic and static settings contradict each other, dynamic settings are given higher priority. The following two keys are used to store dynamic settings:

- HKLM\Software\Policies (the preferred location)
- HKLM\Software\Microsoft\Windows\CurrentVersion\Policies

Policy settings stored in these specific locations of the Registry are known as *true policies*. Similarly to HKCU keys, users are only allowed to read these settings. Let's briefly review the computer environment settings, which are configurable using group policy objects. In the Group Policy Object Editor, the computer environment settings in Administrative Templates are divided into four sections, as follows:

- **Windows Components**   This contains the same categories of settings as Windows Components in the user configuration section, except that computer configuration settings are specifically tailored for computer objects that are more closely related to computers than users, or which must be set earlier in the boot process. For example, if you compare Windows Update settings in the user and computer configurations, you will find that the user configuration only allows administrators to restrict user access to Windows update features, whereas the computer configuration exposes settings such as whether reboot should be performed automatically upon installation of updates. Some other computer configuration settings are also featured in the user configuration settings section; if there is a conflict in values for the same setting in both sections, the computer configuration value becomes effective.

- **System**   This contains the bulk of system settings, most importantly Remote Assistance, User Profiles, Disk Quotas, Net Logon, and Logon. Remote Assistance specifies whether terminal services access should be allowed on the computer and whether remote assistance requests should be permitted. Although terminal services is not new to the Windows world, you need at least the Windows XP client operating system to support this functionality on a desktop computer. The User Profiles section contains configuration settings associated with roaming and local user profiles—for example, whether roaming profiles should be cached locally. You cannot, however, turn the user profile into a roaming profile just by using group policies. This needs to be configured using the Active

Directory Users and Computers snap-in. The Disk Quotas section allows management of disk quotas in a way that is similar to configuring this feature locally on a client computer, with the only exception that group policy quotas are applied to all NTFS disks and you cannot set individual user quotas. The Net Logon section provides several dozen settings that deal with the logon process and how client computers look for domain controllers. In a majority of situations, you will not have to modify these settings. Finally, the Logon section allows you to set which applications should be launched automatically upon user logon, and which "Run" Registry keys should be processed at start-up.

- **Network** This section offers offline synchronization, DNS client, network connections, QoS, and SNMP settings manipulation.

- **Printers** This final section allows you to control printer-related settings such as printer publishing in Active Directory, printer browsing, directory pruning, and we o-based printing.

Figure 6-17 shows the Group Policy Object Editor interface with the Computer Configuration container expanded.

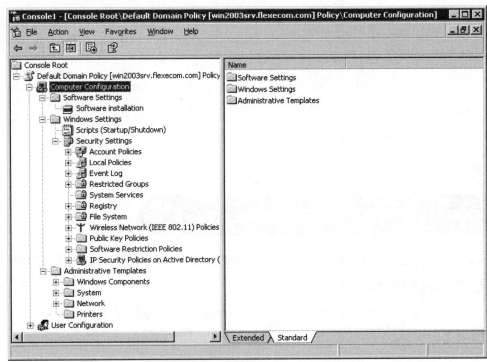

FIGURE 6-17

Computer configuration in the Group Policy Object Editor

EXERCISE 6-1

CertCam & MasterSim ON THE CD

Creating, Editing, and Applying Group Policies

In this exercise, you use the GPMC console to create a group policy object that makes some user environment modifications, and you assign this policy object to all domain users. Note that this exercise assumes you have installed the GPMC tool, which can be downloaded from www.microsoft.com.

1. Log on to the network using the administrator account.

2. Click Start | Run, type in **gpmc.msc**, and press ENTER.

3. Switch to the Group Policy Object container.

4. In the menu, select New and create a new policy, giving it a descriptive name.

5. Switch to the policy object you just created and click Edit. In the User Configuration section, expand Administrative Templates, and go to the Desktop container. Select Remove Recycle Bin Icon from Desktop.

6. Double-click the setting and choose Enabled on the property page that appears. Then click OK.

7. Now select your domain in the GPMC console, and in the context menu select Link An Existing GPO. Then pick the policy you just created and apply the change.

Policy configuration and association is complete. Now to test the setting, log off from the machine and log on using one of the user accounts that belongs to the domain in question. If all goes as planned, the recycle bin icon should be hidden from the desktop.

CERTIFICATION OBJECTIVE 6.02

Configure the User Environment by Using Group Policy

In planning your group policy strategy for the user environment, one of the most valuable functionalities to implement is making a particular user environment independent of a particular computer. In case the computer breaks down and has to be replaced or serviced, administrators want to spend the least amount of time moving their files and applications to another machine. To solve this issue, group policy offers user software distribution and folder redirection technologies.

In addition to making the user environment independent of computers, you will want to ensure that your organization's security level is enforced—users may need to be certain that their email messages are not intercepted or maliciously sent on their behalf, that no one else is able to register on the network using their credentials, and so on. You can configure security-related settings, such as digital certificate enrollment and encryption, through group policy as well.

User Software Distribution

Prompt software installation is one of those tasks administrators are likely to perform at least once a week, depending on the size of a company. Traditional methods of rolling out applications (attending each machine and installing software manually) no longer satisfy even midsize, dynamic environments. The disadvantages of attended installations are many: the need to install applications using administrator accounts, lack of removal mechanisms and procedures, application vulnerability due to inadvertent file removal or Registry modification, and the need to answer a batch of technical installation questions, which users may not be able to answer on their own. Furthermore, productivity of administrative personnel is affected throughout the life cycle by requiring them to attend client desktops again and again every time an application must be upgraded or patched.

Windows Server 2003 continues automated software distribution traditions established with Windows 2000. Windows Installer and group policies remove the burden of attended software installation. Windows Installer consists of three major components: a client component that requests software to be installed, an installer component implemented in msiexec.exe, and application packages (also called MSI packages, *.msi files) and software modification templates (called transform packages, *.mst files).

Windows Installer

Windows Installer is part of Windows 2000/Windows Server 2003/Windows XP operating systems and may also be offered as a separate add-on for older Microsoft operating systems. When a client requests a software package to be installed, removed, upgraded, or repaired, Windows Installer uses information contained in the appropriate MSI package to apply or roll back changes in the Registry and in the file system. In case of a request to repair an application, it checks file versions and copies original files over to replace their modified versions. The list of programs that shows up in Control Panel | Add/Remove Programs is also maintained by Windows Installer.

Detailed settings for Windows Installer are available in the group policy object, in both the User and Computer Configuration sections, Administrative Templates\ Windows Components\Windows Installer. Additional settings that apply to the Add/ Remove Programs applet are located in the User Configuration section, Administrative Templates\Control Panel\Add Remove Programs.

MSI Installation Packages

Software developers who want to take advantage of Windows Installer functionality (which also includes automated group policy software rollouts) need to ensure that their applications are compatible with MSI technology; this usually requires shipping an MSI installation package with the application distribution files. If an application you have to deploy through group policies does not have an MSI package provided by the software company, or you wish to deploy this application preconfigured with certain settings, you can create your own MSI package using tools such as WinINSTALL LE, which is provided on the Windows Server 2003 distribution CD, in the Valueadd\ 3rdparty\Mgmt\Winstle directory.

WinINSTALL LE, and other applications with similar functionality, takes a snapshot of the system before and after the software installation process, and compares deltas between the two snapshots. This allows WinINSTALL to analyze file system changes, Registry settings, system services, and INI files added as a result of the installation process. It then compiles this information into an MSI package, which could be used to roll forward the same changes on another system, or roll them back on the system where the application has been installed.

One drawback of this method is that you are just mirroring changes between computers; you cannot change any of the settings, such as the installation drive and directory, in the process. It is therefore recommended that you set up a "clean" workstation that most adequately represents your average workstation, and use it to assemble MSI packages.

If you are rolling out a mission-critical application that is fairly large and complex, you may find it difficult to install this application on every type of workstation in your organization without being able to customize MSI packages. This is where transforms (.mst) come in. Transforms contain a set of changes that need to be applied to the main MSI package, effectively adjusting execution of developer-provided MSI packages. You can associate one or more transforms with the same

MSI package using the command line-interface or using group policies (shown in Figure 6-18). The following sample msiexec.exe command can be used to launch the MSI package installation along with a set of transforms:

```
msiexec /i C:\MSIPackageName.msi TRANSFORMS=TransformList
```

MST transforms can be used to achieve any of the following:

- Indicate which components contained in the MSI package you want to deploy
- Define how users will be allowed to interact with the installation process—whether to hide it completely or allow users to answer installation questions interactively
- Define a set of valid answers to installation questions, if users are allowed to interact with the process
- Define the application installation directory
- Define how icons should be added to the user environment
- Select any other files you wish to deliver as part of the installation process, if necessary

FIGURE 6-18

Associating transforms with MSI packages using group policy

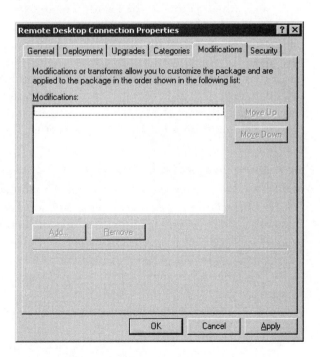

If MSI packages are not provided by the software developer and it is not possible to create your own MSI packages using WinINSTALL LE, you won't be able to take full advantage of Windows Installer functionalities, but it would still be possible to publish applications using group policies. To achieve this, administrators need to create a ZAP file in any text editor, such as notepad.exe, and place it into the setup directory where setup.exe or install.exe are located. ZAP files are similar to INI files; they must contain an [Application] section and may also contain an [Ext] section. Each section contains parameters and their respective values. Sample ZAP file content would look similar to the following:

```
[Application]
FriendlyName = The Olde Software
SetupCommand = \\servername\sharename\appname\setup.exe
DisplayVersion = 1.0
Publisher = The Olde Software Shoppe
URL = TheOldeSoftwareShoppe.com
[Ext]
ABC =
```

The key parameter here is SetupCommand = \\servername\sharename\appname\setup.exe, which points to the location of an executable setup file that should be launched on the client machine. The remaining parameters are relatively unimportant and are used to modify the appearance of the published application. Note that the installation application published using ZAP files cannot be launched using nonadministrative privileges, and therefore administrators will need to execute these files manually in cases where protected Registry keys must be modified as part of installation. This sort of defeats the purpose, but ZAP files are not really advertised as complete substitutes for Windows Installer technology.

Installing Software Using Group Policies

When you use a software distribution policy to install applications via group policy, MSI packages are executed on computers and for users affected by the policy using the System account context (note that ZAP files are outside of this category). This ensures smooth execution even for users who have restricted privileges in the system and are not allowed to install applications themselves. This also has no effect on the restriction, since only group policy–published or assigned applications will be executed using the System account.

on the !
ⓙob

If your organization uses Microsoft SMS Server, software publishing through SMS offers several advantages over group policies, such as the ability to perform scheduled rollouts, support for legacy operating systems, and independence from Active Directory. Installation of SMS is a complex task and is certainly not recommended specifically for software management if group policy functionality is already in place.

When it comes to making your software available via group policies, you have two choices: publishing and assignment. When you *publish* an application, it becomes available for installation in the Add/Remove Programs applet, as shown in Figure 6-19. Software can only be published for users, because the computer itself cannot determine whether it needs an application or not.

Contrary to publishing, software can be *assigned* to both users and computers. When you assign applications to computers, they get installed as part of the operating system boot process, after the OS is loaded but before the logon prompt is displayed. When you assign applications to users, application icons are placed on the desktop and in the Start menu, and are installed the first time the user attempts to launch an assigned application. (As we progress through this discussion, you'll see how the new "Install this application at logon" feature available in Windows Server 2003 can be used to trigger application installation upon user logon.)

FIGURE 6-19

Published applications in the Add/Remove Programs applet

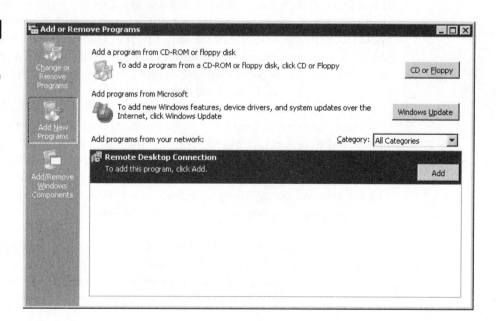

If your MSI package allows, some larger applications (such as MS Office) can be installed in several stages. For example, when a user accesses it for the first time, only a basic set of features is installed, and additional features are published within the application but are not made available on the computer until the moment the user invokes that particular function. In addition, users can initiate software installation if they try to open a file that has an extension associated with one of the published or assigned applications.

Before you can proceed with software policy configuration, you will need to set up a network share, assign appropriate permissions, and copy your MSI packages to that location. Note that you can use several locations at the same time for load-balancing needs. When ready, open your favorite group policy editor (GPMC or GPEdit; if you use GPEdit, make sure you select Default Domain Policy to edit). Expand Software Settings in the User Configuration or Computer Configuration section, right-click on Software Installation, and click properties.

You are presented with four groups of preferences: the General, Advanced, File Extensions, and Categories tabs. Use the General and Advanced tabs to set default settings for your installation packages, specifying options such as whether you will publish or assign packages, or let a wizard ask this question every time you create a software distribution package; and whether or not ZAP and 32-bit applications should be made available to 64-bit clients. The File Extensions tab lets you select the order of application preference when working with file types supported by more than one application. This setting may prove useful when you manage two or more applications that are capable of viewing, say, JPEG files. Finally, the Categories tab lets you create application categories for use with Add/Remove Programs. This does not affect software management functionality, only how applications are grouped together in the applet. Figure 6-20 demonstrates this.

Figure 6-21 illustrates the software installation properties on the General tab.

Administrators will need to create deployment packages using the New | Package option in the context menu of the Software Installation policy node. This will invoke a wizard that asks for basic information, such as location of the MSI package and deployment type. After you go through the wizard, you can look through the properties of the newly created deployment package and modify advanced settings, if necessary. Let's review the most important settings available through the deployment package properties.

The Deployment tab, shown in Figure 6-22, allows you to specify the deployment type, such as published or assigned, and deployment options: whether the application should be installed upon logon, whether it should be installed automatically when a user attempts to open a file with associated extension, whether the application

FIGURE 6-20

Using Categories
to group
published
applications

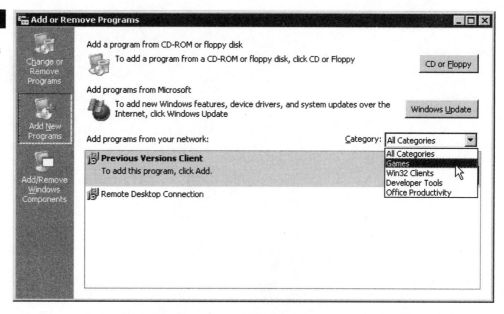

FIGURE 6-21

Software
Installation
Properties,
General tab

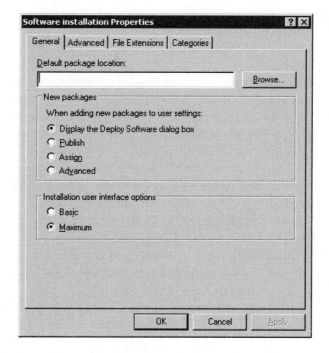

FIGURE 6-22

Deployment tab
in deployment
package
properties

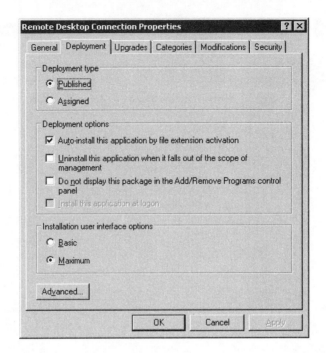

should be removed when it falls out of scope of management, and finally, whether the application should be made available via the Add/Remove Programs applet. The option to install software upon logon is new to Windows Server 2003, and it forces full installation to be performed on the client machine, which will include all the components that would not be made available otherwise. This option is useful for laptop users, who may be logging on to the network specifically to get their software updated before they go on a trip. Finally, on this page you can also set the level of user involvement in the installation process.

The Upgrades tab allows you to define which existing packages, if any, this deployment will upgrade, and also shows which packages, if any, upgrade the current package you are working with. You can click Add to indicate which packages are replaced by this deployment and what should be done with the old packages—if they should be uninstalled first or if the new package should be deployed over the existing application. Note that you cannot manipulate the list of which packages upgrade the current package you are working with; this list is created automatically based on the settings in other packages.

The last tab is Modifications. This is where you specify which transforms should be applied to the base MSI package, in which order. Using MST transforms, you can specify (for example, for applications such as Microsoft Office) which applications from the suite should be installed. Figure 6-19 depicted the interface used to associate transforms with the MSI packages.

One other thing to keep in mind when setting up computer and user software deployment using group policy is that group policy refresh intervals (90 minutes), as well as the manual command **gpupdate**, have no effect on software installation policies. The only two conditions that will apply updated software installation policies are the boot sequence (for computer policies) and the logon process (for user policies).

User Certificate Enrollment and Digital Signatures

As you might have noticed, computing environments have grown in size over the last few decades, and they are no longer isolated, one-off accidents. These environments are huge, and the vast majority of them are interconnected. Corporate administrators need to have a legitimate, truly secure method of dealing with risks associated with information interceptions, misrepresentation, malicious tampering, and break-ins. This is not only true for risks stemming from using the Internet for corporate communications, but also for internal use in medium to large, geographically distributed companies. Thus, security needs can be looked at in two ways:

- The need for strong encryption mechanisms with the ability to decrypt data. Encryption keys used to encrypt the information should be exchanged over the Internet or private network in an open form, but those who intercept this information should not be able to read intercepted, encrypted data.

- The need to guarantee data authenticity and ensure that communicating parties are indeed who they say they are. You need to be sure that the information received, say, through email, is coming from the user who sent it. This will first of all guarantee the communicating party's identity, which as a result, guarantees nonrepudiation (the sending party would not be able to deny that they sent the information). The same holds true for user-server communication: you need to be sure that you are sending information to the intended server, and not to a host impersonating this server.

To achieve all this, you use encryption keys—a set of numbers that make sense in mathematical calculations. As a result of industry progress in the last few years, and based on practical implementation experiences, it has become obvious that public key cryptography is a fairly reliable method of transmitting data in a secure way, in principle. PKI, or Public Key Infrastructure, found its way into Windows technologies and has been used in Microsoft products since the days of Windows NT 4.0.

You don't need to know all the details of public key cryptography, but a little background is relevant to our discussion. PKI is an asymmetrical encryption system that uses different keys to encrypt and decrypt information. Before secure data transactions can be initiated, parties must exchange "public" keys, used to encrypt the information. Public keys are useless for decrypting the information, and that is the main reason why exchanging public keys in the open is not a cause for concern.

Let's say HostA and HostB engaged in a secure transaction, and exchanged their public keys using the Internet. HostA uses HostB's public key to encrypt the information, which is then sent to HostB for processing. If this information is intercepted, along with the public key, an attacker will not be able to read the content of the message. HostB then uses its "private" key that corresponds to the public key submitted to HostA to decrypt the information. There is a mathematical relation between public and private keys that belong to the same set, but when strong algorithms are used, knowing the public key is not enough to deduce the value of the private key. The only thing that an attacker would be able to do with the public key is encrypt his own messages for submission to HostB. This is why it is crucial to make sure no one else has your private key: if it leaks, security is compromised.

This takes care of the first need, but what about authenticity and nonrepudiation? Digital signing comes to the rescue. It works the opposite way: instead of encrypting the information to a public key that belongs to HostB, HostA uses its own private key and a so-called message digest to calculate a digital signature. The *message digest* is the resulting value from hashing the information being transmitted, and it is basically a summary describing this information. Message digests are limited to several hundred bits as specified in the hashing protocol; for example, if MD5 is used, the length of the digest will be 128 bits. Should a single bit value in the transmitted stream of information change, this would result in a totally different message digest value.

HostB receives the information with the signature and performs its own hash calculation, using the same hashing algorithm and supposedly the same information that was submitted. If the resulting hash value matches the one extracted from the signature, HostB sees that the information has not been tampered with in any way. To extract a message digest value from the signature, HostA's public certificate is used. HostA's identity and the authenticity of the submitted information is verified; however, if the two hash values do not match, something has to be wrong with either the source or the information.

A Certification Authority (CA) acts as a third-party in this process. All hosts explicitly trust CAs, and digital certificates are issued by these authorities. CAs also maintain CRLs, or Certificate Revocation Lists, which list all certificates that were invalidated administratively before their expiration. Communicating hosts exchange public keys by submitting digital certificates, and optionally can run them by the CRLs (this will depend on the particular software implementation).

Using PKI in your Active Directory and Windows Server 2003 environment, you can implement the following technologies:

- Smart card authentication
- IPSec communication security
- Encrypted File System (EFS)
- Secure Multi-purpose Internet Mail Extensions (S/MIME)
- Secure web sites using Secure Sockets Layer (SSL) or Transport Layer Security (TLS)
- Digital signatures to ensure nonrepudiation in any of the preceding technologies

You can issue certificates to users, computers, and services in Windows 2000 and Windows Server 2003 environments. Among other things, digital certificates contain public keys, CAs' digital certificates, certificate expiration dates, and the purpose of the certificate.

You can issue digital certificates in Windows Server 2003 either manually, using the Certificates MMC snap-in, or automatically. The process of issuing a certificate involves generating a private key on the client machine and receiving a matching public key from the Certification Authority. Besides these functions, the Certificates snap-in allows you to perform the following:

- Request a certificate to be reissued
- Renew certificates, generating new keys or using existing ones
- Configure automatic enrollment
- Import or export certificates into a file
- Search, delete, and edit certificates

You can also use a web interface to request new certificates. This may be a valuable option if you need to request a certificate from a Certification Authority located outside your Active Directory structure. By default, Certificate Services create an Internet Information Server virtual directory called "certsrv," and you can request your certificates by going to http://servername/certsrv/ using your Internet browser. This feature is called Web Enrollment Support.

New to Windows Server 2003 is the ability to register users with a Certification Authority automatically. In Windows 2000, you could only issue EFS and computer certificates automatically. The new feature is especially useful if you are dealing with environments that have hundreds, if not thousands, of users.

To enroll your users automatically, you need to make sure that the following conditions are met:

- Windows 2000 Server domain controllers, if your company still runs Windows 2000, must be upgraded to Service Pack 3 or later.

- You need to upgrade your clients to Windows XP Professional or Windows Server 2003.

- You need to install the Enterprise Certificate Authority service on a Windows Server 2003 Enterprise Edition or Datacenter Edition server.

Before you can configure automatic enrollment of users with a Certification Authority, you have to install one. Certification Authorities can be either enterprise or standalone. Note that you cannot use a standalone CA for autoenrollment, and to install an enterprise CA, you will need the Active Directory environment.

To install a CA, go to Add/Remove Programs in the Control Panel, switch to Windows Components, and select Certificate Services from the list. Also note that you will not be able to rename your server after certificate services are installed.

Next, you must create certificate templates that will be used to issue certificates. This can, be done using the Certificate Templates MMC snap-in, shown in Figure 6-23. Some certificates will show up as grayed out. These are version 1 certificate templates; they are old and cannot be used for automatic enrollment purposes because they do not contain some of the fields required for this functionality. (In addition to color codes, which are version 2, there is a column that shows which templates can be used for autoenrollment.)

Version 2 certificate templates, appearing in color, can be used for automatic enrollment, and many of the values in these templates can be adjusted. For example, notice that the user template is grayed out, meaning that it is not available for automatic enrollment. To change this, you have to duplicate the template, which will upgrade it to the newer version. Within this upgraded template you can specify how this template should be used by user objects:

- Enroll the subject without requiring any user input. This will enroll users automatically without notifying them.

- Prompt the user during enrollment. This will inform users when the new certificate is requested and then install it. It is possible that some information will be requested—for example, users will be prompted for a PIN number if this certificate is to be used with a smart card.

FIGURE 6-23

Certificate
Templates snap-in

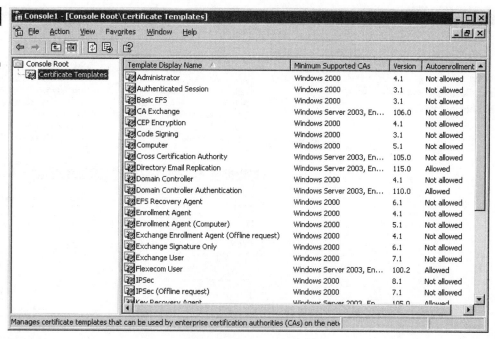

- Prompt the user during enrollment and require user input when the private key is used. This option will also notify users when the certificate is installed and notify them every time their private key is used.

You might want to check out the Security tab in the template properties after you set up all other parameters. Users must have the Autoenrollment right granted to them in order to use automatic enrollment.

On the General tab, you can enable certificate publishing in Active Directory. Optionally, you can also enable "Do not automatically re-enroll if a duplicate certificate exists" in the Active Directory option. Select this option to prevent certificate duplication when users without a roaming profile log on from different machines.

Now that you have a Certification Authority on the network, and a certificate template that you want to use, you need to enable this custom certificate template. Figure 6-24 shows the Certification Authority MMC snap-in. To enable a template, right-click the Certificate Templates container and select New | Certificate Template to Issue.

FIGURE 6-24

Enabling
certificate
templates using
the Certification
Authority MMC

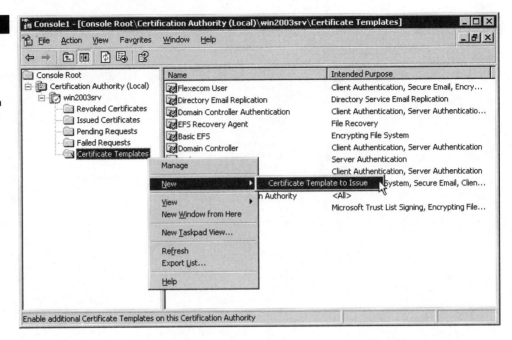

The last step to complete automatic enrollment configuration is to configure
group policy for enrollment of users with the Certification Authority. To do this,
follow these steps:

1. Using the Active Directory Users and Computers snap-in, choose the
   organizational unit containing the users you want to enroll automatically.

2. Right-click this container, and choose Properties. Then switch to the Group
   Policy tab.

3. Click the Edit button.

4. Expand the User Configuration container, then Windows Settings, Security
   Settings, and finally, Public Key Policies.

5. In the right pane, choose Autoenrollment Settings.

6. Make sure that this setting is configured to enroll certificates automatically.
   You may also want to check off one of the boxes to enable automatic renewal of
   issued certificates when they expire. Figure 6-25 shows the Autoenrollment
   Settings window.

7. Click OK to apply your settings and exit the Group Policy Editor. Automatic
   enrollment is now enabled.

FIGURE 6-25

Autoenrollment
Settings
dialog box

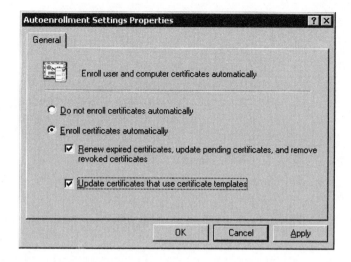

Be aware that certificates have expiration dates. In the certificate template, you
can control the number of days, weeks, months, or years that your certificates will
remain valid. On the same property page, you can also specify how often certificates
should be renewed. By default, this setting is configured to six weeks. The certificate
will be renewed if one of two conditions is met:

- Eighty percent of the certificate validity period elapses
- The certificate renewal period elapses

Finally, if there has been a security compromise, or for any other reason,
administrators can force all automatically issued certificates to be reenrolled.
To do this, open the Certificate Templates snap-in, choose the template or
templates that you wish to change, and click Re-enroll All Certificate Holders
in the context menu.

EXERCISE 6-2

Certificate Enrollment Using Group Policies

In this exercise, you use group policies to issue Basic EFS certificates for a group of users.
To complete this exercise, you need to create an organizational unit—let's name it
"TestUnit." You also need to create a user object, "User," in this organizational unit,
and add it to a newly created group, "TestGroup."

1. Log on to the network using the administrator account.

2. Click Start | Programs | Administrative Tools | Certification Authority.

3. Click Certificate Templates, right-click the container, and choose Manage.

4. In the Certificate Templates MMC snap-in that will appear, select the Basic EFS certificate template. Because this template is based on the old certificate, you need to duplicate it in order to configure it for automatic enrollment.

5. In the context menu of the certificate template, click the Duplicate template.

6. Name your new template using a descriptive name, such as **Basic EFS Autoenroll**.

7. On the Request Handling tab, check that "Enroll subject without requiring any user input" is selected.

8. On the Security tab, add your group to the ACL and grant it Autoenroll rights. Then click OK.

9. Close the Certificate Templates snap-in, and go back to the Certification Authority snap-in.

10. Remember that you have to enable your new template before it can be used for automatic enrollment. Right-click the Security Templates container, and from the context menu, choose Certificate Template To Issue.

11. In the window that will appear, select your newly created template, Basic EFS Autoenroll.

12. Now switch gears and launch the Active Directory Users and Computers snap-in.

13. Select your test organizational unit in the Active Directory structure, and open its properties.

14. Click the Group Policy tab, click the New button, and name your new policy **Certificate Enrollment**.

15. Select the new policy and click the Edit button.

16. Now expand the User Configuration container, then Windows Settings, Security Settings, and finally, Public Key Policies.

17. Double-click Autoenrollment Settings, and check that Enroll Certificates Automatically is selected. Also, enable both of the check boxes and click OK.

18. Log off the network, and then log on using your test user account. You *must* do this on a machine running either Windows XP Professional or Windows Server 2003; otherwise autoenrollment will not issue a certificate automatically.

19. Launch Internet Explorer, and go to Tools | Internet Options | Content | Certificates. Here you can see the list of certificates installed on the system. Check to see that your Basic EFS certificate is listed.

You have two other methods for checking whether the certificate enrollment was successful. One way is to check the local directory C:\Documents and Settings\ user\Application Data\Microsoft\SystemCertificates\My Certificates to see if a new file was created there. A more suitable option for administrators, however, is to log on to the network using the administrator account, and then open the Certification Authority snap-in, switch to the Issued Certificates container, and verify that the user enrollment process for your test user account completed successfully.

Folder Redirection

Most of the user environment settings are saved in user profiles. These settings include things such as the Start menu, My Documents folder, Internet Explorer, and the Application Data folder (which usually contains application-specific settings and data files—most importantly, Microsoft Outlook PST data files).

By default, user profiles are stored locally on client computers, in the C:\Documents and Settings\%username% directory. This may be acceptable in organizations with few employees, where each user has his or her own dedicated computer. This may not be such a great idea in companies where users move between computers, because they will have to set up their profiles on each computer, and some of the data they may have stored on the desktop or in the My Documents folder will not follow them from one machine to another. If administrators have to move users from one machine that is about to fail to another one, they will have to ensure that PST files and all other documents from My Documents in locally stored profiles are also moved to the new machine. Even if your logon scripts are configured to map a network drive, it is still not a trivial task to make sure that all users in your organization remember to save their files on the network. The fact that many office applications default to My Documents when you open or save files is unlikely to help the situation.

Other issues may also contribute to this problem. A centrally administered backup strategy will most likely be useless in the face of storing user data locally on client computers. Although it may be possible to do network backups from a central location, there is no guarantee that users will leave their computers turned on when they leave for the day. By the same token, you cannot assume that all client computers will be turned on during the day. And even if you can make sure that all computers will be turned on during your backup process, it is still very difficult to maintain a backup policy that will include hundreds, if not thousands, of machines, which will probably have to be changed daily. All things considered, distributed backups have very little chance to succeed in the corporate environment.

To address these issues, Microsoft developed roaming profiles that were available as early as Windows NT. The concept of *roaming profiles* is that they are the same user profiles except they're stored on a network share. When a user logs on to the network, this roaming profile is copied to the local drive. Users work with local copies of roaming profiles (with the cached profiles), and upon logoff, changes made to the cached copy are synchronized back to the network location. Despite the fact that this technology effectively solves the problem associated with users floating from one machine to another, it has a number of associated disadvantages. In some circumstances, locally stored profiles may fail to synchronize with the server, resulting in inconsistent profiles and help desk calls. Client computers also need ample disk storage to accommodate profile copies of all users who have to work on a given machine.

Next, some of the files in the Application Data folder (such as Microsoft Access database files and Microsoft Outlook PST files) may take up anywhere between several kilobytes and several gigabytes of space. Synchronizing them with the server may take a considerable amount of time and will consume a lot of network bandwidth. Users will not be able to commence their work on the client computer until their roaming profile has finished loading on the system, which will create an impression that everything is either slow or not working at all. To allow administrators to combine the best features of local and roaming profiles, Microsoft came up with folder redirection.

Folder redirection can be used with group policies to configure some of the profile folders so that they are mapped to a shared folder on the network. Folders that can be redirected are as follows:

- **My Documents**   This folder stores all Microsoft Office files created by users, unless users explicitly save them in another location. The user profile environment variable and some Registry settings point applications to My Documents in the File | Open and the File | Save menus.

- **Desktop**   This includes all icons and folders stored on the desktop. Note that not all icons will work on all computers. Applications must be installed on all computers in the same paths on local drives for this to work regardless of the workstation.

■ **Start Menu** This folder stores all Start menu items maintained for individual users. A portion of files in the Start menu can also apply to all users logged on to this system—these are not included in the Start Menu folder redirection.

■ **Application Data** Application service information that is specific for each user will be stored in this folder. Examples include Microsoft Outlook files, user templates, and temporary files.

When you request access to a folder that is being redirected, you are effectively accessing a network resource. This does not require your profile to be copied in its entirety and is completely transparent for users. This approach allows administrators to save network bandwidth, avoiding unnecessary synchronization between cached profiles and network servers, and speeding up the logon process.

To configure folder redirection, launch the Group Policy Object Editor (Active Directory-based policy), expand User Configuration, then Windows Settings, and then Folder Redirection. This container has four objects, representing each of the folders that can be redirected. In the context menu of each of these objects, you can select properties and use Target and Settings tabs to configure how and where a folder should be redirected. On the Target tab, you can switch the Not Configured setting to Basic or Advanced. Selecting Advanced redirection allows redirecting folders based on security group membership, without having to implement security group filtering for your group policies. Figure 6-26 shows the Target tab where you configure redirection type.

Other than security group filtering, Basic and Advanced settings offer the same folder redirection options:

■ **Redirect to the User's Home Directory** This setting is maintained for backward compatibility with Windows NT 4.0 environments. If your organization already has a user home folder structure in place, you may choose to use it on a temporary basis. If your network still runs applications that use %HOMEDRIVE%, %HOMESHARE%, %HOMEPATH% environment variables, then this may be the best option to go with.

■ **Create a Folder for Each User Under the Root Path** This option will create folders for each user in the network share that you will use. You can specify the network share using the UNC pathname, or a local path. The user subdirectory is created automatically, and access to these folders is restricted using NTFS permissions.

Configuring
folder redirection
using group
policies

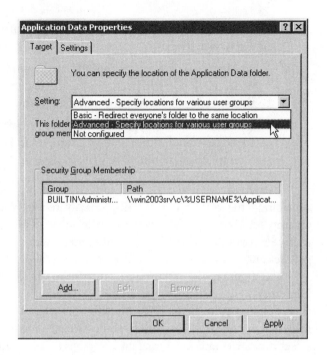

- **Redirect to the Following Location** If your redirected folder locations are already in place, you can specify them by choosing this option. Try to avoid using this option if you can, because not only will you have to create your directory structure manually, but you will also have to assign permissions manually. This may not be possible with a large number of users, unless custom scripting is used.

- **Redirect to the Local Userprofile Location** Setting this option will cancel the effect of redirecting your folders and restore the original functionality, in which user profiles are cached locally. Depending on the Policy Removal settings, you may not need to use this option.

Obviously, for folder redirection to work, the shared network resource used for storing user data must have appropriate share and NTFS permissions assigned to it. If something is not configured correctly and this prevents the system from accessing the location specified for folder redirection, you may see event log records such as the one shown here:

```
Event ID: 101
User: <USERNAME>
```

```
Computer: <COMPUTERNAME>
Description:
Failed to perform redirection of folder <FOLDERNAME>. The new
directories for the redirected folder could not be created. The
folder is configured to be redirected to \\<SERVERNAME>\
<SHARENAME>\%USERNAME%, the final expanded path was \\
<SERVERNAME>\<SHARENAME>\<USERNAME>. The following error
occurred:
Access is denied.
```

Now let's switch from the Target tab to the Settings tab (see Figure 6-27). This tab is used to configure additional options, such as "Grant the user exclusive rights to <foldername>." If this option is selected, only the user and the system account will have access to this folder by default. This of course does not preclude the administrator from taking ownership of the folder and revoking all permissions. The next option, "Move the content of <foldername> to the new location," allows administrators to copy the user folder structure to another location, if that becomes necessary. Administrators are better off using this option, because manual intervention may lead to inconsistent NTFS permissions. You may still need to intervene and add administrators and backup operator groups to the structure's permissions in order to be able to back up the content and perform troubleshooting functions.

Also on the Settings tab, you have Policy Removal options, which dictate whether this setting should still be enforced after group policy is removed. There are two options:

- Leave the folder in the new location when policy is removed.
- Redirect the folder back to the local userprofile location when policy is removed.

Depending on how often changes are made to the group policy, you may prefer one or the other. Note that folder redirection with group policies is only available in the domain environment. Local policies do not allow folder redirection.

on the job *If you're upgrading Windows NT 4.0 workstations, user profiles will still be stored in the %systemroot%\profiles\ directory.*

User Security Mechanisms

User security mechanisms consist of group policies applied to all user objects in a given domain, as well as specific security settings defined in the user section of the group policy that can be applied to individual organizational unit containers.

Settings tab in
folder redirection
properties

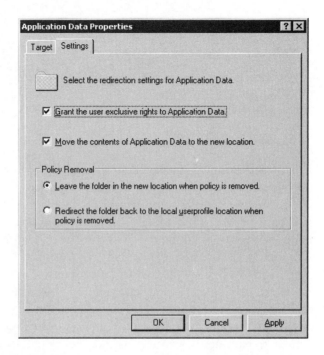

The integrity of your security plan is compromised if your domain users do not log on to the system with their own user accounts, using shared accounts instead of their personal ones. Only when domain user accounts are issued to company employees on an individual basis is it possible to institute and enforce security policies effectively. Outsiders may employ social engineering, dictionary, and brute-force attacks to obtain user logon and password information and gain access to the corporate network. Since one piece of this information is exposed anyway (username information is relatively easy to obtain, for example, by using dictionary attacks against corporate mail servers), security policy in Windows Server 2003 focuses on the second piece of information—passwords—as well as some Kerberos-related settings. You can find associated security policies in the Computer Configuration section, Windows Settings, Security Settings, Account Policies, which contain three main groups of settings: Password Policy, Account Lockout Policy, and Kerberos Policy. These settings cannot be modified on an organizational unit or site level; settings defined in the domain policy will become effective.

First, let's take a look at Password Policy. These settings are used to make it difficult to guess passwords by requiring a certain level of password complexity. Applicable settings are shown in Table 6-9.

TABLE 6-9	Password Policy Settings

Setting	Description
Enforce Password History	Users should not be allowed to reuse old passwords, because chances are good that old passwords have been exposed or compromised. You can configure Windows to remember a certain number of passwords that users defined in the past, preventing them from repeating these passwords.
Maximum (Minimum) Password Age	This setting defines an interval during which users are required to change their password. You can configure the setting to be anywhere between 0 and 999 days. Naturally, the maximum value should be greater than the minimum value. Setting these to 0 days effectively turns this feature off, and users will never be required to change their passwords.
Minimum Password Length	Passwords can only be considered secure if they are not vulnerable to dictionary attacks. If such an attack is launched against your domain controller, and the attacker runs out of dictionary words, he will have to use brute-force, effectively trying all possible combinations of letters, digits, and symbols for any password length. The longer your password is, the harder it is to crack using the brute-force method. As a rule, passwords should not be less than eight characters long.
Password Must Meet Complexity Requirements	Continuing with the brute-force attack, by enforcing password complexity, you increase the number of possible combinations for a given number of characters, because more symbols can now be mixed into a password string. This setting will require your users to mix their passwords with uppercase letters, special characters, and numbers. So instead of 26 characters, your passwords now contain in excess of 100 characters. This will surely give brute-force attackers a hard time.
Store Password Using Reversible Encryption	Windows Server 2003 does not store passwords by default; instead, it stores a value based on a password string, which is called a *hash*. If you use reversible encryption to store passwords, you force the operating system to store actual passwords in encrypted form instead of their hash values, which is considered to be a security risk. However, this may be necessary in certain configurations— for example when you use Microsoft Internet Authentication Server (IAS).

The next category is Account Lockout Policy. The settings shown in Table 6-10 are also very effective against brute-force attacks. Combining all of them makes it practically impossible to crack the password, because attackers won't have the luxury of running their attacks against enabled accounts, and hence the ability to try password combinations against the system is limited.

Kerberos Policy, as the name implies, deals with securing the Kerberos authentication system. After successful authentication, users receive so-called ticket granting tickets

TABLE 6-10	Account Lockout Policy Settings

Setting	Description
Account Lockout Duration	This setting controls how long user accounts should be disabled if the incorrect password entry threshold is exceeded. This setting applies both to console logon attempts and network logon attempts. Note that the built-in administrator account is outside the scope of this setting. This is why administrators must choose the most complex passwords that will be very difficult to guess.
Account Lockout Threshold	This tells the system how many attempts users have to enter their passwords before their accounts are locked out. Most networks should be configured with three to five incorrect password entry attempts. Setting this to less than three is likely to generate a lot of help desk support calls because users often forget to turn off CAPS LOCK and NUM LOCK, and if they changed their password recently, they often forget it.
Reset Account Lockout Counter After	You can also configure the account lockout counter to be reset after a period of time.

(TGTs), also referred to as "user tickets" in the policy settings. When users access network resources, they will need to obtain service tickets by providing this special TGT to a domain controller running the KDC (key distribution center) component. You can limit ticket lifetime and tighten up other Kerberos settings using Kerberos Policy settings, shown in Table 6-11.

Software Restriction Policy

Email and the Internet have become increasingly important for corporate user productivity. Unfortunately, attackers are aware of that, and successful attacks are often launched using harmful attachments in email messages, or using executable components on malicious websites. While some viruses may be nothing more than pranks, others may prove to be very destructive. The majority of users cannot distinguish between harmful and unharmful attachments. For this reason, many companies employ some sort of antivirus software.

However, antivirus software also has its problems, due to the fact that it is impossible for a software vendor to be aware of every single piece of malicious code on the Internet. Without this information, vendors cannot create virus signatures for every virus and hence, detect harmful code effectively. Administrators can take advantage of software restriction policies implemented via group policies to allow only certain types of applications, or specific applications, to be executed. Using software restriction policies,

TABLE 6-11	Kerberos Policy Settings
Setting	**Description**
Enforce User Logon Restriction	Using this Kerberos setting, you can force the KDC to verify user permissions to access the requested resource, before it issues the service ticket based on the user's TGT. If used, this feature will have a performance impact on the authentication process.
Maximum Lifetime Service Ticket	This setting is self-descriptive—it controls how long service tickets issued by key distribution centers should remain valid.
Maximum Lifetime User Ticket, and Maximum Lifetime User Ticket Renewal	These two settings control the validity interval for ticket granting tickets and their renewals.
Maximum Tolerance for Computer Clock Synchronization	Kerberos tickets expire after a while. So if a hacker manages to intercept and crack a ticket, chances are good that this ticket will not be valid anymore. It is also possible for an attacker to tamper with the clock settings on a domain computer. The Maximum Tolerance setting can be used to help prevent attackers from using cracked tickets in this scenario. Computer hosts with time settings outside of the allowed synchronization deviation will not be considered valid. Note that if you have domain controllers—for example, in Japan and the United States—and their time zones are set to JST and EST, respectively, the time difference will not violate this setting.

administrators define a common security level (either Disallowed or Unrestricted) and then create rules to define exceptions from a given security level. These custom rules can be based on one of the following four categories:

- **Hash rule** Administrators can set up rules that allow users to execute certain applications with a known hash. Hashes for each application are calculated when you create this rule, and for as long as executable files remain unchanged, users will be able to launch applications that have matching hashes in the policy.

- **Certificate rule** Using certificate rules, administrators can identify code signing certificates, which are considered safe for the organization. Applications signed with this certificate will be allowed.

- **Path rule** Path rules are used to define locations of applications deemed to be safe. Similar to certificate rules, applications installed in directories that match this setting will be allowed.

- **Internet zone rule** These rules can be used to restrict software based on where it was downloaded from. Zones available for this rule are the same as those defined in the Internet Explorer settings: trusted sites, restricted sites, local intranet, local computer, and the Internet.

If you select the Disallowed security level for your software restriction policy, user applications will not be allowed unless they are specifically permitted by one of the rules. If you select Unrestricted, user applications will be allowed unless specifically prohibited by one of the rules.

By default, when you install Windows, software restriction policies are not created within group policy objects, and the Software Restriction Policies container is empty. Using the context menu of this container in either the User or Computer Configuration section, Windows Settings, Security Settings, you can create a new software restriction policy. This will create a set of containers within the Software Restriction Policies container (see Figure 6-28). The Security Levels container will hold security level configuration, and the Additional Rules container will hold all of the rules created by administrators.

Each of the rules that administrators create also has its own security levels. Thus, if your default security level is Disallowed, you will need to create rules with the Unrestricted security level. The opposite is true—if your default security level is Unrestricted, you will need rules with the Disallowed security level. Each category of rules has its own priority, which is used in case there is a rule conflict. Hash rules

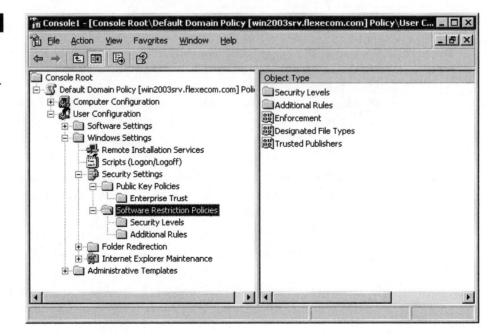

FIGURE 6-28

Software Restriction Policies container

have the highest priority, followed by certificate rules, then path rules, and finally, Internet zone rules. This means that if the same application falls under the scope of more than one rule, the higher-priority rules will become effective.

By default, the system creates additional rules, which allow running programs and system utilities that are part of the operating system. This prevents situations in which you accidentally set the security level to Disallowed and forget to define rules for the operating system files. (This would prevent your computers from booting properly.) Default rules use system variables and wildcards to ensure that they will work regardless of where the operating system is installed.

In addition to rules and default security levels, you can also configure three additional settings:

- **Enforcement**   This setting allows administrators to define the scope of the software restriction policy as it applies to restricted applications. Specifically, you can configure whether a software restriction should be applied to all files of the application in question, or if dynamic link libraries (DLLs) should be excluded from the scope. Controlling access to libraries may be important if you suspect that the system is infected with a virus that targets these files. The downside is that protecting DLLs will slow down application performance, because every time a function stored in a DLL is executed, this policy has to be verified. The Enforcement setting also allows you to exclude local administrators from the scope of this policy. It is not uncommon for companies to have a practice of adding domain user accounts to the local administrators group on workstations, as this may be necessary to support legacy applications.

- **Designated File Types**   Here, you can define which file types are considered to be executable. For example, files such as VBS, BAT, CMD, and EXE are known to be executable, but depending on how you configure restriction policies, you may need to add or remove file types from this list.

- **Trusted Publishers**   This setting should be configured if you are using certificate rules. You can specify which of the three categories of users (domain administrators, local administrators, and users) can add software publishers into the trusted publishers list. Software distributed by companies that were added to the trusted publishers list will not be considered harmful. This applies to Internet downloads as well as ActiveX components that were signed with digital certificates. As mentioned in the PKI discussion earlier, certificate authorities maintain Certificate Revocation Lists (CRLs). Using the Trusted Publishers setting, you can also specify whether this revocation list should be checked. But leaving this option disabled speeds up access to applications.

CERTIFICATION OBJECTIVE 6.03

Deploy a Computer Environment by Using Group Policy

The computer environment consists of installed software and security controls, such as Registry controls, file system controls, service state and security control. Group policy also supports computer-based PKI mechanisms. This part of the chapter covers components that create a computer environment, and how group policies can be used to manage this environment.

Computer Software Distribution

What is the difference between computer software distribution and user software distribution? First of all, the scope of the policy is different: computer software distribution settings apply to computer objects located in the organizational unit that you are working with. Next, computer software distribution finishes before the user logon prompt is displayed, making software available for use right after users log on to the machine. Finally, you cannot publish software for computers; you can only assign software to computers.

EXERCISE 6-3

CertCam & MasterSim ON THE CD

Software Distribution Using Group Policies

In this exercise, you use group policy to install Windows Server 2003 administrative tools on computers located in the IT organizational unit. Before you begin, create a shared folder on your network and copy the adminpak.msi file from the Windows Server 2003 distribution CD.

1. Log on to the network using the administrator account.

2. Click Start | Run, type in **dsa.msc**, and press ENTER.

3. In the Active Directory Users and Computers console, create a new organizational unit, and name it **IT**.

4. Open the properties of this new organizational unit, and switch to the Group Policy tab.

5. Click the Edit button, and using the Group Policy Object Editor console, expand the Computer Configuration container, then the Software Settings container, and click Software Installation.

6. Right-click the Software Installation node, and in the context menu, select New and then Package.

7. In the browser window, go to the network location that you created for this exercise, select the adminpak.msi file, and click OK. Make sure you use the UNC path to access this file in the browser window, otherwise this package will not be found by client computers. You will also get a warning pop-up advising you not to use local paths.

8. Next, select the deployment method for this application. Note that the Published option is unavailable. Your choices are Advanced and Assigned. Click Assigned and click OK. This creates a new software distribution policy.

9. Now move one of your client computer objects into this new organizational unit, and log off the network.

10. Next, you should reboot the client computer object you just moved. You should see an Applying Computer Policy window during the boot phase. When you get the logon prompt, log on to the network.

11. Check to see that your software package was installed on the machine by clicking Start | Programs | Administrative Tools. You should see the familiar administration tools that are available on your domain controller.

Computer Certificate Enrollment

There is no difference between computer certificate enrollment and user certificate enrollment. As discussed earlier, certificates can be used to ensure that communication between two network nodes is private and secure. Certificates can be issued not only to user objects, but also to computer objects and system services.

Using certificates, client computers can verify server identity, ensuring that they are working with a legitimate domain controller, and not a rogue host. The opposite is also true—domain controllers can verify client computer identity, ensuring that they belong to the domain. Certificates issued to computers are also used in IPSec and VPN communications. SSL-secured websites also use computer certificates to encrypt communication between web servers and Internet browsers.

The Public Key Policies container in the computer configuration section of the group policy has four child containers, in addition to Autoenrollment Settings. These containers are described in the following list.

■ **Encrypted File System** This container is used to create recovery agents and configure encrypted data recovery policies. Files encrypted with EFS cannot be taken over by administrators; data will only be available to the user object associated with the appropriate private key. Recovery agents can be used in cases where it is no longer possible to access that private key—for example, when company management or law enforcement agencies need to access files encrypted by a user whose account was deleted.

- **Automatic Certificate Request Settings**   This container, defines a list of certificates that should be issued automatically to every computer object that falls under the scope of this policy. Examples include computer certificates and IPSec certificates.

- **Trusted Root Certification Authorities**   In this container, you can configure which Certification Authorities should be considered as trustworthy in your environment. Companies such as VeriSign and Thawte can issue publicly accepted certificates simply because Internet browsing software has them configured as trusted roots. This makes every certificate issued by either of the two companies trusted. In some cases, you will need to add your own trusted root Certification Authorities—for instance, when you're dealing with a partner organization that uses their own CA, and you want to make sure that computers in your domain can access resources in their domain without getting security warnings.

- **Enterprise Trust**   This container is used to create a certificate trust list (CTL) to be distributed with your group policy. The CTL is a signed list of certificates issued by a third-party CA that the administrator considers acceptable for specific applications, such as client authentication or secure email. CTLs should be used in situations where you want to accept a certain certificate from a third party for, let's say, IPSec communication setup, but would not accept it for any other application.

Although the purpose and template differ, the process of configuring automatic enrollment for computers is no different from that of users.

Computer Security Mechanisms

The last section of group policy that we will look at is computer security. This section can be accessed by expanding Computer Configuration, then Windows Settings, and then opening Security Settings. Figure 6-29 shows the extent of the features you can configure in this section.

Computer security settings can be used to configure computer functionality as well as to restrict access to many of the features available by default. Using these settings, you can configure things such as user rights assignment, auditing and log settings, Registry settings, and communications security levels. You can even select the state of system services, which is useful if you want to disable certain services throughout the domain or OU.

Common logic suggests that the more important a given computer is to your organization, the stricter the security settings should be. By default, domain controllers are configured more strictly than client computers because of their importance to the infrastructure. Let's take a brief look at each of the categories contained in this section that haven't already been discussed.

FIGURE 6-29   Computer security settings in group policy

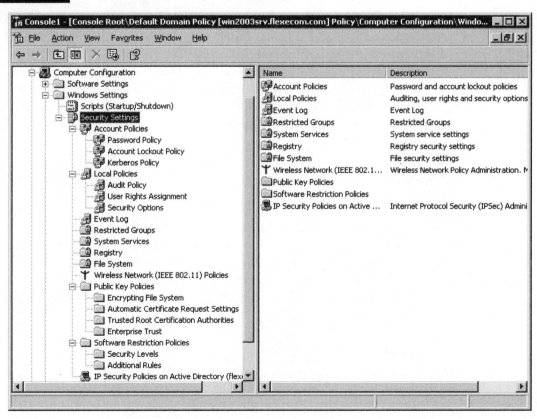

The Local Policies container features three categories, as shown in Figure 6-30, that deal with auditing, user rights assignment, and security options. In the Audit Policy section, you can define which types of system events should be recorded in the event log. You can enable auditing on practically any object that has an ACL. This includes files, directories, services, and Active Directory objects, such as printers and group policies. Before auditing is considered enabled, two things must happen. First, you should enable auditing categories configurable through this audit policy. Second, you should enable auditing on the Security tab of a specific object or group of objects you wish to be audited. Note that while auditing is important from the security standpoint, it should not be abused because excessive audit logging will impact system performance.

The User Rights Assignment policy assigns certain system privileges to user or group objects. Out of several dozen privileges, three or four of them are used frequently, while others may only be necessary in specific situations.

- **Logon Locally**   This allows users to log on to the machine using the console.
- **Log on as Service, Log on as Batch Job**   This allows launching a service or a script in the context of a specific user account. This is widely used for processes scheduled to be executed on the system on a regular basis as part of maintenance, such as backup jobs. To enforce security and prohibit users from using generic service accounts, you can revoke the right to log on locally from a service account, and use that service account to run your scheduled processes.
- **Access this Computer from the Network**   This grants a privilege from anywhere on the network to access resources on a computer where this policy is applied.

The Security Options container features some 70 settings related to system security configuration. It contains settings such as communications security standards, the lowest allowable level of security, what domain authentication protocols should be used when working with third-party or legacy clients, whether the content of the swap file should be cleared before system shutdown, and other settings that harden the system.

Event Log

This container is used to configure the size of each log file (system, application, and security) and what to do when log records fill up (whether to stop logging, overwrite events older than a certain number of days, or overwrite as necessary). Normally, you would want to configure the default log size to be in the neighborhood of 10MB. Too large a size may also hit system performance, but if the file size is too small, it will not have enough space to store a meaningful amount of records, causing logs to be filled up quickly and potentially important records to be overwritten before administrators have a chance to notice them.

System Services

Here administrators can define which services should be started automatically upon system startup, and which should remain disabled. Also note, for each system service, you can specify detailed security settings that can be used to allow or prohibit users from starting or stopping certain services. If you have to disable, say, the Computer Browser service, you might also need to make sure that users are not allowed to restart it.

Registry Rights

You can deploy custom Registry keys and values and configure security rights and auditing settings for any Registry key or hive on client computers. You can use the context menu to add a new key to this container, and go through a simple wizard that will prompt you to configure security settings, and ask how these settings should be propagated to child keys and values. Three main options are available (see Figure 6-30):

- **Propagate inheritable permissions to all subkeys** Will apply security settings to all child keys, preserving existing security settings on client computers. If your settings conflict with the explicit configuration on the client computer, then the explicit configuration will take precedence. Also, child key settings will not be modified if blocking is used. Blocking and inheritance work within the Registry identically with group policies and file system permissions.

- **Replace existing permissions on all subkeys with inheritable permissions** Will replace child key security settings on client computers.

- **Do not allow permissions on this key to be replaced** Will leave security configuration of the key unchanged on client computers.

File System

As with the Registry, you can configure file security and auditing on select files or folders on client machines. If you are working with a folder, after you configure folder security, you can also configure how these settings should be propagated down the structure.

FIGURE 6-30

Registry settings
in security
configuration of a
group policy
object

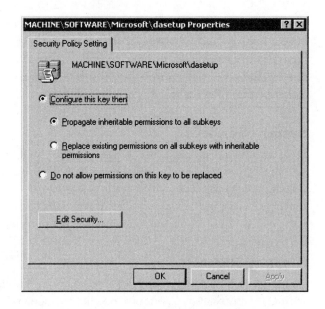

Available options are exactly the same as with the Registry. The only difference is that you are dealing with NTFS ACLs and not Registry key ACLs.

Wireless Network (IEEE 802.11) Policies

Wireless networks can be either infrastructure based, or ad hoc. The former assumes that you have network access devices called access points, which act as a gateway between wireless and wired networks. An ad hoc wireless network is a peer-to-peer network formed by wireless devices. To configure a wireless device to access your network, you have to specify the service set identifier (SSID) value, which is a string of up to 255 symbols that serves as a network identifier, somewhat analogous to subnets in TCP/IP. All devices participating in a wireless network with a common SSID must use compatible wireless authentication and encryption protocols.

Encryption

Without encryption in wireless networks, any passerby with a laptop and a wireless adapter could access your corporate resources. Some research companies conduct regular "war-driving" of downtown areas in North American cities, mapping available networks and publishing this information on the Internet. Presently, the WEP Encryption protocol is used in private wireless networks with a symmetric encryption key. Earlier versions of this technology were found to be flawed, but it still prevents the vast majority of potential break-ins and service theft due to the limited number-crunching power of most attackers' hardware. WEP is also a de facto standard in wireless encryption. If data transmitted over your wireless network is confidential or classified, it is highly recommended that you use a VPN tunnel over the wireless medium.

Windows Server 2003 wireless network policy configuration involves

- Creating a wireless network policy
- Configuring SSID for the new wireless network policy
- Configuring preferred networks
- Configuring authentication and encryption options

IP Security Policy

Configure IPSec parameters using either local policies or group policies. IPSec allows computers to establish an encrypted communication tunnel over the IP network. Setting up IPSec parameters from scratch requires specific knowledge and goes beyond the scope of this exam, and to make things easier Microsoft provided three preconfigured IPSec policies out of the box. In addition to configuring IPSec, IP security policy also allows administrators to configure Internet protocol filtering based on source or destination IP addresses, port numbers, protocol types, and some other parameters.

Three basic policies provided by default are Secure Server, Server, and Client. To establish a secure communication link, one party has to initiate a secure connection request, and the other party has to accept it. Table 6-12 compares the effects of the three policies on communications.

Administrators can also create their own policies and configure encryption and authentication parameters. After your policy is configured, use the context menu of the policy to assign it.

Configuring security components is a fairly tedious task. Microsoft provides security templates that administrators can use to quickly configure environments to a certain predetermined standard. These templates can also be used as a starting point in the configuration process if their settings do not satisfy all of your requirements. As mentioned throughout this chapter, security templates can be viewed with the Security Templates MMC snap-in. Security templates themselves are INF files stored in C:\Windows\Security\Templates. About a dozen templates are provided for specific computer roles—for example, the hisecdc.inf template contains settings suggested by Microsoft for high security on domain controllers. To import a template into your policy, right-click the Computer Configuration, Windows Settings, Security Settings container, and select Import Policy.

TABLE 6-12 | Effects of Default IPSec Policies

IPSec Policy	Can Initiate IPSec Connection	Can Accept IPSec Connection
Client	No	Yes, if connection is initiated by the other party. No in all other cases.
Server	Yes	Yes, if the other party supports IPSec. No, if the other party does not support IPSec.
Secure Server	Yes	Yes, IPSec only. Connections with parties that do not support IPSec will fail.

CERTIFICATION SUMMARY

Group policies are by far the single most important administrative tool provided with Windows Server 2003 for getting your computer and user environments under control.

SCENARIO & SOLUTION

What is the difference between Windows NT 4.0 system policies and group policies?	Group policies are dynamic, meaning that you don't have to explicitly revert the setting for it to be cancelled. It is enough to simply remove the policy object link from an Active Directory infrastructure element (site, domain, OU). System policies also provide only a tiny fraction of what is now possible with group policies.
What is local policy?	Local policy is a subset of group policy settings, which can only be applied locally on a computer. Local policies have the lowest priority in the policy application chain. Some settings, such as Folder Redirection, cannot be applied using local policy.
Is it possible to switch user or computer configuration sections off without reconfiguring your policies?	Yes, you can do this on the General tab in the group policy object properties.
Is it possible to assign a ZAP file–based application to a computer?	No, ZAP files can only be used to publish applications, and applications cannot be published for computer objects.

This chapter covered what user and computer environments consist of and how to use group policies.

It is not a trivial task to memorize and put to use all of the settings configurable through group policies, but the most important thing to remember is how policies on different levels are processed to form the effective policy. You have to keep in mind the domain structure and OU hierarchy when you plan group policies. Recommendations and information in this chapter should help you plan your Active Directory environment more consistently with group policy strategies, which ultimately will define how manageable your environment is.

Fortunately, Windows Server 2003 provides new group policy planning and troubleshooting tools, including RSoP, that dramatically improve administrators' ability to model their planned group policies and see the results before implementing them. RSoP can be used in either planning mode or logging mode. Planning mode allows you to model group policies and see the effective policy by running a simulation; logging mode is used to see the actual applied policy on a given Active Directory object.

Software installation policies, automatic certificate enrollment, and how they differ between user and computer environments were discussed in detail, along with security issues. The last two sections of the chapter reviewed some specifics of working with user and computer environments. From a practical perspective, folder redirection is one of the areas administrators should benefit the most from.

✓ TWO-MINUTE DRILL

Plan Group Policy Strategy

❑ Policy can be applied locally, on the site, domain, and OU levels.

❑ You can adjust default policy processing and application priority using options such as No Override, Block Policy Inheritance, and Loopback Processing.

❑ Group policies consist of User Configuration and Computer Configuration sections. You can toggle each section on and off (both are on by default).

❑ Policies are Active Directory objects; when you apply a policy, you create a link between this object and the Active Directory container.

❑ User Environment and Computer Environment are configured independently of each other, based on the policies effective for a given computer object and a given user object (which are not necessarily the same).

❑ The RSoP tool allows modeling of the policies and viewing policies in effect for different objects.

Configure the User Environment by Using Group Policy

❑ Folder redirection allows storing user data and some application settings in a central network location.

❑ MSI packages can be used with software installation policies and can be further customized using MST transforms.

❑ Autoenrollment only works if your clients are Windows Server 2003 or Windows XP Professional computers. You need to configure certificate templates to support autoenrollment.

❑ Password, account lockout, and Kerberos policies can only be set on a domain level.

Deploy a Computer Environment by Using Group Policy

❑ You cannot publish applications for computers; you can only assign applications.

❑ Software restriction policy is used to block certain programs or types of programs.

❑ Group policies can be used to roll out security settings on Registry keys, system services, and files/directories.

SELF TEST

The following questions will help you measure your understanding of the material presented in this chapter. Read all the choices carefully because there might be more than one correct answer. Choose all correct answers for each question.

Plan Group Policy Strategy

1. On which of the following levels can you apply group policies?
    A. Site
    B. Domain
    C. Domain trees
    D. Organizational units

2. Your OU structure is implemented so that IT personnel and common user accounts are located in the same container. You want to define a policy that will only apply to users, but not to domain administrator members. What group policy features can you use to achieve this without having to restructure OUs?
    A. WMI filtering
    B. Security group filtering
    C. Do nothing—restrictive policies do not apply to administrators
    D. Loopback processing on administrative accounts

3. You created a WMI script to be used with group policies, and tested it on one of the newly installed Windows XP machines. When you implemented it using group policy, the desired settings were not applied to all of your computers. What is the most likely cause of the problem?
    A. WMI filtering can only be used with Windows XP and Windows Server 2003 clients.
    B. WMI filtering may not work depending on computer hardware configuration.
    C. Some computers were not connected to the network.
    D. WMI-filtered policies run according to their own schedule, with a default interval of 24 hours.

4. Your Active Directory OU environment is implemented according to the organizational structure, with the top level being North, South, West, and East containers. In each of the four containers you have an HR OU, where you want to apply the same group policy. How should this be done with the minimum amount of administrative effort?
    A. Apply the policy on the domain level and configure security group filtering.
    B. Create one policy and link it to all HR containers in all top-level OUs.

    C. Use the policycopy.vbs script to duplicate policy objects.

    D. Create a new OU, move HR user objects to this OU, and apply the group policy object on this OU level.

5. Your company is developing a custom office productivity application. Software developers ask your advice on how they should develop a configuration mechanism for a few application parameters. Which of the methods available in Active Directory is preferable from the administrative perspective?

    A. Use schema modification.

    B. Use logon scripts and use group policy to deploy them.

    C. Create a custom ADM Registry file configuration and use group policy to deploy it.

    D. Use the HTTP protocol and code an application mechanism to submit configuration requests to the corporate web server.

6. Your company environment consists of one domain and three OUs that correspond to divisions in Europe, the Americas, and Southeast Asia. Being in charge of the European division, you decide to adjust some group policy settings, including the IE homepage setting. You apply this policy and find that some of the settings are configured correctly, while the IE setting is missing. What might be causing this?

    A. The SMS server was used to configure IE settings.

    B. You cannot use group policies to configure IE settings; instead, use the Internet Explorer Administration Kit (IEAK).

    C. Domain policy enforces this setting using No Override.

    D. The European OU uses the Block Policy Inheritance setting.

7. You configured folder redirection and software installation policy. To avoid rebooting computers, you run **gpupdate** on one of the computers for which these policies were made effective. The **gpupdate** ran without displaying any errors, but neither folder redirection nor software policy appear to have become effective. What is the most likely cause of this problem?

    A. You need to use the **secedit /refreshpolicy machine_policy /enforce** command instead of **gpupdate**.

    B. You did not use appropriate switches with the **gpupdate** command.

    C. Folder redirection and software installation policy are only applied after hours to minimize impact on network traffic.

    D. Some policies cannot be refreshed using **gpupdate**.

8. What is the default policy application order?

    A. Site, domain, OU, local

    B. Local, site, domain, OU

    C. Local, domain, site, OU

    D. Site, local, domain, OU

9. After extensive planning and a bit of tinkering, you created a policy that fits all requirements. Knowing that it will have to be modified sooner or later, you need to make sure that you have a backup in case you ever need to restore this policy. Which of the following is the optimal strategy?

    A. System state backup

    B. SYSVOL folder backup

    C. GPMC policy backup

    D. This cannot be done.

10. What is the purpose of the two RSoP modes, planning and logging?

    A. Planning mode allows you to plan policies for Windows XP clients and Windows 2000 clients.

    B. The planning mode CIMOM database is compiled by an emulator service based on assigned group policies. Logging mode is used to see the content of the CIMOM database that was compiled as a result of actual policy application.

    C. Planning mode does not process security policies.

    D. Planning mode and logging mode differ in how you can view and save the results.

Configure the User Environment by Using Group Policy

11. Which of the following are required to implement certificate autoenrollment?

    A. Windows Server 2003 schema and group policy updates

    B. Windows 2000 Server domain controllers running Service Pack 3 or later

    C. Windows XP Professional or Windows Server 2003 clients

    D. Windows Server 2003 Enterprise Datacenter Edition and an Enterprise CA

12. You work for a consulting and software development firm where most of the users have laptops and often go on business trips to demo company products. You need to configure software installation policy to automatically install the newest version of company products every time users log on to the network. Which of the available methods should you implement?

    A. Publish applications for users.

    B. Assign applications to users.

    C. Assign applications to computers.

    D. Assign applications to users and enable the "Install this application at logon" option.

13. You are deploying a few legacy applications that do not have associated MSI packages. How can you do this?

    A. Create an installation package using Windows Installer.

    B. Use ZAP files.

    C. Use a custom setup script to launch setup.exe.

    D. You cannot install applications that do not have MSI packages.

14. A number of users in the Sales OU have access to confidential information. To harden security, you implemented strict password policy settings. After a while, you discover that some users have plain number sequence passwords, such as 123456. You are not sure if the policy became effective. What might be causing this?

    A. There is a lag associated with policy refreshes.

    B. Password policies must be applied on the domain level.

    C. Password policies must be applied on the site level.

    D. Plain sequence number passwords contain digits and fit password complexity requirements.

15. Why is it necessary to configure a strict password policy?

    A. Long, complex passwords make users more focused.

    B. Passwords are used in the certificate enrollment process.

    C. Long and complex passwords are more difficult to crack.

    D. You may need to configure password storage location preferences.

16. Which of the following events trigger group policy refreshes?

    A. The computer boot sequence and user logon process

    B. Refresh interval expiration

    C. Execution of the Gpupdate tool in Windows XP or Secedit in Windows 2000

    D. Clicking OK in the Group Policy Object Editor

17. Which of the following statements about user environment policies are correct?

    A. User and computer environment policies modify different Registry sections.

    B. User policies are only applicable to Windows 2003/XP clients.

    C. User policies are applied only upon user logon, whereas computer policies are applied at the end of the boot process and upon user logon.

    D. User policies are applied only upon user logon, whereas computer policies are applied at the end of the boot process.

Deploy a Computer Environment by Using Group Policy

18. Which of the following are available for Additional Rules configuration in the software restriction policy?

    A. Hash rule

    B. Certificate rule

    C. Internet zone rule

    D. Path rule

19. You configured auditing using group policies to track AD object and file access events, but you find that AD object access is logged in the security log of Event Viewer, but file access is not. What is the most likely cause of this issue?

    A. Audit is enabled on all Active Directory objects by default. To enable file access audit, you must also enable auditing in file or folder properties.

    B. You can only audit files located on a FAT32 partition.

    C. You cannot audit both AD object and file access. In case of a conflict, AD objects have higher priority, and the file access audit is turned off.

    D. File access events are recorded in the ntfs.log file, located in the root of the system drive; it is not accessible through Event Viewer.

20. You configured folder redirection so that My Documents folders for Group A users are redirected to a network server. A day later users start complaining that My Document folders are empty. What step was omitted that might have caused this?

    A. Selecting the "Move the content of my documents to the new location" option in the folder redirection settings.

    B. Creating and assigning a script that will move folder content when users log on.

    C. Adding appropriate file-level permissions to user folders.

    D. Restoring content from a recent backup into the folder structure implemented on the server.

LAB QUESTION

Branch office managers of a company you work for want to roll out a new application on all domain computers, within their branch only. The software package itself was not huge, so you decided to use the software installation policy and placed the package in a shared folder on the head office network. The link between the two offices is 512 Kbps, so you figured it will take only a few minutes to install the package.

After a few days, you receive a call informing you that this package was installed successfully on some computers but not all of them, and that installations happen irregularly and mostly after business hours or when some of the branch employees are not on site.

You suspect that the problem is caused by inconsistent WAN throughput, move your package to a server on the local network in the branch office, and adjust group policy accordingly; however, you find that it did not address the issue as you hoped it would. What is the most likely cause of this inconsistent behavior?

SELF TEST ANSWERS

Plan Group Policy Strategy

1. ☑   **A, B,** and **D** are correct answers. You can assign group policies to these objects.
   ☒   **C** is incorrect because a domain tree is just a collection of domains and is not subject to policy applications. However, you can link the same policy to all of the domains in a domain tree, or apply group policy to the site if all of the domains are located on the same high-speed network.

2. ☑   **B.** In this situation, you will need to use security group filtering. On the Security tab of the group policy object in question, set the Apply Group Policy right for the domain administrators group to Deny.
   ☒   **A** is incorrect because WMI filtering is used for other purposes, such as querying hardware or software settings. **C** is incorrect; although administrators do get preferential treatment, policies still apply to their user account. **D** is incorrect because Loopback Processing is used to apply user configuration to form a policy assigned to a computer container.

3. ☑   **A.** WMI filtering is not supported for Windows 2000 or earlier clients.
   ☒   **B** is incorrect because inadequate or failing hardware may prevent Windows XP from installing or running, but it does not affect OS feature availability. **C** is incorrect because while this would prevent group policies from being copied from a domain controller, this obviously is not a group policy problem. **D** is incorrect because the WMI script is executed before the policy is applied and is not associated with a schedule.

4. ☑   **B.** You can link one group policy object to several Active Directory infrastructure elements. This requires the least effort and is the recommended approach.
   ☒   **A** is incorrect because this method would require plenty of administrative effort. **C** is incorrect because this script is not a Windows Server 2003 component. **D** is incorrect because this requires OU restructuring.

5. ☑   **C.** An ADM file is flexible, manageable, and a simple enough way to configure client computer Registry settings with group policies.
   ☒   **A** is incorrect because schema modification is a complex process that may or may not be suitable. You will be forced to develop your own way to configure these settings. **B** and **D** are incorrect because these methods are more complex than **C**.

6. ☑   **C.** If a portion of your policy becomes effective, and some settings are missing, it is likely that the No Override setting was used on a higher infrastructure level.
   ☒   **A** and **B** are incorrect because group policies can be used to manage some of the IE settings using the Internet Explorer Maintenance container. **D** is incorrect because **C** is correct.

7. ☑ **D.** Some policy settings that may cause problems if enforced while the user is working are not enforced until a logoff/logon or reboot takes place.
   ☒ **A** and **B** are incorrect because **D** is correct. **C** is incorrect because policies get refreshed regardless of network load.

8. ☑ **B.** LSDOU - Local, site, domain, OU.
   ☒ **A, C,** and **D** are all incorrect because **B** is correct.

9. ☑ **C.** The GPMC allows administrators to back up and restore group policy objects.
   ☒ **A** and **B** are incorrect because copying SYSVOL via SYSTEMSTATE backup or directly from the file system will not allow you to restore group policy objects. **D** is incorrect because it can be done using GPMC. You can restore a policy object using a different name, without overwriting an existing object, if that is necessary.

10. ☑ **A** and **B.** The main difference is how the group policy settings database is compiled.
    ☒ **C** is incorrect because both modes process all applicable policies. **D** is incorrect because both modes allow viewing and saving results in a similar fashion.

Configure the User Environment by Using Group Policy

11. ☑ **A, B, C,** and **D.** All of these are required for certificate autoenrollment.

12. ☑ **D.** The "Install this application at logon" option will force assigned applications to be installed in full, without just advertising application components and then installing them on demand.
    ☒ **A** is incorrect because publishing will require user action in order for the application to be installed. **B** is likewise incorrect because users will have to access the application before it will be installed. **C** is incorrect because user laptops may be turned on before they are connected to the network, in which case the software would not install unless the machine is rebooted.

13. ☑ **A** and **B.** These are the right ways to deal with situations if you have to install an application that did not come with an MSI package.
    ☒ **C** is incorrect because this will not guarantee successful installation, and applications cannot be published this way. **D** is incorrect because you can use methods described in **A** and **B.**

14. ☑ **B.** Password, lockout, and Kerberos policies are applicable to domains only.
    ☒ **A** and **C** are incorrect because **B** is the only correct answer. **D** is incorrect because the password complexity setting assumes symbols, mixed-case letters, and numbers are all mixed together.

15. ☑ **C.** This is the correct answer.
    ☒ **A** is incorrect because password policies are designed to enforce security and protect user information. **B** is incorrect because user certificates are issued based on object common names,

and password complexity has no effect on certificate strength. **D** is incorrect because passwords, or rather hashed values, are stored in Active Directory.

16. ☑ **A, B,** and **C.** All of these events trigger group policy to be refreshed.

   ☒ **D** is incorrect because the GPEdit console does not really have OK or APPLY buttons, which are applicable to policies and not to their properties or specific settings. Only clients can request and apply policy objects. Forced update from a central location would grind the network to a halt if it triggers, say, a few dozen concurrent installations of Microsoft Office.

17. ☑ **A** and **D.** The User and Computer sections of the policy modify different Registry areas and apply at different stages.

   ☒ **B** and **C** are incorrect statements.

Deploy a Computer Environment by Using Group Policy

18. ☑ **A, B, C,** and **D.** All of these rules can be used in the software restriction policy.

19. ☑ **A.** To enable auditing of file and folder access, after switching this type of auditing on using group policies, you also have to explicitly enable auditing on all groups of files to be audited.

   ☒ **B** is incorrect because auditing can only be used on an NTFS partition. **C** is incorrect because audit settings for different types of events are independent. **D** is incorrect because these events are recorded in the security log viewable in Event Viewer.

20. ☑ **A.** This option will instruct the system to copy existing data from the My Documents folder to the newly created structure on a network server.

   ☒ **B** and **D** are incorrect because **A** is a straightforward and simple solution. **C** is incorrect because in case of a permission issue, users would have received an "Access Denied" error message.

LAB ANSWER

Software installation is one of the policies affected by the Slow Link Detection setting. Some of the policies will not get triggered if the total available link bandwidth between the domain controller and a client computer is less than a preconfigured policy value. By default, this value is set to 500 Kbps. Link speed is gauged every time users log on, and there is no guarantee that comparison results will be consistent, depending on how big your pipe is and how heavily it is used at the time of logon. This is why installation was working fine for some users when others were off site; most of the bandwidth was available, in excess of the default setting.

If you place distribution files on a local network (a sensible decision any way you look at it), it still has no effect on slow link detection between a client and domain controller. To increase the likelihood of successful policy application, set a lower threshold for the group policy Slow Link Detection setting located in the Administrative Templates\System\Group Policy folder—for example, 300 Kbps. In the same container, you can select which policies should, or should not, be applied if the slow link is detected.

MICROSOFT CERTIFIED SYSTEMS ENGINEER

7

Managing and Maintaining Group Policy

N ow that we have covered practically every aspect of Active Directory that architects and administrators are likely to face on a daily basis, we need to take a final look at group policies and what methodologies and tools can be used to assist in troubleshooting problems, which are not uncommon in the initial cycles of Active Directory deployment.

CERTIFICATION OBJECTIVE 7.01

Troubleshoot Issues Related to Group Policy Application and Deployment

Chapter 6 described how complex the settings within a group policy object can be, and just how much they cover. Earlier chapters have shown that group policy objects may be applied to Active Directory containers—domains, sites, and organizational units— and discussed in detail how inheritance and blocking work and how administrators can control the mechanism of application of group policy settings. Now, you've established which settings to implement on which levels, you have created a well-organized and logical organizational unit structure that suits the business needs, and created group policy objects and applied them on the respective levels; yet you've found that some of the configuration settings either did not get through as planned, or did get applied, but in the wrong way.

Luckily, there are a few troubleshooting tools administrators can take advantage of. Chapter 6 introduced RSoP—the Resultant Set of Policy MMC snap-in—and its use in planning. This is one of the mainstream tools in Windows Server 2003 when it comes to troubleshooting group policy application problems.

Viewing Effective Group Policy Settings

Determining which policy or policies are in effect is the first thing administrators must investigate if a certain policy is not applied as expected. Windows Server 2003 features at least two GPO troubleshooting tools that administrators are expected to be familiar with—RSoP and Gpresult. In the following exercise, you review how to use the RSoP tool step-by-step.

EXERCISE 7-1

CertCam & MasterSim ON THE CD

Viewing Effective Policy Settings Using RSoP

In this exercise, you use the RSoP console to view group policy object settings applied to the local machine. You run RSoP in logging mode to achieve this.

1. Log on to the network using the administrator account.

2. Click Start | Run, type **mmc**, and press ENTER.

3. In the menu, click File | Add/Remove Snap-in.

4. In the Add/Remove Snap-in window, click Add and find Resultant Set of Policy in the list of installed snap-ins.

5. Select Resultant Set of Policy, click Add, Close, and then OK to close all open dialog windows.

6. Next, in the console, right-click the Resultant Set of Policy node and click Generate RSoP Data. A wizard screen will appear.

7. Click Next on the welcome screen. On the Mode Selection screen, leave the Logging Mode selection unchanged and click Next. The Planning Mode selection would be helpful if you wish to test-apply group policy objects against a certain machine and a certain user to see how that would work if implemented. Logging mode is used to view already applied settings, which is needed in troubleshooting.

8. On the Computer Selection screen, leave the default setting (This Computer) and click Next. Alternatively, you can select another computer if you wish to troubleshoot the policy applied on a remote computer.

9. On the User Selection screen, select which user you will be running the policy settings against. The default setting is the currently logged on user (Current User). Leave the setting unchanged and click Next.

10. You are presented with the final screen of this wizard, which summarizes the RSoP settings. Click Next to proceed with the gathering process and then Finish to close the wizard and review RSoP data.

Note that you can cancel collecting RSoP data for users or computers and just focus on one section of the group policy object. To achieve this, use the corresponding check boxes on either the Computer Selection or User Selection screen.

RSoP presents effective policy settings in a familiar way—containers in the left-hand pane and individual nodes in the right-hand pane. This is similar to how group policy objects are presented in tools like the Group Policy Object Editor, with two slight exceptions. First, you may note that some settings are not shown; this is because they were not configured in the policy object. Second, there is now a Source GPO column next to the configured settings, which shows the group policy object that enforced the settings in question. This is useful in cases where you have to troubleshoot cascading group policies within an OU structure and you want to confirm which policy is in effect.

In addition, RSoP in logging mode can be an effective tool to diagnose policy refresh or processing errors. If there was a problem refreshing or applying the latest version of the policy, RSoP will display an exclamation mark in the appropriate section of the policy, alerting you to the fact (either in user settings or computer settings). If you right-click the section that is displaying a warning sign, and click Properties, you will see the Error Information tab that will list applicable errors and corresponding descriptions. It also presents a time stamp of the latest policy processing run and status of application of various policy sections.

The second troubleshooting tool, Gpresult, can be used to display information about policies in effect on the machine. Gpresult is a command-line utility that produces output similar to the following:

```
C:\Documents and Settings\Administrator.JOVIDUDE>gpresult
Microsoft (R) Windows (R) Oper numbered list 2,wsnl2cy Result tool v2.Worksheet numbered
list,wsnlloft Corp. 1981-2001{Label,lCreated On 10/6/2003 at 10:36:17 AM
{Table Heading,thata for WIN2K3-2\administrator onTable paragraph,tp Mode
-----------------Table spacing,ts----------------------------{neAlert Separator,as
Microsoft(R) WiPicture3 Large 2003, Enterprise Edition
OS Configuration:           Primary Domain Controller
OS Version:                 5.2.3790
Terminal Server Mode:       Remote Administration
Site Name:                  Default-First-Site-Name
Roaming Profile:
Local Profile:              C:\Documents and Settings\Administrator.JOVIDUDE
Connected over a slow link?: No


COMPUTER SETTINGS------------------
    CN=JOVIDUDE,OU=Domain Controllers,DC=sales,DC=flexecom,DC=com
    Last time Group Policy was applied: 10/6/2003 at 10:35:21 AM
    Group Policy was applied from:      jovidude.sales.flexecom.com
    Group Policy slow link threshold:   500 kbps
    Domain Name:                        WIN2K3-2
    Domain Type:                        Windows 2000


    Applied Group Policy Objects
    ----------------------------
```

```
        Default Domain Controllers Policy
        Default Domain Policy

    The following GPOs were not applied because they were filtered out
    -------------------------------------------------------------------
        Local Group Policy
            Filtering:  Not Applied (Empty)

    The computer is a part of the following security groups
    -----------------------------------------------------------
        BUILTIN\Administrators
        Everyone
        BUILTIN\Users
        BUILTIN\Pre-Windows 2000 Compatible Access
        Windows Authorization Access Group
        NT AUTHORITY\NETWORK
        NT AUTHORITY\Authenticated Users
        This Organization
        JOVIDUDE$
        Domain Controllers
        NT AUTHORITY\ENTERPRISE DOMAIN CONTROLLERS

USER SETTINGS
--------------
    CN=Administrator,CN=Users,DC=sales,DC=flexecom,DC=com
    Last time Group Policy was applied: 10/6/2003 at 10:07:36 AM
    Group Policy was applied from:      jovidude.sales.flexecom.com
    Group Policy slow link threshold:   500 kbps
    Domain Name:                        WIN2K3-2
    Domain Type:                        Windows 2000

    Applied Group Policy Objects
    ----------------------------
        Default Domain Policy

    The following GPOs were not applied because they were filtered out
    -------------------------------------------------------------------
        Local Group Policy
            Filtering:  Not Applied (Empty)

    The user is a part of the following security groups
    -----------------------------------------------------
        Domain Users
        Everyone
        BUILTIN\Administrators
        Remote Desktop Users
        BUILTIN\Users
        BUILTIN\Pre-Windows 2000 Compatible Access
        REMOTE INTERACTIVE LOGON
        NT AUTHORITY\INTERACTIVE
        NT AUTHORITY\Authenticated Users
```

```
This Organization
LOCAL
Domain Admins
Group Policy Creator Owners
```

In the three distinct sections, Gpresult lists some basic information about the computer it was executed on, then goes on to collect computer settings and user settings, which represent effective (resultant) settings on the machine in question. Note that Gpresult is simply a command-line tool that uses RSoP APIs to retrieve this information using logging mode. In the Applied Group Policy Objects subsections in computer and user settings, you can see which policy objects are effective on the machine. Also note the filtering sections that list all policy objects that were rejected due to security or WMI filtering. Gpresult can be used with the following switches:

- **/v - verbose mode**   This adds group policy extensions such as ADM Registry-based templates, disk quotas, scripts, IPSec settings, and folder redirection settings, but only those with the highest precedence.

- **/z - super verbose mode**   In addition to the standard output depicted in the preceding listing, and all of the information exposed in the verbose mode, Gpresult will list Registry values applied by the policy, software distribution settings, certificates, and group policy version numbers, regardless of the precedence of these settings.

- **/SCOPE COMPUTER**   Computer settings only. This option will restrict output to settings delivered through the computer settings portion of the policy object.

- **/SCOPE USER**   User settings only. This option will restrict output to settings delivered through the user settings portion of the policy object.

- **/s <system>**   This allows connecting to a remote system.

Finally, there is yet another way to gather similar information that might be helpful when you are troubleshooting an issue over the phone with a user who does not have enough knowledge to do much of the administrative legwork. If you click Start | Help and Support, under Support Tasks, you will find a System Information link. Clicking this link pulls up another menu. Choose View Advanced System Information to continue. In the third menu you are presented with, select View Group Policy Settings Applied. It will take a few seconds for the results to appear on the screen. The resulting information may remind you of the Gpresult output, but then it adds information such as applications listed in the Add/Remove Programs applet, deployment state of software packages, Internet Explorer settings and any scripts enforced by the policy, as well as Registry settings received through ADM templates.

This method also relies on the RSoP engine to gather policy information, but goes one step further than Gpresult. It allows administrators to determine not only which policies are in effect but also how software distribution settings are affecting the machine in question, which Registry settings specifically were applied by which source policy object, and how filtering affected the process. Also note that this method exposes specific security settings that were applied to individual objects and indicates which policy object delivered the setting.

Refreshing Group Policy Settings

By using RSoP-derived tools such as Gpresult, and viewing group policy settings via the Help and Support console, you can determine when the policy was applied. In the initial stages of policy implementation, administrators need to fine-tune their policy settings, which may result in numerous changes applied to group policy objects throughout the day. If a certain setting is not being propagated to client machines as expected, or if a policy is not getting applied in the first place due to other issues that may be taking place elsewhere in the system, checking the latest group policy application time stamp will help establish whether the new setting has been replicated to the machine. If the policy on the client machine was refreshed since it was reconfigured on a domain controller, chances are the setting was overwritten by another policy or setting. Otherwise, the newer policy object has not made it to the client workstation yet. You can confirm whether policy refresh was successful from the Application section of the Event Log, information event ID 1704:

```
Event Type:      Information
Event Source:    SceCli
Event ID:    1704
Description:
Security policy in the Group policy objects has been applied successfully.
```

Remember that the default policy refresh interval is 90 minutes for client computers and member servers, and 5 minutes for Windows 2000 and Windows Server 2003 domain controllers. If administrators make changes to the policy objects, the settings may not become effective for a period of time. Certain settings such as software distribution may not become effective until a reboot or logon event takes place.

To avoid logging off and on or even rebooting your test machine manually while you are experimenting with group policy changes, use the **gpupdate** command in Windows XP or Windows Server 2003 (logoff or reboot in this case only occurs if settings that require these events have been modified). It replaces the **secedit /refreshpolicy** command available in Windows 2000 and serves the purpose of forcibly refreshing policy settings regardless of the refresh interval. The syntax of this command as is follows:

```
GPUpdate [/Target:{Computer | User}] [/Force] [/Wait:<value>] [/Logoff] [/Boot] [/Sync].
```

You can execute **gpupdate** without specifying any parameters, but if you want to test or troubleshoot settings like software distribution, you might need to use some of the parameters provided with the command:

- **/Target** Indicates which portion of the GPO should be refreshed—by default, refreshes both.

- **/Force** Force-applies all policy settings—by default, only changed settings are applied.

- **/Wait** Causes the command line to wait for **gpupdate** to finish processing group policy objects.

- **/Logoff** Forces a logoff if the policy refresh implemented changes that are normally applied in the foreground mode (during logon). Note that logoff will not be forced if settings implemented with the latest policy do not require it.

- **/Boot** Forces a reboot if the policy refresh implemented changes that are normally applied during computer start-up. Note that reboot will not be forced if settings implemented with the latest policy do not require it.

- **/Sync** Results in the next foreground process (computer bootup or user logon updates) to be performed synchronously; that is, the user interface will not start loading until policy processing and application is complete.

Network-Related Issues

Network-related problems are often overlooked when dealing with group policy issues, but it is vital that every aspect of network communication between client and server is configured and operating as prescribed. In addition to most basic network connectivity that must be in place, DNS resolution should be functioning correctly for the client to be able to resolve server names to IP addresses.

Network troubleshooting is a subject perhaps deserving of its own discussion; for the purposes of this chapter, only the most common tools, introduced in Chapter 2, will be covered: NSLOOKUP and the **ipconfig** and **ping** commands. The NSLOOKUP command-line utility is used to verify DNS functionality and resolve DNS fully qualified domain names into IP addresses. The **ipconfig** command outputs the interface configuration with pertinent connection parameters. Finally, the **ping** command can be used to send test packets and verify end-to-end connectivity.

Traditional network troubleshooting is based on a seven-layer OSI model that takes the guesswork out of the process. If network connectivity is the suspect, you should first run the **ipconfig** command to see if the network interface is disconnected. If that is not the case, you proceed to **ping** and its three tests—pinging the loopback address 127.0.0.1, then pinging the local IP address, and finally, pinging the default gateway address. (You will find these addresses in the **ipconfig** output.) To wrap it up, you should verify connectivity to the DNS server by pinging its IP address, and then run the **nslookup** command to resolve domain controller names. In firewalled networks, this may not be acceptable because pings in many cases are filtered out. In this case, you would need to use telnet to connect on port 53 to verify connectivity to the DNS server and check availability of the service.

This being said, administrators often begin from the last step of this process; if it works, all underlying troubleshooting steps immediately become redundant. If you are able to telnet to the DNS server on port 53 using its hostname, you have tested all seven OSI layers successfully. This means your interface is connected to the network and you can ping the loopback, local IP, and, depending on the DNS server location in the network, the default gateway address as well. In other words, network connectivity problems are ruled out. You just have to make sure that the IP address returned by the DNS server is indeed the right address (DNS configuration may also be a problem). And in more complex routed networks, you might also want to run the **tracert** command from the client to the domain controller in question to make sure there are no routing loops and to see that packets are taking expected routes.

on the **job**

Recall the Netdiag utility from Chapter 4. It may save you time to start network troubleshooting with this tool. Depending on the results, you may need to fall back to other tools mentioned in this section, but if no problems are detected by Netdiag, it would make sense to proceed to the next phase in your troubleshooting—replication.

Correct name resolution is paramount in the group policy application process simply because clients need to be able to locate domain controllers in order to locate policy configuration and copy policy files. They use DNS to locate hostnames and IP addresses of the servers providing network services, preferably in their local Active Directory sites—services such as Active Directory. If there is a name resolution problem in the network, most likely group policy will not be the only component of Active Directory that will be affected.

Policy Replication Issues

After you establish that network connectivity and name resolution are functioning as expected, the next thing to look at would be replication. Remember that group policy files are stored in SYSVOL shares on domain controllers, and the content of these shares must be consistent throughout your Active Directory environment. The File Replication Service (FRS) is used to replicate the content, so it is not actual Active Directory replication that you should be focusing on while troubleshooting group policy replication. That said, it is vital to ensure that Active Directory replication also works, due to the fact that FRS uses the same connection objects (created manually and automatically), the same topology, and the same replication schedules as Active Directory.

Most of the tools that administrators use to troubleshoot AD/FRS replication are discussed in Chapter 4, in the section "Monitor Active Directory Replication." The tools listed here can assist in obtaining a variety of diagnostic information regarding the health of the domain controller, replication partners, topology information, the latest replication attempts and outcomes, and so forth.

- **Dcdiag**   This tool runs a series of diagnostic tests on a domain controller; these tests include replication and topology integrity checks.

- **Repadmin**   This tool is used to analyze replication mechanisms in great detail. Repadmin exposes information such as the time stamp of the last successful replication, error codes if it was not successful, the history of all replication metadata, and replication settings, among many other things.

- **File Replication Service log in Event Viewer**   The log provides a very convenient and fast way to verify whether FRS is having problems replicating SYSVOL data to other domain controllers.

- **FRS debug logs**   Ntfrsapi.log files and Ntfrs_000X.log files (where X is a sequential number) located in the %systemroot%\debug folder also expose FRS configuration and diagnostic information that may capture detailed information as to what is causing the problem. These logs are not enabled by default. For more information on how to configure FRS logging, see the "Monitor File Replication Service" section in Chapter 4.

- **Ntfrsutil**   This utility is used to view FRS tables, memory, and thread information, and may be helpful in troubleshooting complex FRS issues. It also allows for listing transactions from the FRS database (%systemroot%\ntfrs\jet\ntfrs.jdb).

- **Replmon**   This allows you to view replication topology and replication information and settings, such as connection object properties, using a convenient GUI application.

■ **Sonar.exe**   Sonar is a GUI-based tool written specifically for FRS monitoring and troubleshooting. Administrators can use it to gather statistics on replicas and monitor traffic levels, backlogs, free space, and other parameters. This tool presents read-only information per each replication partner, not per connection or per session, so you might think of it as a more convenient way to get a view of your FRS landscape from 30,000 feet.

on the **Job**

Sonar.exe is not included in Windows Server 2003 Support Tools, but it is featured in the Windows Server 2003 Resource Kit. You can also download it separately from www.microsoft.com, Windows Server 2003 Downloads/Tools section. Along with the tool, when downloaded separately from the Resource Kit, Microsoft includes a lengthy white paper dedicated to troubleshooting FRS issues and providing an in-depth overview of how the service works and where and how it can be used.

Recovering from Group Policy–Related Disasters

There are several ways to back up and restore group policy objects. The SYSVOL share, located on all domain controllers and replicated by means of FRS, is used, among other things, for storing files that implement group policy settings. You should include SYSVOL shares in your backup routines and perform backups regularly. Microsoft discourages administrators from modifying SYSVOL share content and structure manually, even by restoring it from a backup. Microsoft knowledge base article 324175 discusses this in a fair bit of detail; it has to do with so-called juncture points.

You will want to avoid tampering with the structure of this share, so if you must restore group policies from a backup, it is recommended that you use advanced options in NTBACKUP (or use the appropriate option in backup software used in your company) to restore SYSVOL content to another directory and then copy actual policy files into the SYSVOL directory.

A more elegant solution to group policy backup and restore problems may be implemented using the Group Policy Management Console (GPMC). This console allows backing up and restoring individual group policy objects, giving administrators a flexible mechanism to implement GPO backups before and after policy object modifications are performed. This may also be indispensable in change management processes, in addition to disaster recovery, where administrators may require a quick and reliable way to back out of an unsuccessful policy change. Although it does not back up "external" configuration of group policy objects, such as WMI filtering, it does save GPO configuration information, which administrators can view later on when they restore GPOs.

Follow these steps to back up group policy objects (assuming that the GPMC is already installed):

1. Log on as domain administrator, click Start | Run, type **gpmc.msc**, and press ENTER.

2. In the left-hand pane, expand your forest, expand the Domains container, expand domain GPOs that you want to back up, and then expand the Group Policy Objects container. You should see at least two GPOs listed there—Default Domain Controllers Policy and Default Domain Policy. Any additional GPOs you created in this domain should also appear in the list.

3. Right-click the GPO you wish to back up, and click the Back Up option in the context menu. The Back Up Group Policy Object dialog box will appear next.

4. Type in a backup location where you wish to save the group policy object, provide a description if necessary, and click Back Up. The Backup progress window will appear next.

5. When the process finishes, you will be presented with warning and error messages (if any). Click OK to finish.

Note that a GPO, when backed up, is not saved as a single file. Instead it is saved as a structure of folders, representing different configuration sections, and several files inside this structure.

The process of restoring a group policy object is likewise pretty straightforward:

1. Log on as domain administrator, click Start | Run, type **gpmc.msc**, and press ENTER.

2. In the left-hand pane, expand your forest, expand the Domains container, expand the domain GPOs that you want to restore, and then expand the Group Policy Objects container.

3. Right-click the policy object you wish to restore, and in the context menu, choose the option Restore From The Backup. A wizard welcome screen will appear.

4. Click Next to continue. You will be prompted to provide a location of the backup folder. Type in the path to the root of your backup folder and click Next.

5. The wizard will read the content of the folder provided and display existing backups for the group policy you are performing a restore on. Select the backup version you wish to restore, and click View Settings if you wish to examine external configuration of this object. Click Next to continue.

6. The next screen provides a confirmation of what the wizard is about to do. Click Finish. The Restore progress window appears next. Once the restore operation is finished, you will be presented with warning and error information if applicable. Click OK to exit.

If you are trying to restore a group policy object that is no longer listed in the Group Policy Objects container, you may want to create a new group policy object and then use the context menu to import GPO settings from the corresponding backup. Just like restoring, importing does not re-create external settings such as WMI filtering, delegation, or GPO links; you would have to reconfigure this manually. Alternatively, you can restore any GPO from an existing backup, regardless of whether this GPO exists in Active Directory. To do this, you need to call up the Manage Backups screen by selecting the Manage Backups option in the Group Policy Objects container context menu.

Managing backups and restores in an organization of significant size may get more complicated than backing up one or two policy objects. To back up all of the policies at once, you can choose the Back Up All option in the Group Policy Objects container context menu. From the same context menu, you can also invoke the Manage Backups dialog box to take a look at all existing GPO backups and to view their "external" configuration at the time the backup was created.

on the **job**

Keep in mind that the GPMC delivers a set of COM objects that implement functionality delivered through the user interface tool. Administrators can write their own scripts or otherwise automate group policy management using the same objects. More information on this can be obtained from www.microsoft.com/windowsserver2003/gpmc/.

Finally, if an outage damaged the SYSVOL share or otherwise disabled your existing group policy objects, and you do not have a backup of SYSVOL or a backup of individual group policy objects, you will need to resort to the DcGPOFix utility, which restores the Default Domain Policy and Default Domain Controllers Policy to their original post-Dcpromo state. As you can see from the following code, this option should only be used in terminal cases where nothing else can be done to recover current versions of policies.

```
C:\Documents and Settings\Administrator.JOVIDUDE>dcgpofix
Microsoft(R) Windows(R) Operating System Default Group Policy Restore Utility v5.1
Copyright (C) Microsoft Corporation. 1981-2003
Description: Recreates the Default Group Policy Objects (GPOs) for a domain
Syntax: DcGPOFix [/ignoreschema] [/Target: Domain | DC | BOTH]

This utility can restore either or both the Default Domain Policy or the
Default Domain Controllers Policy to the state that exists immediately after
a clean install. You must be a domain administrator to perform this operation.

WARNING: YOU WILL LOSE ANY CHANGES YOU HAVE MADE TO THESE GPOs. THIS UTILITY
IS INTENDED ONLY FOR DISASTER RECOVERY PURPOSES.

You are about to restore Default Domain policy and Default domain Controller policy for
the following domain
sales.flexecom.com
Do you want to continue: <Y/N>?
```

Policy Application Issues

When troubleshooting policy application issues, you will need to determine what is causing group policies to conflict or what is causing them to be ineffective.

Application, Inheritance, Blocking, No Override, and Loopback Processing

Inheritance and blocking are the most obvious places to start sorting out conflicts in complex Active Directory environments where one or two policies just don't cut it. Remember how group policies are applied: local policy is applied first (although it is not really a "group" policy, it may have an effect on local computer security settings), then site policy, followed by domain policy, followed by the OU policy. Policies on all four levels are processed and overwritten by those GPOs applied later in the process. Therefore, it would make things easier if group policies were designed to apply the bulk of settings on the least specific level—that is, site or domain—with only a few more particular settings applied on the most specific level—organizational units. If your OU structure features several levels and each of those levels has a link to its own GPO, policies will be processed in the order from least specific OU (parent levels) to the most specific OU (child levels).

Settings not explicitly defined in the policies that are applied in the later stages are inherited either from defaults, or from the policies applied earlier in the process, unless administrators modify the Blocking and No Override options. The No Override setting takes precedence over policy blocking. Of course, to quickly determine which policies are in effect, you can use Gpresult, as noted earlier in the chapter—it explicitly lists all effective policies for a given user and computer.

You have to keep one more thing in mind when figuring out the order of application of group policy settings: some setting areas between user and computer configurations overlap. If you configure the same setting in the computer configuration section and user configuration section, the end result will be determined based on the User Group Policy Loopback Processing Mode setting, as described in Chapter 6. Merge will add user settings to computer settings, Replace will cancel user settings and apply computer settings; by default, if there is a conflict of settings between user and computer configuration sections, computer settings receive higher precedence.

Security and WMI Filtering

Next, you need to look at GPO ACEs, also known as security filtering, and WMI filtering. Users need at least two rights granted to them, such as Read and Apply, in order to be able to apply policies. Not only that, you also need to make sure that none of the users who need to access the policies in question have membership in security groups that were assigned an explicit Deny on the group policy ACL list. Explicit Deny will prevent users from reading the policy, and therefore it will not be applied. You can access either the GPMC (if it is installed), or Active Directory Users and Computers (ADUC)/Active Directory Sites and Services (ADSS) consoles, to modify security filtering settings for each individual group policy object.

WMI filtering has similar effects on policy application in the sense that if your WMI filter does not match the user or computer in question, the policy will not be applied. To determine whether a policy was filtered out because of a WMI filter match (or lack of it), use Gpresult.

Disabled GPOs or Configuration Sections

Disabled GPOs or turned-off user or computer configuration sections also present a potential problem. GPOs can be disabled entirely or in portions, only affecting either user or computer configuration sections. You can check to see if these conditions are true using the same tools—Gpresult and ADUC/ADSS or GPMC (by checking properties of the respective policy objects).

GPO Links and Object Location in AD

Finally, GPO links should also be verified. First of all, they need to exist—that is, the policies should be applied to containers where you expect them to be applied. Second, if you are working with policy links that span several domains, you need to make sure that at least one domain controller is available in each domain. The reason is rather straightforward: cross-domain policy links need trust relationships and authentication available to them in order to access a GPO not located in their own domain.

Another consideration when verifying group policy links is user or computer location in the OU structure. If it changes, the client may not be aware of the fact for about 30 minutes, because client computers cache their domain location information. If you need to enforce policy settings immediately, you must make sure that the user logs off and logs back on (if the user account location changed), or reboot the client computer (if the computer account location changed).

Policy Tattooing

Last but not least, you might want to ensure that policy tattooing is not preventing your settings from becoming effective on target machines. The concept of policy tattooing needs to be explained a little further. *Tattooing* refers to custom Registry settings applied with group policies that are persistent in nature. Administrators who worked with System Policies in Windows NT 4.0 should remember how this older implementation of group policies used to work: when you configure settings using poledit.exe and distribute these settings in ntconfig.pol files through NETLOGON shares, they are committed to the Registry and will not revert to their original state, unless another policy is applied that explicitly assigns original values. In other words, user logoff, computer reboot, and removal of policy assignment would have no effect on the modified Registry values on client machines—settings are persistent.

In contrast to Windows NT 4.0-style policies, Windows 2000 (and Windows Server 2003) group policies distribute nonpersistent settings: user configuration is removed every time the user logs off, and computer configuration is likewise lost upon reboot. If you revoke an assigned policy, client systems will likewise pick it up upon the next policy refresh. All is well then, right? Not if you use custom administrative templates that apply Registry settings to keys that are not maintained by the group policy engine.

<table>
<tr><td>

exam

⚠ atch   ***An easy way to distinguish these settings is that nonpersistent settings appear in a GPO with a blue icon, and persistent/tattooed policy settings appear with a red icon.***

</td><td>

If you apply computer settings to HKEY_LOCAL_MACHINE\SOFTWARE\Policies or HKEY_LOCAL_MACHINE\SOFTWARE\Microsoft\Windows\CurrentVersion\Policies, and user settings to HKEY_CURRENT_USER\SOFTWARE\Policies or HKEY_CURRENT_USER\SOFTWARE\Microsoft\Windows\CurrentVersion\Policies, then tattooing

</td></tr>
</table>

will not be a problem in your network. However (and you've probably guessed it by now), this depends on how the software you manage with group policies has been engineered. If your applications were not written to store their settings in the keys mentioned here, you may have to deal with occasional tattooing problems.

Logging Policy Processing Information

Policy processing logging may shed light on internal errors that happen during the processing and application of policy files. What you are looking for is the userenv.log log file located in the %systemroot%\debug\usermode folder. By default though, this log file is disabled. To enable it, you need to modify Registry settings to add the UserenvDebugLevel value to the HKEY_LOCAL_MACHINE\Software\Microsoft\ Windows NT\CurrentVersion\Winlogon Registry key. You need to assign this REG_DWORD setting a value of 0x10002. This modification kicks in on the fly, and you should start seeing some diagnostic information logged in the userenv.log file the next time a policy refresh is performed (every 90 minutes, or whenever triggered manually).

For performance reasons, the active log file will rotate during the logon if its size is over 1MB. A new userenv.log file is created while the existing one is saved as userenv.bak. Userenv.log will keep growing in excess of 1MB during the user session. Here is an example of what you should expect to see in the log:

```
USERENV(1b8.168) 20:37:30:262 ProcessGPO:  Searching
<CN={6AC1786C-016F-11D2-945F-00C04fB984F9},CN=Policies,CN=System,DC=sales,DC=flexecom,DC=c
om>
USERENV(1b8.168) 20:37:30:262 ProcessGPO:  Machine has access to this GPO.
USERENV(1b8.168) 20:37:30:262 ProcessGPO:  GPO passes the filter check.
USERENV(1b8.168) 20:37:30:262 ProcessGPO:  Found functionality version of:  2
USERENV(1b8.168) 20:37:30:262 ProcessGPO:  Found file system path of:
<\\sales.flexecom.com\sysvol\sales.flexecom.com\Policies\{6AC1786C-016F-11D2-945F-00C04fB9
84F9}>
USERENV(1b8.168) 20:37:30:272 ProcessGPO:  Found common name of:
<{6AC1786C-016F-11D2-945F-00C04fB984F9}>
USERENV(1b8.168) 20:37:30:272 ProcessGPO:  Found display name of:  <Default Domain
Controllers Policy>
USERENV(1b8.168) 20:37:30:272 ProcessGPO:  Found machine version of:  GPC is 1, GPT is 1
USERENV(1b8.168) 20:37:30:272 ProcessGPO:  Found flags of:  0
USERENV(1b8.168) 20:37:30:272 ProcessGPO:  Found extensions:
[{827D319E-6EAC-11D2-A4EA-00C04F79F83A}{803E14A0-B4FB-11D0-A0D0-00A0C90F574B}]
USERENV(1b8.168) 20:37:30:272 ProcessGPO:  ==============================
USERENV(1b8.168) 20:37:30:272 GetGPOInfo:  GPO Local Group Policy doesn't contain any data
since the version number is 0.  It will be skipped.
USERENV(1b8.168) 20:37:30:272 GetGPOInfo:  Leaving with 1
USERENV(1b8.168) 20:37:30:272 GetGPOInfo:  ******************************
USERENV(1b8.168) 20:37:30:272 ProcessGPOs: Logging Data for Target <JOVIDUDE>.
```

```
USERENV(1b8.168) 20:37:30:302 ProcessGPOs: OpenThreadToken failed with error 1008,
assuming thread is not impersonating
USERENV(1b8.168) 20:37:30:302 ProcessGPOs: ----------------------
USERENV(1b8.168) 20:37:30:302 ProcessGPOs: Processing extension Registry
USERENV(1b8.168) 20:37:30:302 ReadStatus: Read Extension's Previous status successfully.
USERENV(1b8.168) 20:37:30:302 CompareGPOLists:  The lists are the same.
USERENV(1b8.168) 20:37:30:302 CheckGPOs: No GPO changes and no security group membership
change and extension Registry has NoGPOChanges set.
```

This is just a tiny portion of the full log, and the amount of detail it delivers about the processing, as you can see, is remarkable. You don't want to keep it logging for no reason though. As you know, excessive logging and auditing is taxing, and small things tend to add up and slow the system down.

If your environment relies heavily on group policy, and its functionality is critical while group policy files are modified quite often, you may also want to enable verbose group policy logging in the Event Log to see a bigger picture. To achieve this, you need to add a REGDWORD value RunDiagnosticLoggingGroupPolicy to the HKEY_LOCAL_MACHINE\Software\Microsoft\Windows NT\CurrentVersion\ Diagnostics Registry key and assign it a value of 1.

This will cause a significant portion of diagnostic group policy information to be logged in the Application log; so depending on your log settings, you might want to increase its size or change the log record retaining mode to overwrite as needed. Otherwise, this Registry setting will cause your application log to fill up rather quickly.

Administrators are better off troubleshooting GPO problems using userenv.log because, even with verbose logging, information logged in the Event Log will not reveal some errors and warning messages that are logged in userenv.log.

Generally, this log should be used to confirm that there are no group policy core failures or client-side extension failures. Core failures result in total loss of group policy processing and application due to reasons outlined earlier in this chapter: network connectivity problems, DNS resolution issues, or inconsistent SYSVOL content (replication issues). Client-side extension failures may result in individual policy sections being skipped. Areas that may be affected by this problem include software distribution, scripts, folder redirection, IPSec settings, administrative templates, and security settings, all of which are implemented using separate client-side extensions. Userenv.log will help you confirm whether each of these extensions was processed correctly, whether changes in policy were detected, and so on. A typical example of a problem that may cause script client extension errors is incorrectly defined script paths.

Troubleshoot Group Policy Software Installation Issues

In the final section of this chapter, we will look into some aspects of using group policy objects and software management, as well as troubleshooting of problems commonly associated with this technology. You may recall from Chapter 6, in the section "Installing Software Using Group Policies," that administrators need to use MSI packages (or ZAP files in worst-case scenarios) in order to install software, and that the software can be assigned or published (assigned to users or computers, or published to users).

If your software package is assigned to a computer object, it will install the next time the workstation is rebooted, before the logon prompt is displayed. If the package is assigned to a user object, administrators can either force software installation upon user logon or trigger installation if the user clicks application icons or attempts to open files associated with the yet-to-be-installed application. Publishing software packages is only available to users, and applications published through group policies can be found in the Add/Remove Programs applet in the Control Panel.

When dealing with software installation issues, potential problems can be divided into three main categories: client-side extension problems, group policy processing or application problems, and Windows Installer problems. Since group policy processing and application problems were reviewed earlier in the chapter, we will skip to client-side extensions and Windows Installer.

A large portion of the errors and warnings generated from software distribution–related processes is published to the Event Log, Application log section. The source of these events appears as Application Management. Typical software distribution errors, such as those generated during installation due to insufficient free space or inability to access the distribution point, are logged by MsiInstaller, also in the Application section of the Event Log.

However, if the logging level configured by default does not reveal enough details about why the installation is failing, you may need to enable verbose logging. This can be achieved by adding the REGDWORD value Appmgmtdebuglevel to the HKEY_LOCAL_MACHINE\SOFTWARE\Microsoft\Windows NT\CurrentVersion\

Diagnostics Registry key and assigning it a value of 0x0000009b. Doing so will force the software installation client-side extension of the group policy engine to perform extensive logging using the %windir%\debug\usermode\appmgmt.log file.

MsiInstaller can also be configured to perform verbose logging. To enable this, add the following values to the HKEY_LOCAL_MACHINE\SOFTWARE\Policies\Microsoft\Windows\Installer key:

- Debug = REGDWORD 0x00000003
- Logging = REGSZ "voicewarmup"

Once these values are configured, MsiInstaller will start logging in two separate directories, depending on what sort of installation is being performed:

- %systemroot%\temp\MSI*.log
- %temp%\MSI*.log

Outside of logging and all other troubleshooting methods, and group policy application, replication, and refresh concerns discussed to this point, keep in mind the following information:

- Paths to distribution shares should not contain IP addresses or domain names. They should be UNC paths made up of hostnames and sharenames, as in \\servername\sharename.

- The software distribution point must be accessible to client computers. If there is a network problem or permissions issue, installations will most likely fail. Computers use the local system account when accessing distribution shares.

- Distribution shares should not be hosted by Windows NT 4.0 or later servers. They are not supported by software installation in group policies.

- The distribution share must be in the same Active Directory forest.

- Software distribution (publishing) will not work on servers running Terminal Services in application mode.

- If you assign applications to users, desktop icons may not appear until the user logs off and logs on again.

- MsiInstaller installations triggered by group policy are executed with elevated permissions. ZAP installations of legacy applications require users to have either Power User or Administrator privileges on the local machine.

Software Update Services and Windows Update

Patch and service pack distribution may be somewhat troublesome using group policies for several reasons. First, Microsoft may not always provide MSI packages; most commonly, patches are released as executable files. This creates more work for administrators if they are to create their own MSI packages. Second, it would not be practical to maintain a list of dozens, if not hundreds, of patches in your group policies. Group policy objects would take more space and network bandwidth and would be more resource intensive to process and nearly impossible to manage, as some patches get revised and updated, and others are added almost on a daily basis.

An optional workaround to using group policies is to manually download all the patches into a centralized location and create an install script that applies these patches. Although acceptable, depending on the size of the network, this may also be counterproductive. Microsoft originally came out with the Automatic Update service that can be set to check for updates on a periodic basis, alerting users to the fact that new updates are available for their platform, and optionally downloading and installing the patches. This service, at the time, was the best alternative, and here's a piece of good news: it is fully configurable through group policies.

Still, two problems existed in the early going. First, Microsoft did not initially provide an option not to reboot computers automatically after the patches were installed. It was a good alternative to manual installation, to MSI packages, and to asking users to run Windows Update, but it did create the problem of user workstations running important overnight processes getting rebooted without warning. The second problem with individual patch download from the Internet is bandwidth—it has to be available, and it has to be sufficient for all computer nodes to download those latest service pack distributions. That's 120+ MB times the number of managed computers—not very efficient.

Enter Software Update Services (SUS). The SUS concept is essentially the same as Windows Update and Automatic Update combined, but it introduces some important improvements to the patch management process that may suit many production environments. It replaces the Windows Update online servers with an internal company server running SUS. This eliminates the need to download patches more than once, thus preserving bandwidth. In addition, individual servers no longer need the Internet connection and the ability to talk to the outside world, communicating directly with the Microsoft update services (and this is not to mention MSBLAST-type worm scenarios when Microsoft's online servers are offline).

The new process essentially allows system administrators to review, download, and test patches locally. Once approved, they are published on the internal SUS server, and become available to Windows clients and servers. The SUS server is implemented as a system service called Software Update Services Synchronization Service. It is provided with an HTML-based management console where administrators can define the synchronization schedule (when your SUS server should poll updates from Microsoft).

The first synchronization cycle needs plenty of time and bandwidth, as your SUS server will be downloading hundreds of megabytes of updates. From that point onward, it is practical to set up the synchronization process to occur nightly. You will also use this HTML console to review and approve patches and service packs. Nothing will be made available to local clients by default, unless updates have been approved by an administrator. By default, this management console is configured on the local IIS server and is accessible through http://servername/SUSadmin.

On the client side (with clients being desktop or server systems), the Automatic Update service is configured to work with the local SUS server. SUS needs either Active Directory or, in the absence of it, a slight modification in the Registry that tells the update service on client systems where to look for updates. Since our discussion is Active Directory-centric, we will continue accordingly.

on the
job

The SUS server is available for free from www.microsoft.com/sus/. As of this writing, the latest version is SUS 1.0 SP1. The SUS client is called Automatic Update, it runs as a system service, and it is configurable using its own Control Panel icon. The SUS client is included in Windows 2000 SP3 and later, and in Windows XP and Windows Server 2003. It is also downloadable. You must update the Automatic Update client on pre-SP1 Windows XP computers in order to include pre-SP1 Windows XP computers into your SUS management game plan.

Let's fire up GPEdit.msc and see how to configure Windows Update using group policies.

EXERCISE 7-2

CertCam & MasterSim ON THE CD

Using Group Policies to Configure the Windows Update/SUS Client

In this exercise, you use the GPOE console to view and modify group policy object settings as they pertain to Windows Update.

1. Log on to the network using the administrator account.

2. Click Start | Run, type **gpedit.msc**, and press ENTER.

3. The settings we are after are located in the computer configuration portion of group policies, Administrative Templates, Windows Components, and finally, Windows Update. Go ahead and expand these containers.

4. Configure the Automatic Updates option. This is the main configuration setting for choosing the mode of operation for Automatic Update and defining the polling schedule. This configuration works with or without an intranet SUS server. In the absence of an intranet server, it will simply configure the Automatic Update client service to poll Windows Update servers maintained by Microsoft (unless Windows Update is disabled—see the following information). Options available for the mode of operation are Notify For Download And Notify For Install, Auto Download And Notify For Install, and Auto Download And Schedule The Install.

5. Use the Specify Intranet Microsoft Update Service Location option to add your intranet SUS server. Here, you need to specify two URLs: one for the patch download and another one for the statistics upload.

6. The Reschedule Automatic Updates Scheduled Installations setting can be used to reschedule the installation process N minutes after the system boot process is complete in cases when a previously scheduled installation was missed.

7. The No Auto-Restart for Scheduled Automatic Updates Installations setting is useful if you want to prevent automatic reboots upon patch installation. Enable it to reduce the stress level of users who leave important processes running on their workstations overnight.

8. One last group policy setting that concerns Windows Update can be found in the user configuration section, Administrative Templates, Windows Components, Windows Update. If you switch to this container, you will see one setting: Remove Access To Use All Windows Updates Features. If this setting is configured, it effectively removes the Windows Update/SUS Client functionality from your clients.

Remember that these settings are only supported by Windows 2000 SP3 or later, Windows XP Professional SP1 or later, and Windows Server 2003 computers. Microsoft did not support installing service packs prior to SUS SP1.

SCENARIO & SOLUTION

What is the difference between logging mode and planning mode in RSoP?	Logging mode is used to display actual permissions applied for a specific computer and specific user during the natural course of group policy processing and application, whereas planning mode is a simulation process of applying a given policy to a selected user and computer. Logging mode is useful in troubleshooting, while planning mode is more suitable for designing group policy settings and hierarchy.
What is policy tattooing?	Tattooing refers to custom Registry settings applied with group policies that are persistent in nature. They are committed to the Registry and will not revert to their original state, unless another policy is applied that explicitly reverts original values.
Why is it important to ensure that FRS is healthy and file replication works well?	FRS is responsible for replication of the SYSVOL share content between domain controllers. In terms of group policies, if SYSVOL shares are inconsistent, the client will get unpredictable results when attempting to apply policy settings.
How do you restore default group policies in the event that they are deleted?	First, try restoring individual policies from a recent backup using the GPMC. If none exist, restore the SYSVOL share to an alternate location and copy policy files into the actual SYSVOL share. If no SYSVOL share backups exist, you will need to use DcGPOFix to revert to post-Dcpromo versions of default policies.

Using SUS and group policy together can fully automate patching and make prompt deployment of the latest security updates enterprise-wide a breeze. The only portion of the process that administrators will still have to take care of is patch QA testing and timely approval using the SUS console.

CERTIFICATION SUMMARY

The closing chapter of this book described troubleshooting techniques and mechanisms available in Windows Server 2003. We started with an exercise on how to use the RSoP tool in logging mode to collect effective user and computer settings from a machine you are troubleshooting, and then covered details of the Gpresult tool. We then moved on to look at tools for refreshing group policy settings, such as Gpupdate.

If a problem persists after reviewing effective settings, modifying group policy objects, and refreshing policy settings, you may need to move on to the next stages of troubleshooting. Network troubleshooting steps and tools were discussed, and then you learned why replication problems and FRS are important factors when troubleshooting group policy.

You need to ensure that there is a backup of every piece of the system you are dealing with; however, having a full backup of everything may not necessarily satisfy various recovery scenarios. In the event of a lost policy, you want to have a quick and efficient way of restoring the necessary files from a backup, certainly avoiding downtime, or even worse, Active Directory rollbacks. The GPMC tool allows backing up and restoring individual policies in a way that is transparent to the rest of the system and its users.

Next, you need to go through the group policy application process with a fine-tooth comb. Concepts such as inheritance, blocking, no override, loopback processing, security and WMI filtering, disabled GPOs or configuration sections, failed or missing GPO links, object location in Active Directory, and finally, policy tattooing all have distinct effects on the end result. If the environment you are dealing with is complex due to its nature and/or poor planning, collecting information that deals with these concepts and how they are being used in your environment would be step one of any troubleshooting initiative. You may also need to look into the internals of group policy processing (verbose logging of various components will help achieve this).

The final section of the chapter covered some basic information pertinent to software installation troubleshooting and the advantages of using Software Update Services (SUS) in Windows Server 2003 networks.

✓ TWO-MINUTE DRILL

Troubleshoot Issues Related to Group Policy Application and Deployment

❑ Use RSoP in logging mode to get a full set of effective permissions.

❑ Gpresult should be used to collect policy information on a machine; it can identify specific policies that were applied and filtered out.

❑ Gpupdate is the Windows Server 2003 equivalent of **secedit /refreshpolicy** on Windows 2000.

❑ For troubleshooting network issues related to group policy application, you can use tools like Netdiag, Dcdiag, NSLOOKUP, and the **tracert** and **ping** commands.

❑ FRS is used to replicate SYSVOL content (and group policies) between domain controllers. It uses the same replication engine as Active Directory.

❑ Backup and restore of individual policies is possible using the GPMC. You should also back up the SYSVOL share, but it is not recommended to restore its contents directly from the backup to the original location.

❑ When troubleshooting policy application issues, pay special attention to inheritance, blocking, no override, loopback processing, security and WMI filtering, disabled GPOs or configuration sections, failed or missing GPO links, object location in Active Directory, and policy tattooing.

❑ Userenv.log can be enabled through the Registry to expose detailed information about group policy application and processing.

❑ The Event Log can be switched to display verbose information about group policy application and processing.

Troubleshoot Group Policy Software Installation Issues

❑ When troubleshooting issues related to software installation with group policies, look at group policy processing, client-side extension problems, and Windows Installer issues.

❑ MsiInstaller and software installation client-side extensions keep separate logs, but they are not enabled by default. A limited amount of information is posted to the Event Log.

❑ You can use the SUS server with Automatic Updates on client machines to distribute patches and service packs automatically. Group policies can be used to configure Automatic Update on client machines to get Windows updates from your intranet server.

SELF TEST

The following questions will help you measure your understanding of the material presented in this chapter. Read all the choices carefully because there might be more than one correct answer. Choose all correct answers for each question.

Troubleshoot Issues Related to Group Policy Application and Deployment

1. You are troubleshooting group policy application issues. Objects in one of the OUs do not get the settings from the Default Domain Policy. Clients from that OU do not complain of any problems logging on or accessing Active Directory search functions. What is likely to be causing this issue? (Choose all that apply.)

    A. Failed GPO link

    B. Policy is blocked

    C. Client-side extensions fail to process policy

    D. Policy is disabled

2. You want to enable detailed logging of group policy processing and application. How would you achieve this? (Choose all that apply.)

    A. Use the Event Log.

    B. Turn on verbose logging.

    C. Use the userenv.log log.

    D. Turn on userenv.log.

3. You are troubleshooting a policy application issue, and you need to find out which policies were applied on a client computer. Which of the following tools can you use? (Choose all that apply.)

    A. RSoP in planning mode

    B. RSoP in logging mode

    C. Gpresult

    D. Help and Support console

4. You need a list of all custom Registry settings applied to a client machine. How would you do this using Gpresult?

    A. Use the /z switch.

    B. Use the /v switch.

    C. Don't use any switches.

    D. Gpresult cannot collect this information.

5. Your company is developing a custom office productivity application. Software developers ask your advice on how they should develop the configuration mechanism of a few application parameters. You want to manage this application using group policy. What should you suggest? (Choose all that apply.)

    A. Use schema modification.

    B. Use logon scripts and use group policy to deploy them.

    C. Create a custom .adm Registry file configuration, and use group policy to deploy it.

    D. Store application Registry settings in keys supported by the policy engine to avoid tattooing.

6. You want to enable userenv.log logging. How should you configure values in the HKEY_LOCAL_ MACHINE\Software\Microsoft\Windows NT\CurrentVersion\Winlogon key to achieve this? (Choose all that apply.)

    A. Set Appmgmtdebuglevel to 0x0000009b.

    B. Set Debug to 0x00000003.

    C. Set UserenvDebugLevel to 0x10002.

    D. Set RunDiagnosticLoggingGroupPolicy to 1.

7. Your company has offices on three continents. You are an administrative delegate responsible for group policy implementation in the South African branch. The Active Directory environment is implemented as one domain with three sites and a comprehensive OU structure. You attempt to open one of the group policy objects in the Group Policy Object Editor but get an error. You verify group policy permissions and confirm that you have Read access. What is the most likely cause of this problem?

    A. In order to use the Group Policy Object Editor, you have to have the Full Control access right for the group policy objects in question.

    B. You must be a member of the Domain Admins security group in order to use the Group Policy Object Editor.

    C. In addition to Read rights, you need Change permission in order to modify object settings.

    D. None of the domain controllers are available in your local site. Check whether they are online and accept connections as expected.

8. You are troubleshooting a policy application issue. Some of the settings you expect to be applied on the site level are not becoming effective. Upon further investigation, you find out that there are domain and OU policies that apply similar sets of settings. What is the most likely cause of this problem?

    A. There is no problem; this behavior is by design.

    B. There is not enough information to diagnose the problem. You should enable userenv.log logging and look into GPO processing.

C. Set the No Override option on the site-level policy to enforce its settings.

D. You should enable verbose logging in the Event Log to collect more information about client-side extension processing of policy settings.

9. After extensive planning and a bit of tinkering, you have created a policy that fits all requirements. Knowing that it will have to be modified sooner or later, you need to make sure that you have a backup in case you ever need to restore this policy. Which of the following is the optimal strategy?

A. System state backup

B. SYSVOL folder backup

C. GPMC policy backup

D. This cannot be done.

10. What is the purpose of RSoP planning mode and RSoP logging mode?

A. RSoP planning mode allows you to plan policies for Windows XP and Windows 2000 clients.

B. RSoP planning mode CIMOM database is compiled by an emulator service based on assigned group policies. RSoP logging mode is used to see the content of the CIMOM database that was compiled as a result of the actual policy application.

C. RSoP planning mode does not process security policies.

D. RSoP planning mode and RSoP logging mode differ in how you can view and save the results.

11. You are troubleshooting a group policy application issue. You notice that group policy is not applied to some members of the security group, which is located in one of the OUs that is a child of a parent OU where the policy is applied. What is the most likely cause of this problem?

A. Check to see if the policy is blocked on the child OU level.

B. Check to see if the policy is disabled.

C. This is by design—policies are not applied to security groups, only to users and computers.

D. You need to link the child container to the GPO in question for the policy to become effective.

12. You work for a consulting and software development firm. You need to troubleshoot a group policy application issue for one particular user. The rest of the users in the same OU have no problems applying this policy. Upon investigation, you discover that the policy in question is not getting to the client computer, but there are no network problems reported or observed on this machine. What is the most likely cause of this problem?

A. The policy may be blocked for this particular user.

B. Check user membership in security groups, especially if some of them have Deny on the ACL of the policy in question.

    C. The user configuration section may be turned off.

    D. Check to make sure that the policy is not disabled for this user.

13. You are deploying a few legacy applications that do not have associated MSI packages. How can you do this? (Choose all that apply.)

    A. Create an installation package using Windows Installer.

    B. Use ZAP files.

    C. Use a custom setup script to launch setup.exe.

    D. You cannot install applications that do not have MSI packages.

14. You are troubleshooting a group policy issue. The Default Domain Policy and Default Domain Controllers Policy appear to be corrupt. Upon investigation, you determine that there are no backups of policy taken using GPMC or by direct file backup of the SYSVOL share. What should you do to resolve the issue?

    A. Use the Dcpromo utility.

    B. Use the Ntdsutil utility.

    C. Use the Dcdiag utility.

    D. Use the DcGPOFix utility.

15. The concept known as policy tattooing is best described by which of the following?

    A. Applying Registry settings to keys not maintained by group policy

    B. Applying custom Registry settings

    C. Applying system policies using *.pol files

    D. Applying custom ADM administrative templates

16. Which of the following events trigger group policy refreshes?

    A. Computer boot sequence and user logon process

    B. Refresh interval expiration

    C. Execution of the Gpupdate tool in Windows XP or **secedit** in Windows 2000.

    D. Clicking OK in the Group Policy Object Editor.

17. Which of the following statements about user environment policies are correct?

    A. User and computer environment policies modify different Registry sections.

    B. User policies are only applicable to Windows 2003/XP clients.

    C. User policies are applied only upon user logon, whereas computer policies are applied at the end of the boot process and upon user logon.

    D. User policies are applied only upon user logon, whereas computer policies are applied at the end of the boot process.

Troubleshoot Group Policy Software Installation Issues

18. Your network is running an SUS server, and group policy is used to configure client computers to retrieve updates daily. However, after a while you notice that SUS updates are not taking place, and whenever you try running Windows Update manually, you get an error. What is the most likely cause of this problem? (Check all that apply.)

   A. Policy loopback processing is configured incorrectly.

   B. Remove Access To Use All Windows Updates Features has been enabled.

   C. The SUS server is not synchronized with Microsoft Windows Update servers.

   D. The SUS administrator has not approved any updates yet.

19. You are configuring software distribution packages for your organization. You verified that group policy objects are applied on client machines successfully and that they are up-to-date, yet somehow software distribution changes are not becoming effective on user workstations. What is the most likely cause of this issue? (Choose all that apply.)

   A. For published software distribution changes to become effective, users have to log off and log on again.

   B. For assigned software distribution changes to become effective, computers have to be rebooted.

   C. There may be something wrong with policy processing. Enable userenv.log to gather details.

   D. User accounts must be able to access software distribution shares in order for software packages to be downloaded successfully.

20. You are troubleshooting MSI package installation problems. You log on using the administrator account and enable MsiInstaller logging using the Registry settings. What are the locations of these log files? (Choose all that apply.)

   A. C:\Windows\System32\LogFiles\MsiInstaller\MSI*.log

   B. C:\WINDOWS\Debug\UserMode\MSI*.log

   C. C:\Windows\temp\MSI*.log

   D. C:\Documents and Settings\Administrator\Local Settings\Temp\MSI*.log

LAB QUESTION

Sergio is an administrator working for a startup company that is going through the group policy planning and implementation phase of their Active Directory deployment project. After planning and testing, the company"s administrators decided to implement their changes in production environment: They created new group policy objects, implemented security and filtering configuration, and deployed their plan successfully. Company backup policy was implemented so that full system state backups and file system backups are performed nightly.

HR personnel is responsible for all user account changes, but they do not have anything to do with group policy links or administration. After approximately three days after the changes were made, administrators received numerous helpdesk support calls and reports that the settings that were recently implemented were no longer effective. Sergio conducted a thorough investigation of the issue and concluded that the newly implemented policy wass configured properly but became corrupt. He restarted one of the domain controllers in DRSM mode, performed system state restore using the previous night's backup, marked domain naming context as authoritatively restored, and rebooted the domain controller.

Now group policy functions as expected; however, a massive amount of user account changes implemented by HR personnel that morning were lost. What went wrong, and what could have been done to avoid this?

SELF TEST ANSWERS

Troubleshoot Issues Related to Group Policy Application and Deployment

1. ☑ **B** is correct. In this scenario, the policy is most likely blocked for this individual OU.
   ☒ **A** is incorrect. The Default Domain Policy is applied on the domain level by default and not on the individual OU level; hence, OUs do not have a GPO link, and the policy settings are applied by virtue of inheritance. **C** is incorrect because client-side extensions are only responsible for subcomponents of the group policy, such as scripts and folder redirection, and not the bulk of standard settings. **D** is an unlikely candidate here due to the fact that the policy is only having problems in one of the OUs.

2. ☑ **C** and **D** are correct answers. In this situation, you will need to use the userenv.log log file, but since it is not enabled by default, you will also need to turn it on.
   ☒ **A** is incorrect because the Event Log does not provide enough information about group policy processing; it may log severe errors and warnings of major significance, which only alerts you to a problem and carries no information about policy processing. **B** is incorrect. Although verbose logging through the Event Log will reveal more details about the process, it still will not log all of the errors and warnings, and in addition, it will result in the Event Log flooding, putting additional stress on the system.

3. ☑ **B, C,** and **D** are correct answers. All of these tools can be used to display information about effective group policies, with varying levels of detail.
   ☒ **A** is incorrect because planning mode only runs a simulation and does not present actual applied settings.

4. ☑ **A.** The Gpresult /z switch enables super-verbose output and will display required Registry information with any level of precedence.
   ☒ **B** is incorrect. Although the /v switch will enable verbose output and result in extensive information being displayed, it may not list all of the settings, depending on their precedence level. **C** is incorrect because you need to use one of the verbose switches to see this information. **D** is incorrect because Gpresult can be used for this purpose.

5. ☑ **C** and **D** are correct answers. The ADM file is flexible, manageable, and a simple enough way to configure client computer Registry settings with group policies. By applying these settings to dynamic Registry keys serviced by group policies, administrators can avoid tattooing policy settings elsewhere in the Registry.
   ☒ **A** is incorrect because schema modification is a complex process that may or may not be suitable. You will be forced to develop your own way to configure these settings. **B** is incorrect because this method is more complex than **C** and **D**, and it may not perform consistently 100 percent of the time.

6. ☑ **C.** Setting UserenvDebugLevel to 10002 (hex) in the Registry key presented in the question will achieve the desired result.

   ☒ **A, B,** and **D** are incorrect. All of these values are valid for other logging purposes and not for the Registry key in question.

7. ☑ **A.** To be able to open a group policy object in the GPEdit.msc console, you need to have Full Control rights on the object in question.

   ☒ **B, C,** and **D** are incorrect. Domain Admin membership would achieve the desired result, but in this case it may not be desirable to add a remote administrator to the Domain Admin group if all he or she needs to do is edit a group policy object. Likewise, if domain controllers are not available in the local site, an attempt will be made to access domain controllers in remote sites.

8. ☑ **A.** Remember LSDOU: Local, Site, Domain, OU. The later in the process the policy is applied, the more effective it is. In this case, OU policy may be overwriting some of the settings set on higher levels.

   ☒ **B, C,** and **D** are incorrect because **A** is correct.

9. ☑ **C.** The GPMC console allows administrators to back up and restore group policy objects.

   ☒ **A** and **B** are incorrect because copying SYSVOL via SYSTEMSTATE backup or directly from the file system will not allow you to restore group policy objects, but may help fix policy file corruption issues. **D** is incorrect because it can be done using GPMC. You can restore a policy object using a different name, without overwriting the existing object, if that is necessary.

10. ☑ **A** and **B.** The main difference is how the group policy settings database is compiled.

    ☒ **C** is incorrect because both modes process all applicable policies. **D** is incorrect because both modes allow viewing and saving results in a similar fashion.

11. ☑ **C** is correct. Group policies are not applicable to security groups, only to user and computer objects.

    ☒ **A, B,** and **D** are incorrect because **C** is correct.

12. ☑ **B.** It is very likely that the user in question may be affected by some form of group policy filtering, either WMI or security. Checking to see if the user belongs to any security groups that may have an explicit Deny defined in the ACL of the group policy object in question would be step one.

    ☒ **A** is incorrect because it is not possible to block policy on the user level. **C** is likewise incorrect because the question suggests that the policy, in general, works as expected for the majority of users. **D** is incorrect largely for the same reason.

13. ☑ **A** and **B**. These are the correct ways to deal with situations if you have to install an application that did not come with an MSI package.

☒ **C** is incorrect because this will not guarantee successful installation, and applications cannot be published this way. **D** is incorrect because you can use methods described in **A** and **B**.

14. ☑ **D**. The DcGPOFix utility is the intended solution in this question.

☒ **A, B,** and **C** are incorrect because none of them are designed to restore default policies. Ntdsutil may be used to restore the domain controller's SYSVOL and Active Directory to its predisaster state, but this is a very dramatic approach to the problem. Likewise, Dcpromo will fix the policies, but if there is only one domain controller, it will destroy the existing Active Directory environment. If there is more than one domain controller, then Dcpromo will copy corrupt policies from other domain controllers.

15. ☑ **A**. This is the correct answer that summarizes the rest of the options in the most generic way.

☒ **B, C,** and **D**, are incorrect. **B** is incorrect because it is possible to apply custom Registry settings without tattooing them into Registry keys not serviced by group policy. **C** is incorrect. While system policies are applied in a static fashion, they are not the best description of what tattooing is. **D** is incorrect because it is possible to apply ADM templates in a dynamic fashion, as long as they modify dynamic Registry keys.

16. ☑ **A, B,** and **C**. All of these events trigger group policy to be refreshed.

☒ **D** is incorrect because the GPEdit console does not really have OK or APPLY buttons that are applicable to policies and not to their properties or specific settings. Only clients can request and apply policy objects. Forced update from a central location would grind the network to a halt if it triggers, say, a few dozen concurrent installations of Microsoft Office.

17. ☑ **A** and **D**. User and Computer sections of the policy modify different Registry areas and apply at different stages.

☒ **B** and **C** are incorrect statements.

Troubleshoot Group Policy Software Installation Issues

18. ☑ **B** is correct. If you configure Remove Access To All Windows Updates Features, Windows Update will get disabled on the computers affected by this policy.

☒ **A** is incorrect because loopback processing has no effect in this case, due to the fact that the policy settings in question do not overlap. **C** and **D** are incorrect because, although they are required before any internal update will take place, they would not be causing an error message or preventing users from running a manual Windows Update process using the Internet.

19. ☑ **A** and **B** are correct. In order for the software distribution changes to become effective, a logoff/logon event or a reboot event must occur first, depending on the distribution method.
☒ **C** is incorrect, because **A** or **B** should be done first before any troubleshooting takes place. **D** is incorrect because user accounts are not used to access distribution shares; local system accounts are used to download packages.

20. ☑ **C** and **D** are correct. These are the correct locations for log files, providing that default environment variables and Windows amd user profiles locations have not changed.
☒ **A** and **B** are incorrect because MsiInstaller log files are not maintained in these directories.

LAB ANSWER

Technically, nothing went wrong. Sergio performed authoritative restore using the system state backup made the night before. It overwrote SYSVOL share content and Active Directory database, reverting all the changes to AD objects that occurred since the backup run. This behavior is by design.

In this particular situation, though, it wasn't the best approach to the problem of corrupted policy files. The lab question mentioned that Sergio did not find any group policy object configuration issues; hence the AD GPO should be intact. It could be a problem with actual policy files stored in SYSVOL share. Sergio could have restored system state backup to an alternate location and attempted to copy the policy files back into production SYSVOL shares. An even better solution would entail using GPMC console to restore the policy from policy backup.

A

Windows Server 2003 Network Port Reference

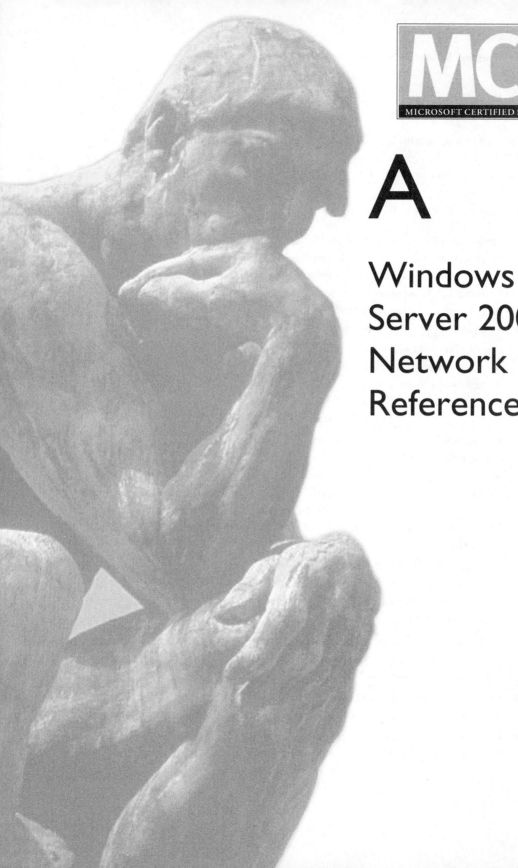

T he first part of this appendix lists TCP/IP ports used by Active Directory services in Windows 2000 and Windows Server 2003. The second part lists ports that may be opened on a domain controller.

Here are the Active Directory ports:

- **88/tcp and 88/udp-Kerberos**   Kerberos is an industry-standard distributed authentication system that is implemented in Windows Server 2003 as its default authentication mechanism. Kerberos is implemented as a KDC (Key Distribution Center) service, which runs on domain controllers. KDC listens on port 88 for ticket requests.

- **123/udp-NTP**   NTP stands for Network Time Protocol. Windows Server 2003 domain controllers need to synchronize time and ensure that no Kerberos client on the network has a time deviation of more than five minutes (configurable). Time stamps are used by a mechanism in Kerberos that is responsible for preventing replay attacks.

- **135/tcp and 135/udp-RPC**   RPC, the Remote Procedure Call protocol that is Microsoft's implementation of the RPC protocol developed by Open Software Foundation (OSF), adds Microsoft-specific extensions. The RPC protocol allows Windows applications to communicate over the network and execute system calls remotely. When you manage DNS or DHCP servers from the same network location using the MMC, you are using the RPC protocol. RPC is a program-level protocol (Application Layer of the OSI model), and it uses TCP/IP as its networking vehicle.

- **389/tcp-LDAP**   Port 389 is used by the LDAP service. The Lightweight Directory Access Protocol is used to access directory services provided by domain controllers. LDAP is the primary way for Windows computers to access the information stored in Active Directory.

- **445/tcp and 445/udp-SMB**   SMB stands for Server Message Block, and it is used for file sharing and transfer. SMB is used directly with TCP/IP and removes another dependence on NetBIOS.

- **464/tcp-Kerberos Password**   This port is used by the Kerberos authentication protocol whenever users of the system attempt to change their passwords.

- **636/tcp-LDAP over SSL**   Port 636/tcp serves the same purpose as 389, except it is used when LDAP traffic is encrypted over Secure Sockets Layer (SSL).

- **3268/tcp-Global Catalog** Microsoft uses port 3268 on domain controllers that are configured to provide global catalog services to the network. Global catalog servers are used by users and applications who need to find certain information outside of their own domain.

- **3269/tcp-Global Catalog over SSL** Port 3269 is used for the same purpose as 3268 by global catalog services, except traffic is encrypted over Secure Sockets Layer.

The following ports may be opened on a domain controller, depending on the services it is configured to provide to the network. Note that some of these services do present a security risk and must be carefully planned and configured to avoid potential compromises and disruption.

- **21/tcp-FTP** Port 21 is used by FTP, or File Transfer Protocol, to transfer files over the network. FTP is inherently weak because it relies on plain-text passwords. It is a big security risk to run and use this service on a domain controller, or any network node for that matter. SFTP protocol uses SSH or SSL to encrypt FTP traffic, but Microsoft has not implemented SFTP support in its IIS service. When you install IIS on a domain controller, carefully evaluate FTP alternatives, and only use FTP if it is an absolute requirement.

- **25/tcp-SMTP** The Simple Mail Transfer Protocol server, implemented as part of Microsoft's IIS, is used by the Windows Server 2003 domain controller for replication, if you configure SMTP as your replication transport. You may need to enable this service if your replication design requires it.

- **53/tcp-DNS** Port 53 is used by the domain name system to service queries and transfer requests. Port 53/tcp is used for zone transfers (unless the zone is integrated in Active Directory) and for queries that generate answers larger than 512 bytes.

- **53/udp-DNS** Continuing from port 53/tcp, port 53/udp is used by clients to query DNS servers (clients submit requests to these ports).

- **80/tcp-HTTP** Port 80 is used by IIS's web server component to serve website content.

- **119/tcp-NNTP** Port 119 is used by NNTP server, also a part of IIS. NNTP stands for Network News Transfer Protocol, and it is used by server components such as Microsoft Exchange Server, which in the case of smaller organizations will, in many instances, reside on a domain controller.

■ **137/udp-NetBIOS Name Server**   The NetBIOS Name Server protocol is one of the NetBIOS over TCP/IP (NetBT) suite of protocols, and it is used to provide hostname-to-address mapping on networks that still support NetBIOS.

If your Windows Server 2003 does not require NetBIOS, it is recommended that you disable it in TCP/IP properties on servers and workstations. This can also be configured through the DHCP service.

■ **138/udp-NetBIOS Datagram**   Like the NetBIOS Name Server protocol, the NetBIOS Datagram service is part of the NetBIOS over TCP/IP (NetBT) suite. NetBIOS Datagrams are used for network logon and network browsing.

■ **139/tcp-NetBIOS Session Services**   NetBIOS Session Services are likewise part of the NetBIOS over TCP/IP suite of protocols. They are analogous to SMB in NetBIOS-free networks. They are used for file sharing, file transfer, and printing.

■ **443/tcp-HTTPS**   Microsoft's IIS service, if configured on a domain controller, can serve content securely using digital certificates and Secure Sockets Layer (SSL). Port 443 is used by the web server component for the Hypertext Transfer Protocol over SSL (HTTPS).

■ **500/udp-ISAKMP**   ISAKMP, or Internet Security Association and Key Management Protocol, implements a mechanism that performs encryption key exchange when establishing a secure IPSec network connection.

■ **563/tcp-SNEWS**   The Secure News (SNEWS) protocol implements NNTP over SSL and may have to be configured on a domain controller that also runs Exchange Server services.

■ **1723/tcp-PPTP**   Point-to-Point Tunneling Protocol (PPTP) is one of the protocols used to establish VPN connections between a VPN client and a VPN server in Windows operating systems.

■ **3389/tcp-RDP**   A Remote Desktop Protocol (RDP) implementation uses port 3389 by default. Microsoft implements this technology in Terminal Services on a Windows Server 2003 or Windows 2000 Server. The RDP client is implemented in Remote Desktop Connection (RDC), is shipped as part of Windows XP and Windows 2003 Server, and is available separately for other operating systems. It used to be called Microsoft Terminal Services Client (MSTSC) in Windows 2000. Terminal Services/Remote Desktop Connection allows users to access servers remotely as if they were logged on locally using a console session; these are indispensable tools for administrators as well.

B

Deploying Active Directory in Firewalled Networks

This appendix discusses strategies that may be used to deploy Active Directory in DMZ networks or in distributed environments that use firewalls or router access lists to provide internal security segmentation. One of the scenarios where this information may prove useful is in the case of an extension of the domain environment into the DMZ network in order to include web or email servers into a common, centralized management environment.

Preparations for Deployment

We start with a list of ports that must be allowed through the firewall:

- 135/tcp, 135/udp-RPC endpoint mapper
- Dynamic RPC port range (or one RPC port; see "Deploying Active Directory in Firewalled Networks Using Static RPC" later in this appendix)
- 445/tcp, 445/udp-SMB
- 389/tcp-LDAP
- 636/tcp-LDAP over SSL
- 3268/tcp-Global Catalog
- 3269/tcp-Global Catalog over SSL
- 88/tcp, 88/udp-Kerberos
- 53/tcp, 53/udp-DNS
- 123/udp-NTP

Ports such as 53 and 123 are optional, which means that you don't necessarily need to allow these services through the firewall between the DMZ and corporate network. Depending on your needs in particular situations, DNS query traffic may be localized in the DMZ using one of the following methods:

- Use the hosts file to set up static mappings of hostnames to IP addresses. Hostnames can be configured to include a centrally administered hosts file.
- Use the DNS server that is local to the subnet, and allow zone transfer traffic only between the two DNS servers involved in zone replication.
- Use the DNS server that is local to the subnet, and integrate zones into Active Directory. Replication traffic will use RPC instead of DNS ports to replicate zone information.
- Use the DNS server that is local to the subnet, and maintain a separate zone manually.

Depending on how many hosts you have in the DMZ network and how often your environment changes, some of the items in the preceding list may not be practical in the long run, but DNS integration with Active Directory does allow the biggest of zones to replicate without using DNS ports while localizing DNS query traffic in the subnet.

Furthermore, the NTP service that is used for time synchronization between domain controllers and members of the domain is not entirely necessary, although it is secure and rather convenient. Some companies may instead configure their domain controllers in the DMZ network to synchronize time with public services, such as those provided by university servers. Alternatively, administrators may need to ensure that time is set correctly on DMZ domain controllers.

Deploying Active Directory in Firewalled Networks Using Dynamic RPC

The RPC protocol needs to be permitted in order for RPC-based replication and services to work across firewalls. The way RPC works, the initiating host contacts the destination host first on port 135 to request which port is used by a service of interest. The destination host's RPC port mapper service returns the port number assigned to the service in question, and the initiating host then reestablishes a connection on that port.

The problem is that, by default, RPC can map dynamically to any port number in the range of 1024 to 65,535. If your firewall between the DMZ and corporate network allows dynamic inbound connections on any port within this range, then RPC replication will work without further firewall reconfiguration.

However, this scenario is extremely insecure, and in most networks this functionality should not be permitted. If dynamic RPC is allowed, it opens up a huge security hole.

Deploying Active Directory in Firewalled Networks Using Static RPC

Instead of opening up your firewall to incoming connections on thousands of ports, you may opt to hardcode the dynamic RPC port to a single value using the Registry and open just one port. This solution makes Active Directory in firewalled networks a more feasible concept, but it requires a bit of configuration work on the part of domain controller administrators.

First, you need to decide which port should be used by your domain controller to replicate. Anything over 50,000 is a valid choice, providing that your selection does not conflict with another custom process or service that is implemented in your network. IANA reserves ports over 49,152 for dynamic allocations.

Next, you will need to add a value to the Registry on domain controllers that will be involved in replication across firewalls. You can take the following script and save it as a *.reg file; then execute this file on the domain controllers in question, and it will add the value as configured. This process eliminates manual configuration and the potential for human error.

```
Windows Registry Editor Version 5.00
[HKEY_LOCAL_MACHINE\SYSTEM\CurrentControlSet\Services\NTDS\Parameters]
"TCP/IP Port"=dword:0000C350
```

The dword value represented in this Registry script is in hexadecimal format and equals 50,000 in decimal.

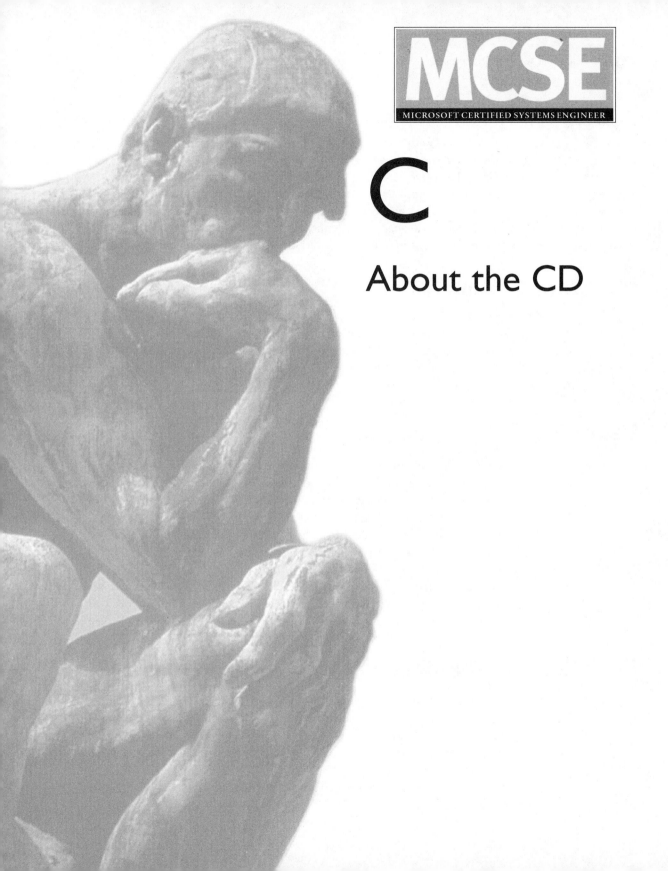

MCSE
MICROSOFT CERTIFIED SYSTEMS ENGINEER

C
About the CD

T he CD-ROM included with this book comes complete with MasterExam, MasterSim, CertCam movie clips, the electronic version of the book, and Session #1 of LearnKey's on-line training. The software is easy to install on any Windows 98/NT/2000 computer and must be installed to access the MasterExam and MasterSim features. You may, however, browse the electronic book and CertCams directly from the CD without installation. To register for LearnKey's online training and a second bonus MasterExam, simply click the Online Training link on the Main Page and follow the directions to the free online registration.

System Requirements

Software requires Windows 98 or higher and Internet Explorer 5.0 or above and 20 MB of hard disk space for full installation. The Electronic book requires Adobe Acrobat Reader. To access the Online Training from LearnKey you must have RealPlayer Basic 8 or Real1 Plugin, which will be automatically installed when you launch the on-line training.

LearnKey Online Training

The **LearnKey Online Training** link will allow you to access online training from Osborne.Onlineexpert.com. The first session of this course is provided at no charge. Additional Session for this course and other courses may be purchased directly from www.LearnKey.com or by calling 800 865-0165.

The first time that you run the Training, you will required to register with the online product. Follow the instructions for a first time user. Please make sure to use a valid e-mail address.

Prior to running the Online Training you will need to add the Real Plugin and the RealCBT plugin to your system. This will automatically be facilitated to your system when you run the training the first time.

Installing and Running MasterExam and MasterSim

If your computer CD-ROM drive is configured to auto run, the CD-ROM will automatically start up upon inserting the disk. From the opening screen you may install MasterExam or MasterSim by pressing the *MasterExam* or *MasterSim* buttons. This will begin the installation process and create a program group named "LearnKey." To run MasterExam or MasterSim use START | PROGRAMS | LEARNKEY. If the auto run feature did not launch your CD, browse to the CD and Click on the "LaunchTraining.exe" icon.

MasterExam

MasterExam provides you with a simulation of the actual exam. The number of questions, the type of questions, and the time allowed are intended to be an accurate representation of the exam environment. You have the option to take an open book exam, including hints, references, and answers, a closed book exam, or the timed MasterExam simulation.

When you launch MasterExam, a digital clock display will appear in the upper left-hand corner of your screen. The clock will continue to count down to zero unless you choose to end the exam before the time expires.

MasterSim

The MasterSim is a set of interactive labs that will provide you with a wide variety of tasks to allow the user to experience the software environment even if the software is not installed. Once you have installed the MasterSim you may access it quickly through this CD launch page or you may also access it through START | PROGRAMS | LEARNKEY.

Electronic Book

The entire contents of the Study Guide are provided in PDF. Adobe's Acrobat Reader has been included on the CD.

CertCam

CertCam .AVI clips provide detailed examples of key certification objectives. These clips walk you step-by-step through various system configurations. You can access the clips directly from the CertCam table of contents by pressing the CertCam button on the Main Page.

The CertCam .AVI clips are recorded and produced using TechSmith's Camtasia Producer. Since .AVI clips can be very large, ExamSim uses TechSmith's special AVI Codec to compress the clips. The file named tsccvid.dll is copied to your Windows \ System folder during the first auto run. If the .AVI clip runs with audio but no video, you may need to re-install the file from the CD-ROM. Browse to the PROGRAMS | CERTCAMS folder, and run TSCC.

Help

A help file is provided through the help button on the main page in the lower left hand corner. Individual help features are also available through MasterExam, MasterSim, and LearnKey's Online Training.

Removing Installation(s)

MasterExam and MasterSim are installed to your hard drive. For BEST results for removal of programs use the START | PROGRAMS | LEARNKEY | UNINSTALL options to remove MasterExam or MasterSim.

If you desire to remove the Real Player use the Add/Remove Programs Icon from your Control Panel. You may also remove the LearnKey training program from this location.

Technical Support

For questions regarding the technical content of the electronic book, MasterExam, or CertCams, please visit www.osborne.com or email customer.service@mcgraw-hill.com. For customers outside the 50 United States, email international_cs@mcgraw-hill.com.

LearnKey Technical Support

For technical problems with the software (installation, operation, removing installations), and for questions regarding LearnKey Online Training and MasterSim content, please visit www.learnkey.com or email techsupport@learnkey.com.

Glossary

A record   Same as host record, this is a DNS entry that is used to point a DNS name to an IP address and provide name-to-address resolution information.

access token   A descriptor, calculated each time a user logs on to the system, that contains an object's SID, GUID, and group membership information. An access token is attached to each process launched in the security context of the corresponding user account.

account   An object in Active Directory that represents a user or a computer.

account domain   In terms of older Windows NT 4.0–style environments, an account domain is a domain that is used to define and store user accounts.

Account Lockout policy   Part of the Account Policies group of settings in group policy object that defines how accounts should be locked out if a password is entered incorrectly a certain number of times.

ACE   Short for access control entry. An entry on an access control list that specifies a security principal and the level of permissions that principal is allowed or denied.

ACL   Short for access control list. A list of ACEs for a given resource. Allows administrators to define permissions used in controlling access to directory objects and file system resources.

Active Directory   LDAP-based information system used to store objects and provide network services such as centralized authentication, common namespace, and security context.

Active Directory Domains and Trusts console   Active Directory MMC-based management snap-in for performing domainwide operations, such as managing UPN suffixes and setting up trusts.

Active Directory Migration Tool   A GUI wizard used to perform account migration between Microsoft Windows domains (Windows NT 4.0, Windows 2000, and Windows Server 2003).

Active Directory Schema console   Active Directory MMC-based management snap-in for modifying schema classes and attributes manually, controlling which attributes should be replicated to the global catalog, and moving the Schema Master FSMO.

Active Directory Sites and Services console   Active Directory MMC-based management snap-in for configuring intersite and intrasite replication schedules and objects.

Active Directory Users and Computers console   Active Directory MMC-based management snap-in for performing most day-to-day tasks involving objects, group policies, and organizational units.

administrative templates   Section of a group policy object that allows administrators to implement Registry settings and control the appearance and functionality of applications.

administrator account   Built-in user account that, by default, is the most powerful security principal in the system. It is added to Enterprise Admins, Domain Admins in each domain, and the local Administrators group on each machine.

ADSI   Short for Active Directory Service Interfaces, a set of libraries that allows administrators and developers to access and manipulate Active Directory data programmatically.

ADSI Edit console   Active Directory MMC-based management snap-in for modifying all of the attributes and objects stored on a given domain controller, regardless of whether attributes were created manually or if they are accessible using other (standard) MMC-based tools.

allow permission   A condition on an ACE that grants a certain type of permission to a certain security principal. (See *deny permission.*)

Anonymous Logon   A system group that represents all users connecting to the system without providing logon credentials.

Application Data folder   A folder in the user's profile that can be redirected to a network location using the group policies folder redirection feature.

application log   A portion of system logging information available through the Event Log that contains application and service-specific information, warning, and error messages.

application partition   Also known as application naming context, this partition is a segment within the Active Directory database that is used to store application data (such as DNS records) and is replicated forestwide but only to designated servers.

AS   Short for authentication service; in the context of Active Directory it is a portion of the KDC service that is responsible for initial user authentication.

attribute   A property of an object stored in Active Directory. For example, a username is an attribute of a user object.

auditing   A mechanism that monitors and logs certain system security events, such as which security principals are attempting to access which objects.

authentication   A process that establishes the identity of a security principal by matching provided logon credentials with objects stored in Active Directory.

authoritative name server   In the context of DNS, a name server that is authorized to answer queries for a certain DNS zone—for example, a primary or secondary server.

authoritative restore   Active Directory recovery operation that copies data from a recent backup and marks it as authoritative, increasing USN values artificially so that restored data will overwrite more recent data on other domain controllers during subsequent replication cycles.

authorization   A process whereby user identity, established in the authentication stage, is verified against access control lists of individual objects in order to determine the effective level of access.

BDC   Short for backup domain controller, a secondary, read-only replica of the user and computer account database designed to balance the query load and provide fault tolerance.

BIND   Short for Berkeley Internet Name Domain, a prominent DNS service implementation on theUNIX/Linux platform.

blocking   A mechanism that prevents default inheritance of settings from parent containers in the Active Directory structure. This refers to both object security settings and group policy settings.

bridgehead server   A server that is used to replicate changes from one site to another across a site link.

bridging   A concept that refers to transitiveness of site links. If Site A has a link to Site B, and Site B has a link to Site C, if links are bridged, then Site A will be linked to Site C.

CA   Short for Certification Authority, a network service that implements PKI infrastructure in the enterprise and is used to issue digital certificates.

certificate   Same as digital certificate and X.509 certificate. A certificate is a binary value or file that contains information such as public key, expiration date, and root certificate authority. This information is used in asymmetric cryptography.

child domain   A lower-level domain joined to an existing domain tree or forest. For example, sales.corp.com is a child domain of corp.com.

class   An object type defined in the Active Directory schema. All objects are instances of existing classes.

CNAME record   Canonical name record, a record used in the DNS to assign aliases, or secondary names, to hosts such as www or ftp.

computer account   Same as computer object; an entry in the Active Directory database that represents a domain-participating computer.

computer configuration   A section of a group policy object that manipulates computer-specific settings.

computer object   See *computer account.*

conditional forwarding   A new feature in Microsoft's DNS implementation that directs DNS queries to different name servers based on the requested information.

configuration partition   Also known as configuration naming context, a segment of the Active Directory database that contains forest and domain configuration information and is replicated to all other domain controllers in the forest.

connection object   An object that represents a connection between two domain controllers in the replication topology.

contact   An object that is used to specify contact information for someone outside the organization. It is not a security principal.

container   An object class that can contain other objects, forming a parent-child relationship.

CSVDE   Short for Comma-Separated Value Data Exchange, a command-line tool that enables administrators to extract and import Active Directory objects from, and to, the database.

DACL   Short for discretionary access control list, a section of an ACL that lists security principals and their respective resource access rights.

database   In the context of Active Directory, a set of files that stores Active Directory data and transactions. Windows Server 2003 uses the ESE database engine. The name of the Active Directory database is ntds.dit.

Dcdiag   A command-line tool used for domain controller diagnostic operations.

Dcpromo   A GUI-based wizard used to promote a server to become an Active Directory domain controller or to demote a server to remove Active Directory.

Default Domain policy   A default group policy object that implements settings for all computers and users in the domain.

Default Domain Controllers policy   A default group policy object that implements stricter settings on domain controllers. Domain controller policy is applied on the OU level and overrides domain policies.

default-first-site-name   A site object created by default when you first install Active Directory.

defragmentation   A process of arranging data in a sequential manner to improve performance. Applies to databases and file systems alike.

delegated zone   A portion of the DNS namespace that has been delegated to another name server.

delegation   A process of enabling certain security principals to perform specific tasks on a group of objects. In reference to DNS, delegation assigns authority for a portion of a namespace to another name server.

Delegation of Control Wizard   A GUI-based wizard used to perform delegation in Active Directory.

delegation records   NS records on higher-level DNS servers that identify which lower-level name servers are responsible for serving the given zone authoritatively.

deny permission   A condition on an ACE that revokes a certain type of permission from a certain security principal. (See *allow permission*.)

Desktop folder   A folder in a user profile that can be redirected to a network share using group policy folder redirection.

DFS   Short for Distributed File System, it allows creation of a single shared resource tree without regard to where actual shared folders are located. Can be standalone or Active Directory–integrated.

DHCP   Short for Dynamic Host Configuration Protocol, this technology allows administrators to assign dynamic IP addresses based on need, at boot time.

digital certificate   See *certificate*.

directory schema   A blueprint of Active Directory database content that specifies exactly what kinds of objects can be created and which properties they should have.

directory service   A network service provided by directory servers that implements directory infrastructure and facilitates access to its resources.

directory service log   A portion of system logging information that pertains to directory services operations and is accessible through the Event Viewer.

disaster recovery   A process of recovering from a catastrophic failure of a system. In terms of Active Directory, this involves recovering the AD database.

distribution group   A user group that has no security identifiers and is used exclusively for maintaining mailing groups.

DNS server   A server that provides domain name resolution services by providing clients' IP addresses in response to hostname queries and vice versa.

domain   In Windows Server 2003, it is a logical network structure that has a common security boundary.

Domain Admins   A built-in security group in Active Directory that is added to the Administrators local group on all computers participating in the same domain. It has most of the administrative privileges, except for those necessary to perform operations affecting the entire forest.

domain controller object   An Active Directory object representing a computer that is also a domain controller.

Domain Controller Security Policy console   A Group Policy Editor MMC-based snap-in that opens the default domain controller group policy.

domain controllers   Network servers that maintain Active Directory databases and services such as KDC.

domain local group   A user group that has domain scope. It can contain global and universal groups from anywhere in the forest or trusted domains, but can only be used within its own domain. Its purpose is primarily to assign permissions to resources.

domain mode   Also known as functional level, this defines which types of domain controllers are still operating in the domain and hence, which functions should be available or restricted.

domain model   Architectural structure of domains in the same enterprise. More common to older Windows NT 4.0 infrastructures, where each domain was a completely separate unit for organizing resources.

domain name   A string used to identify a domain in DNS or NetBIOS namespaces.

Domain Naming Master   Forestwide operations master that is responsible for operations involving adding or renaming domains in the forest.

domain partition   Also known as domain naming context, this is a segment of the Active Directory database that is used to store objects belonging to the same domain. This partition is replicated to all domain controllers only in same domain.

domain tree   A set of parent and child domains that are organized hierarchically to form a contiguous namespace, where child domains append parent domain names to their own name.

Domain Users   A built-in security group that contains all newly created users by default. It carries plenty of restrictions that prevent certain system tasks yet allow most of the functionality for users to do their work.

DSA   Short for Directory Service Agent, it is a software component that provides access to Active Directory data.

Dsquery   A command-line tool for querying Active Directory for information.

DSRM   Short for directory services restore mode, a mode that must be chosen when booting a domain controller in order to perform Active Directory restore operations.

dynamic DNS   Domain name system implementation that supports dynamic registrations of hostnames coming online.

effective permission   A concept that refers to actual applied permissions as opposed to formally assigned ones. Group membership and user actions in the system affect effective permissions.

empty root domain   A way of building your Active Directory forest so that the root domain is maintained only to form the namespace.

Enterprise Admins   The most powerful built-in security group. Members of this group receive Domain Admin privileges in each domain in the forest, and some other enterprise privileges like setting up forest trusts.

Event Log   A central logging facility in Windows operating systems.

Event Viewer   An MMC-based tool that is commonly used to view the content of Event Logs.

Everyone   A special identity, also called system group, it includes all users of the system, except the Anonymous Logon group.

filtering   A concept that refers to selective application of settings based on a common characteristic. In the case of group policies, their application can be filtered based on security group membership.

folder redirection   A mechanism, controlled through group policies, that allows administrators to map folders in user profiles to network shares.

forest   A collection of Windows 2000 or Windows Server 2003 domains organized in one or more treelike domain structures.

forest root domain   Top-level domain in the Windows domain structure.

forest trust   A trust relationship between two Windows Server 2003 forests. Trust relationships allow accounts in one forest to authenticate to another forest and request access to resources located in that forest.

forward lookup zone   In DNS, forward lookup zones are used to create hostname-to-IP address association and to service hostname-to-IP resolution requests.

FQDN   Short for fully qualified domain name, which is a full DNS name that includes the hostname and full parent domain name (DNS suffix)—for example, server1.corp.com.

FRS   Short for File Replication Service, it is a component of Windows Server 2003 that is used to replicate file system resources across several domain controllers.

FSMO   Short for flexible single master operation. In highly distributed environments, certain domain roles must be performed by a single server. In Windows Server 2003 and Windows 2000, these are five roles that ensure stable and consistent environment operation.

Full Control   A type of permission in Active Directory that grants Read, Write, Modify, Delete, and Take Ownership rights.

functional level   See *domain mode*.

garbage collection   A housekeeping process in the Active Directory database that removes all objects that were marked as tombstoned (were deleted) 60 days ago (by default).

global catalog   One of the Active Directory partitions that is replicated to all domain controllers in the entire forest and contains a partial replica of all objects in the same forest (not all object attributes are included in this partition). Serves the purpose of locating objects in a timely manner. By default, the GC partition only exists on the first domain controller in the forest; additional GCs on domain controllers need to be enabled manually.

global group   A type of group that can contain only those security principals located in the same domain as the group, but can be used to assign permissions in any domain in the forest.

GPMC   Group Policy Management Console, a standalone Group Policy management snap-in for performing GPO management and maintenance with one tool (editing is still done using GPEdit).

Gpresult   A command-line tool that displays the resulting set of group policy settings on a given computer.

Gpupdate   A command-line tool available with Windows XP and Windows Server 2003 that triggers a refresh of group policy settings on a computer.

group policy   A set of settings that are applied to users and computers based on their membership in domains, sites, and organizational units.

group policy link   An association between a group policy object and an Active Directory container (site, domain, OU) that makes GPO settings effective for a group of users or computers.

group policy object (GPO)   An object in Active Directory that implements group policies.

group policy object Editor console   Sometimes referred to as GPEdit, this tool is used to modify settings in a given group policy object.

groups   Can be distribution or security, these are used to group security principals based on a common characteristic (such as department or role) for the purpose of streamlining permissions management or maintaining distribution lists.

GUID   Short for globally unique identifier, it uniquely identifies an object to Active Directory. No two automatically generated GUIDs can ever be the same.

hash   A calculated value in which an algorithm is applied to data such as passwords to create a unique digital value that is of a fixed length and cannot be reverse-engineered. A hashed value minimizes the chances of successful interception, tampering, or source spoofing, depending on the application of sensitive information, which can be transferred over an insecure medium.

host record   See A *record*.

inetOrgPerson   A new standard object class implemented in Windows Server 2003 Active Directory in order to support interoperability with other X.500 directory systems.

Infrastructure Master   One of the five FSMO roles that is responsible for handling group membership changes and updating SID-to-DN mappings in multidomain environments.

inheritance   A concept that refers to a child object receiving security or group policy configuration settings from its parent, effectively "flowing" settings assigned at higher levels down the structure.

in-place upgrade One of the migration paths from earlier versions of the operating system to Windows Server 2003.

integrated zone In the context of DNS, this is a forward or reverse lookup zone that is integrated into Active Directory. DNS stores its information in AD, and it is available on all domain controllers that have DNS service installed, unless the application partition is used and is configured otherwise.

intersite replication A process of submitting the latest changes to the Active Directory database over to domain controllers located in a different site. It is performed according to a replication schedule and through bridgehead servers only.

intrasite replication A process of submitting the latest changes to the Active Directory database over to domain controllers located in the same site. It is performed between pairs of servers in accordance with an automatically generated topology.

IPSec Short for IP Security, a protocol that specifies how TCP/IP encryption is performed.

ISTG Short for Inter-Site Topology Generator, it is a component of the KCC, or Knowledge Consistency Checker, which maintains connection objects linking bridgehead servers.

KCC Short for Knowledge Consistency Checker, it is a component that runs on every domain controller and generates replication topology using the same algorithm.

KDC Short for Key Distribution Center, a service that implements the Kerberos authentication protocol on the network.

Kerberos An authentication protocol developed for the purpose of secure authentication on a public network.

key A value used in mathematical formulas to encrypt or decrypt data.

LAN Manager One of the first DOS network environments in Microsoft networks.

LDAP Short for Lightweight Directory Access Protocol, it is a protocol that made it possible to use X.500-like directories on existing TCP/IP networks.

LDIFDE   Short for LDAP Data Interchange Format, Data Exchange, it is similar to CSVDE in that it is a command-line tool that allows extracting and importing objects into Active Directory. It uses LDAP format and also can be used to apply modifications to existing objects.

Ldp   This is a GUI-based tool that can be used to browse the LDAP directory and perform modifications and some other operations.

local group policy   A partial set of settings available through AD-based group policy. Local group policies are stored and applied on computers locally.

loopback processing   This feature is used to overwrite computer configuration settings from the group policy object that applies to a user, with the computer configuration settings inherited by the computer object based on its position in the structure.

LSA   Short for Local Security Authority, it is a process that interacts with the user and Kerberos to authenticate users and construct access tokens.

mandatory profile   A user profile that is read-only, meaning that no user environment modifications (such as files saved on the desktop) are saved. Every time the user logs on, he or she gets the same profile.

migration path   A reference to one of three recommended upgrade processes: in-place upgrade, restructure, upgrade then restructure.

mixed mode   A reference to a domain functional level other than Windows 2000 native or Windows Server 2003. Older domain controllers (Windows NT 4.0) are allowed to participate in mixed mode domains.

MMC   Short for Microsoft Management Console, it is a wrapper application for plugging in different management modules called snap-ins, which are in turn used to manage the infrastructure.

MSI   Short for Microsoft Installer, a technology that is used for software distribution with group policies, in addition to application management on local computers. Also, MSI installation package (*.msi file).

MST   A reference to an *.mst file called a transform, which may be used to modify the standard MSI installation package.

My Documents folder   One of the four user profile folders, which is the default location for user data to be stored, and can be redirected using group policies.

MX   Short for mail exchanger, this is a DNS record that is used to specify which IP address SMTP mail should be directed to.

namespace   A common environment with a consistent naming convention, can be flat (NetBIOS) or hierarchical (DNS).

naming context   Also known as Active Directory partition, a certain segment of the Active Directory database stored on a given domain controller.

native mode   The opposite of mixed mode, native mode precludes Windows NT 4.0 or Windows 2000 domain controllers running in mixed mode from participating in the Windows Server 2003 functional level domain.

nesting   A concept of making groups members of other groups of the same type— for example, placing global groups into other global groups.

nonauthoritative AD restore   Active Directory restoration process that copies data from a recent backup and does not force it to propagate to other domain controllers. The restored domain controller will receive and commit updates from other controllers upon reboot.

NS record   Short for name server, in DNS this is one of the two structure-forming records of major importance that point to authoritative servers.

Ntdsutil   A command-line interface program that allows administrators to manipulate and analyze Active Directory databases. It is commonly used for authoritative restores, semantic analysis, and defragmentation of the Active Directory database.

NTLM   An authentication protocol used in LAN Manager and Windows NT up to and including version 4.0. Windows Server 2003 supports it but defaults to a more secure Kerberos protocol.

object   Commonly used to refer to an instance of the object class, or in other words, an actual entry in the Active Directory database. User accounts and printers are objects.

offline defrag   A process of booting a domain controller into directory services restore mode and running the **ntdsutil** command to perform physical rearrangement of data chunks within the database file to set them up in a sequential order. This improves performance.

OID   Short for object identifier, a unique series of numbers in a certain order that identifies country, company, perhaps product or technology, and then assigns a random set of numbers.

online defrag   Similar to offline defrag, but administrators do not interfere with the process; it runs every night by default, without taking domain controllers offline.

Operation Master   See *FSMO*.

OU   Short for organizational unit, this is a container that can be used to form a structure within a domain that closely resembles the business organization. Group policies and delegation are also applicable on the OU level.

owner   Someone who created an object, or took ownership of it later on (special identity).

parent   A container that houses an object. Objects, when added to a container, form a parent-child relationship.

partition   In Active Directory, also known as naming context. (See *naming context*.)

PDC   Short for primary domain controller, a concept used in Windows NT 4.0 and older systems whereby domain controllers adhered to a single master replication model—that is, one write copy of the database and many read copies.

PDC Emulator   One of the five FSMO server roles that is responsible for emulating PDC functions and performing some other management tasks—for instance, assigning SID numbers from a pool or urgently replicating security-sensitive changes (password change, locked-out account).

permission (privilege)   A condition or operation that is allowed or denied based on user identity and matching ACEs on an ACL.

PIN   Short for personal identification number, used together with smart cards to avoid unobstructed use of lost or stolen cards.

PKI   Short for Public Key Infrastructure, it is a distributed system that uses digital certificates, private and public keys, and asymmetric cryptography to dramatically reduce the chances of successful information or identity theft.

primary name server   In standard DNS zones, this is the first DNS server serving a given zone, usually by means of the only read/write copy of the zone.

primary zone   The first, read/write instance of a DNS zone on the primary name server.

private key   In PKI, this is a value used in mathematical formulas to decrypt information encrypted to a corresponding public key.

propagation   A process of copying changes from one server to another in a distributed environment.

PTR record   Short for pointer record, this is a DNS record that is used to provide reverse mappings of IP addresses to hostnames.

Read permission   A type of permission in Active Directory that grants a user the right to access the file in read-only mode.

realm   A Kerberos/UNIX term similar to "domain" in Windows.

realm trust   A trust relationship established manually between a Windows 2000 or Windows Server 2003 domain or forest, and a realm.

recovery   See *disaster recovery*.

Registry   A local system repository of all system and program settings.

Repadmin   A command-line tool for managing and troubleshooting Active Directory replication.

replication   Same as propagation, it is a process of synchronizing changes between all relevant AD domain controllers.

replication topology   A common replication schema or structure that is calculated by the KCC process on each domain controller.

Replmon   A GUI-based tool that allows monitoring, managing, and troubleshooting replication topologies and issues.

resource domain   In Windows NT 4.0 terminology, resource domains are used to store resources such as file sharing servers and printers.

restore   A process of copying information from a backup. (See also *disaster recovery*.)

reverse lookup zone   The opposite of forward lookup zone, this type of zone is used to perform reverse lookups of DNS hostnames by IP addresses.

RID Master   One of the five FSMO server roles that is responsible for assigning globally unique number pools to domain controllers.

roaming profile   A user profile that is saved on the server each time the user logs off, and is loaded on a machine each time the user logs back on, even if the logon machine is a different workstation.

root domain   A root is the highest domain in the DNS namespace or name hierarchy. In DNS terms, this is the "." domain that is appended after the TLD in each FQDN. In AD terms, see *forest root domain*.

root hint   A list of preconfigured IP addresses that are authoritative for the root domain. In order to start the domain resolution process, the DNS server must know the IP where it will submit the root domain request for TLD NS IP.

root server   In DNS terms, this is one of the servers on the root hint list.

RPC   Short for remote procedure call, this is a protocol used by most of the Windows management applications and intrasite replication.

RSoP   Short for Resultant Set of Policy, this is a GUI tool, integrated into other Active Directory management tools, which allows easy troubleshooting of group policy settings by calculating or displaying effective settings. It is also found as a standalone snap-in for an MMC console.

SACL   Short for system access control list, one of the control lists that form the ACL. SACLs are used to define auditing settings for an object.

SAM   Short for Security Account Manager, a legacy user account database employed on Windows NT 4.0 domain controllers and still employed locally on Windows Server 2003 computers.

schema   Full blueprint of all possible object classes and attributes that can be used in Active Directory.

Schema Admins   A built-in universal group, members of which receive schema administrator privileges.

Schema Master   One of the five FSMO server roles that is used to make changes to the schema.

schema partition   A segment in the Active Directory database that contains schema configuration information and is replicated to all domain controllers in the forest.

secondary name server   In the context of DNS, a backup name server that is used for load balancing and fault-tolerance purposes.

secondary zone   In the context of DNS, it is a read-only copy of the primary zone.

security descriptor   A piece of data that contains security information for an object that can be secured.

security group   Security groups have their own SIDs and participate in the security scheme.

security log   Portion of the system log that displays security-related events, such as success and failure auditing events.

security principal   An object that has its own SID and therefore can be featured on an ACL. Examples are users, computers, and security groups.

semantic database analysis   In Active Directory, this is a logical scan of database integrity, performed through Ntdsutil.

service account   A user account created for the purpose of running system services.

session ticket   An identifier that a client requests from the KDC TGS service, which is later submitted to the server in question in order to authenticate the user and server to each other.

shared secret   A secret key that must be preshared, or communicated in a secure fashion, between two parties involved in a communication process in order to establish their identity.

shortcut trust   An optimization feature of Active Directory whereby administrators create explicit trust between two deeply nested child domains, especially if they are in different trees, in order to improve LDAP performance.

SID   Short for security identifier, a string that uniquely identifies a security principal within the forest.

SIDHistory   A security principal object attribute available in native domain modes that tracks the history of SID values assigned to an object, which helps retain permissions when moving objects between domains.

site   A structural component in Active Directory that allows administrators to distinguish computers that are located on the same LAN segment from those located across slow and/or unreliable WAN links.

site link bridge A concept of transitiveness of site links. See *bridging*.

SiteLink An Active Directory object that represents a link between one or more sites.

smart card A credit-card-sized device with an integrated chip that can store digital certificates and be used to authenticate to Windows 2000 and Windows Server 2003 domains.

SMTP Short for Simple Mail Transfer Protocol, which is the standard protocol used to send email messages.

SOA record Short for start of authority record; in DNS it is used to configure zone settings such as default TTL, and also to indicate authoritativeness of the zone.

special permissions A custom set of rights that can be included on an ACE that are not covered by standard permissions.

SRV record This record is critical to Active Directory operation. It is used to locate services on the network—services such as LDAP (domain controller), KDC (Kerberos), and some others.

SSO Short for Single Sign-On, which allows users to authenticate just once and then access all resources in the same domain that they have access to, without additional authentication steps.

standard permissions Similar to special permissions, this is a predefined set of permissions that enable Read, Write, Change, Take Ownership, or Full Control access to the object and all its attributes.

Start Menu folder One of the user profile settings that contains shortcuts for applications and system settings, and can be redirected to a network share using the group policy folder redirection feature.

stub zone A DNS concept similar to shortcut trusts in Active Directory that is used to optimize the DNS resolution process. It effectively sets up an empty zone on the server and copies NS records from the authoritative server, establishing a "pointer" to authoritative zone servers.

SYSVOL   System volume share that gets created on each domain controller. It is used to store files necessary to service user logons—group policy files and logon scripts, for example.

TCP/IP   Transmission Control Protocol/Internet Protocol, the industry-standard communication protocol used in the vast majority of networks, including the Internet.

TGS   Short for ticket granting service, it is a part of the KDC service that implements ticket distribution service on the network.

TGT   Short for ticket granting ticket, this is a value encrypted to a key that only KDC knows, and then encrypted again using a shared long-term key between client and KDC, which is used to verify a user's identity.

tombstone   A marker that is placed on an Active Directory object once it gets deleted. Tombstoned objects are removed from the directory 60 days after they are deleted (by default) as part of the garbage collection process.

topology   See *replication topology*.

transaction log   A set of files that are used to store changes to the Active Directory database.

transform file   A custom set of application settings that can be bundled with a corresponding MSI package.

transitive trust   A concept used to establish the pass-through nature of trust relationships. If domain A trusts domain B, and domain B trusts domain C, domain A will trust domain C through two transitive trust links.

tree root   A top-level domain that forms a new domain tree.

trust   An association established between two domains or forests that allows accounts from the trusted domain to use resources in the trusting domain.

universal group   A group that can contain user and group accounts from any domain and can be assigned resources in any domain.

universal group membership caching   Global catalog servers are used to look up universal group membership upon logon. If you cache this information on domain controllers, logon requests will still be processed when the global catalog becomes unavailable.

UPN   Short for universal principal name, which is used as a suffix in Windows 2000 logon names, such as user@domain. The default list of UPNs equals all domain names in the forest, but they can also be added manually.

user account   Same as user object.

user configuration container   A portion of group policy settings that provides user configuration.

user object   An entry in the Active Directory database that represents a user of the system.

user profile   A set of folders and files that store user data and settings pertaining to the same user account.

USN   Short for update sequence number, it is a serial number that corresponds to each object for the purposes of selective replication.

Windows Installer   See MSI.

Write permission   A standard permission in Active Directory that allows writing information to objects or attributes.

WSH   Short for Windows Scripting Host, a scripting language environment built into Windows operating systems, which has the ability to interpret VBScript and JScript scripts.

X.500   A standard that defines common rules for directory services.

X.509   A standard that defines common rules for digital certificates.

ZAP file An alternative to an MSI file that does not contain actual installation files and can only be installed by someone with administrative permissions if Registry modifications must be made.

zone In the context of DNS, this is a common storage database (text file) that contains DNS zone configuration and records for a given namespace. It can contain more than one DNS domain if subdomains were not delegated.

INDEX

I

S

U

INTERNATIONAL CONTACT INFORMATION

AUSTRALIA
McGraw-Hill Book Company
Australia Pty. Ltd.
TEL +61-2-9900-1800
FAX +61-2-9878-8881
http://www.mcgraw-hill.com.au
books-it_sydney@mcgraw-hill.com

CANADA
McGraw-Hill Ryerson Ltd.
TEL +905-430-5000
FAX +905-430-5020
http://www.mcgraw-hill.ca

**GREECE, MIDDLE EAST, & AFRICA
(Excluding South Africa)**
McGraw-Hill Hellas
TEL +30-210-6560-990
TEL +30-210-6560-993
TEL +30-210-6560-994
FAX +30-210-6545-525

MEXICO (Also serving Latin America)
McGraw-Hill Interamericana Editores
S.A. de C.V.
TEL +525-1500-5108
FAX +525-117-1589
http://www.mcgraw-hill.com.mx
carlos_ruiz@mcgraw-hill.com

SINGAPORE (Serving Asia)
McGraw-Hill Book Company
TEL +65-6863-1580
FAX +65-6862-3354
http://www.mcgraw-hill.com.sg
mghasia@mcgraw-hill.com

SOUTH AFRICA
McGraw-Hill South Africa
TEL +27-11-622-7512
FAX +27-11-622-9045
robyn_swanepoel@mcgraw-hill.com

SPAIN
McGraw-Hill/
Interamericana de España, S.A.U.
TEL +34-91-180-3000
FAX +34-91-372-8513
http://www.mcgraw-hill.es
professional@mcgraw-hill.es

**UNITED KINGDOM, NORTHERN,
EASTERN, & CENTRAL EUROPE**
McGraw-Hill Education Europe
TEL +44-1-628-502500
FAX +44-1-628-770224
http://www.mcgraw-hill.co.uk
emea_queries@mcgraw-hill.com

ALL OTHER INQUIRIES Contact:
McGraw-Hill/Osborne
TEL +1-510-420-7700
FAX +1-510-420-7703
http://www.osborne.com
omg_international@mcgraw-hill.com

Sound Off!

Visit us at **www.osborne.com/bookregistration** and let us know what you thought of this book. While you're online you'll have the opportunity to register for newsletters and special offers from McGraw-Hill/Osborne.

We want to hear from you!

Sneak Peek

Visit us today at **www.betabooks.com** and see what's coming from McGraw-Hill/Osborne tomorrow!

Based on the successful software paradigm, Bet@Books™ allows computing professionals to view partial and sometimes complete text versions of selected titles online. Bet@Books™ viewing is free, invites comments and feedback, and allows you to "test drive" books in progress on the subjects that interest you the most.

Prepare

Get the books that show you not only what—but *how*—to study

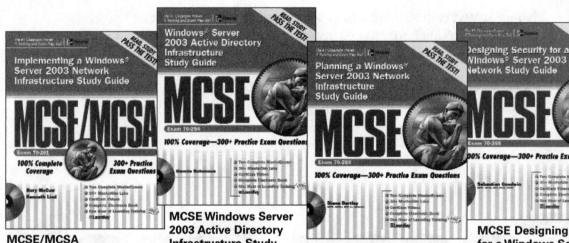

MCSE/MCSA Implementing a Windows Server 2003 Infrastructure Study Guide (Exam 70-291)
MCCAW & LIND
0-07-222566-1
$49.99
Available: October 2003

MCSE Windows Server 2003 Active Directory Infrastructure Study Guide (Exam 70-294)
SUHANOVS
0-07-222319-7
$49.99
Available: October 2003

MCSE Planning a Windows Server 2003 Network Infrastructure Study Guide (Exam 70-293)
BARTLEY
0-07-222325-1
$49.99
Available: November 2003

MCSE Designing Security for a Windows Server 2003 Network Study Guide (Exam 70-298)
GOODWIN
0-07-222747-8
$49.99
Available: December 2003

- **100% complete coverage** of all official objectives for each exam
- **Exam Readiness checklist** at the front of each book
- **Step-by-step exercises** are linked to MasterSims and CertCams on the CD-ROM—so you can watch, listen, and try the exercises live
- **Inside the Exam** sections in every chapter highlight key exam topics covered
- **Simulated exam questions** match the format, tone, topics, and difficulty of the real exam

On the CD-ROMs
- MasterExam Practice Tests
- MasterSim Labs
- CertCam Videos
- Complete Electronic Book
- LearnKey Video Training
- Flash card study program for your PC or Pocket PC

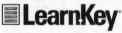